History And Description Of The Manchester Waterworks...

John Frederic La Trobe Bateman

Nabu Public Domain Reprints:

You are holding a reproduction of an original work published before 1923 that is in the public domain in the United States of America, and possibly other countries. You may freely copy and distribute this work as no entity (individual or corporate) has a copyright on the body of the work. This book may contain prior copyright references, and library stamps (as most of these works were scanned from library copies). These have been scanned and retained as part of the historical artifact.

This book may have occasional imperfections such as missing or blurred pages, poor pictures, errant marks, etc. that were either part of the original artifact, or were introduced by the scanning process. We believe this work is culturally important, and despite the imperfections, have elected to bring it back into print as part of our continuing commitment to the preservation of printed works worldwide. We appreciate your understanding of the imperfections in the preservation process, and hope you enjoy this valuable book.

*H.E. The President of the Argentine Republic 1884
with the compliments of
the author.*

HISTORY OF
THE MANCHESTER WATERWORKS.

J. F. Bateman
1859

HISTORY AND DESCRIPTION

OF THE

MANCHESTER WATERWORKS.

BY

JOHN FREDERIC LA TROBE BATEMAN,

F.R.S.S., L.&E., PAST PRESIDENT OF THE INST. C.E., F.G.S., F.R.G.S., ETC., ETC.

MANCHESTER:
T. J. DAY, 58, MARKET STREET.
LONDON:
E. &. F. N. SPON, 16, CHARING CROSS.
1884.

418652

Dedication.

TO SIR JOSEPH HERON, Knight,

TOWN CLERK OF MANCHESTER,

THE FOLLOWING PAGES ARE DEDICATED, AS A SLIGHT ACKNOWLEDGMENT OF
THE AUTHOR'S ADMIRATION OF HIS CHARACTER AND ABILITY,
AND OF THE FRIENDSHIP HE HAS ENJOYED
FOR NEARLY FORTY YEARS.

PREFACE.

THE works for the supply of the City of Manchester and its neighbourhood with water from Longdendale, are not only in many respects the largest which have ever been executed in this country, but they have been attended with so many difficulties in their construction, and present so many points of novelty and interest, that it is conceived a somewhat detailed account of them may not only be due to their relative importance among the great engineering works of the age, but may also contain matters of much local interest and of considerable value to the Student in Hydraulic Engineering.

The first or Historical Part was written in Scotland, during a period of enforced leisure, in December, 1858, and January, 1859. It brings up the history of the Waterworks to the time at which the second Act for authority to construct the works in Longdendale was obtained, namely, in July, 1848, and to the transfer of the works from a Company to the Corporation.

At the time I then wrote the works were not finished, and I therefore delayed a description till they should be entirely completed.

When the works were first laid out, I had acquired considerable experience in the construction of large works of a similar description, and had collected much information—a great deal of it from actual observation—upon the fall of rain, the quantity of water flowing from the ground, and other kindred subjects, which were intimately mixed up with the question of the water-supply of towns.

Since then I have been largely engaged in other works, as well as in the construction of those which form the subject of the following History, and I have consequently still further added to the information I possessed.

The first project for the supply of water to Manchester from the Pennine chain of hills was laid out in 1844. The works in Longdendale were commenced in 1848, but I was not able to report them completed till the spring of 1877. Up to the present time, therefore, they have occupied nearly forty years of my life.

It is not everyone who commences so great a work at so early an age, or who is permitted to continue his labours for such a period; and I have much reason to be thankful for the health and life which have been granted to me, and for the unshaken confidence which the Manchester Corporation have always reposed in me.

In this long period I have of course gained much practical knowledge, and I can now look back to the inexperience and faults of my early years with the hope that they have all been corrected, and with the consciousness that I have been mainly instrumental in conferring on the inhabitants of Manchester and the neighbourhood one of the greatest blessings which it is possible for a town to enjoy.

I had not intended to have written any description of the works until they were finally completed; but various circumstances have contributed to postpone that period, and I find so many things which are deserving of record passing from my mind, that much of the material which now exists for a tolerably full description will soon be lost for ever.

It would be a tedious business, and probably uninteresting to the general reader, if every detail of the work were described, and I have therefore simply related, in the second or Descriptive Part, the main features of the undertaking, and such difficulties, peculiarities, or novelties as it has presented.

I should perhaps observe that the descriptive part has been written during the last five or six years, at such times as I could devote to the undertaking from the more important calls of an active professional life; and I must therefore claim the reader's indulgence for the disjointed narrative, for some repetition, and for the apparently inconsistent dates of some parts of the work.

16, Great George Street, Westminster, London, S.W.,
    January, 1884.

LIST OF ILLUSTRATIONS.

Map shewing the original design for the Manchester and Salford Waterworks in 1844.
Map shewing the Works in Longdendale and *en route* to Manchester, as constructed by the Corporation.
Map shewing Storage Reservoirs in the Valley of Longdendale.
Section shewing Reservoirs and lines of Mains.

WOODHEAD RESERVOIR.

Plan shewing old and new Embankment, Discharge Tunnel, &c.
Longitudinal and Transverse Sections of Embankment.
Details of Waste Watercourse, &c.
Sections of Valve Shaft and Valve House.
48 in. Sluice Valve and original gearing.
Details of Large Valves.
Gearing for Large Valves, General Drawing ... ... Sheet 1.
    ,,   ,,   Details of Gearing, all Framing omitted .. ,, 2.
    ,,   ,,   Details of Framing, all Gearing omitted ,, 3.
    ,,   ,,   Details of Floor Plates and Girders ... ,, 4.
Diagrams of Rainfall at Embankment, Sheet 1.
   ,,   ,,   ,,   ,, 2.
   ,,   ,,   ,,   ,, 3.

CROWDEN BROOK.

Weir for separating pure and turbid Water.
Details of Crowden Weir.
Pivot Sluices at Crowden Weir.

TORSIDE RESERVOIR.

Plan of Embankment, Discharge Tunnel, &c.
Longitudinal Section of Embankment, and Section on line of Syphon Pipe.

RHODES WOOD RESERVOIR.

Plan of Embankment, Discharge Pipes, &c.
Longitudinal and Transverse Sections of Embankment, and Section on line of Syphon Pipe.

VALE HOUSE RESERVOIR.

Plan of Embankment, &c., and Sections of Waste Watercourse.
Longitudinal and Transverse Sections of Embankment, &c.

BOTTOMS RESERVOIR.
Plan of Embankment, Waste Weir, Discharge Tunnel, &c.
Longitudinal and Transverse Sections of Embankment.
Sections across Waste Weir.
Details of Valve Shaft, showing arrangement of Hydraulic Engines for working Valves.
Details of Test Basin.
Details of Ironwork in Test Basin.

MILLOWNERS' AUXILIARY RESERVOIR.
Plan and Sections.
Details of Weirs and Shuttles.
Self-acting Floodgates and Details.
Details of Sluice Gearing.

MOTTRAM TUNNEL.
Longitudinal Section and Details.

GODLEY SERVICE RESERVOIR.
General Plan of Works.
Plan and Sections of Straining Frames. Sheet 1.
Sections of Straining Frames ...   „ 2.
Details of Straining Frames and Strainers. „ 3.
Details of Discharge Orifices.

WORKS AT AUDENSHAW AND DENTON.
Plan of Old and New Reservoirs.
Sections of New Reservoir Embankments.
Plan and Sections of Inlet Wells.
Plan of Outlet and Straining Wells.
Sections and Details of Straining Wells.

PRESTWICH SERVICE RESERVOIR.
General Plan.

MISCELLANEOUS.
Skeleton Map of intended Water Mains in 1849.
Diagrams of Water Supply to Manchester, and Rainfall at Gorton Reservoirs.
Self-acting Ball Air Valves, and Hydrants.
Self-acting Closing Valve for 36-in. Pipes.
Horizontal Sluice Valve and Reflux Valve.
Reversing Tumbler in Discharge Troughs, and Gauge Sluice in Watercourses.
Sections of Joints for 12-in. Pipes.
Map shewing proposed Line of Aqueduct from Thirlmere.
Plan shewing intended Works at Lake Thirlmere.

[The right of Publication and of Translation with respect to the whole of this Work is reserved.]

J. F. LaTrobe Bateman

1884.

HISTORY OF THE WATER-SUPPLY TO MANCHESTER.

PART I.—HISTORICAL.

THE city of Manchester has risen upon and around the site of the old Site of Manchester. Roman station of *Mancunium*, near the confluence of several rivers and streams of water which, taking their rise in the high lands to the east and north-east of the city, descend through what were formerly well-wooded and picturesque valleys, but which are now for the most part filled with towns, villages, mills, and all the busy manufacturing establishments which are connected with the great seat of the cotton trade of England.

A well-watered place it must have been in former times. The Irwell, the Medlock, the Irk, and various smaller streams, all abounding with fish, were never-failing sources of excellent soft water. The superficial beds of drift sand and gravel yielded copious springs, and the new red sand-stone rock which lay beneath the town contained an almost inexhaustible supply of pleasant drinking (though hard) well-water. There was enough and more than enough for all the ordinary wants of a large population, and not until the streams were fouled by manufactories, and the sands and gravels covered by buildings, and the water they contained drained off or spoiled by the attendant operations, was it necessary to resort to artificial means for a supply of water.

Hence, beyond here and there a discovery of an ancient Roman or Early Records. British well, there are no early records or remains of any means for supplying the town with water. Historical research shows that there were a few public wells or fountains, which were guarded from injury and repaired from time to time by the public authorities; but the few scanty notices which exist do not go beyond the beginning of the sixteenth century and are principally found in the old records of the Manchester Court Leet. From these it appears that there was one principal spring or fountain rising in what is now about the centre of

Early Conduit and Fountain.

the city, and from which the name of "Fountain-street" has been derived, which for a very long period—viz., from 1506 to 1776—continued to supply water to the inhabitants, being apparently, during a large portion of that period, almost the only public supply of that nature which existed. The water was conveyed from the spring by a conduit to what was the Market Place, now principally occupied by Victoria-street. The conduit was, however, neglected and allowed to get into disrepair, and the supply which it yielded was often so inadequate to the wants of the people, that stringent rules were from time to time established regulating the quantity which each householder was to be permitted to take. Thus in October, 1578, the Leet Jury order that "no person shall take water from the conduit [as it was "termed] in any vessel of greater value [capacity] than one woman is able to "bear filled of water, and but one of every house at one time, and to have "their cale [call or turn] as hath been accustomed"; and officers were appointed to see the order enforced. This limited supply would probably not exceed four or five gallons, and if that was all that one household received in one day, obtained with difficulty by a woman waiting perhaps for hours for her proper "cale," and then carried on her head for all distances in all weathers, it forms a strong contrast to the constant and unlimited supply which is now delivered into the smallest house and poorest cottage—where the average consumption is at present about 50 or 60 gallons per day.

The fountain above alluded to sometimes yielded "more generous liquor" than water. It is related in a letter from William Heawood, steward of the Court Leet, which was copied into "Acton's Guide to Manchester, 1804," that, on the occasion of the rejoicings for the Coronation of Charles II., on the 23rd April, 1661, after the authorities, inhabitants, troops, &c., had attended divine service at the Collegiate Church, "the "Boroughreeve, Constables, and the rest of the burgesses of the town not "then in arms, accompanied Sir Ralph Assheton, knight and baronet, and "divers neighbouring gentlemen of quality, together with the said Warden "and Fellows of the said College, and divers other ministers, with the town "musick playing before them upon loud instruments through the streets to "the cross, and so forward to the conduit, officers and soldiers in their "order, the gentlemen and officers drank his majesty's health in claret, "running forth at three streams at once of the said conduit, which was "answered from the soldiers by a great volley of shot, and many great "shouts, saying, 'God save the king!' which being ended, the gentry and "ministers went to dinner, attended with the officers and musick of the "town, the auxiliaries dining at the same place. During the time of dinner "and until after sunset, the said conduit did run with pure claret, "which was freely drunk by all that could, for the crowd, come so near "the same."

Towards the close of the last century Manchester had become a large town, and the local supplies from springs having failed or been injured from causes inseparable from the rapid extension of buildings and population, artificial means of supply appear to have been established by Sir Oswald Mosley, the Lord of the Manor, who put down a pumping engine for raising water from the river Medlock at Holt Town, a short distance above the town. From the geological character of the district over which the river ran the water of the Medlock must always have been soft, and at that time very good and pellucid. It was raised by the pumping engine to the high parts of the town, and conveyed to the Shudehill pits and the Infirmary pond—all now swept away—where it was stored, and from whence it was distributed by pipes to the lower parts of the town for the use of the inhabitants. The accommodation so afforded could only have been partial, and the remainder of the inhabitants must, after the failure of the Fountain-street conduit and the destruction of the springs in the superficial sands and gravels, have procured their supplies from wells sunk into the hard red sand-stone, from which the water had to be raised by pumps. The water from this source, though, as has been stated, pleasant to drink, was very hard and unfit for general domestic use, and was alleged by a high medical authority of the day—Dr. Percival—to be injurious to health. He states in an Essay dated November, 1771, and entitled "Experiments "and observation on Water, particularly on the hard Pump Water of "Manchester," written for the purpose of showing the injurious effect of impure and hard water in various complaints and disorders, that "the pump "water of Manchester is in general very impure. It is impregnated with "a large quantity of selenite, or earthy, astringent salt," and "that it "contains also no inconsiderable quantity of alum." He says that he "cannot omit one observation," "that the inhabitants are peculiarly subject "to glandular obstructions and scrofulous swellings, and that water loaded "with stringent, earthy salts, hath a direct tendency to produce such

Waterworks of Sir Oswald Mosley.

Quality of Water. Opinion of Dr. Percival, 1771.

"complaints." The necessity for obtaining a better and more abundant supply had therefore become urgent, and soon after the commencement of the present century several rival schemes seem to have been projected.

Rival Schemes, 1808.

In 1808 two schemes were prepared, and were intended to be brought before Parliament in the ensuing Session, for supplying the town with water to be chiefly taken from the Medlock and the Irk or their tributaries.

Public Meeting on same.

A public meeting of the inhabitants was called upon the subject, which was held in November, 1808, and by adjournment in the following month, the Boroughreeve in the chair, when, *inter alia*, the following very important resolution was passed:—

Committee appointed.

"That a Committee be appointed at this meeting for taking these schemes into consideration; and that it be an instruction to such committee to inquire whether the object of supplying the town with water may not be effected in a way more eligible for the inhabitants at large, and less injurious to the private property of individuals, by drawing such supply from the river Irwell or other sources; and also to inquire whether it is worth while for the inhabitants of Manchester to take the management of such a concern into their own hands, and apply the profit arising from it to the improvement of the town, or other public purposes, and, if so, by what means can this be best effected."

Thus early did the inhabitants of Manchester appreciate not only the advantage of a good supply of water, but that very enlightened principle of legislation (which was not, however, acted upon till forty years subsequently) that "the furnishing and control of this important article of "food and cleanliness, on which the health and comfort of the inhabitants "depend, ought to be under their own direction, and not entrusted to "persons whose sole object would be the promotion of their own private "interest."

Public Meeting to receive Report from Committee, February, 1809.

The Committee thus appointed laid their Report before a Public Meeting called for the purpose of receiving it, on the 2nd February, 1809. This Report is a very remarkable document. It contains a short description of two alternative schemes, either of which in the opinion of the Committee was preferable to those proposed by the private companies. One of these alternative schemes is remarkable as being a suggestion to take the supply of water from the river Irwell, within or adjoining to the town of Manchester, to be raised by a steam-engine and filtered for the use of the inhabitants; a tolerable proof of the then comparative purity of the stream and the little apprehension which at that time existed of the horrible condition into which, within a comparatively short period, the same stream would be converted by the growing trade and population. It is, however, chiefly noticeable for the sound views it enunciates on the advantage of the supply being in the hands of the inhabitants themselves, and as containing the germ of those judicious resolutions which were subsequently carried into effect, by which the Gasworks, many years ago, and the Waterworks and Manorial Rights more recently, have become the property of the town. It is worth re-printing in full, and is as follows:—

"Your Committee have taken into consideration the two schemes proposed by individual adventurers to be brought into Parliament in the present session, for supplying the town of Manchester with water; and they are of opinion that the sources from which such supply is intended to be taken are insufficient for that purpose, and that even if such sources were adequate, the application thereof would be highly injurious to private property, inasmuch as the same would cut off many of the springs and feeders which now supply large and extensive printing, bleaching, and dyeworks with water, and afford to numerous cotton factories and other works condensing water for their steam-engines. [*Report of Committee.*]

"Your Committee are also of opinion that the supply of the town of Manchester with water ought to be under the direction of its own inhabitants, and that it would be contrary to sound policy to intrust the furnishing and control of this important article of food and cleanliness, on which the health and comfort of the inhabitants depend, to persons whose sole object will be the promotion of their own private interest, and who are induced to the undertaking from no other motive.

"Your Committee are further of opinion, that an ample supply of water for the use of the inhabitants of Manchester may be afforded from other sources than those mentioned by these undertakers, and in a manner which will not in the least degree injure or affect private property. One of these sources may be derived from the river Irwell, the water of which below the town of Manchester is more than sufficient to supply the mills and locks of the navigation on that river. The water may be advantageously taken in several places adjoining to the town, and may be filtered through beds of sand and gravel, either natural or artificial, at a very small expense.

"The water may be raised to a proper height to supply every part of the town, by means either of a steam-engine or a fall of the river Irwell not now occupied; and this may be effected either separately or in conjunction with

Report of Committee—continued.

a proposed plan to continue St. Mary's-gate, by a regular descent, to Chapel-street in Salford, and from thence to Bolton, Bury, and other places north of Manchester and to render the Irwell navigable to Hunt's-bank, and by means of warehouses and wharfs on each side of the new intended bridge, to place the termination of the navigable communication from Liverpool to Manchester in the centre of the latter town. The weir, which would be required in that case to extend the navigation, would produce a fall of the river more than sufficient in power to raise the requisite supply of water for the use of the town.

"Another source from which the town of Manchester may be adequately supplied with pure water, and which we think best, is through the Ashton Canal. The water may be taken from the river Tame, at the Dukinfield weir, in times of flood only, and may be preserved in reservoirs to be made in lands of very little value near that weir.

"From these reservoirs it may be conveyed through the Ashton Canal, by regulated gauges, to a reservoir near the town of Manchester, where it may be filtered and rendered pure for the use of the inhabitants. In its course, it will supply the Ashton Canal Company with lockage water for the use of their navigation, and will be particularly valuable to them in dry seasons. The mill-owners will also be benefitted by a diminution of the inconvenience they at present sustain from back-water in times of flood. The filtering reservoir may be made near Holt Town, where the water will be supplied at the height of twelve feet above the level of the street at New-cross, and may be made to flow into the highest apartments of every house in the town of Manchester.

"As the latter scheme will not require a steam-engine, or any other expensive apparatus in its commencement or extension, it may be begun on a limited scale, and extended in proportion to the funds which may be raised for its establishment. It may be commenced without even the expense of the proposed reservoir at Dukinfield weir, because the waste water which flows from the Ashton Canal on the level of the Stockport branch, and at present is of no use, would be sufficient to supply a considerable part of the town of Manchester. If in the execution of the plan an intermediate reservoir should be deemed necessary, an advantageous situation may be had in the lands of Mr. Green, in Clayton, from whence the water may be brought to the town of Manchester through either the Ashton Canal or a separate tunnel.

"The means of raising money for carrying into effect this important plan, as well as the mode by which it may be effected most beneficially for the inhabitants of the town, have necessarily occupied the attention of your Committee. The supply of the rich with good water will form but a small part of the object which the inhabitants of the town have in view. They will be anxious to communicate this gratuitous blessing of Providence to the poorest individuals. In this pursuit, their interests and their inclinations will unite. They will, by preserving the health of the poor, prevent an increase of the rates for their relief; and by adding to their comforts and happiness, procure for themselves the gratifying sensations of benevolence. This consideration necessarily connects the scheme with the legal institution for the relief of the poor, and places the distribution of the profits in the hands of the Churchwardens and Overseers. When the funds are so applied, and the rates (which at present are so severely felt by the public) will be relieved by this new source of income, there can not be wanting a motive with any inhabitant of the town to prefer this supply of water to any other which may be equally or more expensive and less eligible with respect to its purity.

"But although the distribution of the profits ought to rest with the Churchwardens and Overseers, there is another consideration which may render it more eligible to place the management of the Waterworks in other hands. To effect these works it will be necessary to carry pipes under all the principal streets, and occasionally to interrupt the passage of carriages. That this interruption may be as small as possible,—that the damages done to the streets may be effectually repaired,—that no disputes may arise respecting the amount of damages or the mode of repairs, and that the public may in this respect suffer the least inconvenience, it is advisable that the management of the works should be placed under the Surveyor of the Highways, and particularly so when the offices relating to the highways and the police are united.

"With respect to the means of raising money to carry the same into effect, your Committee apprehend that a fund may be raised without any burden upon either the landowners or inhabitants. The Churchwardens, in their corporate capacity, may be authorized by the new Police Acts to issue transferable notes, bearing interest, payable yearly. These notes may either be made a perpetual loan, or be payable at a stated period. In either case they will serve as a circulating medium, and will have this advantage over cash and bank notes, that they will bear interest. The Legislature has already granted the privilege of issuing notes like these to many canal companies, and it cannot be supposed that the privilege would be refused to the first manufacturing and commercial town in the kingdom, if the extent of that circulation were limited to a sum which is necessary to be raised for the preservation of the health and comfort of its inhabitants. The interest, as well as the principal, would necessarily, in such a case, be made a charge upon the poor-rates raised in the town of Manchester. If this mode of raising

Report of Committee—continued.

money should be deemed ineligible by the inhabitants of the town, other easy means may be readily suggested.

"It may be expected that your Committee should state the probable profits or loss from the execution of the scheme. To do this accurately would require much more time than has been taken by your Committee, and a considerable degree of information arising from practical knowledge. Your Committee, however, have not been inattentive to this part of the subject. It is notorious that the profits of the New River Company in London have exceeded those of any other scheme ever instituted in this country. The two companies of proprietors of waterworks in Liverpool have had the goodness to communicate statements of their expenditures and incomes to your Committee, from which it appears that, although these are rival schemes, and very expensive ones, they are likely to prove of great advantage to the proprietors, and they afford indisputable evidence that if only one well-conducted plan should be adopted in Manchester, supported by the inhabitants at large, and operating to the benefit of every individual, it must be crowned with ultimate, and probably with immediate success.

"JAMES BATEMAN,
"Chairman of the Committee.

"Manchester, February 2nd, 1809."

The Meeting then passed the following Resolutions:—

Resolutions of Meeting.

"That it is the opinion of this Meeting that the two schemes proposed by individuals to be brought into Parliament in the present Session, for supplying the towns of Manchester and Salford with water, are ineligible;—that the sources from which the supplies of water are intended to be taken are insufficient for that purpose;—and that even if such sources were adequate, the application thereof would be highly injurious to private property, inasmuch as the same would cut off many of the springs and feeders which now supply large and extensive printing, bleaching, and dye-works with water, and afford to numerous cotton factories and other works condensing water for steam-engines.

"That it is the opinion of this Meeting that the supply of the towns of Manchester and Salford with water ought to be under the direction of their own inhabitants; and that it would be contrary to sound policy to entrust the furnishing and control of this important article of food and cleanliness, on which the health and comfort of the inhabitants depend, to persons whose sole object will be the promotion of their own private interest, and who are induced to undertake their schemes from no other motive; and that the profits of such an undertaking ought in justice to be received by the inhabitants, to go in aid of the poor-rate or other public rates of the town.

"That a Committee be appointed to oppose the above two schemes in Parliament, and that it consist of the following gentlemen, viz., the Borough-reeve and Constables, Messrs. J. L. Philips, George Duckworth, John Kennedy, Thomas Entwistle, James Bateman, Jonathan Beever, John Drinkwater, Thomas Belcher, William Myers, Otho Hulme, John Railton, Roger Farrand, Peter Ewart, Thomas Hoyle, jun., Charles Mc.Niven; and that any five of the Committee be competent to act.

"That this Meeting approves of the plan suggested by the Committee for supplying the towns of Manchester and Salford with water, taken in times of flood only from the river Tame, into large reservoirs, to be brought from thence through the Ashton Canal to a proper situation near Manchester, where it may be filtered previous to its being conducted through pipes to the houses of the inhabitants; and that the Committee be directed to communicate with the Ashton Canal Company for that purpose.

"That it be referred to the Committee before appointed, to employ proper engineers to digest a plan, and form an estimate of the expenses attending the above undertaking, and of the probable profits to arise therefrom; and that the same be laid before a future town's meeting, in time to enable them, in case they should approve thereof, to obtain powers in the intended police act for carrying the same into effect.

"That the expenses of the above opposition be paid from the police rates, and that a clause be inserted in the new police bill to authorize the payment thereof.

"That letters, with copies of these Resolutions and the Report of the Committee, be sent to the following members of both Houses of Parliament, [10 peers and 16 members of the House of Commons] and to such other members as the Committee may think necessary, requesting their attendance in Parliament to oppose the above schemes, and to support such plan as may be adopted by the inhabitants of Manchester.

"That the thanks of this Meeting be given to the Committee, for their zeal and attention in forming their able Report."

It is much to be regretted that the efforts of the town at that time were unsuccessful—they strenuously opposed the two Bills in Parliament, and though they seem to have received much valuable assistance from the local members and from many others, one of the Companies, commonly called the "Stone-pipe Company," but properly the "Manchester and Salford Waterworks Company," succeeded in carrying their Bill.

Then commenced the perpetration of one of the most barefaced and nefarious pieces of jobbery which has ever disgraced the annals of private companies, replete as they unhappily are with instances of dishonesty.

Stone-pipe Company.

For many years the general body of proprietors of the Waterworks Company and the town of Manchester and its inhabitants were, by clever trick and management, given over to the tender mercies of a small body of men, who were the owners of a quarry of oolitic sandstone in the West of England, from which they manufactured stone pipes, trading under the name of the "Stone-pipe Company."

This company acted under the authority of a patent granted to Sir George Wright, baronet, of Ray Lodge, in the county of Essex, in 1805, for "cutting pillars or tubes out of solid wood or stone."

In the year 1808 the following men constituted the Company—Sir George Wright, bart., and Messrs. William Mainwaring, Samuel Hill, Henry Wright, and Richard Hill; and with a view of extending the sale of their pipes, they projected the scheme for supplying the town of Manchester with water. As a groundwork for a company to start upon, and to prevent competition, they agreed with Sir Oswald Mosley, the Lord of the Manor, for the purchase of his interest in the waterworks which then existed for a yearly rent of £624. 10s. 1d. It was this company so inaugurated which succeeded in carrying their bill through Parliament in spite of the opposition of the town.

Manchester and Salford Waterworks Act, 20th June, 1809.

The Act was passed on the 20th June, 1809. It empowered the company to raise £60,000. in shares, and an additional sum of £50,000. on mortgage, and to erect and complete works for supplying the town with water from the river Medlock at Holt Town, but restricted them to the taking of not more than 120,000 gallons per day, unless water was running to waste in the Bridgewater Canal, and not more than one-fourth of the whole stream in dry weather. This quantity of 120,000 gallons is stated to have been the quantity which Sir Oswald Mosley had for some time previously taken for the use of the waterworks.

The Act having been passed, the first general assembly was held on the 12th July, 1809, in Manchester, at which the whole of the members of the Stone-pipe Company contrived to get appointed officers for executing the Waterworks Act. Thus Sir George Wright, Samuel Hill, Richard Hill, and George Bolton Mainwaring were appointed directors; William Mainwaring was appointed treasurer, and Henry Wright solicitor of the company. The remaining directors were relatives or friends of the shareholders in the Stone-pipe Company. A resolution was passed empowering the directors or any three of them to draw on the treasurer for what money was necessary, and the treasurer was authorized to pay the same.

The assembly was adjourned to the 4th January, 1810, to be held not in Manchester but in London, where all the members of the Stone-pipe Company resided. Previous to this adjourned meeting Sir George Wright had died and the vacancy in the direction thus occasioned, together with four others, as required by the Act, were filled up by the re-election of those going out of office (two of whom were members—a third the son of a member, and the fourth the brother of a member, of the Stone-pipe Company), and a friend of the parties;—thus giving a preponderating influence to the Stone-pipe Company over the funds of the Waterworks Company. At this meeting Mr. Henry Wright, the solicitor, was appointed chief clerk of the undertaking, and a resolution was passed committing the care and custody of the common seal to the chief clerk. All preliminary arrangements being now made business commenced, and a resolution was passed at the same meeting to the following effect:—

"That it would be highly desirable to prevent any other persons from carrying on works for supplying Manchester and Salford with water; and that, as it appeared the Stone-pipe Company were the owners of the old waterworks for supplying the inhabitants with water, and that they had the power of making additions and improvements the better to enable them to supply the town with water;—

"It was moved, seconded, and resolved unanimously:—

"That it be and it is hereby referred to the court of directors, to purchase of and from the said company of proprietors of the Stone-pipe manufactory the whole of their right, title, and interest of, in, and to the said waterworks, aqueducts, and reservoirs now belonging to them in the said town of Manchester, at the most reasonable price at which the same can be had and obtained."

At a meeting of proprietors held on the 5th July, 1810, at which only fourteen were present, of whom seven were interested in the Stone-pipe Company, one of them being appointed chairman, a report was read which contained the following piece of information:—

"Your directors have to state to you that, in pursuance of the instructions given to them at the last general assembly, they have purchased from the Stone-pipe Company the whole of their right, title, and interest in and to the ancient waterworks at Manchester. For these they have given the sum of £14,000., which has been paid by instalments to the said Company."

Sir Oswald Mosley was under the belief that the purchase from him had been made on behalf of the Waterworks Company, for whom the Stone-pipe Company merely acted as agents; and from the words of the Act of Parliament reciting the agreement with him, it would certainly appear that the purchase had been made by the Waterworks Company, who thus seem to have been entrapped into paying for the original works twice over. No part of this sum was paid to Sir Oswald Mosley. Even the rent, which had been agreed for, and which the Stone-pipe Company ought to have paid to entitle them to sell the concern, was transferred to the broad shoulders of the Waterworks Company, who seem to have paid it from the commencement as if they had been the original purchasers. The whole of the £14,000. went into the pockets of the few proprietors of the Stone-pipe manufactory, being paid, according to the directors' report, to Messrs. Samuel Hill, Henry Wright, and Richard Hill, in their characters as partners in the Stone-pipe Company. It appears that about this time some of the partners had sold their shares at 200 or 300 per cent. premium.

This transaction having been satisfactorily completed, the directors also reported at the same general assembly, on the 5th July, 1810, that they had contracted with the Stone-pipe Company for fifteen miles of main and forty-five miles of service pipes for the supply of the town, and that the pipes were in course of delivery, to be paid for within two months of being delivered. By the agreement between the two companies, an engineer of the Waterworks Company was to see the pipes proved at Gloucester or Tewkesbury prior to their delivery; but this seems to have been artfully omitted, and the pipes were never proved at all. The following prices were

<small>Price of Stone-pipes.</small>

agreed to be paid:—18in. bore, 45s. per yard; 15in., 35s.; 12in., 30s. 9d.; 9in., 18s. 8d.; 8in., 16s.; 7in., 13s. 9d.; 6in., 11s. 6d.; 4in., 7s. 8d.; and 3in. bore, 4s. 11d. per yard.

From a subsequent investigation, it appeared that at this time iron pipes could have been procured for 30 per cent. less cost, and later on for 70 per cent. less. The pipes were bored and turned out of blocks of soft stone, cut into lengths of about 2 feet, with spigot and socket joints, which were united with Roman cement. The pipes would, of course, vary in thickness, but those which are still occasionally dug out of the ground are generally from 2in. to 4in. thick.

The work now went on merrily. The pipes were delivered as rapidly as they could be furnished; and they were laid in the streets of Manchester under the immediate superintendence of two partners of the Stone-pipe Company, who were also directors in the Waterworks Company. The laying was well managed to prevent the discovery of any faulty pipe, or rather, the utter worthlessness of the whole for the purpose they were intended to serve;—they were laid in different streets, placed apart from each other, and junctions avoided, so that no trial of them could be made with the water in the river till long after the Stone-pipe Company had obtained payment to the extent of £36,984. At last, however, in July, 1812, a trial was made,—the pipes burst and were proved unable to bear the pressure. Mr. Rennie, C.E., was called in and recommended that stone-pipes should be used only where the pressure did not exceed 30 or 40 feet, and that in the lower parts of the town iron pipes should be substituted. At a special general meeting on the 15th September, 1812, it was resolved that no more pipes should be sent to Manchester without the orders of a general meeting. But the Stone-pipe Company were not to be beaten;—they were the managing directors and held the seal of the Waterworks Company. Pipes continued to be sent and paid for, till at length, at a special meeting in London, held without previous notice on the 26th November, 1813, the directors reported that the Waterworks Company were in great pecuniary difficulties; and a Committee of Inquiry was appointed of seven proprietors who presented their report on the 17th December following. They reported that "it was "fully understood that the pipes were to be equal to a pressure of 150 feet, "the Reservoir being 100 feet higher than parts of the service of the streets." They stated that though the pressure was reduced under 25 feet the pipes proved defective, and that if suffered to remain the great object of the works would be defeated. They pointed out that the plans and instructions of the Waterworks Company were entirely frustrated by the Stone-pipe Company not having delivered good, sound pipes, according to their engagement, and they declared their opinion that the Waterworks Company were entitled to redress from the Stone-pipe Company. The Committee also showed that the price of the stone-pipes very largely exceeded that of iron-pipes, and in conclusion they "stated their complete and unanimous conviction that "unless the stone-pipe system be abandoned the inevitable ruin of the "concern must be the consequence."

In the face of all this, the directors still urged the laying of the pipes "with all expedition." The company was in great pecuniary difficulties; but the acting directors, who were composed of members of the Stone-pipe Company, carried on the undertaking by accommodation paper and by misapplying the common seal of the Waterworks Company. They had run the company into a debt of upwards of £50,000., and the concern was on the eve of bankruptcy. Yet on the 15th September, 1814, at a meeting in Manchester, only eleven proprietors present (the majority being connected with the Stone-pipe Company), the directors speak of an "amicable arrangement;" and after referring to "the incontestable proofs which your directors have "of the *efficiency* of stone-pipes," they order as many of different bores "as can be laid with expedition."

At length the Stone-pipe Company, which is stated to have consisted at this time of four persons only (Samuel and Richard Hill, Henry Wright, and G. B. Wainwaring), had obtained all the money they could from the Waterworks Company; and accordingly, at a special meeting in London on the 13th December, 1814, it was resolved that the Stone-pipe Company agree that their contract with the Waterworks Company should cease, to all intents and purposes, from that date, and that mutual releases should be given. These releases, however, were not prepared, and the Stone-pipe Company soon after became embarrassed. It is almost impossible to believe that so small a body of men could for so long a period have retained such a fatal influence over a company intimately connected with the welfare of shrewd and enterprising Manchester, and numbering some at least of its townspeople amongst its proprietors.

[margin: Meeting in London, 13th Dec., 1814. Contract of Stone-pipe Company with Waterworks Company to cease.]

The extraordinary apathy with which the town seems to have looked on all this time may, perhaps, in great part be accounted for by the trouble into which it was brought by its parliamentary opposition to this very company and its rival in 1809. When the fight was over, the Commissioners of Police ordered the payment of all expenses incurred by or on behalf of the town in opposing the water bills. These orders were appealed against by Sir Oswald Mosley and the Bridgewater Trust; and though the appeals were at first dismissed, they were subsequently (under mandamuses granted by the Court of King's Bench) heard at the Salford Quarter Sessions in October, 1810. The majority of the magistrates on the Bench were of opinion that the Police Commissioners had no power to apply the police fund in a parliamentary defence of the rights of the

[margin: Orders to pay Expenses of Town in opposing Waterworks Company in Parliament appealed against by Sir Oswald Mosley and Bridgewater Trust.]

inhabitants, though such defence be directed and carried on by the inhabitants at large; and, therefore, the orders of the Commissioners for the payment were set aside. The Parliamentary Committee, in reporting the result, thus point out the consequences of the decision of the Quarter Sessions:—

> "The inhabitants of Manchester have no public rate or income expressly appropriated to the defraying the expenses of any application to Parliament, either to obtain or amend a police Act, or other Act for the improvements of the town; and it is to be regretted that they are equally destitute of any pecuniary fund for their protection in Parliament against any individual, or any set of individuals, who may apply for powers exceedingly injurious to its interests. For instance, a power to make waterworks, and break up the streets (not either limiting the price or stipulating the quality of the water), has already been obtained, contrary to the wishes of the inhabitants. In some other towns (for want of opposition from the inhabitants), Acts have been obtained compelling the inhabitants to purchase the water. If the present waterworks in Manchester should prove unprofitable, or if the proprietors should not be satisfied with a profit of two or three hundred per cent., an application may be made for an Act to compel the inhabitants of Manchester to pay the proprietors such sums as may be satisfactory to the latter; and if the inhabitants are (by appeals like the present) deprived of the means of being heard in Parliament against such an application, Parliament may presume a tacit consent; and although none of the future proprietors of the waterworks may happen to be inhabitants of Manchester, it is possible that some one of them may have a tenant or servant in whose name he can prosecute an appeal. Your Committee, therefore, beg leave to submit to your consideration the high importance of immediately providing some adequate means for the support of your rights, your property, and your independence.
>
> "On behalf of the Committee,
>
> "J. LEIGH PHILIPS, Chairman."

Report of Parliamentary Committee.

The unhappy dilemma in which Manchester found itself has not unfrequently been experienced by other places, even down to the present time, in cases where corporations or other public authorities have endeavoured to oppose objectionable or to carry out beneficial measures affecting the interest of the towns they represented. It is an anomaly in the state of the law which ought to be removed.

The affairs of the Waterworks Company were now in a deplorable condition. They were involved in litigation of all kinds; they had been compelled to apply for power to raise more money, and had obtained an Act for that purpose in 1813, empowering them to raise amongst themselves any sum not exceeding £100,000. In April, 1815, their affairs were handed over to trustees, who continued in receipt of the water-rates till August, 1819. Sir Oswald Mosley had made a distress for his rent. The taxes were in arrear. There was not a penny to pay labourers' wages, and no person would sell the company anything upon credit. The Stone-pipe Company were represented to be insolvent, and there appeared to be no way of extricating the company from its difficulties. But, according to an Irish proverb, "when things are at the worst they are sure to mend." The proprietors determined to change the management of affairs, and to appoint directors residing in Manchester, where in future they should hold their courts, and where the entire management should be carried on. This gave some confidence to the town, and several gentlemen residing there consented to become directors. The directors in Manchester held their first court in Manchester in August, 1816, and from that time a new state of things was introduced. With great difficulty they obtained possession of the books and documents in the hands of the London directors and the Stone-pipe Company, and they then investigated the accounts, and resisted the payment of the balance alleged to be due to the Stone-pipe Company, having become aware of their illegal transactions. They obtained an Act of Parliament in 1816 for further powers to raise money and to protect the company from a repetition of the evils under which they had so long suffered. They determined to substitute iron pipes for stone ones, and directed the engineer, Mr. Ruddock, to make an estimate of the cost. His estimate, presented on the 14th May, 1817, amounted to £21,920. 6s. 2d.; and by 1823 the Company had expended upwards of £16,000. in this process of substitution. The Manchester directors being of opinion that the Company could not flourish until the numerous debts due to their "*bonâ fide*" creditors were satisfied, suggested that money should be raised for that purpose by the creation of an additional number of shares, which suggestion was carried into effect; and by the proceeds thereof, with a sum of £20,000. borrowed from the commissioners for the issue of exchange bills, the "*bonâ fide*" creditors of the Company were paid, and in August, 1819, the directors were again in receipt of the water-rates.

The foregoing is substantially an abridgment of a very interesting account of "Old Manchester and its Supply of Water," which appeared in the *Manchester Guardian* newspaper in the month of November, 1850, from the pen of one of the very able editors of that journal. It is compiled from very careful research into old documents and records, and as it contains many things of interest, which have not been introduced here, it is printed *in extenso* in the Appendix. Account of "Old Manchester and its Supply of Water."—*Manchester Guardian*, November, 1850.

The singular narrative of the gross mismanagement and jobbery which marked the career of the Manchester and Salford Waterworks Company could not be passed over without notice in a history or description of the Manchester Waterworks. It has been given as briefly as possible; for though it is not without interest and instruction, yet it seems hardly creditable to a town which could publicly entertain, and resolve to act on, such sound and judicious views of local administration as those which are contained in the recommendations of the committee and in the resolutions of the public meetings in 1808 and 1809.

The town, however, has fully redeemed its character since that time, and in fulfilment of the views then entertained it has led the way to the establishment of that sound principle, now almost universally acted upon, that everything which affects the material well-being, and the comfort, health, and prosperity of a town, should be under the control of the inhabitants themselves. The Corporation are now the owners of the Waterworks, and under their enlightened and liberal management a most abundant supply of excellent water is delivered at cost price to every inhabitant. Corporation, Owners of Waterworks.

From the time at which the Stone-pipe Company ceased to control the actions of the Waterworks Company the affairs of the Waterworks Company were conducted regularly and steadily enough, but it was long before they could recover from the lamentable and depressed condition into which they had been brought. The supply from the Medlock was much too limited in quantity, and the water was gradually becoming deteriorated by printing and bleaching establishments and other trading operations.

The town was rapidly increasing in size and importance, and in 1821 the company again applied to Parliament for power to raise more money and to extend the limits of the district to be supplied. No new sources of supply seem, however, to have been obtained, and finding that the water they had was quite inadequate for the district they had included, they Manchester and Salford Waterworks Company's Act, 1821, authorizing additional capital.

D

resolved to apply to Parliament for powers to construct additional works on an entirely fresh source of supply.

Act 1823 authorizing construction of Gorton Reservoirs.

In 1823 they obtained an Act for constructing large reservoirs in Gorton, about four miles from Manchester, on ground high enough to supply the whole town by gravitation, although it was at first contemplated to carry the water only to the existing reservoirs at Beswick. This was an important step in the right direction; and, considering the limited views which then existed as to the requirements of a town, and the losses which the company had sustained, it was a bold and highly creditable undertaking.

Beswick Reservoirs.

Up to this time the waterworks had consisted of a couple of small reservoirs or settling ponds at Beswick, into which the water from the Medlock was received, and a larger reservoir, about seven acres in extent, and containing 5,404,311 cubic feet, about 67 feet above Piccadilly in Manchester, into which the water from the settling ponds was pumped by a stationary single-acting condensing engine of 45 horse-power, made by Bolton and Watt. From this reservoir, which formed the service reservoir of the town, the water was conducted by pipes,—first wooden ones, then stone ones, and finally cast-iron. The quantity which the company was permitted to take from the river was still limited to 120,000 gallons per day, except in times of flood. Upon these works they had managed to spend and throw away, from 1809 to 1823, no less a sum than £228,000., and upon this outlay they had not yet received a single dividend.

Gorton Reservoirs.

The reservoirs at Gorton were to be placed on a stream of water which derived its supplies from about 1,500 acres of surface drainage. By the Act of 1823, which authorized their construction, the company were empowered to take flood waters only—the ordinary stream being required to pass to the parties entitled to it through gauges to be constructed for that purpose. This principle of division or arrangement was the same as that on which most canal reservoirs had been constructed. It required large reservoirs to contain all the water which flowed from the ground in floods, and with that view the reservoirs, two in number, appear to have been laid out. They covered, with embankments and other works when constructed, about $61\frac{1}{4}$ acres of ground with a water surface of $56\frac{1}{4}$ acres, and contained about 35,000,000 cubic feet of water, about 31,000,000 of which were available for the supply of the town. It is difficult to determine how much of all the water which flowed from the district passed into the reservoirs so as to become available for the supply of Manchester. The elevation of the ground from which the water was collected was slight, nowhere rising to more than 334 feet above the level of the sea; while that of the lower reservoir itself was 244 feet, and the upper one 259. The drainage ground consisted partly of pastoral and partly of moss land, 212 acres of Droylsden or Ashton Moss being included within the area. Several small villages and many detached farms and houses were scattered over the district, so that it presented no very favourable features for the collection of water for the supply of a town. It was however the nearest high land suitable for the purpose which could be found, and it enabled the company to obtain a great addition to their supplies, and most materially to improve the position of their waterworks. The average quantity of rain was about 36 inches per annum. If of this 18 inches flowed from the ground and down the streams, the gross produce would be equal to an average quantity of about 1,780,000 gallons per day. From this must be deducted the quantity which would pass through the gauges. There would probably remain something more than 1,000,000 gallons per day for the use of the waterworks if nothing was filched from the gauges. In process of time, however, as water became valuable to the company, no more was permitted to run past the reservoirs than was absolutely necessary for the wants of the landowners and other parties below; and the gross supply at the command of the company, including what was taken from the Medlock, was estimated at 1,400,000 or 1,500,000 gallons per day. *Quantity of Water from Gorton Reservoirs.*

The works at Gorton were completed about 1825 or 1826 and the water was conveyed from thence to Beswick, a distance of about three miles, by a cast-iron pipe of 18 inches in diameter. At this time the population of Manchester and Salford and the district within the limits of the water supply would be nearly 200,000 persons; but as a very large number of these were not supplied with water by the company, the supply they had now obtained might be considered, as compared with what had previously existed and as compared with other places, tolerably abundant. *Works at Gorton commenced 1825 or 1826.*

The Gorton reservoirs and the works for conveying the water to Beswick were constructed by the late Mr. Nicholas Brown, of Wakefield, an engineer who had had considerable experience in the formation of canals and the reservoirs for supplying them with water. The reservoirs appear to have been well constructed, but all the details, which were essentially of *Constructed by Mr. Nicholas Brown, of Wakefield.*

a waterworks character were ill designed, and had to be materially altered and improved in after years by Mr. Simpson, C.E., of London, who subsequently became the engineer of the Waterworks Company. When the reservoirs where finished the quantity of water supplied to the town, according to an experiment made by Mr. Nicholas Brown in May, 1826, appears to have been 943,250 gallons per day. From this time there appears to have been nothing done towards extending or improving the supply of water for many years. The consumption gradually increased and the rental and position of the company consequently improved. In 1831 they first paid a dividend, twenty-two years after the first establishment of the company.

<small>Mr. Simpson's Report, May, 1842.</small>

In 1842 the company, feeling that they had carried on without alteration as long as possible, and experiencing great difficulty in meeting the demands for water which pressed upon them from the rapid growth of the town, called in Mr. Simpson to advise them as to the best means of improving the waterworks and obtaining more ample supplies of water. Mr. Simpson presented his report on the 31st May, 1842. He found the works in very bad condition;—the 18-inch main pipe from Gorton to Beswick, which ought, if properly laid, to have been capable of conveying 2,385,000 gallons in twenty-four hours, had been laid with so little attention to curves and levels and other details, that it did originally convey, according to a memorandum left by Mr. Brown, only 1,966,000 in that time, and when Mr. Simpson examined it in 1842 it could convey only 1,506,900 gallons in the twenty-four hours. This reduction in delivery, he attributed, in part, to an obstruction at the rose of the pipe in the Gorton reservoir, but principally to incrustation and to accumulations of sediment inside the pipe. He recommended various important improvements in the details of the reservoirs and the piping, so as to enable the company to deliver the water with more ease and certainty and in better condition, and, without suggesting any locality or direction in which he thought it likely an additional supply of water could be obtained, he urged upon the attention of the directors the importance of procuring large additional supplies from some place at a distance from Manchester, where the land was of little value, and where large store reservoirs could be constructed at a sufficient elevation to permit the water to flow from them into the Gorton reservoirs.

Although Mr. Simpson at this time estimated that the two reservoirs at Gorton contained together 226,000,000 gallons, (or 35,160,000 cubic feet,) of water, yet, after making what he considered proper reductions for evaporation during long droughts and other circumstances, the total store which could be considered available for the town was 133,000,000 gallons, which at 1½ million gallons per day, assumed as the quantity then supplied, would last out only 88 days. If the tenants who then took the water were *well supplied*, the quantity required would be increased 20 per cent. and then the store would last out only 74 days. He estimated that the available quantity of water in store should be equal to at least 120 days' service.

His report was accompanied by several tables and calculations, and amongst the rest the following estimated average quantity of water (received from Gorton and from the river Medlock at Beswick) in each year from 1836 to 1841, inclusive :— *Mr. Simpson's Estimate of quantity supplied.*

	Gallons per diem.	Received from Gorton.	Raised by Beswick Engine.	Total in Years.
		Gallons.	Gallons.	Gallons.
1836...	1,294,000	345,523,000	59,499,000	405,022,000
1837...	1,325,000	362,750,000	51,975,000	414,725,000
1838...	1,340,000	398,828,000	20,592,000	419,420,000
1839...	1,355,400	390,827,700	33,412,500	424,240,200
1840...	1,400,000	411,965,000	26,235,000	438,200,000
1841...	1,433,000	418,433,000	30,096,000	448,529,000

Looking at the increase which had taken place in the population of the district within the limits of supply, and assuming 1,500,000 gallons per day to have been the supply in 1841, he made the following calculation :—That the supply then required, making good deficiencies, was 1,800,000 gallons per day; that in 1851 it would be from 2,340,000 to 2,412,000, according as the future progressive increase of population was continued; in 1861 from 3,042,000 to 3,400,920; and in 1871 it would amount to from 3,954,600 to 5,033,361 gallons per day. The lower numbers are computed on an increase of 34 per cent. in each decennial period; the higher numbers on 34 per cent. for the first period, 41 per cent. for the second, and 48 per cent. for the third decennial period. The result far outstripped these calculations. By the year 1858 the actual consumption of water amounted to 11,000,000 gallons per day, almost four times the highest quantity Mr. Simpson had looked forward to as likely to be required at that time. *His Estimate of future requirements.* *Actual result four times as much.*

Mr. Simpson's recommendations carried out.

The alterations which he recommended in the details of the works were carried out. The mode of discharging the water from the reservoirs and the facility of accomplishing it were materially improved. A new line of pipes, 24 inches diameter, was laid from the Gorton reservoirs along the Hyde-road direct to Manchester, and several larger mains were laid and other improvements were effected in the town. No additional supply of water, however, being obtained, the pressure of increasing demand was only the more severely felt by the greater facility which these improvements afforded to the inhabitants for drawing water. No suitable or comprehensive scheme was projected, and so urgent became the necessities of the company that, as a temporary expedient, they applied for and obtained a supply of water for several years from the Ashton canal. The water was run from the canal at Fairfield into the upper reservoir at Gorton at convenient periods, and there allowed to settle and clarify until it was considered fit for use, after which it was passed into the lower reservoir and supplied to the town.

Supply from Ashton Canal.

Shaft or well in new red sandstone at Gorton.

At length Mr. Simpson recommended that a shaft should be sunk into the new red sandstone which lay beneath the Gorton reservoirs, although it was there covered for some depth by sand and clay, in expectation that a considerable quantity of water might be procured by that means. This expectation was grounded on his recent experience in sinking the Green-lane well in Liverpool, and in similar undertakings which had been carried out there and elsewhere in the same geological formation. The town of Liverpool had, for many years, been supplied with water principally obtained from wells sunk into the new red sandstone on which the town is situated, and Mr. Simpson was at this time engaged in sinking the most successful well which has been formed there, and which was then yielding water of very good quality and in great abundance—upwards of 1,000,000 gallons per day, which were pumped out by a steam-engine. Encouraged by this success he advised the Manchester Waterworks Company to adopt similar measures, as the geological formation of the country was the same and there appeared good ground for supposing that the quantity yielded would be equal in amount. Indeed a larger quantity was anticipated, for it was expected that the additional supplies to be obtained by this course would be from 2,000,000 to 4,000,000 gallons per day. Mr. Simpson was supported in his views by the local mining and geological knowledge of the late Mr. Bradbury, of the

Clayton collieries, near Manchester, and not many miles from the site of the well at Gorton.

The proposition was one which particularly recommended itself to the adoption of the directors of the company, for the works could be undertaken without the necessity of applying for parliamentary powers; the well or shaft could be commenced at once on ground already belonging to the company, and could be prosecuted as rapidly or as slowly as might be thought desirable. The cost would not be great, and there was a certainty of finding some supply of water, which, although it might not be so large as was anticipated, and would be hard in quality, would yet be pleasant drinking water, bright and colourless, and a valuable addition to the limited quantity they were already in possession of. The work was therefore determined upon. It was commenced in the Autumn of 1845,—suspended for some time during the time that the company applied to Parliament for powers to carry out a much larger scheme which will by-and-by be noticed,—then recommenced when that scheme was abandoned, and finally completed in the year 1849, after the commencement of the works since executed by the Manchester Corporation.

As this, and the pumping engine connected therewith, formed the last work constructed by the Manchester and Salford Waterworks Company, it will be convenient to give a short description of them here, although it comes somewhat out of place in the regular order of events. Between their commencement and completion other important steps had been taken for obtaining a more abundant supply of water, but they form altogether a new era in the history of the works, and must be treated separately. The well is 12 feet in diameter, it is sunk to a depth of 212ft. 6in., and from the bottom galleries are driven in various directions. The well was sunk through clay and sand for 131ft. 6in. before it reached the rock. Before reaching the rock a good deal of water issued from the granite sand passed through, and from a bed of coarse gravel 5 feet thick which lay upon the rock; but these supplies gradually decreased. After reaching the rock the quantity yielded increased as the depth became greater. The water was pumped out during the sinking, and the excavated material raised by an engine of 25 horse-power, until the water produced was more than the engine could raise. When this occurred the well had been sunk 194ft. 6in., and the further sinking was suspended until a new and more powerful engine was erected. This engine was a very beautiful and excellent single-acting condensing engine made by the Hayle Foundry Company, in Cornwall. The nominal power was 160 horses. The diameter of the piston was 60 inches and the length of stroke 10 feet. It was furnished with two sets of pumps—one a plunger pump of 24 inches in diameter and 10 feet stroke, and the other a bucket pump of 28 inches in diameter and 7ft. 6in. stroke, only one set of pumps being intended to work at once.

After the engine was completed and set to work, the well was sunk 18 feet deeper and the tunnels driven. The principal increase of water was obtained by the driving of the tunnels which crossed various cracks or fissures, each of which yielded a copious supply of water. These fissures were in some cases 8 inches in width; they ran in a direction from North-East to South-West. This was in a direction nearly at right angles to the line of junction which the red sand-stone is supposed to make on its Eastern margin with the coal measures, and upon which it rests or abuts unconformably. This line of junction or outcrop of sandstone is covered by diluvium or boulder clay, but it is ascertained to pass within a few hundred yards of the well and to the East of it, and forms the Eastern or North-Eastern boundary of this portion of the new red sand-stone basin. It is evident, therefore, that a well sunk into the new red sandstone so near its outcrop, and where it was so thickly covered by impervious clay, was not in a well-chosen site for yielding a large supply of water, but during the sinking it amounted at one time to 1,500,000 gallons per day.

Quantity yielded by well.

Cost.

The engine commenced working in February, 1847, and continued regularly at work till the beginning of 1851. After that time it was occasionally employed, in periods of exigency, during the early construction of the Corporation works, and before they had been so far completed as to supply the town without aid from other sources. The quantity yielded by the well had fallen to 1,200,000 gallons per day in 1850, and to 750,000 gallons a-day in 1852, according to daily measurements taken previous to the pumping being discontinued. The cost of lifting the water a height of 193 feet was 1·819 of a penny per 1,000 gallons, with coal at about 12s. per ton. The total cost of the well, engine, buildings, and all attendant expenses was about £20,300.

We now come to a period at which the supplies of water for domestic purposes began to be regarded on much broader bases. The commission for inquiry into the health of large towns in 1844, had revealed how deplorably deficient their supplies of water generally were, and how much the health of the inhabitants depended on an abundant supply of good and wholesome water, and on the proper sewerage and cleansing of the towns they lived in. The rapidity with which populations had increased in Great Britain, especially in the manufacturing districts and the great seats of industry, had been such that no adequate provision had been made for the wants and comforts of the people, who were thus herding together in great communities; and the necessity of undertaking bold and comprehensive measures for improving the sanitary condition of towns generally, and especially of those which had been suddenly created or enlarged, was fast forcing itself upon the attention of the country. This was nowhere more evident than in the manufacturing towns of Lancashire and Yorkshire. In both these counties the supply of water had already received more than ordinary attention, and many works of importance had been constructed within a comparatively recent period. The peculiar geological and geographical position of many of the towns in these districts had naturally led to the construction of waterworks on the gravitation principle, most of them on an inadequate scale, but still forming good starting points for subsequent extension, and supplying much useful information.

Health of Towns Report.

The manufacturing district of Lancashire lies on the western slope, and the manufacturing district of Yorkshire on the eastern slope of the Pennine chain of hills commonly called the "back-bone of England." These hills occupy a position about midway between the Irish channel and the German ocean. Commencing in the mountainous district of the northerly portion of the west riding of Yorkshire, they extend, as bold and rugged hills, in a direction due south, and finally die away, in more gentle eminences, about Ashbourne, in Derbyshire. They form not only the highest land and the natural watershed or summit of the country, reaching in various parts an elevation of nearly 2,000 feet above the sea, but they are also the geological summit or anticlinal ridge of the different strata which have been raised or exposed to view by the original elevation of the ground. In the Peak Forest district near Castleton on the south, and in the neighbourhood of Skipton on the north, the carboniferous limestone has been thrown up and forms the summit of the country. In the intermediate

Manufacturing Districts.
"Back-bone of England."

Water from Mill-stone Grit.

distance, the highest ground is composed of the mill-stone grit and the strata of the lower coal measures. As the ground gradually falls away to the east and the west, the lower strata dip under the coal measures, and the valuable beds of the Lancashire and Yorkshire coalfields come in and form the principal geological features on their respective sides of the summit of the country. The water which is found in the millstone grit formation, and in the shales and sandstones of the lower coal measures, is not only abundant but soft and pure, the springs yielding the most sparkling water, fit for all purposes of life or trade. The upper part of the hills is bleak and sterile, almost wholly moorland, generally capped with peat moss, covered with heather, and abounding with grouse. The slopes are cut up into deep, narrow and picturesque valleys, down which an infinite number of small streams find their way to the level country at the foot, and are there gradually collected into important rivers.

Cotton and Woollen Trades.

The establishment of the two great staple trades of the Cotton and Woollen manufactures in these districts is no doubt owing to many of these local peculiarities and advantages. The innumerable small streams of excellent water fed by the copious rain which fell on the hills above,—the abundance of coal,—cheap and excellent building materials,—a native population, eminently intelligent, hardy and industrious, and the many natural facilities for communicating with the great markets and seaports of the country, all combined to create and foster that extraordinary commercial prosperity, and that rapid growth of population, which are now the distinguishing features of these parts of England.

Waterworks at Sheffield, Ashton, &c., established in 1825.

Most of the waterworks, of any noticeable character, which had been constructed for the accommodation of the inhabitants of the populous places in these districts, had been established by joint-stock companies in the speculative period of 1825, and had been generally attended with very successful pecuniary results. The establishment, or material enlargement, of the waterworks at Sheffield, Ashton, Oldham, Bolton, and Preston are, with many others, all to be referred to this period. All these places were supplied by works laid out on the same principle—that of collecting the springs or the surface drainage of a neighbouring upland district, storing the water to some extent in reservoirs at a point higher than the district to be supplied, and conveying it thence by iron pipes for distribution. Previous to this period, at the end of the last and at the commencement of the present century, the speculative rage of the country had expanded itself in the formation of canals. The construction of these works had brought about the formation of large reservoirs for the purpose of supplying them with water, and in this way much valuable experience and information (all having an intimate bearing on the construction of town waterworks) might have been acquired and collected. It is surprising, however, how little had been done to turn to good account the opportunities for obtaining information which these works afforded. Scarcely anywhere had observations been made on the fall of rain or the quantity of water which could be collected from any given area. A rain-gauge, except in the hands of a philosophical observer, was a thing unknown. All was guess or "rule of thumb." It is believed there were no observations from which any definite conclusions could be drawn which had at that time been obtained by any canal company or waterworks in the country. The earliest, and indeed the only, information capable of being turned to practical account, which existed for many years, was the result of observations by the late Mr. Thom, of Rothesay, in Scotland, and unfortunately very little of the knowledge he accumulated has been made public. In a paper, which he contributed to the Institution of Civil Engineers, he gave the measurements of the rain which fell at the Shaws Waterworks, above Greenock, and the quantity of water which was collected during the years 1826 and 1828 in the large reservoirs he had constructed there for the joint supply of the town of Greenock and for driving the machinery of mills. These measurements will be referred to hereafter. Canal Reservoirs.

Observations of Mr. Thom, of Rothesay.

The construction of these works seems to have been the first systematized attempt to render *all* the water of a district available for useful purposes. Millowners' reservoirs, whether constructed by themselves for their own benefit, or by canal or waterworks companies as compensation for interfering with their supply of water, had been frequently before constructed both in England and in Scotland, but their size and their capability had been the result of bargain or of accident, and had no where been laid out with reference to the fall of rain and the water flowing from the collecting area, so as nicely and accurately to adjust their proportions to the supply which might be expected.

Some of the reservoirs of the Shaws Waterworks were amongst the largest artificial sheets of water which had been constructed. The success Shaws Waterworks.

of the work seems to have created—or, perhaps, rather revived—a desire on the part of millowners in other districts, to impound the surplus water of floods and wet seasons for use in increasing the volume of the streams which drove their machinery in seasons of drought. The Turton and Entwistle reservoir, near Bolton, in Lancashire, was the first large work undertaken by millowners themselves, which followed the construction of the Shaws Waterworks. The undertaking was no doubt prompted by the advantage which had been derived from a large reservoir in the adjoining valley called the Belmont reservoir, which had been constructed (as the result of a very hard bargain, by the Bolton Waterworks Company) for the benefit of the millowners on the river Eagley, in lieu of a valuable spring which that company obtained parliamentary powers to take for the supply of the town. Both these reservoirs were in very favourable situations for holding a large quantity of water. The Belmont reservoir was formed by an embankment in a narrow gorge 70 feet in height, and the company were required to discharge from it, for the benefit of the millowners, a stipulated and guaranteed uniform quantity of water for twelve hours in each working day.

Turton and Entwistle Reservoir.

Belmont Reservoir.

The Turton and Entwistle reservoir was formed by an embankment in an equally convenient and advantageous position. The embankment was projected to be 128 feet in height, but was only completed to a height of 108 feet. At this height it proved large enough to hold all the water which could be collected, when the quantity discharged was properly regulated and the reservoir worked to the full extent of its power.

Other reservoirs, on the same principle as the Turton and Entwistle reservoir, were constructed about the same time, or soon after, in other parts of the country, but these two reservoirs furnished the best and almost the only reliable information which existed for calculating the probable water produce of a district in the Lancashire hills, at the time to which we have brought the history of the Manchester Waterworks.

Bann Reservoirs.

In the year 1835, in association with Mr. Fairbairn (afterwards Sir William Fairbairn), I was engaged by the millowners on the river Bann, in Ireland, to survey and lay out the necessary works for the construction of storage reservoirs on that river, and an Act of Parliament for their construction was obtained in 1836. In the course of the three following years the works were completed according to my designs and under my direction as engineer to the company.

These works consisted of a large reservoir in the Mourne mountains in the county of Down, which, when completed, held nearly 300,000,000 cubic feet of water, supplied by the water draining from 3,300 acres of mountain land—and of a smaller reservoir on a lower portion of the river to hold occasional floods and night water.

Here was a good opportunity for obtaining accurate and valuable information, and accordingly rain-gauges were put down at Lough Island Reavy, the name of the largest reservoir, about 400 feet above the level of the sea, and on Spelga mountain, a hill 1,400 feet in height and selected as likely to represent the mean fall on the mountains. These gauges were continued for several years, and when the reservoir was finished the quantity of water which was received by it was also accurately observed. The general result was that the rain, in an average year, amounted to about 72 inches per annum at Lough Island Reavy reservoir, and to 74 inches on the Spelga mountain, and of this quantity about 48 inches reached the reservoir besides allowing a quantity to run to waste.

A year or two subsequently I was engaged in laying out a series of reservoirs, of which one was shortly afterwards constructed, called the Glossop reservoirs, for the purpose of impounding the floods and regulating the flow of water in the streams in the neighbourhood of Glossop, in Derbyshire. Here again was a good opportunity for obtaining information as to the fall of rain upon the Pennine chain of hills, and particularly as to the comparative fall at various heights from the foot of the hills on the westerly side right across the hills, over the summit to the foot of the easterly slope, which, by the assistance of friends who undertook to superintend the observations, I was enabled to obtain. One rain-gauge was put down near Glossop, at the westerly foot of the hills, about 500 feet above the level of the sea;—another at the head of Hurst Brook valley, near the summit of the hills on the westerly side, about 1,500 feet above the sea;—a third on the easterly side of the summit, about 1,600 feet high, on the flank of Kinder Scout, the highest hill in the district, and at the head of Ashop-dale; and a fourth in the valley of the river Derwent, at Bamford-cum-Hathersage, about 300 feet above the sea. The results of these observations were given in a paper which was contributed to the Literary and Philosophical Society of Manchester, in 1844, entitled—" Observations " on the relation which the fall of Rain bears to the water flowing from

(margin notes: Glossop Reservoirs. Rain-gauges on Pennine chain of hills.)

"the ground." The observations had not been very regularly kept, but the mean annual results, as recorded by the gauges, are as follows:—

At the westerly foot of the hills, for 2¼ years	45 inches.
At the westerly edge of the summit plain, 4 years...	61·7 inches.
Ditto mean of 1840 and 1841	67·8 "
Ditto in 1842, dry year...................................	47·1 "
Easterly edge of summit plain, mean of 1840 and 1841	77·45 "
Easterly foot of hills in the valley of the Derwent, mean of 1840 and 1841	40·85 "

These years were all below the average, judging from Dr. Dalton's observations for 47 years at Manchester.

The gauges were all placed within about 9 inches or a foot of the ground, in open situations, and consisted of a cylinder, sunk into the ground, about 36 inches long and 7 inches diameter, with a receiving funnel of the same diameter. The depth of rain received by the gauge was indicated by an index rod attached to a float which rose as the gauge filled, the rod passing through a small hole at the bottom of the funnel. The gauge was emptied from time to time, but objections were subsequently taken to the accuracy of the results, on the ground that the index rod as it rose above the top of the funnel would expose a larger surface and so increase the area for collecting rain. To some extent this objection was well founded, and it is probable that the depths shown are a little in excess of the rain which actually fell. Still, they were a near approximation, and they were the first gauges which showed that a much larger quantity of rain fell on the hills in this locality than on the plains below.

Various previous experiments had been made with rain-gauges raised abruptly from the surface,—by Dr. Dalton on St. John's Church in Manchester,—by Professor Phillips on York Minster, and by others; and a few isolated observations had been taken on the rain falling on high points of hill as compared with what fell at the foot; and as these observations showed that less rain was received by a gauge the higher it was raised from the surface of the earth, it had been erroneously concluded by many that less rain fell on elevated land than on low land. The observations which I had made, however, led me to form a very different opinion, and as the fact was one of great importance in all questions relating to supplies of water, my attention was especially directed to it, and I lost no opportunity of obtaining accurate information.

In the Parliamentary Session of 1838 I had been employed, by some objecting landowners, to oppose a scheme for obtaining additional supplies of water for the town of Oldham, and had consequently examined the engineering merits of the proposed extension. The original waterworks had been established for nearly 15 years. No rain-gauge had been put down, and consequently no record of what rain fell in the district had been kept. No measurement of the water, which was received from the drainage ground of the reservoir, had ever been taken, and, therefore, nothing was known either of the probable rain or the probable quantity of water which the scheme which had been laid out would produce for the supply of Oldham. All was mere surmise. Under these circumstances, and with the aid of the late Mr. Leather, of Leeds (with whom I was associated in the inquiry), all the information which could be obtained of the fall of rain in neighbouring localities was hunted up. The most important was a series of many years' observations along the line of the Rochdale Canal and over the Pennine chain of hills by Blackstone Edge. They embraced the whole mass of hill, from Middleton and Rochdale on the westerly foot, over the summit by the Whiteholme and Blackstone Edge reservoirs, to Ripponden and Sowerby Bridge on the easterly foot. From the proximity and similarity of the districts they seemed to be exactly what was required. They had been regularly furnished by the Canal Company to Dr. Dalton, and by him contributed to the Manchester Literary and Philosophical Society, in whose Memoirs they were published.

Opposition to Extension of Oldham Waterworks, 1838.

Rochdale Canal Rain-gauges.

Taking these observations as the ground-work of calculation, it was clearly proved that there was not water enough to fill the reservoir which had been projected, and that the works contemplated, while they would have injured the landowners, who were opposing the measure, would have been useless for the purpose of the company. The scheme was accordingly defeated and the Bill lost.

A few years after this, the various hill observations which I had established in different parts of the country, unquestionably proved that much more rain than had been registered by the Rochdale canal gauges must have fallen on the hills above Rochdale and Oldham, and I accordingly directed my attention to the character and position of the gauges which had been employed. I found that they were all fixed in the ridging of the roofs of the houses of the persons in whose custody they were placed. This was at once sufficient to explain the discrepancy. No doubt this position had been chosen from the impression that, being the most exposed situation which could be found, it would necessarily catch all the rain which fell, in ignorance of the ascertained fact, that less rain fell on the top of a house than on the ground, and less on the top of a tower than on the top of a house; and overlooking the circumstance, which would have been obvious on reflection, that every wind which blew would be deflected upwards by the sloping roof of the house,—would rush with increased velocity over the ridging, and carry away the rain which ought to have fallen into the gauge.

Many years of observations were thus worse than useless, for they had been issued to the world with the high authority of Dr. Dalton, who would be ignorant of the position of the gauges. They would be implicitly believed in by all who were not acquainted with the circumstances, and had already been the means (in the case of Oldham) of preventing the passing of a useful Act of Parliament. The subject was therefore brought under the notice of the Manchester Literary and Philosophical Society, in whose Memoirs, as already stated, the returns had been published. A committee of that body was formed, consisting of Mr. Peter Clare, Mr. Stanway, and myself, for the purpose of testing the accuracy of the observations, not only on the line of the Rochdale canal, but also on the lines of the Ashton and Peak Forest canals, where observations had been going on for some time, and where similar errors had, in some cases, been committed. Of this committee I was the only acting member. Everything was done under my direction, and beyond the first cost of the rain gauges, which was borne by the Society, all the expenses of observation were defrayed by me. It was determined to put down gauges within a few inches of the ground, in exposed situations, as near as possible to those of the Canal Company, which were still to remain on the ridges of the houses on which they were placed. The gauges were of the cylinder form already described. They were sunk into the earth to within about 8 or 9 inches of the top, within a strong box to prevent injury, and to permit their being taken out for repairs or emptying. The observations were made monthly and the gauges then regularly emptied.

The first year's observations produced the following results:—

	According to Rochdale Canal Company's Gauges placed on the ridges of the Lock-keepers' or other houses.	Average fall according to same Gauges.	Number of years of average.	According to the Society's Gauges put down in open situations nearly on a level with the ground.	Difference in Inches.	Excess per cent. over Company's Gauges.
	In. dec.	In. dec.		In. dec.	In. dec.	
Slattocks, or Lane Side, near Middleton	18·14	30·88	8 years.	28·8	10·66	58·76
Moss Lock, near Rochdale	20·50	29·10	16 "	30·3	9·80	47·8
Whiteholme Reservoir, Blackstone Edge	22·64	34·27	21 "	35·1	12·46	55
Toll Bar, Blackstone Edge	23·45	36·35	10 "	34·2	10·75	45·84
Blackhouse, near Ripponden	24·89	......	......	35·9	11·01	44·28
Sowerby Bridge	16·77	27·61	18 "	23·8	7·03	41·92

Rochdale Canal Company's Rain Gauges and those of Literary and Philosophical Society.

This was clear proof that the Canal Company's gauge did not show the real quantity of rain.

Looking, however, at all the observations which had been made during the year, there appeared to be a pretty regular ratio between the falls registered by the two different gauges at the same place, the variation from which was confined within much narrower limits than might have been expected. By applying a corresponding correction to the past observations of the Canal Company, it was believed that a tolerable approximation to the truth might be arrived at. This ratio might be taken as two to three for the gauges on the summit of the hill and for those on the westerly side (being that most exposed to the winds which were accompanied by rain), and at six to eight for the gauges on the easterly side of the summit.

These corrections made, the following would represent the probable average rain which would annually reach the earth at the respective places, *Corrections.*

which, from one year's observations, it appeared we should be justified in assuming:—

    At Slattocks ....46 inches per annum.
          (450 feet above level of the sea.)
        Moss Lock 44   "   "
          (500.)
        Whiteholme Reservoir 51   "   "
          (1,200.)
        Toll bar, Blackstone Edge..................54   "   "
          (1,000.)
        Sowerby Bridge 37   "   "
          (300.)

These observations were continued for many years, the particulars of which will be found in the Appendix. The average result was as follows:—

    At Moss Lock, Rochdale ....$34\frac{1}{4}$ inches.
        Whiteholme Reservoir......................................51·4   "
        Toll bar, Blackstone Edge ....51·6   "
        Blackhouse ....52·0   "
        Sowerby Bridge ....31·73   "

Doubts were thrown on the observations at Moss Lock by the return from other gauges carefully kept in the immediate neighbourhood, from which it appeared that the mean fall of rain at Rochdale during 16 years was $46\cdot\frac{3}{8}$ inches.

When these facts were clearly ascertained it was a source of great regret that I had, by taking the inaccurate data of others as the basis of calculation, been instrumental in defeating the Oldham Waterworks Bill in 1838, and it was consequently with no little satisfaction that, 17 years later, I assisted in laying out and carrying through Parliament for the Corporation of Oldham, into whose hands the waterworks had passed, a large and much more important measure for increasing the supply to the town, than had been originally designed, and which, I trust, will prove a blessing and a benefit to the inhabitants for many years to come.

Bolton Waterworks. In the year 1842 I was engaged by the Bolton Waterworks Company to prepare for Parliament, and to carry out, an extension of the waterworks for supplying that town. These works consisted, principally, in the enlargement of the Belmont reservoir, already alluded to, for the purpose of giving an increased quantity of water to the millowners on the river Eagley, as compensation for various springs, surface drainage, and other privileges which were to be ceded to the company.

It was important to ascertain accurately what amount of water could be safely guaranteed. The extent of collecting ground, the depth of rain which fell upon it, the quantity which would flow from the surface, the proper capacity of the reservoir to hold it, and the length of drought during which the supply from the reservoir must be kept up without assistance from rain, were all important elements of calculation. There was very little certain knowledge for our guidance. The nearest rain-gauge was at Bolton, where one had been very carefully kept for many years by Mr. Henry Hough Watson, an old pupil of Dr. Dalton. A large quantity of water had run over the waste-weir of the existing Belmont reservoir, but no measurements had ever been taken. Here it was that the observations of Mr. Thom at the Shaws Waterworks, and the four years' experience of the working of the Turton and Entwistle reservoir, came in as useful guides in determining the question. Beyond these and the limited information afforded by the Bann reservoirs, there was no other definite knowledge obtainable at the time. Rain-gauges were put down at the commencement of the year 1843 on the drainage ground of the Bolton Waterworks, but all points of dispute or arrangement between the parties had to be decided before one year's return could be obtained. As far, however, as the rain observations went, we were warranted in assuming that a much larger fall of rain occurred on the hills above Bolton, where the waterworks were situated, than at Bolton, although the average rain there for 10 years was nearly 50 inches.

Rain Gauge of Mr. Henry H. Watson at Bolton.

Turton and Entwistle Reservoir.

Mr. Thom's information, in his own words, is as follows:—

Mr. Thom's observations.

"*Rain in Bute, from 1st April, 1826, to 1st April, 1827.*

	Inches.
"Depth of rain that fell from end of March to October 1st, 1826	12
"Of which there found its way to the reservoir	1·5
"Taken up by evaporation, vegetation, &c.	10·5
"Depth of rain that fell from October 1st, 1826, to March, 1827	25·2
"Of which there found its way to the reservoir	15·3
"Taken up by evaporation, absorption, vegetation, &c.	9·9

	Inches.
"Depth of rain that fell in March, 1827	8·2
"Of this there found its way to the reservoir	7·1
"Taken up by evaporation, vegetation, &c.	1·1
"Depth of rain from 1st April, 1826, to April, 1827	45·4
"Of which there found its way to the reservoir	23·9
"Lost to the reservoir	21·5

"Note.—The above was from a drainage of more than 4,000 Scots acres.

(Signed) "R. Thom."

"*Rain available for Greenock Reservoirs.*

"Square feet of surface draining into Greenock reservoirs	217,700,000
"Depth of water which fell thereon, year ending September 30th, 1828	6 feet.
"Cubic feet of rain which fell on the drainage	1,088,800,000
"Cubic feet of rain which flowed into the reservoirs	744,594,165
"Cubic feet evaporated, absorbed by vegetation, &c.	344,205,835

(Signed) "R. Thom."

In the year 1826 there was the smallest fall of rain in this country of which we have any record, and probably one of the longest droughts. The year 1827 was also below an average, but it was followed by one in which the gross amount of rain was very high, being, however, principally due to an excessive fall of rain in the month of July. The two years, therefore, to which Mr. Thom's observations refer, viz. 1826 and 1828, were especially valuable—one indicating the result in an excessively dry year, and the other in a wet one considerably above the average. In the dry year little more than one-half of the small quantity of rain which fell reached the reservoirs, and during the six summer months only $1\frac{1}{4}$ inch out of 12 inches which fell flowed off the ground. In the year 1828, which must be considered a wet one, the water flowing from the ground into the Greenock reservoirs was a trifle above two-thirds of the rain which fell. The quantity taken up by vegetation, or lost by evaporation or other causes, was in 1826 equal to a depth of $21\frac{1}{4}$ inches; and in 1828 to $22\frac{3}{4}$ inches. The quantity collected in the first year was $23\frac{9}{10}$ inches, in the second $49\frac{1}{4}$ inches.

The general character and position of the districts in which these observations were made, and the annual fall of rain, were all sufficiently similar to the Bolton waterworks district to permit their being safely used for approximate calculations.

At the Turton and Entwistle reservoirs, the drainage ground of which adjoined the drainage ground of the Belmont reservoir, no register of rain had been kept, but measurements of the quantity of water which had been collected and discharged had to some extent been made. The collecting area to this reservoir was ascertained to be 2,036 statute acres, and the capacity was estimated by Mr. Thomas Ashworth, who had constructed it for the millowners, at about 100,000,000 cubic feet of water, being in the proportion of nearly 50,000 cubic feet of storage for every acre of collecting ground. It was large enough to impound all floods.

Turton and Entwistle Reservoir. Measurements.

Mr. Ashworth, in reporting to the commissioners of the reservoirs in September, 1836, stated that the quantity of water which had been discharged from the reservoir during the first year, all of which had been passed through an iron-gauge fixed for the purposes of measurements, had amounted to 250,865,600 cubic feet, and there were at the end of the period 50,000,000 cubic feet impounded in the reservoir. The quantity actually discharged was equal to a depth of 34 inches over the whole drainage ground. If the impounded water had been caught within the year, it would require to be added, and that would increase the depth of water flowing from the ground, besides that required for evaporation from the surface of the reservoir, to about 41 inches.

These observations appear to have been taken from the summer of 1835 to the summer of 1836, a period in which the rain-fall was probably a little below an average. At Bolton it was 3 inches less than Mr. Watson's ten years' average of 49·2 inches.

Mr. Ashworth again reported on June 30th, 1837, that during the preceding year of 365 days, 289,404,000 cubic feet had been discharged from the reservoir. This quantity would be equal to a depth of 39 inches collected from the drainage ground. The rain at Bolton for the year was 1-49th less than the mean fall of 49·2 inches.

The rain-fall on the drainage ground above the reservoir not having been ascertained no calculations could be made upon the proportion which the water flowing from the ground bore to the rain which fell. But the rain-gauge at the Bolton Waterworks, which was fixed on the 13th January, 1843, to some extent supplied this deficiency. The rain at Belmont in this year, which, according to the Bolton gauge, was as nearly as possible an average year, exceeded 60 inches, and supposing the rain in the Turton and Entwistle district to have been the same, the 40 inches of water collected in that reservoir in the average years of 1836 and 1837 would be nearly two-thirds of that which fell. This agreed with the observations of Mr. Thom at the Greenock reservoirs in 1828, and with those at the Bann reservoirs, in Ireland, in average years.

<small>Rain at Belmont, 1843.</small>

But there was also another fact connected with the Turton and Entwistle reservoir which was of importance in determining what quantity of water could be safely guaranteed from any given district.

<small>Turton and Entwistle Reservoir.</small>

The great object of the reservoir was to regulate the supply of water by impounding the floods and increasing the quantity in dry weather, and the water had, therefore, been discharged regularly at a uniform rate during certain hours of every working-day. There had now been 6 or 7 years' experience. The quantity which had been discharged in every year had exceeded 20 cubic feet per second during 12 hours of every working-day.

Returning to the Bolton Waterworks, it was proposed to raise the embankment of the Belmont reservoir 10 feet, by which it would be rendered capable of holding about 78,000,000 cubic feet. The drainage ground measured 1,820 acres, so that the amount of storage was equal to about 43,000 cubic feet for every acre of collecting ground. This was rather less than that provided by the Turton and Entwistle reservoir, but that was considered to be somewhat in excess of what was necessary.

<small>Bolton Waterworks.</small>

With these materials before them, the Directors of the Bolton Waterworks, on the advice which I ventured to give, considered themselves justified in guaranteeing to the mills a uniform discharge from the reservoir of 15 cubic feet per second for 12 hours of every working-day, a quantity just equal to 30 inches in depth of water collected from the whole surface of the drainage ground.

The experience of 15 or 16 years fully established the safety and wisdom of the decision, notwithstanding that several years during this period had much less than the average amount of rain, and the supplies from reservoirs elsewhere generally failed. Indeed, from an accidental circumstance which will be referred to hereafter, much more than the stipulated quantity was discharged from the reservoir.

Such, then, was the whole amount of knowledge on these subjects which existed in a tangible form, or at all events all that I was in possession of, at the time I was requested, in the summer of 1844, by the late Thomas Cooke, Esq., the chairman, and the late George Murray, Esq., the largest shareholder, in the Manchester and Salford Waterworks Company, to advise them upon the best means of obtaining an ample additional supply of water for Manchester and its neighbourhood.

Mr. Cooke was also chairman of the Bolton Waterworks Company and had in the course of the severe parliamentary struggle which had occurred in obtaining the Act for that town, in the preceding year, become acquainted with the general particulars and principles on which that scheme had been based.

I was tolerably prepared for the duty I was then called upon to perform. I was intimately acquainted with all the surrounding country, more especially with that hilly district to the east of Manchester to which I naturally looked for an increased supply of water. I lost no time, therefore, in devising a sufficient scheme for what I considered the requirements of the town, on as large a scale as I could venture to bring under the notice of the Company; and in June I presented a report, addressed to Mr. Cooke and Mr. Murray, of which the following is a copy :— *Mr. Bateman's Report to the Manchester and Salford Waterworks Company, 1844.*

"Manchester, 12th June, 1844.

"To Thomas Cooke, Esq., and George Murray, Esq.

"*Manchester Waterworks.*

"Gentlemen,—In further explanation of the views I had the honour of laying before you a few weeks ago, upon the means of increasing the supply of water to the town of Manchester, I beg to submit the following report.

"I propose to show, first, the quantity of water required for the full supply of the inhabitants, and the trading wants of the town, with the probable rate of increase. Secondly.—The insufficient means you have at present for meeting the demand for water. Thirdly.—The sources from whence an abundant supply may be best obtained and the cost of procuring it; and Fourthly, the probable return of the outlay.

"First.—The towns of Manchester and Salford contain upwards of

300,000 inhabitants; the manner in which they are distributed and the progressive increase will be shown by the following table of the population of the townships comprised within the powers of your Act, and to all of whom the supply of water may be easily extended :—

Township.	1801.	1811.	1821.	1831.	1841.
Manchester	70,409	79,459	108,016	142,026	163,667
Cheetham	752	1,170	2,027	4,025	6,080
Newton	1,295	1,784	2,577	4,877	6,127
Bradford	94	108	95	166	910
Beswick	6	14	35	248	345
	72,556	82,535	112,750	150,842	177,129
Salford	13,611	19,114	25,772	40,786	51,522
Pendleton	3,611	4,805	5,948	8,435	10,905
Broughton	866	825	880	1,580	3,793
	18,088	24,744	32,600	50,801	66,020
Chorlton-upon-Medlock	675	2,581	8,209	20,569	28,822
Hulme	1,677	3,061	4,234	9,624	26,819
Ardwick	1,762	2,763	3,545	5,524	9,906
Gorton	1,127	1,183	1,604	2,623	2,422
Openshaw	339	459	497	838	2,280
	5,580	10,067	18,089	34,178	69,749
Summary	96,224	117,346	163,439	235,821	312,898
Rate of increase per cent. in each decennial period	...	21·95	39·28	44·28	32·68

"The steam-power employed in manufactories, &c., was in 1888 :—

"In Manchester .... 7,926½ horse-power.
Salford .... 1,998 "

Total .... 9,924½ "

"There are upwards of forty dyeworks, printworks, bleachworks, and other establishments requiring a large and constant supply of pure water for the purposes of their trade, in addition to the supply to steam engines.

"The quantity of water required for a full supply for these various purposes will be as follows:— Population and water required in 1844.

	Gallons daily.
"300,000 inhabitants at 10 gallons per day each, which includes a supply for ordinary trading purposes equal to the present ..	3,000,000
"To steam engines—say a partial supply to one-half or 5,000 horse-power, which are now inadequately supplied in dry seasons—the supply may principally be given by increasing the volume of the streams on which they are situated, say ...	2,500,000
"Dyeworks, printworks, &c., say	1,500,000
"Total daily if *all* supplied	7,000,000
"Deduct one-fourth for those not taking the water.....................	1,750,000
	5,250,000

"Should the town go on increasing in the same proportion in which it has done for the last 20 years, the supply required will probably be in—

1851 ....7,000,000 gallons daily.
1861 9,333,000   "

"Large as the quantity here assumed appears to be when compared with the actual consumption at present, it is still considerably under the average supply of the London Water Companies, and not more than sufficient to meet all the demands of a town like Manchester.

"Secondly.—The quantity of water which is at present supplied from the Gorton reservoirs is, I am informed, something more than 1,500,000 gallons per day. The distribution of it is attended with the greatest economy, the average consumption per house, taking all the circumstances into consideration, being probably less than any well-supplied town in the kingdom. That this quantity is pretty nearly the extent of your resources will be apparent not only from the exhausted state of your reservoirs at the present time, but from the following calculation :— Supply to Gorton reservoirs.

"The supplies to the Gorton reservoirs depend solely upon the surface water of rain flowing from a tract of flat cultivated land about 1,600 statute acres in extent. The rain of an average year in this locality will not exceed 36 inches, of which not more than one-half will ordinarily flow off the ground and reach the reservoirs, to be there impounded. Assuming 18 inches as the available depth of rain, and that the capacity of the reservoirs is sufficient to impound it all, the quantity will be 104,544,000 cubic feet per annum, equal to a daily supply for 365 days of 1,784,409 gallons per day, *but just* sufficient to keep you safe in the supply of your present tenants, and only one-third of the quantity which the town is now actually in a condition to take.

Water from red rock.

"I am aware that an attempt is now being made to increase the supply by sinking into the red rock and pumping up the water which is there met with. Some water will no doubt in this way be gained, but I do not think it possible that the additional 3,500,000 gallons per day, which are *now* required, to say nothing of future wants, can ever be procured. It is equal to nearly 7 cubic feet per second, night and day, a greater quantity of water than has hitherto been supplied to the river Eagley from the Belmont reservoir, and equal to the produce from springs of 8,000 or 10,000 acres of mountain land abounding with a supply of water.

"If, however, this amount should be obtained at the depth to which your present shaft is sunk (and it would be absurd to expect such a quantity to force its way through the pores of close red sandstone and rise spontaneously to the surface) it would require an engine of 140 horse-power, working 24 hours in a day, to lift it. The annual cost of this cannot be taken at less than £20. per horse-power, making a gross cost of £2,800. per annum, to which must be added the interest upon the outlay, altogether, probably, equal to the interest at 5 per cent. on £60,000. or £70,000.

Proposed supply.

"Thirdly.—Let us now consider the sources from whence an abundant supply may be procured.

"Within ten or twelve miles of Manchester, and six or seven miles from the Gorton reservoirs, there is a tract of mountain land abounding with springs of the purest quality. Its physical and geological features offer such peculiar facilities for the collection, storage, and supply of water for the use of the towns in the plain below, that I am surprised they should so long have been overlooked. There is no other district within reasonable limits, nor any other source from whence water may be obtained which will bear comparison with it.

Elevation of hills.

"The hills I allude to are those which rise abruptly behind the town of Stalybridge, forming an advanced outpost, as it were, of the main chain of hills behind them. Harridge Pike and Shaw Moor, the most advanced summits, are nearly as high as the more distant hills, being upwards of 1,200 feet above the level of the sea, and between 800 and 900 feet above the town of Stalybridge, this elevation being gained in the short space of a single mile. They are so situated as to be the first to interrupt the progress of the clouds borne by the westerly winds from the most rainy quarters. The clouds thus stopped will become embayed in the deep ravines and trough-like valleys which lie behind these summits, from whence they can scarcely escape until they have deposited their contents. The quantity of rain in this locality will, therefore, be unusually abundant, while the absence of flat land on the tops, and the steep declivities of the sides, will cause a very large proportion to run rapidly off in useless floods and torrents. The water thus flowing from the surface, and which may be collected in reservoirs constructed for the purpose, will be nearly as pure as it comes from the heavens; for the comparative absence of peat within the limits of the drainage ground, and the small extent of flat land on which the water may lie, will prevent it being tinged in colour and spoiled in quality, like many mountain streams which derive their first supplies from the gradual draining of flat bog-topped summits, while the bare uncultivated ground, never subjected to manure or tillage, and never loaded with vegetation, will allow the water to pass off uncontaminated by the decay of animal and vegetable substances, which a more cultivated and richly manured country invariably engenders. The animalcules which abound in the Gorton reservoirs are an example of this.

"The geological character of the district also contributes essentially to the purity and abundance of the water. It consists of the lower portion of the coal measure formation, below the coal and mineral springs, and, therefore, secure from injury by mining operations. The tops of the hills are principally capped with gritstone, resting on alternating beds of shale and stone, the whole of the strata dipping towards the west. Wherever the sandstone rests upon the shale the water is thrown out in pure and copious springs; a great proportion, owing to the inclination of the strata, being derived from sources far beyond the limits of the surface drainage.

"The combination of all these causes must contribute to the production of a large supply of water of the utmost purity.

"The area of the country from which supplies might be gathered is almost unlimited, but the district to which I wish now to draw your attention, and which will afford a plentiful supply for many future years, consists of about 3,700 statute acres. Its situation will be best understood by reference to the coloured portion of the accompanying Ordnance Map. The part coloured pink, shows the extent of surface which naturally drains to a point, the site of a suggested reservoir on Swineshaw brook,—the upper darker coloured portion showing that, to the surplus water of which the Huddersfield Canal Company are entitled, if they choose to avail themselves of powers obtained some 50 years ago. The land coloured green, drains to a point on Car brook, near the foot of Bucton Castle hill, from which the surplus water may be diverted to the Swineshaw valley. The water from the land coloured brown, between the Car brook valley and the Swineshaw valley, may be intercepted by the water-course conveying the water from Car brook. The small part coloured blue, on the south of the Swineshaw valley, may be rendered tributary to the reservoir by a catch-water drain. The part coloured purple, draining to the Hollingworth brook, which flows into the river Etherow, in

Area of district.

the valley of Longdendale, is separated from the Swineshaw valley by a high ridge of land, but a tunnel of about half a mile in length through this ridge will bring the water from that land also. In this valley, then, may be collected the whole or a portion of the water flowing from the districts just described. Impounding reservoirs may be here constructed, from the lowest of which water may be conveyed to the Gorton reservoirs, a distance of six miles, through iron pipes, with a pressure of 330 feet.

"The measurement of the drainage ground of these several districts is as follows:—

	Statute acres.
"Pink—To the Swineshaw reservoir, the site being the property of the Huddersfield Canal Company	550
"Ditto—To the suggested reservoir at Walker wood, below the Swineshaw reservoir	765
"Total natural drainage in the Swineshaw valley	1,315
"Green—To point of diversion on Car brook to Hoarstone clough	925
"Brown—Will be intercepted by a water-course from Car brook to the reservoir at Walker wood	390
"Blue—Will be intercepted by a catch-water drain on the south side of the Swineshaw valley	65
"Purple—To the point of proposed diversion on the Hollingworth brook and to the mouth of the tunnel from that valley	980
"Total	3,675

Rainfall. "From observations which were made under my direction, upon this very chain of hills above Glossop, during the years 1839, 1840, 1841, and 1842, it has been ascertained that the depth of rain, in average years, will exceed 70 inches, and the result of other observations, upon a large scale in similar districts, proves that upwards of two-thirds of the rain which falls in an average year will flow off the ground and reach the valleys. We shall, therefore, be safe if in this locality we take two-thirds of the rain which falls, or 4 feet over the whole surface, as the quantity available for collection in reservoirs.

"Four feet upon 3,675 acres will yield 640,332,000 cubic feet per annum, equal to a daily supply for 365 days of 1,754,334 cubic feet, or 10,929,500 gallons. From this gross quantity must be deducted the requisite supply to the mills on the streams, or that required to be given as compensation for the right to abstract the remainder.

"The present supply to the mills on Swineshaw brook, when unaffected by recent rain, is from 1½ to 2 cubic feet per second. Supposing this quantity to be more than doubled, and the mills guaranteed a constant quantity during working hours (or 12 hours in the day) of 5 cubic feet per second, there will be required for this purpose 216,000 cubic feet or 1,345,680 gallons per day.

"In Car brook the ordinary stream, when not swollen, affords about 1 cubic foot per second. Suppose 3 to be guaranteed during working hours, it would require 129,600 cubic feet or 807,408 gallons per day. To be enabled to guarantee this quantity would require the construction of a reservoir to contain a supply of 1 foot per second for 60 days—say 3,000,000 cubic feet.

"If the surplus water *only* of this brook were taken, the mills would be left in their present state, and the quantity available to the company would probably be less than by adopting the principle of a guarantee, as much water would run to waste. A guarantee would, therefore, be better for both parties.

"On Hollingworth brook the stream at the point of the proposed diversion is, in ordinary dry weather, about 1 cubic foot per second, and at the site of a suggested compensation reservoir, at the foot of the part coloured yellow, from $1\frac{1}{2}$ to 2. Suppose the guarantee to be 5 feet.

"The drainage ground to the site of the proposed compensation reservoir, below the point at which the brook is proposed to be diverted to the Swineshaw valley, coloured yellow in the Map, is 460 statute acres. Taking the available rain upon this land at only 3 feet per annum, on account of the lower elevation of part of it, it will yield 60,112,800 cubic feet per annum—equal to a supply of about $4\frac{3}{4}$ cubic feet per second during working hours for 300 days in the year. If to this be added the half-foot of spring water, it will bring the whole amount to a trifle more than the assumed guarantee of 5 feet. To render the whole of the water which may be collected available, the reservoirs should contain about 15 million cubic feet, supposing the whole of the water to be taken out of the valley at the point of the proposed diversion, at the foot of the land coloured purple.

"These deductions will produce the following results:—

	Gallons.	Gallons.	Total supply.
"Gross daily supply		10,929,500	
"Deduct—To supply the mills on Swineshaw brook at 5 feet per second	1,345,680		Compensation.
"On Car brook at 3 feet per second	807,408		
"On Hollingworth brook, if the compensation reservoir be constructed, nothing	... ...	2,153,088	
"Will remain		8,776,412	Will remain for Manchester.

"In the quantity remaining is included the water from the 550 acres above the Swineshaw reservoir, to the surplus portion of which the Huddersfield Canal Company is entitled. It is desirable that the Canal Company's rights should, if possible, be purchased, not only for the purpose of obtaining the entire command of the stream, but because the site of their reservoir is the best which can be found in the valley, and, without it, there may be some difficulty in procuring sufficient storage room. There are the remains of the embankment which they originally constructed, which from gross negligence in not constructing a waste weir, was allowed to be swept away. It has never been repaired. If no arrangement can be made with them, there will be the further deduction of the water to which they are entitled. This may probably amount to about 1 million gallons per day. Taking 4 feet of rain and, allowing for the proportion of its contribution to the supply of the mills, it would be 1,072,873 gallons per day, which, deducted from the 8,776,412 gallons, would leave the net residue available to the Water Works Company for the supply of Manchester, 7,703,539 gallons per day.

"This, irrespective of what the Gorton reservoirs will yield, is 2,500,000 gallons per day more than is now required according to the calculations I have made;—700,000 gallons per day more than the probable demand in 1851, and, with the assistance of the supply to the Gorton reservoirs, sufficient for the probable wants in 1861; but having once established a footing in the hills it will be an easy matter to make arrangements for additional drainage ground whenever it may be required.

"Having now shown that the resources afforded by the district recommended are sufficient for all present and future wants, let them be ever so large, the next question is, the cost of procuring that which will meet the demands of the present time and some twenty years to come.

Storage required.

"The first point under this head is the extent of storage room required. The present Gorton reservoirs contain, I am told, about 220,000,000 gallons or about 35,300,000 cubic feet. To ensure the mills the guaranteed quantities I have assumed, and to supply, for the consumption of the town, 5,000,000 gallons per day, would require in average years, from calculations upon the monthly fall of rain, and the produce of the springs and surface drainage, according to the season of the year, storage for about 50 million cubic feet, and in unusually dry seasons, like the one we have just witnessed or the summer and autumn of 1842, about 75 million cubic feet, assuming of course that the supply is obtained from the hills.

"It will be necessary, therefore, in the first instance to construct reservoirs which shall contain 40,000,000 or 50,000,000 cubic feet, and to obtain powers for a further extension of 20,000,000 cubic feet to meet future demands as they may arise.

"I have made the necessary surveys and calculations to enable me to estimate the capability and cost of accomplishing these objects.

"The Swineshaw valley, although the best for the purpose in that district, does not afford many good sites for large reservoirs. A reservoir upon the site of the Huddersfield Canal Company's may be made to contain about 26,000,000 cubic feet; one lower down, at Walker wood, about 24,500,000 cubic feet, and intermediate ones from 10 to 15 million more, to which may be added one to the extent of from 5 to 10 millions on Car brook—altogether about 70 million cubic feet, which added to the Gorton reservoirs, would make a total storage space for 105,000,000 cubic feet.

"If it is found that no arrangement can be made with the Huddersfield Canal Company for their reservoir, the deficiency, when it arises (for a substitute would not be immediately required) may be supplied by obtaining power to construct a reservoir of equal capacity in a tolerable convenient situation near the foot of the hills, behind Mr. Wilkinson's mill at Stalybridge. Terms might be proposed to the parties immediately interested, which would be advantageous at no loss to the Company.

"The other works required would consist of a water-course from the Car brook to the Swineshaw valley,—a short water-course and filter beds on the south of that valley,—a water-course and tunnel from the Hollingworth brook, —a compensation reservoir on that stream, and a line of iron pipes from the lowest reservoir on the Swineshaw brook to communicate with the discharge pipes from the highest reservoir at Gorton.

"The surface of the water in the lowest reservoir on Swineshaw brook is about 330 feet higher than the Gorton reservoir. The great pressure which this difference in level gives will enable a comparatively small pipe to discharge a very large quantity of water. A 21 inch main will discharge into the Gorton reservoir 8,750,000 gallons in 24 hours; a 24 inch main 12,224,000 gallons in the same time. The advantage in many respects, which this increase of pressure would give in the service of the town if the water were taken direct from the Swineshaw reservoirs, particularly for the extinction of fire, and for supplying some parts of the town, in which the pipes are now too small, is well worth consideration, but I will not overload my report by entering into that part of the subject.

"The estimate for the completion of all the works I have now described _{Estimate.}

will be as follows. Details of the estimates and other particulars will be found in the Appendix. I have every confidence that the prices allowed are more than ample:—

"Swineshaw reservoir on the site of the Huddersfield Canal Company's	£12,496	0	0
"Walker wood reservoir	11,632	10	0
"An intermediate reservoir	6,226	0	0
"Water-course from Car brook	2,130	10	0
"Water-course and tunnel from Hollingworth brook	3,124	0	0
"Catch-water drains, roads, filter beds, and other work in the Swineshaw valley	3,000	0	0
"Compensation reservoir on Hollingworth brook	7,500	0	0
"Reservoir on Car brook	2,500	0	0
"Compensation for injury to water privileges above the compensation reservoir on Hollingworth brook, say £100. per annum—20 years' purchase	2,000	0	0
"Cast-iron main, from the Walker wood to the discharge pipe of the highest reservoir at Gorton, if 21 inches diameter... If 24 inches diameter, £27,600.	22,700	0	0
	£73,809	0	0
"Say for additional works to meet future demands	10,000	0	0
"Say cost of Act of Parliament and arrangements with millowners	5,000	0	0
"Subsequent, legal, engineering and incidental expenses, 10 per cent. upon £80,000	8,000	0	0
	£96,809	0	0

"Of this sum not more than between £60,000. or £70,000., including the cost of the Act of Parliament, need be laid out within the next 8 or 10 years, unless the demand for water increases beyond what I have anticipated.

"In addition to the works here estimated, there will be the cost of additional pipes consequent upon the increased supply.

Return for outlay. "Fourthly.—The last thing I proposed to consider was the probable return for the outlay.

"On this subject the want of information upon many points essential to a right estimate of rental will prevent my giving you more than approximate means for ascertaining the net amount yourselves by comparing what it should be with what it is.

"In investigating the cost of supplying water to the neighbouring large towns and the profit derived therefrom, I have been led to the conclusion that, generally, where the outlay does not exceed £1. per head, the net return will be from 7 to 10 per cent., or in other words that the profit will be about 2s. for each inhabitant.

"In Manchester, therefore, upon this rule the sum applicable as a dividend should be about £30,000.

"Again, the gross rental for domestic consumption, including a limited supply for other purposes, may be estimated by the average rate paid by each tenant. Three-fourths of the houses may be considered as water tenants, and the rate per tenant will be found to vary from 15s. to 20s. There were in Manchester and Salford in 1841 upwards of 60,000 dwelling houses. Taking the water tenants at 45,000 and the rate at 15s. only, the rental would be £33,750. per annum. *[Probable Revenue from domestic consumption.]*

"The rates, however, in Manchester are higher, and the necessity for water greater than in the neighbouring towns, and, therefore, a larger return than this may be expected. The gross rental for domestic consumption should not be less than £40,000.

"But there are sources of emolument connected with the scheme I have laid before you which are not included in the calculations of rental I have given, and from which, I believe, you have never yet received a sum worth consideration;—I mean the supply to be afforded to large consumers for all trading purposes, and such a supply for the extinction of fire, that any room in a mill or warehouse may in a moment be deluged by pipes conducted into them commanded by a valve on the outside of the building. This plan, where there is a high pressure of water, supersedes the necessity of fire engines, and is practically put into operation by Mr. Jones, of Oldham, who saves the whole of the insurance upon his extensive mills at Wallshaw.

"That a supply of water for this purpose may be made the source of a considerable revenue, will be apparent from the two following facts:—

"In Liverpool they are now spending £40,000. or £50,000. in engineering works alone, in a project confined entirely to watering streets and extinguishing fires.

"The amount of insurances effected on warehouse property alone in Manchester is, I am informed on good authority, £1,600,000.

"I will now attempt to estimate the probable annual return from these sources, exclusive of the extension in domestic consumption:— *[Probable Revenue from trade, &c.]*

"For an occasional supply of condensing water to steam engines, and for increasing the quantity of water in dry seasons in the small streams from which condensing water is now procured, say at least	£1,500	0	0
"Dyeworks, printworks, breweries, &c., say 30 establishments at £100. each	3,000	0	0
"For a supply of water to mills and warehouses, for the extinction of fire upon the principle alluded to, say one-tenth of £30,000., a low estimate of the saving in insurance	3,000	0	0
	£7,500	0	0

"This estimate is founded upon the present wants of the town, and may be taken as the rental from these sources upon an outlay of £70,000. or £80,000. The future rental will keep pace with the progressive increase in mercantile establishments.

"In concluding this part of the subject I may observe that the population of the town is increasing at the rate of 8,000 persons yearly, which ought not only to increase the profit £600. or £800. per annum, but it should warrant the yearly outlay of £8,000.

"I have now, I think, gone through all the facts and figures which bear upon the question, but I must not omit to draw your attention to one feature of the scheme which does not come within the limit of calculation,—the great extension in manufacturing establishments requiring water which may be expected to result from a pure and abundant supply. Large establishments which are now carried on inconveniently at a distance from the town for the mere purpose of obtaining pure water, would be brought home, and a large proportion of the trade of the district would become concentrated within the bounds of the borough. An increasing impulse would be given to the rapid growth and prosperity of the town, and more beneficial results may be expected to flow from an unlimited supply of pure water than from any project of the day.

"I have the honour to remain,
"Gentlemen,
"Your very obedient servant,
(Signed)   "J. F. BATEMAN."

Reasons for giving Report in full. This Report has been given in full because it contains the germ of what was subsequently carried out, and was the commencement of experiments and observations which were finally elaborated into the valuable information which we now possess.

Recommendations adopted, and Plans, &c. prepared for Parliament. The recommendations it contained were adopted by the Company. The surveys and plans were prepared with some additions (the most important of which was a service reservoir in Openshaw on a higher level than the Gorton reservoirs) which suggested themselves in the course of preparation, and a Bill for obtaining power to construct the works was brought into Parliament in the following Session. It was violently opposed

Opposition of Mill-owners. by the mill-owners and others interested in the streams proposed to be interfered with. No reasonable compensation would satisfy them, and after it had passed through the House of Commons, the Company deemed the measure so burdened with obligations—which they doubted their power to fulfil with advantage to themselves, and were so disgusted with restrictions ^{Bill abandoned.} which had been insisted on by the Committee—that they determined to abandon it.

Previous to this determination I addressed to them the following report, from which it will be seen that my feeling was in favour of their taking the Bill as it was and securing a footing in the hills :—

"London, 29th May, 1845.

"To the Chairman and Directors.

"*Manchester and Salford Waterworks.*

"Gentlemen,—The Bill having now passed through Committee, I am enabled to inform you of the position in which the measure stands with reference to the quantity of water which you may expect to obtain for the supply of Manchester after deducting that which the Committee have decided shall be supplied to the mills on the streams interfered with.

"Had the measure passed through Parliament without alteration in its engineering features, the water at the command of the Company would have been, in ordinary years, 9,968,000 gallons daily, after deducting for the supply of the mills on Swineshaw and Car brooks,—for the stipulated supply, if required, to the Huddersfield Canal, and for occasional waste, 5 feet per second constantly, or about 11 feet per second for working hours. In years of drought there would have remained a daily supply of about 6,800,000 gallons.

"No deduction was necessary for the Hollingworth and Arnfield brooks, as the compensation to be given to these streams would have been obtained from a district independent of that which could be made available to the use of the Waterworks Company.

"The reservoir space contemplated by the Bill, added to the existing Gorton reservoirs, would have ensured a daily supply throughout the most trying period of the last 12 months, which from March, 1844, to March, 1845, is the driest year on record, of 7,000,000 gallons, besides affording the guaranteed quantity to the Huddersfield Canal Company, and 5 feet per second for 12 hours a-day to the mills on the Swineshaw brook.

"This quantity may, therefore, be taken as that beyond which it would not have been prudent for the Company to extend their supplies, as, although a larger average might have been calculated upon, it would have required increased reservoir accommodation to have ensured it.

"The supplies to Ashton for trading, and to Stalybridge for domestic purposes, are not deducted because the sum to be paid for them is sufficient to pay the interest at 5 per cent. of the cost of additional works to meet those calls.

"As the Bill now stands, 2 feet per second for working hours are to be supplied to the mills on the Hollingworth brook more than the district will afford, independent of that which it was intended to appropriate to the use of the Company. Two feet per second for working hours, also, are to be given to the mills on the Swineshaw brook, and ¾ foot per second to a Mrs. Waring, more than had been calculated upon; and the volume of the Car brook before any surplus is to be taken has been fixed so high, that a considerable deduction must be made on that account.

"The gross amount of these deductions, including the Huddersfield Canal and occasional waste, if reduced to a constant stream, will be about 8¼ cubic feet per second. This quantity deducted from what the district will afford will leave at the command of the Company, for ordinary years, 8,800,000 gallons daily, and in years of drought about 5,000,000 gallons daily. An outlay of from £5,000. to £10,000. will be necessary on the Hollingworth brook to enlarge the reservoirs, and the Company may then calculate upon the remaining reservoirs, as contemplated by the Bill, being sufficient to meet all other demands and ensure a supply to Manchester of about 6,000,000 gallons per day.

"The water to be supplied to the mills on the Swineshaw brook, under penalty for failure, may be taken from any one of four reservoirs, and arrangements may be made to supply those on the Hollingworth brook from any one of three. It is scarcely possible, therefore, that by any misfortune a penalty can be incurred.

"The other material points on which unexpected alterations have been made, are, the obligations to afford constant supply, and the low amount to which the water rates have been reduced, particularly in respect of water closets, for which no charge is to be made in tenements of less value than £15. per annum.

"With reference to the 'constant supply,' I am convinced that the statements which have been made as to the cost which it would entail upon the Company will, only to a small per centage, prove well founded or correct upon examination.

"The only expense will be a partial remodelling of some of the piping. The mains, which are stated to be only just sufficient to supply the quantity of water which is now sent to Manchester, will require enlarging to convey any greater quantity, and that expense must, therefore, form a consequent and an essential part of the proposed scheme of increased supply. Even supposing, therefore—what is denied by many men who have had the opportunity of judging by experience—that each tenant will use more water under the 'constant' than the 'intermittent' system, the enlargement of mains cannot be laid to that account, when the operation is rendered absolutely necessary, under any system, by the increased quantity of water which will be brought to Manchester for distribution. If, however, it should require, under the 'constant' supply, a little increased area in the mains, this will be counterbalanced by the decreased size of the service pipes, which may be diminished in proportion to the greater length of time during which a given quantity of water would be drawn by the tenants. The water which is now supplied in 1 or 2 hours, for 24 hours' consumption, would not probably be drawn under the 'constant' supply system in less than 10 or 12 hours, thus enabling a smaller pipe to do the work. The pipes would not require to be stronger, and a great saving might be effected in the number of turncocks. The renewal of inefficient lead services and taps would fall upon the tenant and not upon the Company. The tenant would be amply repaid for such a cost by the convenience of the 'constant' supply, and would, therefore, have no cause for complaint if compelled to incur the expense of putting all into good order.

"The only circumstance which, in reference to Manchester, induces me to take a view adverse to the 'constant' supply system, without previous preparation, is the probability of robbery in the poorer districts. I think there is sufficient ground for this apprehension to render the obligation disagreeable and objectionable to the proprietors. If, upon trial it should be found to be groundless, it would be the interest of the Company to afford the supply in the most convenient and least expensive manner, thereby encouraging the consumption and increasing their tenants.

"On the remaining point, the reduction in the rates, with the accompanying restrictions, I am not so well able to give an opinion as those who have more particularly considered the subject of tariff: without the power of rating all or the bestowal of any corresponding advantage, it appears an oppressive infliction;—with the power of rating the owners or occupiers of *all* houses, I believe the rates fixed by the Committee would afford an ample return for whatever outlay might be required to carry out the most extended and perfect scheme.

"The question of a compulsory rate is one of great importance to waterworks companies, and one which would be attended with great public benefit. It is one for which the public mind is gradually becoming prepared, and which, there is reason to believe, would be supported by Government. The delay of a year might facilitate the acquisition of such a power; and while I do not think that in any respect, except the rating classes, the Company have reason to be dissatisfied with the Bill in its present shape, it is worth their consideration whether it would be most prudent to take the good they can obtain this session and secure a footing in the hills, or try to obtain a more perfect and enlarged measure next year.

"The resources of the hill district and the unparalleled purity of the water have been thoroughly established,—the temper of the millowners has been tried, and the amount of compensation determined would form a basis for future arrangements, while the struggle with them has induced a disposition to treat on a larger scale for more extended supplies. The Etherow district alone would yield for the use of the Company upwards of 20,000,000 gallons of water a day, and, though the scheme now before Parliament, is sufficient to meet all present wants, and undoubtedly includes that portion of the district which should be primarily secured and occupied, it would be a matter of much importance and advantage to the Company to prevent the preoccupation, by other parties, of the district to which they must look for future extension. Such an occupation is rendered probable, by the attention which the millowners, who are the parties most immediately interested, have necessarily directed to the subject, and the conviction they must have acquired of the advantage which reservoirs would give them of securing a regular instead of an irregular and uncertain supply of water.

"I have the honour to remain,

"Your very obedient servant,

(Signed) "J. F. BATEMAN."

"P.S.—Daily measurements have been taken of the streams included within the limits of the Bill, since the commencement of this year. The season has been unusually dry, but from the 1st January to the end of April the water at the command of the Company, after deducting what is now required to be supplied to the mills and streams, would have been 4,600,000 gallons per day. This is quite confirmatory of the accuracy of my previous calculations, and would, independent of any other measurements, warrant the anticipation of a supply by the aid of reservoirs, at the least, equal to 6,000,000 gallons per day."

<small>Subsequent experience showed calculations to be too favourable.</small>

Notwithstanding the views adopted in this Report, and the calculations it contains, subsequent experience has unquestionably proved that the scheme had been laid out on too sanguine an expectation of results which would not have been altogether realized. Both the probable rain-fall and the available quantity of water which would flow off the ground, were assumed at higher figures than observations since taken would have warranted; and the length of drought which it was considered requisite to provide storage for, after allowing for the ascertained produce of springs, viz., 60 or 70 days in average years and 100 days in dry years, was below what several severe dry periods have since shown to be requisite. Still, the scheme, if carried out, would, even hampered as it was by heavy and unreasonable compensations, have produced very nearly all that had been promised, though most likely some additional storage room must have been provided.

The scheme had been laid out so as to take possession of the nearest high land and unappropriated streams, and in such manner and on such levels as would have allowed subsequent extension up the valley of the Tame towards Greenfield and up Longdendale towards Woodhead, two districts abounding with fine water and affording many facilities for the construction of works. The Swineshaw brook, which formed the nucleus of the scheme, is still the finest stream as to quality and quantity of spring water, in proportion to the area drained, with which I have become acquainted, in any part of the same geological formation. *Scheme had been laid out so as to be extended towards Greenfield and Woodhead.*

When the measure was abandoned, the Company resumed the sinking of the well at Gorton into the new red sandstone; and the extraordinary press of professional employment, which resulted from the railway mania of that year, 1845, prevented my turning my attention to the question again for some time. This suspension of activity on the part of those interested in the existing waterworks induced other parties to enter the field. It was an age of speculation and bold adventure. Men's views were rapidly expanding, and schemes which would not have been thought of a few years before were not now considered too great to be undertaken. *Sinking Well at Gorton resumed.*

The Commissioners of the Turton and Entwistle reservoir, so often referred to, who were the millowners on the stream below the reservoir, and who were subject to rather a heavy annual tax in proportion to the fall upon the river which they occupied, for the payment of the interest on the cost of the reservoir, acting principally under the advice or at the instigation of Mr. James Hardcastle, who, with some of the mortgagees, was the principal promoter, conceived that they might by some additional works convert their undertaking into one for supplying Bolton, Salford, and Manchester with water, and relieve themselves from the payment of the disagreeable impost to which their works were liable. They called in Mr. Hawksley to their aid, and dignified their scheme with the title of "The Lancashire Waterworks." The district was very favourable, both for the construction of reservoirs *"Lancashire" Waterworks.*

and the collection of water. Mr. Hawksley laid out a good and well-digested scheme, and a Bill was brought into Parliament in the Session of 1846, for supplying the places named and a large district besides. The Bill was well supported, and the Manchester and Salford Waterworks Company, whose courage had been exhausted by their unsuccessful attempt of the previous year, ran great danger of having to compete for the custom of the district with a powerful rival with a much larger and better supply at command.

They durst not face again the greedy millowners of the Stalybridge district, and they, therefore, looked about for some place from whence they could obtain an additional supply of water, where they would be likely to meet with less opposition. Their eyes had in some measure been opened, and they could now see as far as the hills. They accordingly entered into negotiations with Mr. Legh, of Lyme Park, in Cheshire, a few miles beyond Stockport, whose property lay on an advanced spur of the Buxton or Peak Forest hills, and in a favourable position for collecting and storing a limited quantity of water. Having made conditional arrangements with him, they hastily got up a scheme which they laid before the Parliamentary Committee, in opposition to "The Lancashire Waterworks," and which they professed their intention to introduce in the next session of Parliament, if the scheme then before the Committee, were thrown out. They would probably, however, have been unsuccessful in preventing that measure being carried—for Manchester and its neighbourhood were in urgent need of a better supply of water—if the Manchester Corporation had not also opposed the Bill.

Lyme Park Scheme.

Opposition of the Manchester Corporation to the "Lancashire Waterworks."

The Corporation had come to the conclusion that the supply of water was of that public character, and so intimately connected with the health and welfare of the town, that it ought to be in the hands of the inhabitants themselves, and they had therefore determined to apply to Parliament for powers to buy the existing waterworks, to obtain additional supplies, and to levy a compulsory rate on all householders for a constant and unlimited supply for domestic purposes. This determination on the part of the Corporation of Manchester was stated to the Committee, and, chiefly owing to the powerful advocacy of their very able Town Clerk, Mr. Heron (now Sir Joseph Heron), the Bill was defeated. He objected to the powers applied for being granted to the Lancashire Water Company, on the ground that it would be necessary for the Corporation to become the sole distributers of water within the borough, in order to carry out what they intended, and that as it would be necessary as a preliminary step to become the proprietors of all existing waterworks; the granting of powers to a second company would involve the purchase of two companies instead of one, and might prevent the Corporation undertaking a project which was so obviously for the good of the town. The consequence of this opposition was, that the Committee agreed to require, if the Bill then before them was proceeded with, the insertion of a clause restraining the Company from any interference whatever within the Borough of Manchester for a period of three years from the passing of the Act; and if upon the expiration of that period such steps had been taken, either by the Corporation or the Manchester and Salford Waterworks Company, as would satisfy the Board of Trade that the required supply of water would be obtained for the borough of Manchester, then the Lancashire Waterworks Company would be shut out for ever. The result of this clause was that the Bill was abandoned. The quantity of water which the Company would have been able to bring to Manchester would not have exceeded six or seven million gallons a day, and the lowest price at which it could have been sold there would have been 2¼d. per 1,000 gallons, or about £22,000. per annum for six millions daily—an excessive price compared with what it could have been obtained for elsewhere. The quantity was not sufficient for the wants of the two boroughs of Manchester and Salford; and what the rest of Lancashire, with its million of inhabitants, must have done for its share of the supply from the "Lancashire Waterworks," it would have been difficult to say. *"Lancashire Waterworks" Bill abandoned.*

The Corporation of Manchester immediately applied themselves to carrying out the obligations they had thus voluntarily imposed upon themselves. Before the Committee appointed to oppose the "Lancashire Water Bill" left London, where I had been assisting them in their opposition, I received an intimation that they would look to me for suggestions as to the best mode of remedying the deficient supply under which the town was notoriously labouring. *Instructions to lay out Works for Corporation.*

I had, in fact, been for some time considering the question, and I was prepared with a scheme which I believed would fully meet all requirements. It was an extension of that which had been projected two years before for the Manchester and Salford Waterworks Company. Nothing had occurred to shake my confidence in that being the right district to go to. The greatest quantity of water could there be obtained for the least money.

It was of unexampled purity when properly treated by the separation of that which, in heavy rain, was occasionally turbid and discoloured, and the country afforded facilities for almost unlimited extension of works for collecting and storing water. The observations upon the fall of rain and the quantity of water that poured from the ground, which had been commenced on behalf of the Water Company in 1844, had been regularly continued, at my own expense, after the company had abandoned their Bill. The accurate information which had thus been acquired had confirmed the general accuracy of my previous impressions, and it afforded the means of calculating, with confidence, what water the district would afford.

Observations on rain-fall.

But all the streams below the ground which could be appropriated for waterworks purposes were employed as water-power by cotton-mills, or afforded supplies to dyeworks or printworks, and the opposition of rich and powerful millowners would have to be encountered.

Opposition of millowners.

In the waterworks scheme of 1844, two sets of millowners had to be dealt with—those upon the river Tame and those on the river Etherow—and the difficulties of the company were thus increased. In order to simplify the arrangements which would have to be made, I very unwillingly determined to relinquish that part of the scheme of 1844 which included the Swineshaw work and the drainage to the river Tame, and to concentrate the whole of the water in the valley of the Etherow, including so much of the upper part of that valley, there called Longdendale, as would yield the requisite quantity of water, laying out the works on such levels as would permit the ultimate occupation of the whole of that portion of the valley upon which no mills had been erected.

Scheme proposed.

In the upper part of the valley, near Woodhead, there were some tempting and apparently excellent sites for large reservoirs, and the first idea which was worked into shape was—in imitation of the Bolton waterworks—to make a large reservoir at Woodhead, to impound flood waters for the purpose of increasing the working power of the stream in dry weather, which should be handed over to the millowners for their use, in full compensation for the right to take away all the water of the district on the northerly side of the valley which lay between this reservoir and the Hollingworth brook, at the lowest point at which the water could be conveniently diverted to Manchester. It would have to be carried by tunnel through a high ridge of hill at Mottram, to Godley and Hyde, from whence it could easily be conveyed to the Gorton reservoir, and to Manchester.

Before bringing this project formally before the Corporation, I communicated with the solicitor of several of the more influential millowners who had opposed the Water Company in their application to Parliament in 1845, with a view of ascertaining whether such a scheme would be likely to meet with their approval. I was of opinion that they were far too enlightened, and too much alive to their own interests, to stand long in the way of a scheme which could be proved to be one of material benefit to them.

The following is the letter which was addressed to Mr. Vaughan, of Stockport, the solicitor referred to :—

"Manchester, 30th July, 1846.

"My dear Sir,

"I promised a short time ago to communicate with you as soon as I had matured a scheme which I then mentioned to you for taking the water for the supply of Manchester from the valley of the Etherow, upon the principle of compensating the millowners, liberally, by large compensation reservoirs. *Letter to Mr. Vaughan solicitor to millowners.*

"I have been detained so long in London that I have not been able to turn my attention to it as early as I could have wished. I now find there is a strong set in favour of the Lyme scheme, in the belief that the Etherow district swarms with unreasonable and impracticable millowners.

"I believe, however, that this arises from a misapprehension on both sides, and I think a good, sound scheme, mutually advantageous, only requires to be clearly laid before them.

"What I propose is, that the waterworks should be allowed to take the Crowden brook, the Armfield and Hollingworth brooks, with such waters as they may intercept between them ; that Mr. Ralph Sidebottom, and any other parties on these streams before they join the main river, shall be compensated in money; that the millowners on the Etherow shall receive a large reservoir, to contain say 80 or 100 million cubic feet of water (as large as can reasonably be made), to be constructed solely for their use, as their compensation.

"The streams to be taken by the waterworks will yield, in dry weather, 5 or 6 cubic feet per second; and their full working volume, measured to the full extent to which the water can be employed, will be about 10 or 12 cubic feet per second, flowing constantly.

"A reservoir of 100,000,000 cubic feet will yield, for 6 days a week, a constant quantity of 20 cubic feet per second for 10 weeks, in addition to the natural stream, or 40 feet per second for 12 hours in the day.

"Put into horse-power, the difference will be a gain to the river of about $1\frac{1}{4}$ or $1\frac{3}{4}$ horse-power to each foot of fall on the average yearly flow, and in dry weather a gain of about $2\frac{1}{4}$ horse-power to each foot for 12 hours in the day.

"This is a rough outline, without any pretension to very accurate detail of the scheme I was thinking of, and I shall be glad to have your opinion of the spirit in which such a proposition would be met by the millowners.

"I may mention that a reservoir of the size named is about ten or eleven times the size of the Glossop reservoir, and about the same as the Turton and Entwistle reservoir; but it will be far more efficient than that, inasmuch as it will have, if placed at Woodhead, about four times the extent of ground from which to receive its supplies.

"I have not yet brought the subject before the waterworks' party, because I am desirous of learning the feeling of the principal millowners first.

"I think, if they will calmly consider the measure, they will see that it is their interest to support it. They will be materially benefitted, and the town of Manchester will obtain, though at considerable outlay, water from the best source for the supply of the inhabitants, looking both at present wants and future extension. There must, however, be hearty coöperation, or the opportunity will be lost.

"Pray make what use you like of this letter, and let me hear from you as early as convenient. I am obliged to return to London on Sunday, for about a week, and should like to be able to take some definite steps on my return.

"The Lyme district, if not taken by Manchester, will come in well, as I have before recommended, for Stockport. It is the natural direction in which that town should look for water.

"Believe me, dear Sir,

"Very truly yours,

(Signed) "J. F. BATEMAN."

Instructions to prepare for Parliament. I subsequently saw Mr. Vaughan, and millowners whom he did not represent, and the result of our communications was an impression on my part that the millowners were disposed favourably to entertain the scheme. I then submitted it to the Corporation, and received their instructions to prepare for Parliament.

On further survey and more mature consideration, the reservoir at Woodhead was much enlarged from what had been originally contemplated; and it was resolved to offer to the millowners the guarantee of a certain fixed quantity of water per day from the Woodhead reservoir, as compensation, instead of making over to them the reservoir itself.

The scheme was laid out on the assumption that 10,000,000 gallons of water per day was then required for the full supply of Manchester and the district proposed to be included within the operation of the Act, or the "limits of supply" as they are usually called. During the time that had elapsed since the project for the Water Company was designed, the estimates of what water was required for a town had gradually enlarged, and 20 gallons per head per day was now the lowest estimate of what was necessary for public and domestic purposes. This was, to a great extent, the result of experience in places where a constant full supply of good water had been given, and probably owing, in a slight degree, to the recommendations of the Board of Health, whose writings had attracted very general attention to the sanitary condition of towns.

The rain and stream observations on Swineshaw brook showed that in the year 1845, which was a year of just average rainfall, $40\tfrac{3}{4}$ inches had flowed off the ground, out of a rainfall of $59\tfrac{3}{10}$ inches; and in the year 1846, which was a dry year, $33\tfrac{1}{4}$ inches, out of $42\tfrac{3}{10}$. *Rain and stream observations on Swineshaw brook in 1845 and 1846.*

The general character of the water will be best understood from the following description, which was written for the information of the surveying officers appointed under the Preliminary Enquiries' Act, 1846 (which was then, for the first time, put in force), to enquire into the merits of this and other competing schemes which were projected for supplying Manchester with water:—

"The inadequacy of the present means for supplying water to the borough of Manchester and the adjacent district being on all hands admitted, as well as the impossibility of meeting the wants of the district by any extension of the present works of the Manchester and Salford Waterworks Company, it is unnecessary to dwell on the particulars of those works, or to say anything to urge the immediate necessity of securing a more abundant supply of pure water. Suffice it to say, that the most sanguine calculations of the means at the disposal of the Waterworks Company do not exceed 3,000,000 gallons of water per day, while the population of the district included within the powers of their Acts, amounts, at the present time, to 400,000 persons, and is *Description of proposed works for surveying officers.*

increasing at the rate of 10,000 persons in a year, the whole of whom are almost wholly dependent upon artificial means for a supply of water. For domestic consumption, and public sanitary purposes in the hands of the Corporation, the lowest estimate that can be made upon the present requirements of the district will be from 6,000,000 or 8,000,000 gallons of water per day; and it is not improbable that, for these purposes, before the expiration of 20 years, when the population may be expected to reach 600,000, the demand will amount to from 12,000,000 to 15,000,000 gallons daily. There are, in addition to the domestic and sanitary wants of the community, various and important trading establishments in the town, requiring a constant and abundant supply of pure water; and it is believed that, at the present time, anything short of 10,000,000 gallons per day would be insufficient for all purposes.

"The works proposed by the Corporation are laid out upon the basis of obtaining 20,000,000 per day in average years, and 15,000,000 in dry ones.

"It is proposed to connect them with the existing reservoirs and pipes of the present Waterworks Company, so as to make the best use of the money already sunk in these works.

"The district from which the water will be collected is a very elevated and percipitous portion of the Pennine chain of hills lying directly east of Manchester, and beyond the Gorton reservoir of the present Water Company.

"It extends over upwards of 15,000 statute acres; the nearest point in a straight line being about 9 miles, and the furthest about 19 miles distant from Manchester.

"Its elevation varies from 550 feet (the level of the lowest reservoir in the hills) to 2,000 feet above the sea, the great bulk of the ground being 1,400 feet and upwards.

"It consists of the lower strata of the coal measures, below the coal, the well-known rock called 'millstone grit' forming the cap of the hills and the precipitous sides of a large portion of the district.

"It abounds in the purest and most abundant spring water; and the rain, which falls there in large quantities, flows in torrents off the steep declivities of the mountains. The superficial character of the country, particularly of that portion which is to be specially allotted to the service of the town, is peculiarly favourable for the collection of the purest water.

"A large portion of it consists of bare and steep declivities, on which no water can rest; another large portion, of high mountain pasture, a small quantity of enclosed and cultivated land, and some decayed peat moss, no longer vegetating, but, by being carried away in small quantities in heavy rain, occasionally discolouring the water. The objectional tract of this description, within the district from which water will be collected for the town, consists of about 1,500 acres. The water flowing from it will be collected by catch-water drains, and separated from that to be supplied to the town, being either allowed to run to waste or stored in reservoirs for filtration.

"The bulk of the water to be collected will consist of floods, which are now totally useless for all purposes.

"The streams, when unaffected by recent rain, form little more than one-third of the whole quantity which flows down, and the dry weather measure is not one-fourth of the average volume.

"About one-half of all the water which flows off the ground runs off at present in a perfectly pure and colourless condition, notwithstanding that good and bad are now indiscriminately mixed together.

"The average rainfall over the whole district is about 60 inches, but there not unfrequently occur years when it only amounts to between 40 and 50. Of the rain falling, about two-thirds flow off the ground, the remainder being absorbed by evaporation, vegetation, &c.

"The excessive floods of very wet years cannot be made useful except by very large impounding reservoirs; and a quantity something under the average must, therefore, be calculated upon as the produce of the district.

"This quantity may be taken at three feet in depth of water over the whole surface of the drainage ground.

"This depth, upon 15,000 acres, will yield 1,960,200,000 cubic feet per annum, or 5,370,410 cubic feet or 38,565,062 gallons per day.

"From this quantity must be deducted that which it is proposed to give to the millowners as compensation for the right to abstract the remainder.

"It is proposed to guarantee to them 60 cubic feet per second, in all seasons, for 12 hours each working day, equal to 25¾ feet per second constantly throughout the year.

"Taking this quantity, there will remain for the use of the town as follows:—

	Cubic feet.
"Total daily quantity, at 3 feet per annum, from 15,000 acres......	5,370,410
"Supply to mills, at 25¾ feet per second, for 24 hours, equal to 60 feet per second, for 12 hours, during working days	2,215,627
"Leaving..........................	3,154,783

"Or 19,717,890 gallons per day, for the supply of the town.

"The water is to be stored in capacious reservoirs of the following capacities:—

	Cubic feet.
"Reservoir on Crowden Brook	18,493,602
"Ditto on Armfield Moor	13,072,581
"Ditto in Armfield Brook, near Woolley Mill	38,755,556
"Ditto in Hollingworth Brook	12,348,100
"Ditto at Tetlow Fold in Godley	8,849,810
"Service Reservoir at Denton	9,481,050
"Ditto at Pendleton	849,100
"Ditto at Broughton	630,180
"New works for storing water for supply of town	102,479,479
"The existing Reservoirs of the Waterworks Company at Gorton	35,800,000
"Compensation Reservoir for the millowners at Woodhead	154,573,420
"Total	292,852,899

"The daily supply of the streams intended to be appropriated to the use of the town will, in the severest drought, yield about 3¼ million gallons per day, without the assistance of reservoirs.

"The average of a 10 weeks' drought will be about 6 or 7 million gallons per day.

"By the assistance of the above reservoirs, and proper arrangements in the collection and separation of the water, with filtration when required, the whole of that required for the supply of the town may be obtained in the greatest purity.

"In this state, the hardness, according to Dr. Clarke's test, is about one degree, and it is perfectly colourless and tasteless.

"All the water will finally be collected in the reservoirs near the junction of the Hollingworth and Armfield brooks. From thence it will be sent in a covered watercourse and tunnel to the reservoir at Tetlow Fold, near Godley, a distance of about 3¾ miles.

"From the Tetlow Fold reservoir, which is intended for the regulation of the pressure upon the pipes, the water will be conveyed in a cast-iron main-pipe to the service reservoir at Denton, a distance of 6,336 yards, and to the present Gorton reservoir of the Waterworks Company, a distance of 7,848 yards.

"From these reservoirs the water will be supplied to the town.

"From Denton service reservoir to Ardwick, at the entrance of the borough, the distance is 6,730 yards.

"From the Gorton Reservoir the pipes are now laid.

"The pressure above Piccadilly, one of the highest parts of Manchester, will be, from the Denton reservoir, 170 feet, and from the lowest Gorton reservoir 91 feet, and the supply is intended to be constant.

"About one-third of the town will be supplied from the Gorton reservoir, and the remainder and more distant and higher parts from the Denton reservoir.

"The service reservoirs at Pendleton and Broughton are intended to be filled during the night, and the district immediately surrounding them supplied from these reservoirs respectively, during the day, so that the mains which are employed in the supply of Manchester during the day will be made available for the supply of more distant parts during the night."

The estimate of the works necessary for bringing the water to Ardwick (the junction of the London-road and Hyde-road), at the commencement of the town, was £210,000., and of carrying the pipes through the town to the service reservoirs at Pendleton and Broughton, including those reservoirs, was £45,000., making a total of £255,000. To this £10,000. were subsequently added for auxiliary reservoirs for the accommodation of the mill-owners, and for additional extra cost in the tunnel under Mottram hill.

Original estimate.

"ESTIMATE.

"Compensation reservoir, land, and works £24,255 0 0

"*Remainder of Works—Engineering Cost:—*

"Watercourse from Enterclough to Crowden reservoir	£620	0 0		
"Crowden reservoir	10,100	0 0		
"Watercourse from Crowden reservoir to Armfield reservoir..	3,600	0 0		
"Armfield reservoir	17,065	0 0		
"Hollingworth reservoir	5,500	0 0		
"Waste weirs and watercourse at the two last reservoirs	1,100	0 0		
"Armfield moor reservoir	8,100	0 0		
"Catch-water drains on the moors	2,700	0 0		
"Watercourse from Hollingworth reservoir to mouth of tunnel.....................................	5,183	0 0		
"Tunnel	13,860	0 0		
"Watercourse from end of tunnel to Tetlow Fold reservoir..	1,650	0 0		
Carried forward.........	£69,478	0 0	24,255	0 0

"*Remainder of Works—Engineering Cost*—continued:—

Brought forward......... £69,478 0 0	£24,255	0 0
"Tetlow Fold reservoir 6,500 0 0		
"Millowners' gauge............................... 1,000 0 0		
"Main pipes from Tetlow Fold reservoir to Denton service reservoir and the present Gorton reservoir................................. 30,536 0 0		
"Denton service reservoir 5,515 0 0		
"Main pipe from Denton service reservoir to Ardwick 30,298 0 0		
	148,327	0 0
"Land and contingencies, including the land for the compensation reservoir and purchase of water rights	55,400	0 0
"The cost of bringing the water to Ardwick, including land, works, and contingencies	210,000	0 0
"Service reservoirs at Pendleton and Broughton, and main pipes from Ardwick to them......................................	45,000	0 0
	£255,000	0 0

"Estimate of water power now enjoyed in ordinary states of the river at the following establishments, compared with what there will exist after the abstraction of water for the supply of Manchester, and the construction of the compensation reservoir:—

Name.	Fall.	Present Water Power.		Future Water-power regular.	Gain above Maximum.	Gain above Minimum.
		Minimum.	Maximum.			
	Feet.	Horse-power.	Horse-power.	Horse-power.	Horse-power.	Horse-power.
Mr. Rhode's mill, occupied by Mr. Winterbottom............	14	25	35	84	49	59
Mr. Winterbottom	20	40	60	125	65	85
Messrs. Sidebottom, Waterside.	19	40	60	128¼	68¼	88¼
Mr. Dalton	10	25	30	65	35	40
Mr. Sidebottom, Broadbottom..	20¼	70	140	160	20	90
Mr. Andrew, Compstall	49¼	800	360	500	140	200

"Mr. Andrew's reservoirs enable him to make more efficient use of the water than other millowners."

The Corporation were not to carry their Bill without opposition. The Etherow millowners, by way of putting themselves into a better position, as they supposed, for extorting terms from the Corporation, projected a scheme of reservoirs for regulating and increasing the available supply of the stream, to be constructed at their own cost, one of the reservoirs being on the same site as the Woodhead reservoir of the Corporation.

The Manchester Sheffield and Lincolnshire Railway Company had recently purchased the Ashton, the Peak Forest, and the Macclesfield canals, and they projected a scheme for applying the surplus water of the two latter navigations to the supply of Manchester, Salford, and Stockport. The Manchester and Salford Waterworks Company also prosecuted the Lyme Park scheme, which they had got up in the preceding session in opposition to the "Lancashire Waterworks." This was done by arrangement with the Corporation, to cover the contingency of their scheme being lost, and the possibility of the arrangement for the purchase of the waterworks falling through. Mr. Hawksley was the engineer to the Etherow reservoirs or millowners' scheme, Mr. Homersham to the Railway Company's project, and Mr. Simpson to the Waterworks Company. All these schemes were referred to the surveying officers, who were as follows:—Henry Robert Goldsmit, Esq., Barrister-at-Law, and George Rennie, Esq. Civil Engineer, to inquire into the Etherow Reservoir Bill; and George Wingrove Cooke, Esq., Barrister-at-Law, and James Meadows Rendel, Esq., Civil Engineer, to inquire into the Manchester Corporation Waterworks Bill, the Manchester Sheffield and Lincolnshire (supply of surplus water) Bill, and the Manchester and Salford Waterworks Company Amendment Bill.

Although the appointments were separate, the bills were all so intimately connected that all the four gentlemen agreed to sit together, and they met for that purpose at the Town Hall in Manchester, on the 26th January, 1847, and continued their sittings until all the evidence upon the various bills had been gone through.

The inquiries which took place at this time in various parts of the country were the first experience of the working of the Parliamentary Inquiries Act. In some places, from a dislike or unwillingness to give any information, prematurely, when it was known that the parties must still appear before a Committee of the House of Commons, the very baldest evidence was submitted to the surveying officers, and in many cases the subsequent parliamentary contact was rendered more severe than it would have been had no preliminary inquiry taken place. In other places the full merits of the schemes were gone into and ample information given, and it not unfrequently happened that differences were in consequence amicably arranged in the country. In Manchester all parties prepared for going thoroughly into the question. Evidence was given on all sides as if it were a final tribunal before which they were appearing, and *there* certainly great advantage resulted from the public and open discussion of the merits of the various projects which were submitted for consideration.

Reports of surveying officers.

The reports of the surveying officers were open to considerable question as to the soundness of the conclusions at which they arrived, and like those made by their colleagues upon schemes in other places, and like the Board of Trade Reports on Railways which had been made a year or two before, they seem to have had little effect in guiding the determinations of the Committees of the two Houses of Parliament, to which the reports, as well as the schemes to which they referred, had subsequently to be submitted.

After a few years' experience the preliminary inquiries on local matters were discontinued. They were not considered to have been attended with much general benefit, and the feeling of the country—or at all events of those who had to do with such questions—was decidedly against them. Their object was to reduce the expense and the trouble of obtaining local acts, by instituting inquiries upon the spot, and by that means obtaining more general and accurate information than could be submitted to Parliamentary Committees; but as the Committees were not to be bound by the reports of the surveying officers, and there was nothing to prevent the evidence which was taken in the country being repeated in Committee, both the labour and expense attending the application for an Act were frequently increased.

Etherow Bill.

When the surveying officers met, the Etherow Reservoir Bill was the first Bill inquired into. This scheme consisted of two large reservoirs,—one at Woodhead Chapel, with an embankment 87 feet 9 inches in height, forming a reservoir of 126¼ acres in extent, and estimated to contain 174,000,000 cubic feet; another at Torside, a little lower down the valley, with an embankment of 62 feet, being about 72¼ acres in extent, and containing 79,000,000 cubic feet. The two reservoirs together would cover about 200 acres of ground, and would contain 253,000,000 cubic feet of water. They would receive the water draining from 12,838 acres of the mountain land above them.

Mr. Hawksley estimated the cost at £49,750. The Bill contained power to raise a capital of £60,000., and to levy rates upon the mill falls for the payment of interest and working expenses, with a limitation in the rates to 7½ per cent.

Mr. Hawksley's estimate of the Etherow Bill.

In estimating the quantity of water which the district would produce, Mr. Hawksley took as the basis the working results of the Turton and Entwistle reservoir, all the particulars of which he had ascertained in working out the probable capabilities of the "Lancashire Waterworks Bill" of the previous session. He computed the quantity which had been regularly discharged from that reservoir at 42 inches over the whole of its collecting ground out of an annual rain-fall of 58 or 60 inches. Regarding the two districts as much alike, except that the shed from the Etherow district would be more rapid, he took it "as a practical fact" that this quantity of water would be impounded in the Etherow reservoirs and rendered available for the supply of the millowners.

There was one point of difference which he did not take into account. The capacity of the Turton and Entwistle reservoir was equal to 50,000 cubic feet for every acre of collecting ground, having "accidentally," as Mr. Hawksley correctly expressed it, been so proportioned as to retain the whole quantity of water which came down from the area shedding into it. The capacity which he had provided in the Etherow reservoirs was equal to only 20,000 cubic feet per acre of collecting ground. It was evident, therefore, that unless the Turton and Entwistle reservoir was very much too large a good deal of the Etherow water must run to waste in floods, which could not be stored and rendered useful to the mills. The reservoirs, by the assistance of the natural stream, which he first correctly estimated at about 1½ cubic feet per second for every 1,000 acres of drainage ground in ordinary summer weather, was, however, equal to ten weeks' supply of the quantity of water which he estimated they would afford to the river, viz.:— 120 cubic feet per second, or 10 horse-power, to every foot of fall for 12 hours of every working day. He was of opinion that though the reservoir might fail in extreme droughts, they would afford the quantity named for six years out of seven. At that time it must be admitted that it was generally considered sufficient by engineers to calculate for ten or eleven weeks' drought in the hilly districts of the North of England; but it was not usual to take the full average produce of the year's rain-fall, except where the reservoirs were large enough to store all the water which ran off the ground *in wet seasons* as well as in average ones and dry ones.

<small>Probable rates under the Etherow Bill.</small>

The evidence which was adduced on this Bill by the promoters themselves completely demolished it. It had been well devised and supported on its engineering merits, but it had been hastily concocted, no doubt for the purpose of hampering the Corporation, and without due consideration of its effects upon the millowners, should it pass into a law. The whole occupied fall sought to be benefitted was but 252 feet. The rate payable in respect of each foot, supposing the works would be executed for the money they were estimated to cost, would be nearly £20. per annum, be the benefit small or great, and no matter for how short a period of the year the additional water power which the reservoirs might contribute would be really required and useful. The mills near the reservoir would generally be great gainers, but as you descended the river its volume was swelled by contributions from other sources, till, within the limits to which the rating was intended to extend, it became so large that the natural stream was generally sufficient for the working of the mills without any extraneous aid. When, therefore, gentlemen whose mills were in this position found, as the evidence gradually unfolded itself under the searching cross-examination of the Town Clerk, that they would be liable to rates of from £200. to £800. a year and to all consequential damages in the event

<small>Bill abandoned.</small>

of the bursting of a reservoir, they were too glad to abandon all connexion with the scheme and to endeavour to come to terms with the Corporation, who offered them a guarantee of more water than any of them (with one or two exceptions) could usefully employ, and to take upon themselves all liability in the event of accident. The Bill did not proceed further than the inquiry before the surveying officers. The millowners, however, carried their opposition into Parliament and made a hard fight with the Corporation, but they finally arranged the question of compensation on terms exceedingly advantageous to themselves.

The Corporation scheme which was next gone into before the surveying officers, has already been pretty fully described.

<small>Opposition to the Corporation Bill.</small>

It met with the most virulent opposition, both by the millowners and by those who represented the railway rival project for supplying Manchester with the surplus water of their Peak Forest and Macclesfield canals. The most extraordinary evidence was brought against it, and though it is charitable to suppose that it was really believed in by those who gave it, yet, in almost every respect the result has proved the gross inaccuracy and the utter fallacy of almost everything which was asserted in condemnation of the project and in the attempt to prove it absurd and impracticable.

The rain observations and the measurements of the streams, which had been carefully taken for years for the purpose of obtaining correct information for our guidance, were ridiculed and treated as worthless. The idea that more rain fell on the high moorlands than on the plains below was treated as a monstrous absurdity, and the rain gauges on the line of the Rochdale canal, published by Dr. Dalton in the Memoirs of the Manchester Literary and Philosophical Society, although it was well known at that time that they were not to be relied upon, because they had been placed in the ridges of the roofs of houses, were brought forward to disprove the large fall of rain which was anticipated and to prove that less rain fell on high land than on low. *Rain and stream returns ridiculed.*

From actual measurement it had been ascertained that the produce of an average year in the Swineshaw district would exceed a depth of water flowing off the ground of 40 inches, and that there was both more rain and more produce in Longdendale than in the Swineshaw valley. For purposes of calculation I had taken 36 inches. Mr. Hawksley had taken 42 inches. It was asserted, however, that the rain would not exceed 36 inches in a dry year, and that not more than 24 inches would flow off the ground, and that owing to the small storage provided, 16 inches was all that could be rendered available. It was a fact which could have been ascertained at the time that the spring water alone, in the dryest weather, without any storage at all, yielded what was equivalent to half this quantity.

Rain gauges were put down, and so contrived to show a small quantity of rain, in furtherance of the theory that less rain fell on high land than on low, that they proved at Woodhead a fall of 33 inches of rain only when $49\frac{1}{2}$ inches had actually flowed off the ground. Calculations were made to prove that so far from the Corporation being able to get any water at all for Manchester, they would have to bring some from other sources to give the compensation to millowners which it was proposed to guarantee.

The whole drainage ground, or nearly the whole, was alleged to be peat; the water which flowed down the streams was said to be never used for domestic purposes; cattle would not drink it; in flood it could be smelt *Statements as to bad quality of water.*

a field off, and it was asserted that if the flood-water were used it would poison the whole population of Manchester.

Samples.

Samples of water, which it was stated were fair samples of the water we were proposing to collect for the supply of the town, were exhibited before the surveying officers, and gravely put in and sworn to, which had been collected—not from the streams themselves, but from deep holes dug into the peat on the flat tops of some of the hills in dry weather, and the bottles filled from the drops which gradually oozed out of the peat from the sides of the hole and accumulated at the bottom.

Accident to two gentlemen.

Two zealous gentlemen, in their eagerness to ascertain whether an assertion I had made in my evidence as the result of frequent observation was true or not, took to the hills while the inquiry was going on, and were overtaken by a snowstorm, in which they lost their way and nearly perished from cold and exposure. Long after dark, after wandering about the whole day, they accidently fell or stumbled into a sort of cave at the seal bark rocks, at the head of the Greenfield valley in Saddleworth, which afforded them some protection from the biting wind and storm. The thermometer that night fell to 13° Fahr. in Manchester, and must have been not far from zero in the elevated region in which they were exposed. They were happily enabled to keep each other awake during the night, and shortly after leaving their retreat at daybreak the next morning, they discovered where they were, and were fortunate enough to reach a place of safety without further injury than frost-bitten toes and fingers.

The point they went to ascertain was this:—On being cross-examined as to the character of the water, especially as to water which issued from peat or peat-covered ground, I had stated to the following effect:—that the streams in dry weather were very small and particularly clear and pellucid,—that in walking over the hills wherever I had found water issuing from a swamp or peat bog discoloured or tasting of peat, I had found, by following the stream as it flowed, that it invariably lost all taste and colour within half-a-mile or so of the place at which it escaped from a stagnant swamp; whether this was by admixture with spring water in its course, or by exposure to the atmosphere in a running stream, I did not pretend to say, but it was a fact which I had repeatedly observed, and which anyone might go to the hills and observe for himself.

It is not my intention to go through the evidence which was adduced, and I have only hastily glanced at the extravagant assertions which were made in respect of our scheme, for the purpose of showing the sort of ordeal through which a good scheme, most carefully designed on the best ascertained facts, and most honestly conceived in a spirit of fairness to all, has to fight its way when exposed to interested opposition. Great allowance must be made for inexperience and ignorance, for difference of opinion, and for the different aspect in which two men may regard the same question, but it too frequently happens that feeling is allowed to get the better of judgment, and assertions are made and opinions hazarded which can hardly be reconciled with strict regard to truth. It is unquestionable that professional evidence, of all kinds, is regarded with great suspicion, and the value of a professional opinion and the character of a professional man are correspondingly lowered in public estimation. *Professional evidence.*

The evidence before the surveying officers, which was adduced on the part of the promoters, disclosed the following state of the supply in Manchester and the population within the district to be supplied. *Evidence before surveying officers.*

The tables appended were partly deduced from the Census Returns of 1841, and partly from information carefully obtained by the police officers of the Borough under the direction of Captain Willis the superintendent.

Parliamentary Return of the Population of the Borough of Manchester in the Year 1841:—

Townships.	Houses.			Total of Persons.
	Inhabited.	Uninhabited.	Building.	
Ardwick	1,882	378	84	9,906
Beswick	65	7	...	845
Cheetham	1,146	127	14	6,082
Chorlton-upon-Medlock	5,486	491	54	28,336
Hulme	5,046	494	393	26,982
Manchester	27,055	2,285	134	163,856
	40,680	3,782	679	235,507

Population of Townships not within the Borough of Manchester, but within the limits of the Manchester and Salford Waterworks Company's present Act of Parliament—Census of 1841:—

	Number of Persons.	Houses.		
		Inhabited.	Uninhabited.	Total.
Salford	58,200	10,004	1,243	11,247
Bradford	911	181	9	190
Newton	6,127	1,110	133	1,243
Broughton	8,794	649	31	680
Pendleton	11,082	2,059	91	2,150
Gorton	2,422	484	97	501
Openshaw	2,280	428	43	466
Droylsden	4,938	823	49	872
Audenshaw	5,874	699	62	761
Denton	3,440	604	38	642
	93,513	16,986	1,796	18,782

Population of other Townships or Chapelries proposed to be included within the limits of the Manchester Corporation Waterworks Bill—Census, 1841:—

	Houses.			Total of Persons.
	Inhabited.	Uninhabited.	Building.	
Crumpsall .... Lancashire	589	24	1	2,745
Haughton .... "	577	26	3	3,319
Reddish .... "	206	30	...	1,188
Worsley .... "	1,441	49	3	8,887
Barton-on-Irwell .... "	1,006	62	5	10,965
Prestwich .... "	565	28	3	3,180
Hyde .... Cheshire	1,754	155	11	10,170
Mottram-en-Longdendale "	557	19	2	3,247
Godley .... "	203	7	2	1,389
Newton .... "	1,218	147	...	7,501
	9,056	547	30	51,951

Police Return for the Borough of Manchester for the Year ending February 28th, 1846:—

	Dwelling Houses.		Dwelling Cellars.		Total of Persons dwelling in both.
	Inhabited.	Uninhabited.	Inhabited.	Uninhabited.	
A Division	7,129	162	1,446	82	52,132
B Division	10,809	172	1,564	83	76,997
C Division	14,102	178	1,287	68	81,298
D Division	13,577	349	787	101	82,195
	45,617	861	5,084	334	292,622
					2,655
					295,277

Table showing the Number of Habitable Houses and Habitable Cellars, being separate Tenements, within each Township of the Municipal Borough of Manchester, which are supplied or which are not supplied with Water from the Waterworks Company:—

Townships.	Number of Streets in each Township.	Dwelling Houses.				Dwelling Cellars.				Number of Dwelling Premises supplied by Taps in the Streets.		
		Total Number of Houses.	Supplied with water in the interior.	Supplied with water by a tap in the street.	Not supplied with water.	Total Number of Cellars.	Supplied with water in the interior.	Supplied with water by a tap in the street.	Not supplied with water.	Total Number of Dwellings.	Total Number of Taps.	Average Number of Dwellings to each Tap.
Ardwick	190	2,596	344	1,052	1,200	55	7	29	19	1,081	85	12
Beswick	8	68	9	56	8	...	...	...	...	56	5	11
Cheetham	88	1,487	668	88	686	...	...	...	...	88	13	6
Chorlton	305	6,454	663	495	5,296	259	4	59	196	548	39	14
Hulme	377	8,728	287	363	8,128	201	...	86	115	399	36	11
Manchester	1,885	27,294	8,997	10,888	7,409	4,194	1,041	1,912	1,541	12,800	1,004	12
Totals	2,848	46,577	10,918	12,937	22,722	5,008	1,052	2,080	1,921	14,907	1,182	11

NOTE.—The number of houses which are supplied with water, include the uninhabited as well as the inhabited.

The number of dwelling premises supplied by taps in the streets, which gives the average of 11 houses or premises to one tap, include the cellars as well as houses.

The return does not include the new houses which were in the course of erection and completion, and which were not inhabitable at the time of taking the return.

From the last table it will be seen that the total number of houses in the Borough of Manchester was, in 1846, 46,577. Of these the number supplied with water internally was 10,918, the water, however, being supplied for short periods only during each day. The number of houses supplied by taps in the streets, from which the water was fetched or carried by the tenants, was 12,937, and the number totally unsupplied by the Company was 22,722, which at 5¼ persons to a house would represent a population of 125,000 persons. This was irrespective of a further population of from 25,000 to 30,000 persons who reside in cellars, about 10,500 of whom were totally unsupplied with water. To a slight extent this deficiency was corrected by pumps and wells, most of which, however, were shallow, sunk only into the superficial sands and gravel; but so scarce and valuable was water obtained in this way, that it was kept occasionally in cottages for weeks together, and used over and over again for washing the floors, until the smell produced by it was intolerable.

Dr. R. A. Smith stated that he had analyzed the water of 24 such wells, which, though not a large number, he had to search for over a large portion of the town, and that in every instance he found the waters were polluted with matter from cesspools and sewers, and in some cases from churchyards.

On this subject the surveying officers report:—

"The insufficiency of the present supply, therefore, is evident, and the usual consequences attendant upon such insufficiency are found among the poorer population. Some drink of wells which are polluted by leakage from the sewers and by drainage from grave yards; others obtain a scanty supply by buying from persons who carry water about for sale; some even take for domestic purposes the putrid waters of the canal or of the Medlock, which, used as they are, the latter as a drainage for the sewers, and both for the grosser purposes of the factories, are almost too noisome to be approached. In some parts we find the neighbourhood flocking to catch the water which flows from the condensed water-pipe of a steam engine, and even in the best supplied of the poorer districts there is waste of time and labour, and oftentimes very undesirable contentions in obtaining water from the stand taps of the Company. * * * * All the medical witnesses agree that the large rate of mortality by which Manchester is distinguished is greatly owing to its destitution of water."

The Longdendale waters, proposed to be introduced in substitution of such pernicious supplies, were examined and analyzed by Mr. P. H. Holland

and Dr. Smith. Mr. Holland stated that " they were the purest waters he _{Mr. Holland's opinion of water.}
" had ever seen, that they exceeded even those of the Cumberland lakes,
" and that for all purposes the purer the better, and the softer for drinking
" the better." "This water," he said, "has a peculiarity which is worth
" knowing. Most of the soft natural waters are vapid. Those which run off
" the slate rocks have the taste of rain water, but this water, which filters
" through a soft porous rock, receives in its progress a quantity of common
" air and carbonic acid which gives it the sparkling brilliancy and taste of
" ordinary spring water with the softness of rain water. It is exceedingly
" pleasant to drink."

The hardness of the water in its ordinary state, as ascertained by these _{Hardness of Longdendale water.} gentlemen according to Dr. Clarke's soap test, was as follows :—

Hollingworth brook	1·5
Armfield brook	1·1
Hollins brook	1
Springs under Tintwistle knarr	1
Great Crowden brook	1·2
Little Crowden brook	1·1
Heyden brook	1·2
River Etherow, above the Manchester and Sheffield Railway tunnel	1·2
Water out of the railway tunnel	7·7
River Etherow at Waterside, below the tunnel and below all the above streams except the Hollingworth and Armfield brooks	1·6

A subsequent examination of the water taken in very heavy flood when _{Analyses of flood-water by Professor Graham.} it was much discoloured was, at the request of the surveying officers, made by Professor Graham, of University College, London. His report is as follows :—

"No. 1.—*Labelled 'Water taken from Hollins brook, on the 18th February, by the inspecting officers, during a heavy flood.'*

"Contains 20·2 grains of solid matter, chiefly vegetable fibre or peaty matter, in each imperial gallon, separable by filtration. It filtered immediately, it passes through transparent, but of a sensibly brown tint from peaty matter held in solution, too highly coloured in my opinion for domestic use. But, if the water is freely exposed to the air for a few days, the colouring matter becomes insoluble, and was found to be removable thereafter by filtration. This water I believe, therefore, to contain no impurity which could not be easily separated from it by ordinary mechanical filtration and subsidence, provided it was allowed to remain two or three weeks in a reservoir or settling pond.

"The filtered water is highly pure and soft, and contains no impurity in solution which would render it at all inconvenient for domestic use.

"*No. 2.—Labelled 'Water taken from a small stream near Sprinlow Road, during a heavy flood, by the inspecting officers, 18th February.'*

"Contains only 0·18 grains of solid matter, chiefly vegetable fibre, removed by filtration.

"Filters clear at once, is highly pure and soft, and contains no impurity in solution which would render it at all inconvenient for domestic use. This is by much the least turbid sample of the present series.

"*No. 3.—Labelled 'Water taken from Hollins brook, on the 18th February, during a heavy flood, by the inspecting officers.'*

"Contains 158 grains of solid matter in each imperial gallon, removed by filtration. There is much peaty matter, but the great weight is sand.

"The observations made on No. 1 are all equally applicable to the present sample, and the conclusions respecting it the same.

"*No. 4.—Labelled 'Water taken from Armfield brook, on the 18th February, during a heavy flood, by the inspecting officers.'*

"Contains 27·6 grains of solid matter (peaty matter and mud) in each imperial gallon, removed by filtration.

"In other respects entirely resembles No. 1.

"*No. 5.—Labelled 'Water taken from the Little Crowden brook, on the 18th February, during a heavy flood, by the inspecting officers.'*

"Contains 134·4 grains of solid matter (peaty matter and sand) in each imperial gallon, removed by filtration.

"In other respects entirely similar to No. 1.

"*No. 6.—Labelled 'Water taken from the Great Crowden brook, on the 18th February, during a heavy flood, by the surveying officers.'*

"Contains 184·6 grains of solid matter (peaty matter and sand) in each imperial gallon, removed by filtration.

"In other respects entirely similar to No. 1."

Samples of flood-water, unfavourable specimens. The samples of water collected by the surveying officers, and thus reported on by Professor Graham, were most unfavourable specimens. It would be scarcely possible for the same quantity of rain to produce again such a condition of the streams. An almost continuous frost for three months had suddenly given way. The surface of the peat-covering of the hills—the channels of the streams—and the whole surface of the country had been repeatedly raised by the expanding action of the frost and separated into small particles, which the first flood carried at once into the stream. Probably no other flood in a twelve month would contain so large a quantity of solid matter.

Professor Graham's analysis and report, however, are conclusive as to the excellence of the water even under such circumstances, and the facility with which it may be rendered perfectly fit for domestic use.

The purity of the water in all states, therefore, was undeniable.

The advantage of introducing it into the town was illustrated by Mr. Holland, by a calculation to show the annual saving in soap, as compared with the water supplied by the existing Waterworks Company and with that proposed to be introduced by other parties; taking Mr. Porter's estimate of 9·2 lbs. as the average consumption of soap per head in England per annum:— *Mr. Holland's estimate of saving in soap by use of Longdendale water.*

"*Table showing the probable saving of Soap likely to be effected by substituting the proposed Water from Longdendale for the present supply from the Manchester and Salford Waterworks:—*

	Lbs.	Value. £.	Difference. £.
Total quantity consumed by 350,000 persons at the average of 9·2 lbs. per annum each	3,220,000	72,000	...
Half of present consumption, on which alone it is here assumed the saving will probably be effected—hardness 9, proportion of soap 200	1,610,000	36,000	...
Mixture of Peak Forest and Macclesfield Canal waters, in the proportion of 42 to 22, i.e., as they will be according to the proposed scheme—hardness 7, soap 160..................	1,280,000	28,000	7,200
Lyme Park (according to Dr. Smith's analysis)—hardness 4·9, soap 130 ...	1,040,000	23,214	12,786
Longdendale—hardness 1·25, soap 45......	360,000	8,100	27,900

"*Assumptions.*

"1.—That the population use only the ordinary porportion of soap. It is almost certain they use more in consequence of the smokiness of the town, the comparative wealth of the inhabitants, and the number of works in which large quantities are consumed.

"2.—The population is taken at 350,000, if all are supplied they will be far more numerous.

"3.—That only half of the soap now consumed is used with water as hard as 9°, and that the rest is used with rain-water, or with water softened with soda, or for washing clothes sent into the country. This is equivalent to assuming that about one-fifth of the water used for washing is as hard as 9°.

"4.—That the pipe-water is generally not harder than at present, namely 9°. It is often much harder, as high as 12° or 18°."

So highly did Mr. Holland estimate the value of the water that he gave it as his opinion—"that it would be cheaper for the town of Manchester to "pay many hundred thousand pounds for the Longdendale water than to "have any other water he had heard of for nothing."

<small>Daily measurements of streams.</small> Daily measurements had been made of the streams to be taken, and daily observations upon the colour and condition of the water, and from these it was easy to calculate the quantity of pure uncoloured water which could be collected.

At the time of the inquiry before the surveying officers in February, these observations had extended over a period of seven months, and had, therefore, included the latter part of summer and the whole of the autumn (when the discolouration by the stain of peat is most strongly exhibited), and the winter, during which other causes of disturbance and discolouration are most actively at work, at the same time, that, in the absence of floods, cold weather and hard frost have a tendency to bring the water to the highest state of purity and to exhibit it in its most colourless condition. The observations, therefore, would present a fair average of the year.

From these it appeared that the produce of the whole district to be interfered with, about 15,000 acres in round numbers, was in ordinary dry weather (the water being then perfectly pure and colourless) about 10,000,000 or 11,000,000 gallons per day, and in extreme drought about 6,000,000 gallons per day.

In a full or swollen state of the river in summer, exclusive of floods and discoloured water, the volume of the pure streams from the whole district would, after a flood had washed out the colouring matter, amount to about 70 cubic feet per second or about 38,000,000 gallons per day.

After a long summer drought the streams began to be discoloured after rain, when their united volume reached about 40 feet per second or 22,000,000 gallons per day.

In winter the discolouration was increased when the streams were swollen to about 90 feet per second or nearly 50,000,000 gallons per day, and as the flood subsided the discolouration disappeared at a little more than the same quantity. In two or three days after a flood and the cessation of rain the streams fell to about 40 feet per second.

The average of all the observations during the seven months gave 15,000,000 gallons per day of pure uncoloured water, notwithstanding that in the month of October an unusually large quantity of colouring matter was coming down the stream.

Excluding October, the mean of the remaining months was 17,500,000 gallons per day.

From this it was evident that by properly separating and storing the pure water no filtration would be required, but it was necessary that the Corporation should have entire possession and control of the district, to sort and separate the water as they thought fit, and a sufficient number of water-bailiffs who should reside upon the works and carefully attend to the state of the water.

Hence the determination of the Corporation to give to the millowners a stipulated quantity of compensation water, rather than make over to them any particular reservoir or district, from interference with which the Corporation must necessarily have been excluded.

I pass now to the rival project of the Manchester Sheffield and Lincolnshire Railway Company for applying the surplus water of the Peak Forest and Macclesfield canals to the supply of Stockport, Manchester, and Salford; but as the project has not been carried out, although the Company obtained an Act legalizing the sale of water in bulk, and as it is very fully and accurately described in the report of the surveying officers, which will be found in the Appendix, a brief notice will be sufficient. *Scheme of the Manchester Sheffield and Lincolnshire Railway Company.*

The two canals were supplied with water by the flood-waters of various streams, which the Company were entitled to take for purposes of navigation after certain gauges, which were constructed on each stream for the protection of the millowners, were filled with water. The dimensions of these gauges had been fixed by arbitration in accordance with the respective Acts, and were sufficiently large to pass the streams in all ordinary states of the weather, and also to some extent when they were swollen. The surplus, or so much of it as the Canal Companies chose to take, was stored in large reservoirs for the use of the canals.

It was found there was much more flood-water than the canals required, and the Railway Company, into whose hands the canals had now passed, proposed to make additional reservoirs for the purpose of storing this surplus water, and to obtain parliamentary powers to distribute it and sell it for the supply of Stockport, Manchester, and Salford.

The collecting ground, which extended to nearly 16,000 statute acres, yielded for the most part excellent water, not exceeding $3\frac{1}{4}°$ of hardness. The country was very favourable for the construction of works, and the reservoirs proposed were of large and ample dimensions.

The quantity of water which this scheme would have yielded, for the supply of the districts intended to be included, was very uncertain, as it not only depended upon the amount of rain and the proportion which would flow from the ground, but upon the manner in which the rain fell. A tolerably uniform fall of rain throughout the year during which no great floods occurred, would yield but a small quantity to the reservoirs,—the bulk would pass through the gauges,—while in a year of great vicissitude, although showing probably a less gross amount, a large proportion of the whole might, by reason of sudden rains and heavy floods, be passed to the reservoirs.

The promoters, with little or no data for their conclusions, assumed two-fifths of the annual yield as the quantity which would flow through the millowners' gauges, and that the remaining three-fifths would pass to the reservoirs. After deducting the water required for supplying the navigations, they estimated the residue, available for waterworks' purposes, at about $9\frac{1}{4}$ million gallons per day.

My examination of this district and its capabilities, led me to the conclusion that in certain years 8 or 9 million gallons per day might be obtained, but that in other years the quantity would not exceed 5 millions a day. These computations were made by comparing each stream with the Swineshaw brook, so often already alluded to, upon which daily measurements of the volume had been taken for a considerable period. The character of the district, the fall of rain, and the size of the gauge at which the water had been measured, all concurred in producing a beautiful index of the probable quantity in the Peak Forest and Macclesfield districts. A little allowance for or against, according to the difference in the fall of rain or the difference in the size of the millowners' gauges, corrected the calculations for each stream. This done, it was easy to determine for how many days in the year the volume of each stream would have been more than sufficient to fill the millowners' gauge, and, according to the depth over the gauge above this quantity, to determine how much of the flood water would pass to the reservoirs.

In the year 1845 the produce, according to these calculations, would have been generally three-fifths to the mills and two-fifths to the reservoirs, thus transposing the proportions adopted by the promoters. The total quantity, however, available to the Company, after deducting for the supply of the canal, was about 8,000,000 gallons per day. The year 1845, which gave this result, was especially favourable to the collection of water by the system on which the canal reservoirs were supplied. The fall of rain during the year was just an average, but it was considerably *below* the average during the first six months, and considerably *over* it during the second six months. The excessive floods of the latter period would contribute a large quantity to the reservoirs.

A similar mode of calculation upon the year 1846, showed a nett quantity available to the Company of only 5,000,000 gallons per day, and this was as large a quantity as could, in my opinion, be safely assumed.

It was proposed to convey the water from the reservoirs along the canals for some miles to a convenient point near Marple, four miles from Stockport, where it was to be filtered, received into a service reservoir, and thence conveyed by cast-iron pipes to the towns to be supplied. The water in its passage through the canals became considerably harder, and by being fouled by admixture with clay, more difficult to filter. From being only $2°$ or $3°$ in the reservoirs, the hardness became $6·2°$ in the Peak Forest canal, and $7·6°$ in the Macclesfield canal, at the point at which the water was to be taken out for filtration. This was proposed to be remedied by pitching the canal with stone.

The estimate for the construction of new works was £240,000., including the cost of iron pipes from Marple to Manchester, viz. £90,719.; but to this estimate had to be added a charge for previous outlay in the construction of canal works which were now to be devoted to waterworks purposes. This was taken at £60,000., making the total estimate £300,000.

At the conclusion of the inquiry into the various schemes, and after full discussion on the clauses of the respective Bills, Mr. Heron, Town Clerk, at the request of the surveying officers, handed in the following statement of the objects which the Corporation had in view:—

<small>Statement by Town Clerk of Manchester.</small>

"Power to the Corporation of Manchester to make works, distribute water, and levy water-rates within the borough of Manchester, and to sell any surplus water to any company or other body or person who may be entitled by any Act already passed or hereafter to be passed, to lay down pipes and distribute water in any township or district within ten miles of the borough.

"No. 1.—Manchester Corporation Waterworks Bill. The Corporation of Manchester by this Bill seek to obtain powers to bring from the Longdendale district water for the borough, and believe that 18,000,000 or 20,000,000 of gallons per day can be obtained by the expenditure of about £210,000.

"In order to prevent unnecessary expenditure, and also to avoid any charge being cast upon the rates of the borough, before water can be abundantly supplied to the inhabitants in return for such rates, the Corporation seek to obtain power to transfer, if it appear desirable, all the powers of this Bill to the present Company, in order that the extensions authorized may be carried out in connexion with the existing works.

"No. 2.—Manchester Corporation Waterworks Bill. By this Bill the Corporation seek to obtain the powers necessary to enable them to purchase the works of the Manchester and Salford Waterworks Company, and to have imposed upon them the responsibility and duty of taking the water to every house within the boundaries of the Municipal Borough, and in return to make and levy water-rates.

"Also to have power to make a rate for public purposes, (that is to say) for the supply of water required for flushing and cleansing sewers, for washing and cleansing the streets, and for the extinction of, and also the protection afforded against, fire.

"To have power to sell water for other purposes, by agreement, within the borough, and also for all purposes, either at the rates specified in the Act, or by agreement without the borough.

"The object of the Corporation is to secure an abundant supply and effective distribution of water within the borough (which is at the present time lamentably deficient), and at the lowest possible cost, and, in fact, to obtain, by means of a compulsory rate, an amount which shall be equal only to the actual cost of the water, after giving credit for all sums received for the supply of water beyond the boundaries of the borough, to such parties or districts as may choose to take it, or within the borough by agreement, for other than public or domestic purposes.

"The Corporation are satisfied that the only mode in which they can satisfactorily and economically carry into effect the arrangements suggested is by becoming the owners of the waterworks.

"The Corporation do not, however, seek to become unnecessary dealers or traders in water, and they have already stated to the Corporation of Salford that as soon as that body obtains similar powers for the distribution of water within that borough, and for making rates, they will be quite willing to be shut out altogether from supplying water within the borough of Salford, under any power which they may possess, and will be prepared to sell all pipes laid down at a price to be agreed upon or settled by arbitration, and to supply the Corporation of Salford with the water required for that borough, for all purposes, in bulk, at such a price per 1,000 gallons as may be arranged either by agreement or by reference to any public officer appointed in that behalf.

"The Corporation will be quite willing, in the same way, to be shut out from interfering in all other districts beyond the boundaries of the Manchester Borough, included either in their own Bill (No. 1), or in the present Acts of the Manchester and Salford Waterworks Company, as soon as, under any public or private Act, any other body may be appointed for the purpose of supplying and distributing water within any such district, and of making rates for defraying the expense, and to be bound to sell water in bulk to such body, at such price as shall be agreed upon or settled by arbitration."

The surveying officers reported upon all the projects submitted to them. Their report on the Corporation scheme was open to much question and might easily be shown to be erroneous in many important computations and conclusions, but as these reports had no effect in either hindering or promoting any of the schemes submitted to them, it is not worth while entering into an examination of the correctness of the conclusions they arrived at. In addition to their separate reports, they made a general report on all the schemes, which, as containing a comparative analysis of their opinion of their respective capabilities and merits, and of the manner in which the district ought to be supplied with water, is given at length:—

"Supplemental Report by G. Wingrove Cooke, James Meadows Rendel, Henry Robert Goldfinch, and George Rennie, Esquires, on the Manchester *Supplemental report of surveying officers.*

Corporation Waterworks Bill, No. 1; the Manchester Corporation Waterworks Bill, No. 2; the Manchester Sheffield and Lincolnshire (supply of surplus water) Bill; the Manchester and Salford Waterworks Amendment Bill; and the Etherow Reservoirs Bill.

"To the Commissioners of Her Majesty's Woods, Forests, Land Revenues, Works, and Buildings:—

"My Lord and Gentlemen,—Of five Local Bills, having for their object either the supply of the whole, or a portion, of the boroughs of Manchester, Salford, and Stockport with water, or the abstraction of the waters which were proposed to be converted to that purpose; four were referred to the undersigned surveying officers, Mr. Cooke and Mr. Rendel, and one to the undersigned surveying officers, Mr. Goldfinch and Mr. Rennie.

"The cases were found to be so intimately connected that it was impossible to arrive at any satisfactory estimate of any single scheme, without hearing the evidence upon others. The evidence in favour of any one Bill was part of the evidence in opposition to another, and we found it necessary to sit together upon such parts of the inquiry as could not be disconnected.

"Having drawn up our respective reports upon the separate Bills, we have considered that it will probably be found convenient that we collectively submit a short Supplemental Report upon the whole of them.

"It being fully established that the boroughs of Manchester, Salford, and Stockport are at present very ill supplied with water, the first object of the inquiry is whence a proper supply can be most abundantly and most cheaply obtained.

"This point being settled, we apprehend that the interests of any private parties can be looked upon only as interests for compensation.

"There are three competitors for this privilege of supplying water:—

"First.—The Corporation of Manchester, who propose to include Manchester, Salford, and the surrounding townships, but not Stockport.

"Secondly.—The Sheffield and Lincolnshire Railway Company, who propose to devote the surplus water of their canal gathering grounds to the supply of the three boroughs; and,

"Thirdly.—The present Manchester and Salford Waterworks Company, who propose to increase their works, and in some small degree their districts.

"The water wants of the three boroughs are as follows:—Ten millions of gallons daily for Manchester; five millions for Salford and the townships of Crumpsall, Haughton, Reddish, Worsley, Barton-on-Irwell, Prestwich, Eccles, Bradford, Newton, Broughton, Pendleton, Gorton, Openshaw, Droylsden, Audenshaw, and Denton; and three millions for Stockport,—in the whole eighteen millions of gallons daily.

"We are agreed in opinion that the Corporation scheme cannot be certainly calculated to yield more than ten millions of gallons daily.

"We are also agreed that the Railway Company's scheme cannot be certainly calculated upon for more than from six to eight millions of gallons daily; and we take this large margin on account of the absence of data by which to estimate the probabilities of the occurrence of the extraordinary floods which alone will give water to this scheme.

"The Lyme Park scheme proposed a still smaller supply, and has been withdrawn.

"The Corporation scheme proposes the largest supply at the cheapest rate; it is a perfect scheme for the supply of the borough of Manchester, but not large enough for Salford and the out-townships.

"The Railway Company's scheme offers a smaller supply at a dearer rate. The Corporation can bring ten millions of gallons a day to Manchester for about £13,000. per annum; the Railway Company can bring eight millons to Blackfriars bridge for £27,320.

"This difference does not depend upon any great advantage in point of cheapness, which the Corporation scheme, as an engineer's scheme, has over that of the Railway Company; but simply upon this difference, that the Corporation seek no further return upon the capital expended than the interest for which money can be borrowed upon good security; while the Railway Company look for a trading profit upon the capital invested. Here the Corporation has an advantage with which no trading company can compete.

"The borough of Manchester, however, requires the whole of the water which the Corporation scheme can bring. Every year the water-wants of that borough increase, and every year the difficulty of obtaining water in the neighbourhood for the purposes of waterworks also increases. The active trade which is yearly adding to the population of the borough, is also adding to the value of water-power in its neighbourhood; already it is impossible to find a streamlet which has not been appropriated by some one or more mill-owners; and the longer the accomplishment is delayed, of that which must eventually be done, namely, the establishment of some large and permanent scheme of water-supply equal to the necessities of these towns, the more difficult and the more expensive will such establishment ultimately be.

"Either of the schemes now before us would, we submit, be quite inadequate to the supply of the population which it proposes to serve. When a scheme is brought forward for an object of this importance, it should *permanently* secure the district from the possibility of recurrence to the present disagreeable expedients of receiving into the pipes the drainage of a not very rural district, pumping water from the unwholesome Medlock, or taking it unfiltered from canals. Where a drainage ground is intermixed with peat bogs, giving forth objectionable water, it is especially important that there should be no temptation to the manager of the works to eke out an insufficient bulk of water by admitting the peat-drainage; and the importance of this is still further increased, if it is proposed that the drainage shall pass unfiltered into the pipes.

"Our impression (derived from the evidence), that there is no necessity for the borough of Manchester to restrict itself to an inadequate supply, by sharing this water with places beyond its precincts, is much strengthened by such information as we have been able to obtain as to the cost of the water and the rental of the borough.

"The rental of the borough of Manchester is £1,104,057. A rate of 9d. in the pound would give a return of £41,250., a much larger sum than we can discover to be possibly required for securing the whole of this water to the borough. If we deduct the amount which would be received for the supplies for trade and manufacturing, the rate which would be necessary would probably be not more than 9d. in the pound upon the dwelling houses and shops—assuming that Manchester takes to itself the whole of this water.

"It was stated by the promoters of the Manchester Corporation Bill, that the only object they had in supplying any places out of the borough, was to decrease the expense of water within the borough. We submit that the allowing a corporation to act as a water company beyond the precincts of their borough is inexpedient in principle, and that in this instance it is peculiarly objectionable, because the quantity of water is not greater than they can themselves well consume, and the expense is not more than the borough can reasonably bear.

"If the borough of Manchester were withdrawn, a district would still be left fully sufficient for the remuneration of a water company. If, as we do not anticipate, the rental of that district is not sufficient to pay for the whole of the 8,000,000 of gallons, still the Railway Company's scheme is of a nature to be readily capable of modification.

"Salford and the out-townships had a rental, in 1841, of £414,429., and Stockport has a rental of £102,699. If the little townships of Hyde, Godley, and Newton can maintain an establishment of water-works, upon the principle of constant supply, we submit that it is not probable that, even should the Railway Company abandon their scheme, these large towns will find difficulty in obtaining a supply in bulk, which may be distributed in the manner suggested by the Report of the Health of Towns Commissioners.

"That there are difficulties of detail in recasting these Bills so as to divide the district, in the manner we have ventured to suggest, may not be denied.

The fact of the Manchester and Salford Company's pipes extending beyond the borough would appear to be one of the most serious practical objections. We do not, however, conceive that this would be found insuperable. Any general measure which may enable local administrative bodies to purchase water in bulk, and distribute it by means of water-rates, would probably remove many of the difficulties of detail if the recommendations of the Health of Towns Commission should be recognized in legislation. But we have not thought ourselves justified in pursuing this inquiry further than was necessary to show that neither of these schemes, taken singly, has the capacity of water supply which the Legislature may well require of any body seeking what must be in effect the monopoly of water-supply to this large population.

"We have the honour to be,
"My Lord and Gentlemen,
"Your very faithful Servants,
"GEO. WINGROVE COOKE,
"JAMES MEADOWS RENDEL,
"HENRY R. GOLDFINCH,
"GEORGE RENNIE.

"The Temple, 3rd March, 1847."

The inquiry ended and the reports made, the Corporation and the Railway Company proceeded with their respective Bills to Parliament.

The two Bills of the Corporation were fused into one. Their scheme was opposed solely by their rivals the Railway Company and the millowners on the Etherow, who, although they had abandoned their own measure, fought tenaciously for a large amount of compensation from the Corporation. Terms of arrangements were, however, affected with the latter party, by which the scheme was somewhat modified and materially enlarged, and by which it became necessary to go again to Parliament for additional works and further powers in the following Session. After this arrangement the Bill passed without any essential alteration, but with an obligation to apply for further powers in the next Session, and received the Royal Assent, 9th July, 1847. *Act of 1847.*

The Railway Company also obtained an Act legalizing the sale of water to the three boroughs of Manchester, Salford, and Stockport, and to waterworks companies in bulk, or to other parties for trading purposes, and authorising the formation of a small portion of the works projected, but *Railway Company's Act, 1847, 10 and 11 Victoria, c. 279.*

restraining them from constructing works for the distribution of the water and from acting in any way as a waterworks company. Legal power for selling water was important to them, as they had for some years been disposing of it without any such authority.

<small>Act of 1847, 10 and 11 Victoria. c. 208.</small>

The Act of the Corporation, 1847, empowered them to purchase the Manchester and Salford Waterworks for such price and on such terms as should be mutually agreed upon,—to construct all the works which were shown on the deposited plans,—and to distribute the water within the limits of the Act, which were extended to several places beyond those included in the Acts of the old Water Company. They were required to make certain compensations and accommodation works for the benefit of private parties whose interests were specially affected, and to discharge from the large reservoir at Woodhead, as compensation to the general body of millowners, a quantity of water equal to 60 cubic feet per second for 12 hours of every working day, to be discharged during such hours and in such manner as should be determined by the owners of certain mills mentioned in the Act. They were to be liable to penalties for any failure in this supply, and were also required to make good all damages or injury which might result in consequence of the failure or giving way of any of the reservoirs, the embankments, or other works to be constructed.

No limit of time was imposed for the completion of the works, but the compulsory powers for the purchase of lands were to expire after five years from the passing of the Act.

<small>Compulsory rates.</small>

The most important feature of the Act was the power to levy an unlimited rate upon the owners and occupiers of all property within the borough, for the purpose of paying the interest of the money borrowed for the construction of the works or for the purchase of the old company, and for defraying all other costs and charges attendant upon the supply of water. This rate was to be divided into two kinds, one to be called "The Domestic Water-rate," which was to be made and levied upon the *occupiers* of all dwelling-houses, and of shops and buildings used as dwelling-houses, and of gardens belonging thereto; and the other to be called "The Public Water-rate," to be made and levied upon the *owners* of all dwelling-houses, shops, warehouses, manufactories, or other property within the borough. The rate, in each case, was to be made according to the net annual value, except where the water mains or pipes should not be laid down or properly supplied with water within 50 feet of the wall of any premises liable to be rated, in which event only one-fourth part of a rate was to be levied, and, except in the public rate, in the case of gardens not attached to dwelling-houses, and of arable, meadow, and pasture land, where the rate was to be one-fourth only of the net annual value.

Outside the borough the Corporation had the powers of an ordinary trading water company, to break-up streets, lay pipes, and to supply water to all who wished for it upon rates, for domestic supply, not exceeding 5 per centum per annum upon the annual rack-rent of the premises to be supplied, with a minimum rate of 8s. a year, and a maximum of £10., including water-closets, but not baths, horses, or carriages.

Supplies for trading purposes were to be given, both within and without the borough, by special agreement.

Clauses were introduced by agreement, authorising the Corporation of Salford to buy the water-pipes and other water interest within their own borough, and to purchase water in bulk from the Corporation, and to distribute it for domestic, public, and other purposes, if at any time they obtained Parliamentary authority for doing so and for making and levying compulsory rates, for such supply, within the borough of Salford.

Similar clauses on behalf of the townships of Pendleton and Broughton were also introduced.

Power was given to the Corporation to borrow at interest, for the purposes of the Act, any sum of money not exceeding £650,000., on the credit of the borough-rate and of other rates and property vested in them by virtue of the Act, and they were also authorised to lay by, for a sinking fund, once in every year, any sum out of the rates to be levied which they might think proper, not being more than 5 per cent. on the amount of the principal sums borrowed.

The arrangement which was come to with the millowners on the river Etherow, while the Bill was passing through Committee, involved, as has been stated, considerable alteration and extension of the scheme, and consequently no works were commenced until after the Supplemental Act of 1848 was obtained. *Arrangement for compensation, &c. with millowners.*

It will be remembered that the scheme which had been laid out for obtaining water from the Etherow, in Longdendale, included only so much of the valley as would yield the requisite quantity of water for some years, but that the works were arranged on such levels as would permit the ultimate occupation of the whole of that portion of the river which was unoccupied by mills. This included a district below the Woodhead reservoir of about 3 miles in length, upon which were some very fine sites for large reservoirs, and a very abundant supply of excellent spring water. It was not included in the first instance for fear of making the scheme too large, but the district had been surveyed, the reservoirs had been laid out and estimated, and the additional supply which would be yielded had been ascertained.

The millowners were the first to propose that this district should be included, and that they should, in lieu of it, receive a large guaranteed amount of compensation water to be measured through a gauge, to be removed lower down the river to a point below the lowest reservoir which would be constructed and immediately above the Vale House mills, the highest on the stream.

Compensation. The Corporation were of course prepared at once to accept this proposition, and the compensation was agreed to be raised to 75 cubic feet per second, a quantity which could more safely be guaranteed than the former 60 feet per second, by reason of the greater reservoir storage which would be acquired.

The modifications in the scheme, which this arrangement enabled the Corporation to make, were such as materially to improve the general design and to facilitate the more complete separation of the turbid water from the pure.

Preliminary Inquiry February, 1848. The necessary steps for obtaining an additional Act of Parliament were taken, and a preliminary inquiry was made in February, 1848, by surveying officers appointed under the Preliminary Inquiries Act, 1846. The gentlemen appointed to the duty were George Kettilby Rickards, Esq., Barrister-at-Law, and George Rennie, Esq., Civil Engineer. Their report so fully and accurately describes the proposed extensions that I give it in full:—

Report of surveying officers. "Report by George K. Rickards and George Rennie, Esquires, on the Manchester Corporation Waterworks Act Amendment Bill.

"To the Commissioners of Her Majesty's Woods, Forests, Land Revenues, Works, and Buildings:—

"My Lord and Gentlemen,—We beg to submit to you the following report as the result of our local inquiry respecting the Manchester Corporation Waterworks Act Amendment Bill.

"The object of this Bill, as explained by its title, is to amend the Manchester Corporation Waterworks Act, passed in the last Session of Parliament. By the 53rd section of that Act it is enacted:—

"'And whereas it is expedient, for the more useful application of the water 'to be discharged from the said compensation reservoir, to and for the 'purposes of the said mills and works hereinbefore mentioned, the auxiliary 'reservoirs should be constructed in the course of the said river Etherow. 'And whereas the same cannot be effected under the authority of this Act. 'Be it therefore enacted, that the Mayor, Aldermen, and Burgesses shall apply 'in the next Session of Parliament for an Act to enable the said Mayor, 'Aldermen, and Burgesses to construct, and shall by such Act be required to 'construct, at their own expense such auxiliary and other reservoirs and 'works as may be necessary for the purposes aforesaid.'

"For the purpose of fulfilling the undertaking contained in this section, and of carrying out an agreement entered into with the millowners during the progress of the Act of last Session, the promoters of this Bill, the Mayor, Aldermen, and Burgesses of Manchester, now apply to Parliament.

"The objects contemplated by the present Bill are—1. To increase the quantity of water obtainable for the supply of the district; 2. To increase the quantity guaranteed to the millowners on the river Etherow under the Act of last year.

"The drainage ground secured by the Act of last Session was 15,500 acres.

"By the present Bill 3,400 additional acres of drainage ground would be acquired, making the total 18,900 acres; but, inasmuch, as there will be a partial abstraction of water from about 100 acres, the total net quantity of drainage ground, under the former Act and this Bill together, may be taken in round numbers at 18,000 acres.

"The quantity of water which by the former Act, the promoters bound themselves to discharge out of their compensation reservoir for the supply to the mills on the river Etherow, was 60 cubic feet per second for 12 hours of every working day.

"They now propose, in pursuance of the agreement with the millowners before referred to, to supply to them an additional quantity of 15 feet per second, by altering the situation of the gauge to a lower part of the river, and also to construct certain accommodation works to enable the millowners to obtain the benefit of the arrangement in a more effectual manner.

"The quantity of water obtained from the new drainage ground will be about equally divided between the millowners and the promoters. After deducting the 15 cubic feet to be given to the former, the new drainage ground will yield for the use of the town, according to the fall of rain, the following quantities:—

	Gallons.
"Assuming the available rain at 36 inches.........	3,271,575 per day.
"Ditto ditto 42 "	4,390,125 "

"From the total drainage ground of 18,000 acres, the quantity of water which will remain for the supply of the town, after deducting the 75 feet supplied to the millowners, will be as follows:—

	Gallons.
"At 36 inches of rain.........	23,079,450 per day.
"At 42 ditto	29,792,462 "

"Mr. Bateman, the engineer to the Corporation, stated that he had for the last 12 months, caused rain-gauges to be fixed in the district from which the supply is to be derived, and also daily measurements to be taken of the streams. The mean of all the observations taken from the gauges gave 53¼ inches of rain, and the quantity which by the measurement of the streams appeared to have flowed off the ground was 46¼ inches; last year, however, was rather above the average of years in respect to the fall of rain. Mr. Bateman thought it safe to assume that a quantity of 42 inches would be obtainable year by year. His calculation was based upon observations carried on in a valley, called the Swineshaw valley, immediately adjoining the valley from which the Corporation would derive their supply. His reason for taking the data afforded by the Swineshaw valley, was that his observations there had extended over three years, whereas on the other part of the district they had been limited to the last twelve months; but the last year's experience showed that that valley is less productive in quantity by about one-fourth than the actual locality from which the works of the Corporation would be supplied.

"With a view of providing increased storage for the water, it is proposed, under the powers of this Bill, to construct two additional reservoirs, one to be called the 'Rhodes Wood reservoir,' the other, the 'Torside reservoir;' the two together will contain 319,957,739 cubic feet. It is also proposed to enlarge the Woodhead reservoir, which was included in the scheme of last year, by raising its embankment six feet; by so doing, the total gain in storage room will be 353,838,411 cubic feet. Two other reservoirs, which will be rendered unnecessary by the construction of Rhodes Wood reservoir, being abandoned; the total storage, old and new, which will be obtained, will be 34,000 cubic feet per acre for the 18,000 acres, in all 612,640,587 cubic feet. Mr. Bateman estimates that the reservoir water will be principally used for supplying the mills, and that to a great extent the streams will be sufficient of themselves to supply the town, that is to the extent of 20,000,000 gallons a day.

"By the census of 1841, the population within the operation of the Manchester Corporation Waterworks was found to be 858,654. According to the rate at which the population is estimated to be now increasing, the numbers would amount by the time the works are completed to 454,000, and in 10 years subsequent to that time, according to the same ratio, to 567,000; to supply this population with 20 gallons of water daily per head would require 11,340,000 gallons.

"Whatever may be the excess of supply obtained beyond the domestic and sanitary requirements of the population, the promoters anticipate they will find a ready sale for manufacturing purposes, for which the demand in this district is very great. The profit derived from such a disposal of the surplus water would enable the Corporation to reduce, in proportion to its extent, the price of the water supply to the inhabitants, and would thus redound to the benefit of the district.

"The estimated cost of the works proposed by the Bill, including purchases of land, compensations, and contingencies, is £145,000., this, however, is not wholly in addition to the estimate of last year, as some part of the works then projected will be rendered unnecessary by the new works.

"The additional outlay is estimated at £100,000., as the price of obtaining for the towns an increased supply of about four-and-a-half million gallons per day (assuming the 42 inches of rain), and affording also to the millowners the 75 cubic feet with more certainty of fulfilling the guarantee as to that quantity than as to the 60 feet, according to the former scheme.

"By a self-acting arrangement of the works, explained by Mr. Bateman in answer to question 40, the pure water will be separated from that which may become occasionally discoloured, so as to supply the town only with the pure produce of the streams; the quality of the water, with reference to domestic purposes, was fully established in the investigation of last year.

"The construction of the various water-courses, described upon the plans and in the Bill, for conveying the water to the reservoirs, to the millowners, and to the conduits, and other works already authorised, and also the accommodation works agreed upon between the Corporation and the millowners for the better effecting of the arrangement under this Bill, are fully described by Mr. Bateman in his evidence, to which we beg to refer, and do not seem to require any particular comment in this report.

"The present Bill, as far as our inquiry was concerned, appeared to be virtually unopposed on the part of the Hyde, Werneth, and Newton Waterworks, established under an Act of the 1st William IV., for supplying those townships with water, a solicitor entered an appearance before us, but abstained from offering any opposition, certain other parties on behalf of millowners and others also attended, but apparently rather to watch the proceedings than to oppose the Bill. The only opposition manifested was on the part of Mr. Richard Hyde Clark, a landowner, whose property would be affected by the deviations proposed by the second section at Broomstair bridge and Kingston bridge. The promoters explained that these deviations were proposed, not from any objects of their own, but in order to meet the objections of magistrates of the county of Chester, who had disapproved of the pipes being carried over those bridges, which are county bridges, on the ground that in case of the pipes bursting they might suffer injury; to meet this objection, which, however, the engineer did not consider to be of much objection in itself, an arrangement was come to during the progress of the measure through Parliament last year, which led to the introduction of the 74th section in the Act, and it is to carry out the spirit of that section that the power to make the deviations in question is solicited.

"It was intimated by the promoters that, in case the magistrates should adhere to their objection against allowing the carrying of the pipes over those bridges, they would endeavour to make such an arrangement as might be satisfactory to Mr. Clark.

"It does not appear to us that any other point arose in the course of our inquiry which demands to be noticed in this report; and we beg to submit to you, as our conclusion from the whole evidence, that the Bill is one which would enhance in a material degree the advantages of the scheme which received the sanction of the Legislature, after a full investigation, last year, and is, therefore, entitled to the favourable consideration of Parliament.

"We have only to add, that the objects of this Bill are in no degree affected by the provisions of the Bill for promoting the public health, to which our attention was directed by your instructions of the 19th February.

(Signed)   "GEORGE K. RICKARDS, } Surveying
                         "GEORGE RENNIE,   } Officers.

"8th March, 1848."

The amended Bill was unopposed, and received the Royal Assent, 22nd July, 1848.

By Acts of 1847 and 1848 Corporation empowered to purchase Manchester and Salford Waterworks Company.

By the Acts of 1847 and 1848, the Corporation were to have transferred to them the Manchester and Salford Waterworks, and all the rights and privileges, as well as the responsibilities which had been conferred upon or undertaken by the Company.

The terms on which the existing works, rights, and interests of the Manchester and Salford Waterworks Company were to be conveyed to the Corporation had already been determined.

As early as June, 1846, a conditional agreement had been entered into for ascertaining the price to be paid. This, however, was superseded by a conditional contract fixing the price which was entered into on the 29th March, 1847, during the progress of the first Waterworks Act of the Corporation through Parliament. The price to be paid was based upon a consideration of the net dividends which had for four years previously and which probably might for four years prospectively be paid by the Company.

The Company were to remain in possession of the works till the 1st January, 1851, by which time it was anticipated the new works of the Corporation would be in a sufficiently forward state to supply the town with water. On this day the sale and purchase were to be completed, and the whole of the works and property were to be transferred to the Corporation as they then stood, including all money due to the Company (except dividends and interest due to that day), subject to all the mortgages, debts, and liabilities of the Company.

The price agreed upon was a payment of £3. per annum from 1st January, 1851, on every existing whole share of the Company, of which there were 6,354; and an annual payment on every half-share, of which there were 5,589, at the rate of 5 per cent. on the amount paid-up,—payable half-yearly. These payments were secured on the Borough Fund, with power to the Corporation to buy them off at 20 years' purchase, on giving six months' notice. The Company had a mortgage debt of £97,000.—the rental payable to Sir Oswald Mosley, at 20 years' purchase, amounted to £15,520., and these sums, with the annual payments on the whole and half-shares, formed an aggregate amount for the purchase of £533,760., or an annual payment of £26,650.

The report of the Committee on these arrangements and the agreement with the Company is as follows:—

Agreement of the Corporation with the Manchester and Salford Waterworks Company for the purchase of their works.

"The Committee for General Purposes present the following report:—

"*Waterworks.*

"Your Committee now submit the conditional contract which, in accordance with the authority and instructions received from the Council, they have entered into with the Directors of the Manchester and Salford Waterworks Company, for the purchase of the whole of the works and property of that Company, and which, for the following reasons, your Committee recommend the Council to adopt and confirm:—

"Before referring to the price proposed, your Committee would remind the Council how important it is, on many grounds, that the Council should secure the coöperation and assistance of the Directors of the Company in settling, not the price per share alone, but the terms of the purchase, with reference especially to the time of entering into possession of the property, and becoming liable to the payment of the dividend which may be agreed to be secured; in order that the Council may be enabled so to arrange that no charge upon the Borough Fund shall at any time become necessary, nor any call be made upon the inhabitants until, in return, an ample supply of water can be furnished by the Corporation.

"The Waterworks Company have long since agreed to sell their property to the Corporation, either at a price to be agreed upon or to be fixed upon by arbitration, and have thus voluntarily placed themselves in the only position which could be reasonably asked for or required. It must, however, be obvious that the same coöperation and willingness to meet the views and to suit the convenience of the Council could not reasonably be expected, if the Directors were to be left in a state of suspense and uncertainty as to the price which is to be ultimately paid for their property. Your Committee could only, in such a case, anticipate that the Directors, as trustees for the proprietors, would decline to enter into any arrangement whatever which could by possibility prejudicially affect the value of their property when the price had to be decided by arbitration. On these grounds alone, and irrespective of the question of price, your Committee have felt the great importance of coming to a distinct understanding with the Company, and of now settling the price which shall be paid when the Corporation enters into possession of the property.

"In the early stages of the negotiation, it was considered desirable that the Directors should furnish the Council with a detailed statement of the length and size of the mains and pipes, together with the respective dates at which the same were laid down, so as to enable your Committee to form a proximate estimate of the present value of that portion of the property which is underground. By obtaining this information, it was considered that your Committee would be better enabled to determine the value of the whole property, inasmuch as the cost of the reservoirs, engines, and other similar works, could be, with certainty, ascertained. Subsequent discussion, however, with the Directors, and a closer investigation into the nature of the property, and the different elements to be taken into consideration in forming an opinion of the entire value, fully satisfied your Committee that such information, though on some accounts desirable, was not essential for the purpose of enabling them to determine the price which the Council should be recommended to offer.

"Your Committee, therefore, came to the conclusion that the mode in which a determination as to the price to be given could be most satisfactorily arrived at, was by a consideration of the amount of dividend heretofore and now payable, in connection with the amount which the proprietors considered they had reasonable grounds for anticipating would be shortly received.

"In introducing the Health of Towns Bill into the House of Commons, on the 80th day of March last, Lord Morpeth stated that 'such Bill would 'require that the town councils and the town commissioners should supply 'water to every house, and for this purpose they would be empowered to 'construct waterworks, to contract with water companies, and, if necessary, 'to compel the sale of waterworks, securing the full rate of their dividends to 'those companies from whom it was found necessary to purchase their works.' It thus appears that the principle of ascertaining the price to be paid by reference to the amount of dividend, is to be distinctly recognised in a public general Act, and that upon this basis corporations will be authorized and required to purchase existing works.

"Your Committee, after full and long consideration, have come to the conclusion that the terms now submitted are fair and reasonable as between both the contracting parties; for whilst it is possible that lower terms might be imposed upon the Company if the price had to be *now* settled by arbitration, it is equally possible that the Corporation would be required by any arbitration to submit to higher and less favourable terms, if the price should be left to be *hereafter* determined, when the Council may be prepared to call upon the Company to sell and transfer their works and property to the Corporation.

"Your Committee have endeavoured to effect such an arrangement as would be fair to the Corporation as well as to the proprietors of the Waterworks Company, being fully impressed that whilst, on the one hand, the inhabitants ought not to be called upon to pay more than the property is really worth; on the other hand, the Council have no right to expect that the Company will consent to transfer their present interests and future prospects without having secured to them a full and fair equivalent.

"Fully convinced of the advantages which will result to the Corporation in carrying out their plan, by having secured the coöperation of the Directors of the Waterworks Company, which can only be relied on by now settling the terms of ultimate purchase;—that the terms embodied in the contract now submitted are fair and reasonable to all parties concerned;—and that the interests of the Corporation are not likely to be improved so far as the price is concerned, and would certainly, in other respects, suffer by leaving the question to be hereafter settled by arbitration ;—your Committee do strongly recommend the Council to approve of and adopt the conditional contract now submitted, and to authorize and direct your Committee to take the necessary steps for carrying out the same.

"On behalf of the Committee,

(Signed) "ELKANAH ARMITAGE,

"Town, Hall, "Mayor.
"March 8th, 1847."

Agreement referred to in the foregoing report :—

"Memorandum of Terms of Agreement, entered into the twenty-ninth day of March, 1847, between Thomas Cooke, of Manchester, Merchant, the Chairman of the Directors, and Alexander Kay, Esquire, Samuel Walker, Esquire, and George Faulkner, Esquire, three other of the Directors of the Company of Proprietors of the Manchester and Salford Waterworks, on behalf of the said Company of the first part, and Elkanah Armitage, Esquire, Mayor of the Borough of Manchester, William Benjamin Watkins, Esquire, Alderman of the said Borough, and James Bancroft, Esquire, Alderman of the said Borough, on behalf of the Mayor, Aldermen, and Burgesses of the said Borough, for the purposes of this agreement of the second part, subject to the approval of the proprietors of the Waterworks Company, and also of the Council of the Borough of Manchester, and also to the necessary powers and authority to carry out the arrangements being hereafter obtained from Parliament.

"It is agreed by and between the said Directors, parties hereto of the first part, on behalf of the said Waterworks Company, and the said Mayor and Aldermen, parties hereto of the second part, on behalf of the said Mayor, Aldermen, and Burgesses (hereinafter referred to as the said Corporation), that the said Waterworks Company and the said Corporation respectively shall, on their respective parts, observe and perform the stipulations and agreements hereinafter expressed and contained, that is to say :—

"That the said Waterworks Company shall sell and transfer to the said Corporation, who shall purchase, all the works and property of the said Company as the same shall stand on the 1st day of January, 1851, on which day the said sale and purchase shall be completed, including all moneys, rates, and debts then belonging and owing to the Company (except so much thereof as shall be required for the payment up to the last mentioned day, of such dividend and interest to the proprietors of the whole and half-shares respectively in the said Company as are hereinafter mentioned), subject to all the mortgages, bonds, rents, debts, covenants, engagements, and liabilities, of whatever kind, then owing by or subsisting on the part of the said Company, or to which they, or the Directors or Officers of the Company on their behalf, are or shall be liable, and from which the Corporation shall indemnify the Company, and the Proprietors, Directors, and Officers thereof, and also subject to the payment, by the said Corporation, of all the expenses to be hereafter incurred in carrying out this agreement (except the current expenses of the concern), as well on the part of the Corporation as of this Company.

"That the consideration of such sale and transfer shall be such annual payments to be made by the said Corporation to the proprietors of shares in the said Company, as next hereinafter mentioned, that is to say, an annual payment after the rate of £3. per annum, from the said 1st day of January, 1851, on every now existing whole share in the Company (the total number of such whole shares being 6,354); and an annual payment on every half-share now issued (the total number of such half-shares being 5,589) after the rate of £5. per centum on the amount which shall, for the time being, have been paid up on the same half-shares, such annual payments respectively to commence from the said 1st day of January, 1851, and to be payable half-yearly on the 1st day of January and 1st day of July in each year; the first payment thereof to be made on the 1st day of July, 1851, and to be charged and secured in such manner as shall be approved of by the Counsel of the said Waterworks Company, on the Borough Fund of the said Borough, with proper powers and remedies for recovering the same, with power to the Corporation to buy off each or either of the said annual payments at a price calculated at twenty years' purchase thereon, on giving to the Directors of the said Waterworks Company at least six calendar months' previous notice of the intention of the said Corporation in that behalf, to expire on one of the said half-yearly days of payment. Provided that the said annual payment in respect of the said half-shares or any of them shall not be bought off by the said Corporation at any time before the 1st day of January, 1861, unless with the consent of the proprietor or proprietors thereof.

"That no further issue of half-shares beyond the said number of 5,589 shall be made by the said Waterworks Company, and no further calls made thereon without the consent of the Corporation; and that all moneys raised on such behalf shall be subject to the terms hereinbefore stated.

"That the said Waterworks Company shall, subject as hereunder mentioned, retain the absolute management and conduct of their works, and the supplying of water within the limits of the Acts of Parliament incorporating and regulating the said Company, and the exercise of all the powers vested in them by the said Acts in all respects not hereby expressly restricted, and shall receive the rents, rates, and annual profits arising therefrom, until the said sale and purchase shall be completed; and the payment of the said annual payments as the consideration for such purchase shall be secured as aforesaid; and the said rents, rates, and annual profits, which shall be received by the said Company from and after the 31st day of December next, shall be applied first in the payment of all such charges, expenses, and outgoings incurred, and to be incurred, by the said Waterworks Company as have usually in their accounts been charged to the revenue account, including interest after the rate of £5. per centum per annum on the amount for the time being paid up in respect of the said half-shares; and in the next place in payment of such dividends on the said whole shares as the same may extend to pay, not exceeding £3. per annum on each such whole share; and if there be any surplus income remaining after such outgoings, interest, and dividends as aforesaid, the same shall be carried to capital account in increase of the property of the Company hereby agreed to be sold. That subject to the reservations herein mentioned, as to the capital to be provided, such extensions of mains and pipes within the Municipal Borough as may be required by the Corporation, shall be made and laid down by the said Company in accordance with the plans and directions of the Surveyor of the Corporation, at any time, and from time to time prior to the 31st December, 1850.

"And whereas the said Waterworks Company are the promoters of a Bill now before Parliament, intituled—'A Bill to enable the Company of pro-'prietors of the Manchester and Salford Waterworks more effectually to 'supply the inhabitants of the towns of Manchester and Salford and other 'places with water, and to grant further powers to the said Company of 'proprietors' (and which is hereinafter referred to as the said Waterworks Bill); and the said Corporation are the promoters of two Bills now before Parliament, the one intituled—'A Bill to enable the Mayor, Aldermen, and 'Burgesses of the Borough of Manchester, in the county of Lancaster, to 'construct waterworks for supplying the said Borough and several places on 'the line of the said intended works with water, and for other purposes' (and which is hereinafter referred to as the said Corporation Bill No. 1); and the other intituled—'A Bill to enable the Mayor, Aldermen, and Burgesses of the 'Borough of Manchester, in the county of Lancaster, more effectually to 'supply the said Borough with water, and for other purposes' (and which is hereinafter referred to as the said Corporation Bill No. 2).

"Now it is hereby further agreed by and between the said parties as aforesaid:—

"That if the said Corporation shall in the present or any subsequent Session of Parliament before the said 1st day of January, 1851, obtain powers for constructing the waterworks referred to or contemplated by the said Corporation Bill No. 1, or any part thereof, with or without any additions thereto, and shall also obtain, in or by the same or any other Bill which shall be passed into an Act, powers or provisions for making or effecting such transfer as next hereinafter mentioned, then and in such case, the powers for constructing such last mentioned works, and all other powers, rights, and privileges, which shall by any such Act be given or granted for the construction of such works, the purchasing or taking of lands for the purposes thereof (excepting only all powers which relate to the raising of money therefor or otherwise incident or subservient thereto) shall, in case such transfer shall be considered desirable, and be required by the Corporation in order to the satisfactory carrying out of the agreement hereby entered into be transferred to and vested in the said Waterworks Company, who shall proceed in the execution of the same until the said 1st day of January, 1851, and such last mentioned works shall be so proceeded with under the superintendence of Mr. John Frederic Bateman, the Engineer of the said Corporation, or such other Engineer as the Council of the said Borough shall appoint.

"Provided, and it is hereby agreed, that the said Waterworks Company shall not be bound, or be deemed by the agreement to engage for proceeding in the construction of the said last mentioned works to any greater extent than they shall be enabled to do by the application of such moneys as they shall be able to raise by way of loans on mortgage, or by calling up the amount remaining to be paid upon the said half-shares so issued as aforesaid, under the powers of the said Acts incorporating and regulating the said Company, and which shall not be required for the purpose of continuing and extending the supply of water from the present sources of the said Company, or meeting the other demands upon the said Company, and such other moneys as they shall be able to raise under the powers and authorities proposed to be transferred to or invested in them as aforesaid, or which shall be supplied to them by the said Corporation for the purpose of the said intended new works.

"That the interest of all moneys which shall be raised for the purposes of, or incidental to, the said last-mentioned works, and of such capital as shall be expended at the request of the Corporation, in extending and enlarging the mains and pipes, and the amount of which shall be fixed by the Board next hereunder referred to, shall be paid by and out of the principal of the same moneys, until the said Waterworks Company shall cease to be concerned therein.

"That the said Council of the said Borough shall appoint three members of their body, and the Directors of the said Waterworks Company shall appoint three members of their body, who shall together form a Board for superintending the said proposed new works, and the manner of proceeding therein, and shall give all necessary directions to the engineer and others as to the construction thereof, and shall superintend and regulate all accounts and matters relating thereto, and may appoint a secretary to act under their direction in relation thereto, and the decision of a majority of the members of such Committee present at any meeting thereof, to which all shall be summoned, and at which three at least shall attend, upon all questions before them, shall be binding and conclusive.

"That when the said purchase by the said Corporation of the said works and property of the said waterworks shall be completed, as hereinbefore agreed, the said proposed new works, or so much thereof as shall have been completed, and all lands, hereditaments, property, moneys, and effects, which shall be then vested in or possessed by the said Waterworks Company for the purposes of such new works, and all the powers and privileges which shall have been transferred to or vested in the said Company, for the purposes thereof, or in relation thereto, shall be transferred to and vested in the said Corporation, and shall thenceforth be held, exercised, and enjoyed by them, without any further interference by or on the part of the said Waterworks Company, or the Directors or officers thereof in anywise, subject only to the said annual payments, and the securities, powers, and remedies therefor.

"That the said Waterworks Company and the said Corporation, respectively, shall consent to, and on their respective parts support and promote the introduction into the said Waterworks Bill, and the said Corporation Bills Nos. 1 and 2, or such of them as may be necessary, all such enactments, provisions, alterations, and modifications as may be proper for sanctioning and giving full effect to these terms of agreement, or for embodying the same or any more formal agreement or deed founded hereon, and to be executed as hereinafter mentioned in any of the said Bills, or any other Bill to be promoted, if found necessary or expedient for the purpose. And that neither the said Company nor the said Corporation will be parties to, or promote, or adopt, or support, any Parliamentary or other measure or proceeding which may tend to prejudice or be inconsistent with this agreement, or the spirit or intent thereof. But, nevertheless, either of them, the said Company and Corporation, may present and appear in support of any petition or petitions in opposition to the said Bill or Bills of the other of them, for the purpose only of watching the proceedings thereon, and ascertaining that such Bill or Bills shall, as far as Parliament will permit, be framed in accordance with the spirit and meaning hereof.

"That a meeting of the Council of the said Borough, on the part of the said Corporation, and a special general meeting of the proprietors of the said Waterworks Company, shall respectively be convened for the purpose of adopting or rejecting this agreement, which is hereby declared to be subject to such adoption or rejection; and the same if adopted by the said Council and meeting respectively, shall be embodied in a proper deed to be prepared in accordance therewith, with such provisions as shall be expedient for more fully expressing and carrying into complete effect the objects hereof, and which deed shall be executed under the common seals of the said Corporation and the said Company respectively.

"As witness the hands of the said parties hereto."

By this agreement the Corporation were to become possessed of all the works and property of the Manchester and Salford Waterworks Company on the 1st January, 1851, but the works were practically to remain in the hands of the Company till then, by which time it was anticipated a fresh supply of water would be introduced by the works of the Corporation within the borough of Manchester. The Corporation would from that time levy compulsory rates—a public and a domestic rate—and charge water rents in the out-townships included within the limits of supply in the ordinary manner of a trading company. Salford had made a separate agreement, by which that borough purchased the pipes and other property within their borough, and were to have *a definite* quantity of water delivered to them at the boundary of the two boroughs. Accordingly, we find that the first rates fixed by the Corporation were 3d. for the public rate and 6d. for the domestic rate. The public rate was afterwards reduced to 2d., but the large interest payable by the Corporation for money borrowed and for the purchase of the waterworks was for some time assisted by a moiety of the gas profits. This assistance continued till the year 1861, since which time the whole of the interest and other annual expenses have been paid out of water rents and rates and other profits. The rates in the borough have for many years been 3d. and 9d. respectively on five-sixths of the rental. In the out-districts the water rent has been charged at the rate of 1s. in the £. on five-sixths of the rental.

Other important preliminaries had also been arranged, either prior to the first application to Parliament or between the passing of the first and second Acts.

<small>Arrangements with landowners.</small>

The principal landowners, the Duke of Norfolk and Mr. Tollemache, who together owned nearly all the land to be occupied by reservoirs, and other owners had been agreed with.

Surveys, plans, and working drawings of the more important portions of the work had been prepared, so that when the Act of 1848 was obtained the Corporation was in a position at once to proceed with the undertaking they had thus, after many difficulties and years of untiring perseverance, successfully obtained authority to construct.

The sound and enlightened views which it will be remembered were entertained by the authorities of the time in 1808 and 1809, when the Manchester and Salford Waterworks Company was first established, were thus at length realized, and the opinions then expressed—" that the supply " of water ought to be under the direction of its own inhabitants, and that " it would be contrary to sound policy to entrust the furnishing and control " of this important article of food and cleanliness, on which the health and " comfort of the inhabitants depend, to persons whose sole object will be the " promotion of their own private interest, and who are induced to the under- " taking from no other motive," had, after a lapse of 40 years, been adopted by the unanimous voice of Manchester, and force and reality given to it by the two important Acts of 1847 and 1848.

The example thus set by Manchester has been followed by many of the large cities and towns in the kingdom, and the bold but important and beneficial feature of a compulsory unlimited rate upon all inhabitants, has also, in principle, been largely adopted by the inhabitants of other places with very great success.

<small>Compulsory unlimited rates.</small>

The compulsory unlimited rate renders the security equal to the very best in the land, and therefore enables Corporations to borrow money on the most favourable terms, at the same time that the necessity of paying for water whether they use it or not, induces all parties to avail themselves of the pure and wholesome and unlimited supply placed at their command, instead of penuriously or contentedly drawing from impure or scanty sources the water they require.

In the month of January, 1848, the Corporation applied to the Commissioners for loans to public works for a loan of £250,000, to be advanced by quarterly instalments of £20,000, beginning in April. The loan Commissioners referred the question to Mr. James Walker, C.E., who, having reported favourably on the practicability of the works, though he added somewhat to the estimate and considered 10 per cent. for contingencies too small, recommending 15 per cent. instead, the loan asked for was granted by a letter from Mr. Bickwood, the secretary, dated 10th June, 1848.

<small>Application for loan.</small>

PART II.—DESCRIPTIVE.

THE first works undertaken after the Act of 1848 was obtained were the Woodhead reservoir and the Mottram tunnel. These were soon followed by the Hollingworth and Arnfield reservoirs, the Rhodes Wood reservoir, and the partial completion of the Torside reservoir, the two latter and the Woodhead reservoir being one below the other in the main valley of the river Etherow, and the other two on tributaries of the Etherow, viz.—the Hollingworth and Arnfield brooks. *First works undertaken by Corporation.*

In connection with these reservoirs were various watercourses for conveying water past the reservoirs during their construction, and for carrying the pure water, when collected, to the city of Manchester, for which purpose some of the flood watercourses were subsequently used. Woodhead and Torside reservoirs were intended for the storage of turbid water to be afterwards given as compensation to the river below, or, when sufficiently clarified, to be taken to Manchester. The spring water of the various streams when unswollen by rain, and that issuing from the numberless springs in the valley above the level of the reservoirs were to be separately collected, and, if more than sufficient for the wants of Manchester, were to be stored in the Rhodes Wood reservoir, from which it was to be drawn in times of deficiency.

On the Arnfield and Hollingworth brooks the turbid water, except what was collected in a reservoir below, was allowed to a great extent to run to waste, but all the water intended for Manchester was finally collected below the reservoirs on these brooks, and conveyed partly by conduit, for the most part covered, and by a tunnel under the Mottram hill and by pipes to the Godley reservoir, where it was measured, stored, and strained previous to its passing into pipes of 40 inches in diameter, which conveyed it to the Denton service reservoirs and to Gorton, about 5 miles from Piccadilly in Manchester.

This was the original scheme. It has been altered in some respects and extended. These alterations and extensions will be referred to as the description of the work proceeds.

The Woodhead reservoir was let to Messrs. Richard Thompsons and Sons, of Blackburn, and commenced in August, 1848. The Mottram tunnel was commenced in the same month. The other works enumerated very quickly followed, and water was first passed through the Mottram tunnel and discharged into the river Tame, near Hyde, in October, and delivered in Manchester in December, 1850.

Woodhead Reservoir.

The site of the embankment of this reservoir was at a narrow part of the valley, one side of which consisted of an ancient and extensive landslip, which had pushed over the river and formed a steep escarpment of rock and shale on the other side. The valley itself, in which this as well as all the other reservoirs in the same valley were made, consists of the shales and beds of sandstone which intervene between the millstone grit formation and the limestone, commonly called by geologists the Yoredale rocks.

The turnpike road to Saltersbrook and Sheffield passed on one side of the valley, and the Manchester Sheffield and Lincolnshire Railway on the other. These approached each other at the narrow place selected for the embankment, and the level of the railway fixed the height of the bank. This was 90 feet above the level of the river—30 feet wide at the top, with slopes of 3 horizontal to 1 vertical on the inner or water side and 2 to 1 on the outside. The inside slope was pitched with stone 18 inches thick. The top water level of the reservoir was 777 feet above the mean level of the sea. The reservoir formed by this embankment extended for nearly two miles and submerged a portion of the Enterclough and Glossop turnpike road, which was accordingly diverted and carried over the top of the bank. Two main streams entered the reservoir at its upper end—the river Etherow receiving the water from the long tunnel of the Manchester and Sheffield Railway, called the Woodhead tunnel, and the Heyden brook which flowed down a tributary valley. Across these two streams weirs were thrown which formed residuum lodges, erected for the purpose of arresting the detritus brought down in times of flood. They fully answered their purposes, but they have never been cleaned out.

Through these weirs were sluices for discharging the ordinary volume of water, and at one end of each weir the water was carried off by a channel constructed of dimension sufficient to pass the floods during the construction of the embankment. These watercourses were subsequently used for the pure water of the streams, the upper ends being closed for that purpose and commanded by a sluice and shuttle. When the streams were swollen they were allowed to flow over the weirs into the reservoir.

The reservoir widened considerably in the middle and branched out in two directions,—over one branch, down which the Heyden brook flowed, the Saltersbrook turnpike road was carried by a bridge of nine arches of 30 feet span each.

The puddle trench of the embankment was sunk to a considerable depth, and the water was discharged by two lines of pipes of 48 inches in diameter with valves on the outer ends. On the northerly or turnpike road side of the valley, the puddle was tied into a thick bed of shale and then turned for some distance up the valley until the shale rose to above top-water level. On the southerly or railway side, the puddle trench was excavated for a considerable distance into the clay of the landslip, and in the valley itself the trench was sunk to a depth of about 17 feet below the river into what appeared to be sound ground. The character of the ground was supposed to be ascertained by careful boring before the work commenced. In one case a boring had penetrated 7 feet in stone without a bed or break, and it was, therefore, supposed to be solid rock. On the trench being opened the stone was found to be a boulder 9 feet thick. The boring was consequently very deceptive and the foundations did not prove to be what was anticipated. Great care was taken to secure the watertightness of the reservoir; but when the reservoir was filled with water leakage appeared, which was supposed to be the consequence either of water passing along the outside of the pipes or behind the puddle. Attempts were made to cure the leakage by sinking small cylinders to the pipes and pouring down fine ashes. This operation produced some good, it was evident that the cause of the leakage had been rightly divined and was discovered, but as it still continued, notwithstanding all efforts to arrest it, it was finally determined to construct a new bank altogether. By careful boring, which occupied eight years, a place was at length discovered at which continuous shale existed right across the valley from top-water on one side to top-water on the other, and at this spot a new embankment has been formed, for which an Act of Parliament was obtained in 1863. The embankment crosses the watercourse above the waste weir which had originally been constructed and of which a drawing is given. So that so much of the old work was utilized; there was no occasion to construct a new waste weir. The old bank was left in and the hollow between the two filled up.

The water is now discharged by tunnel driven in solid ground under the hill on the northerly side of the valley. In this tunnel a mass of solid masonry is introduced, through which two pipes are inserted commanded by valves on the outside, within a shaft down which the draw rods pass in a building called the valve house. The valves on the original pipes were 48 inches in diameter, but they were divided into three divisions, each division having a separate valve or door and draw-rod, and raised or lowered by a gun-metal square-cut screw and suitable gearing so that one man could easily open and shut it. Ordinarily the valves were worked by a small turbine-wheel supplied with water from a higher elevation, with arrangements for stopping the action in case of neglect or inattention of the man in charge.

The present mode of discharge differs in some respects from what was originally adopted. Each pipe is now commanded by one valve or door, only raised by power generated by a turbine-wheel of 12 inches diameter, the shaft of which communicates motion by suitable gearing to the draw-rod or screw-spindle working in a cross-head-stock from which are suspended two rods to each valve. On the shaft of the turbine is fixed a grooved pinion which drives a friction-wheel. The pinion on the turbine-shaft revolves at the rate of 600 revolutions in a minute, which is reduced by gearing so that the valve is raised 2 feet 9 inches in 20 minutes. The valves are rectangular, each 15 square feet in area, being 6 feet wide and 2 feet 6 inches deep, with 3-inch brass facing at the bottom of the valve.

The reverse motion for closing the valve is obtained by throwing the pinion on the turbine-shaft *out* of gear with the friction-wheel and *into* gear with a counter wheel, which then imparts motion to the friction-wheel in a contrary direction to that in which it revolves when in connection with the pinion on the turbine-shaft.

Drawings of both of these arrangements and of the winding gear, which are ingenious pieces of mechanism, are given.

Some particulars connected with the formation of this reservoir will be interesting.

Almost immediately after the commencement of the work, the subject of sufficient provision for carrying off floods was carefully reconsidered. A very heavy flood had occurred in the neighbourhood of Blackburn in the previous month of July, of which I was able to ascertain the volume, and I cannot do better than transcribe a portion of the report which I made to the Manchester Waterworks Committee, in October, 1848 :— Flood at Blackburn, July, 1848.

"In determining the sizes of the pipes and watercourses for the purpose of passing floods, when preparing the drawings of this reservoir, I had ascertained that the largest floods which had occurred during the previous four years (over which period constant observations had been made) had not exceeded 700 or 750 cubic feet per second. I, therefore, prepared for the passage of 1,000 cubic feet per second, believing that that would be sufficient to cover all contingencies. This was to be accomplished by forming the watercourse large enough to take 750 feet per second, and by introducing a four-feet pipe through the embankment, which, with 16 feet of pressure, would be able to pass 250 feet per second. As the pressure increased by the gradual raising of the embankment the discharge would also increase. With 50 feet of pressure the discharge through the pipe would be about 420 feet per second.

"Since the drawings were made and the execution of the works contracted for, very considerable damage has been done in the neighbourhood of Blackburn by an unusually heavy flood, which occurred towards the end of July. This flood, which extended over a considerable tract of country, though apparently not equal in extent to the drainage ground of the Woodhead reservoir, was about 150 per cent. greater than any flood measured in that district or in Longdendale. It may be that such a flood does not again occur for years, but I have thought it right to bring the subject before your notice, and to recommend that additional means should be provided for securing the safety of the works, should they unfortunately be subject to such a trial during the time they remain in an unfinished condition. I have thought over the best and cheapest mode of effecting this, and the amount of flood against which it would be prudent to provide. I think if provision were made for 1,500 cubic feet per second during the early state of the works no danger would be incurred. This would be double the largest flood which has taken place during the last four years in that valley, and as the work proceeds, a much greater quantity could be either passed or temporarily impounded.

"The watercourse, as laid out, is already as large as can with safety be excavated out of the steep hill side along which it has to be carried, but I have given instructions that it shall be deepened by the contractor at his own expense, so as to be able to convey about 950 cubic feet per second. He is now excavating it accordingly.

"It would not be prudent to trust to the watercourse only, even if it could be made sufficiently capacious, as there would always be some danger of the newly formed embankment on the lower side giving way under the pressure of heavy floods, in which case, all the water must be passed through the pipe under the embankment, or it must impound, if the work be sufficiently advanced, within the basin of the reservoir. The only safe plan, therefore, is to provide abundant space for allowing the water to escape by pipes through the embankment. * * * * * * * *

I have, therefore, to recommend that two lines of four-feet pipes instead of one be laid through the embankment of the reservoir. The cost, including the fixing of the pipes in their place and the alteration of masonry, will be about £900.

"The means then afforded will pass a flood of from 1,400 to 1,500 cubic feet per second when the embankment is raised about 20 feet across the valley, and from 1,700 to 1,800 when the bank is half finished.

"I am sorry to have to recommend the expenditure of money which must be considered as a mere insurance against risk. I hope the precaution may be unnecessary, but the serious loss and inconvenience which would attend a disaster, would render my conduct wholly unpardonable if with the experience of the Blackburn flood before me I neglected to recommend the adoption of every reasonable provision."

Flood at the Manchester Waterworks, October, 1849.

The recommendations contained in this report were adopted, but notwithstanding these precautions a flood, far exceeding the dimensions assumed, occurred about twelve months after, in October, 1849, which did considerable damage, and the particulars of which are best described in the following report :—

"Manchester, 12th October, 1849.

"*Manchester Corporation Waterworks.*

"To the Waterworks Committee.

"Gentlemen,—I am sorry to have to report serious injury which occurred at the Woodhead reservoir on Sunday last (October 7th). The weir erected across Heyden brook for the purpose of diverting the flood waters, during the execution of the reservoir embankment, along the new watercourse constructed for the same purpose, gave way under the overwhelming force of an extraordinarily heavy flood accompanied by a violent gale of wind, which materially increased the pressure upon the stonework.

"This weir gave way, as nearly as can be ascertained, about two o'clock p.m., after which, the water, no longer able to pass along the new watercourse, impounded in the basin of the reservoir till, at half-past five, it reached the top of the embankment, which had been raised to about 24 feet above the mouth of the discharge pipes, and further raised three feet during the progress of the flood by the utmost exertions of the contractor's men.

"Having reached this point, the water flowed over the top, speedily cutting a breach for the escape of the whole body of impounded water, amounting at that time to 17 or 18,000,000 cubic feet.

"The water, thus let loose, rushed down the valley, destroying fences, crops, bridges, and buildings in its course for about five miles below the reservoir. The damage to the land is not considerable—the more serious injury is to works and buildings.

"Mr. Merritt, the contractor for the Rhodes Wood and Torside embankments, has had a considerable quantity of ashlar stone carried away, besides planks, barrows, waggons, and tools. His works have been otherwise injured and impeded.

"At Vale House mills the injury has been extensive—the goit leading the water to the mill has been partly washed away and filled up. A schoolhouse, the end of a small building, and a good many high fence walls have been washed down. The water got into the cellar of the mill and has damaged a large number of calico pieces. Other damage has been done to the premises, but the machinery has principally escaped. The cottages adjoining the mill have suffered considerably, as well as the gardens belonging to the cottagers. A bridge over the river has been partly washed down.

"At Rhodes' mill, the next below, a timber bridge across the river has been carried away, the water-wheel injured, and some power-looms submerged, besides other damage of no very serious amount.

"At Bottoms mill, the banks of the goit have been damaged and some of the premises partly filled with water, besides injury to roads, fences, &c.

"At Waterside the water got into some cottages and washed down some walls and pigsties, and did other damage of no serious amount.

"At Messrs. Dalton's print-works a wooden bridge across the river has been washed away, and the works damaged to some extent by the water getting into the premises.

"Beyond this point I have heard of no damage of consequence.

"I will now endeavour to explain the cause of the accident.

"When the works were first laid out, provision was made for the passage of about 1,000 cubic feet of water per second by means of the new watercourse and one line of four-feet pipes with a pressure of 16 feet upon it.

"During four years' previous observations there had occurred no flood exceeding 750 cubic feet per second, and as the risk of damage could only exist during the early progress of the work the provision made seemed to be sufficient. In the month of July, 1848, a very heavy flood occurred in the neighbourhood of Blackburn, which you will remember did considerable damage at Darwen, washing down a private reservoir, and drowning 12 or 18 people. I had the means of ascertaining the volume of the flood at the Blackburn Waterworks, and I found that an equal fall of rain would create a flood at the Woodhead reservoir of nearly 2,000 cubic feet per second.

"I considered it, therefore, my duty to bring the subject before you, which I did in a report, dated 28th October, recommending further provision for the passage of extraordinary floods.

"The result of this was, as you will recollect, the addition of another line of four-feet pipes, and an enlargement, as far as practicable, of the flood watercourse.

"Means were thus provided for the passage of 1,500 cubic feet per second when the embankment was raised to a height of about 16 feet, the quantity of water capable of being discharged increasing of course with the increased height of the bank.

"The flood of last Sunday appears at one time to have reached and probably exceeded 4,000 cubic feet per second, and we have the means of ascertaining that for four hours after it attained this height it flowed at an average volume of nearly 2,000 feet per second.

"From marks which are left we can determine that before the weir gave way there were passed at Heyden brook 1,500 or 1,600 feet per second, about 1,000 or 1,100 of which went down the watercourse and the remainder into the reservoir.

"This quantity is exclusive of nearly the whole of the river Etherow and the various other streams which flow into the basin of the reservoir.

"If these streams were equally flooded in proportion to the extent of their drainage the whole volume would have exceeded 4,000 cubic feet per second.

"When the weir gave way, the water was impounded in the reservoir to a depth of 16 feet above the discharge pipe, leaving 8 feet to be filled up before it could reach the top of the bank. The bank was further raised by extraordinary exertions 3 feet, so that the water before it flowed over the top had attained a depth above the discharge pipes of about 27 feet.

"The Heyden brook weir is a strong flag weir capped with large and heavy blocks of ashlar, the top of which is formed into 25 openings of 6 feet in length each, which were partly closed by loose stop planks removable at pleasure, and introduced for the purpose of regulating and controlling the height of the water.

"Had they been partially removed, the weir would most probably have been saved, but the increased quantity of water which would have poured into the reservoir would most likely have produced the same final result, though the breaking down of the embankment would have occurred at a later hour in the day. The rain commenced at ten o'clock on Saturday night and fell in torrents without material abatement till ten o'clock on Sunday night. I have been told by old men, who have lived in the district all their lives, that they never recollect such continuous heavy rain.

"Had the rain ceased at three or four o'clock or had the embankment been 40 feet in height, it is almost certain that no injury would have been sustained.

"The weir was evidently broken down by the continued and violent beating of the waves created by the hurricane which swept straight down the Heyden valley, and which finally shook the ashlar top of the weir so as to allow the water to escape. The work was admirably executed, but was not secured by iron dowells, which had never been considered necessary.

"The contractors are now actively engaged in repairing the damage. The Heyden brook weir will probably be reinstated before the end of next week, and the whole mass of masonry will now be cramped together by strong iron dowells.

"It will take some time to restore the embankment. The pipes have been laid bare from end to end, and must be carefully examined to ascertain if they have sustained any injury, and be firmly embedded in concrete. When this is done, and the base of the bank properly cleared of the wreck, the embankment must be raised with the utmost despatch to a height of 40 feet. Of course, during this operation, risk will be again incurred.   *   *   *

"I have the honour to remain,

"Your obedient Servant,

(Signed)   "J. F. BATEMAN."

On examining the pipes it was discovered that they had been slightly damaged, and I recommended that they should be repaired and strengthened by strong iron clips. I also recommended the erection of a temporary wooden trough or shoot for the passage of flood waters, should another similar flood occur, at a level of about 20 or 25 feet above the mouth of the discharge pipes, firmly bedded in the ground, which would prevent the possibility of water flowing over the top of the newly-formed embankment.

The flood which occasioned the damage, which has been above reported, amounted at its maximum to 50 cubic feet per second from each 100 acres of contributing area.

Such observations are of great value to the hydraulic engineer and to all who have to provide for the safe passage of water. Much depends upon the rain-fall, the character of the country, the extent of the ground from which the water flows, and the distance of mountains. The following results of many observations may be of value:—

Floods.

In the year 1833, a heavy flood occurred in the river Medlock, which did much damage in the lower parts of Manchester. The drainage ground to the river is 12,000 acres. The flood at its maximum height amounted to 2,000 cubic feet per second, equal to 4 inches of rain flowing off the ground in 24 hours. This flood was equal to $16\frac{2}{3}$ cubic feet per second from each 100 acres of collecting ground.

In 1856 occurred a flood in this river which did much mischief in the vicinity of Oxford-road, in Manchester. This flood measured at its maximum 2,400 cubic feet per second, equal to 20 cubic feet per second from each 100 acres.

In 1857 another flood in the river Medlock was measured, which rose to 3,060 cubic feet per second, or $25\frac{1}{2}$ cubic feet per second from each 100 acres.

In February, 1852, the mean flood of the river Etherow, in Longdendale, at the Manchester Waterworks, from 15,400 acres, was during 24 hours at the rate of 10 feet per second from each 100 acres, equal to $2\frac{1}{10}$ inches of water coming off the ground in 24 hours. When at its highest this flood measured from 3,600 to 4,000 cubic feet per second, or 25 cubic feet per second from each 100 acres.

It was during this flood that the Bilberry reservoir, near Holmfirth, was destroyed.

In August, 1856, from a drainage ground of 7,000 acres at the Manchester Waterworks, the mean flow of the streams for 7 hours and 40 minutes was 2,100 cubic feet per second, being equal to 30 cubic feet per second from each 100 acres, and to $2\frac{1}{4}$ inches flowing off the ground in that time, or to 7 inches in 24 hours.

On the occasion of this flood, the river Irwell, in Manchester, was heavily flooded, and much damage done to low lying property.

On May 7th, 1862, from 5 p.m. to 7-30 p.m., 2½ hours, the mean flow of the streams at the Manchester Waterworks, from 7,000 acres, was 2,626 cubic feet per second, being equal to 37¼ cubic feet per second from each 100 acres, and ·93 inches of water over the whole surface, or at the rate of 9 inches in 24 hours.

The average flow of the same flood, from the same ground for 7 hours, was equal to 24·7 cubic feet per second from each 100 acres.

The same flood, for 13 hours, averaged 15¼ cubic feet per second per 100 acres.

In November, 1866, serious injury was done to the low lying parts of Salford and Manchester by a very heavy flood, which occasioned careful investigation.

At Agecroft bridge, above Salford, in the river Irwell, from a drainage area of 132,000 acres, the flood measured 18¼ feet per second from each 100 acres, or 24,500 cubic feet per second in the whole.

In Manchester, the river measured 18·8 cubic feet per second per 100 acres after its confluence with the river Irk, the latter river contributing to the volume of the flood at the rate of 20·4 cubic feet per second per 100 acres.

This flood (viz. that of November, 1866) was carefully measured at the Manchester Waterworks. The water flowing from 14,335 acres there, averaged for 12 hours together 3,347 cubic feet per second, being equal to a depth of 2¾ inches flowing off the ground in that time, and to an average flow of 23·4 cubic feet per second from each 100 acres.

The maximum height of this flood was ascertained at the Bilberry reservoir, near Holmfirth, the drainage ground to which adjoins that of the Manchester Waterworks. It reached 38 cubic feet per second from each 100 acres.

This flood was remarkable as following a very wet season, during which the ground was thoroughly saturated, and springs and streams all swollen. From the beginning of June to the 19th November, 5½ months, the rain at the Manchester Waterworks amounted to 36 inches. During the three days of the flood, viz.: the 16th, 17th, and 18th November, the rain-gauges showed a fall of 4½ inches.

In the flood of August, 1856, already referred to, the rainfall in Longdendale amounted to 3·96 inches in 3 days, but it followed a comparatively dry period, and occurred at a season at which the absorption by the ground would be considerable.

In the flood of February, 1852, the rainfall was equal to 4·6 inches in 5 days, being a little more than that which fell in 3 days in November, 1866.

In October, 1854, at the Glasgow Corporation Waterworks, the volume of water discharged from Loch Lubnaig, from 44,600 acres, averaged 5,500 cubic feet per second during 24 hours, equal to 3 inches in depth of rain flowing off the ground, and to $12\frac{1}{4}$ cubic feet per second from each 100 acres.

At Loch Katrine, on the same occasion, the quantity stored and discharged in 2 days was equal to 6 inches of water flowing off the ground in that time.

In the river Clyde, at Carstairs, the drainage ground being 190,000 acres, the floods in the winter of 1856 and 1857 averaged 20,000 cubic feet per second, equal to $2\frac{1}{4}$ inches flowing off the ground in 24 hours or to 10 cubic feet per second from every 100 acres, besides all the impounded water in the long and gently-sloping valley of the Clyde, which was greatly flooded.

A flood occurred in December, 1879, at the Manchester Waterworks, which was carefully measured. It amounted to $2\frac{1}{4}$ inches of water flowing off the ground in 19 hours, and to $2\frac{3}{4}$ inches in 23 hours, from 14,335 acres: when at its maximum, it flowed at the rate of $32\frac{1}{3}$ cubic feet per second per 100 acres for two hours and 20 minutes.

In March, 1880, another flood at the Manchester Waterworks averaged for 1 hour nearly 27 cubic feet per second both at Woodhead and Torside—the latter having a drainage of 14,335 acres—for 12 hours it averaged $16\frac{1}{3}$ and for four hours $24\frac{1}{4}$ cubic feet per second per 100 acres. This flood, as well as the preceding one, was no doubt moderated by the large reservoirs in which it was measured.

Woodhead Reservoir. To return to Woodhead reservoir. The pipes in the original embankment were supported by a stone pillar under each pipe so as to secure uniform foundation; they were satisfactorily tested in their places by water pressure and then surrounded by and bedded in concrete, and the formation of the bank proceeded with. Much difficulty attended the laying and jointing of the pipes in consequence of the narrow gorge in which they had to be laid. They were passed through the embankment and laid side by side, with a space of about a foot between them.

The puddle trench of this embankment was an expensive and troublesome work. The borings, which were taken before the work was commenced, were, as has been stated, very deceptive. They indicated the existence of rock at a depth of about 20 feet below the surface of the ground on the Derbyshire or south side of the valley, and though it was well known that here there was an ancient landslip—the rock which was supposed to exist was also supposed to be the original ground on which the slip had taken place. Instead, however, of rock being found at this depth large loose stones or blocks of rock were found, sometimes resting on each other; and though the material in which they were imbedded was generally stiff retentive clay, there were beds or "pot-holes" of sand or gravel which it was deemed prudent to follow or cut out. It was, therefore, necessary to go to a much greater depth and distance into the hill than was anticipated.

Delay was thereby occasioned, and as it was clear that the Woodhead reservoir would take a longer time to complete than was expected, it became a matter for consideration whether other reservoirs could not be pushed forward with greater speed.

This was before the flood of October, 1849. The Rhodes Wood reservoir and the partial construction of that at Torside had been let to Mr. Merritt, in April, 1849, and it was, therefore, determined to push these reservoirs forward to obviate the inconveniences of the delay at Woodhead.

Torside and Rhodes Wood Reservoirs.

Arrangements were accordingly made with Mr. Merritt, before the end of 1849, for completing the construction of the Torside reservoir. This reservoir had in the first instance only been intended to have as much of the base constructed as would be laved by the water of the Rhodes Wood reservoir. This involved the construction of the lower part of the puddle wall and the introduction of the discharge pipes. But here, again, difficulties had to be surmounted which further delayed the completion of the works.

In order to convey the flood waters past these two reservoirs, and especially past that at Rhodes Wood, an ancient landslip on the north side of the valley had to be crossed.

At the Torside reservoir a great gap, cut out of the solid rock on the north side of the valley, was constructed for the passage of flood water. Below that, and alongside the Rhodes Wood reservoir, a large channel,

35 feet wide and 10 feet deep was projected and partially executed, when further progress was arrested by the movement of a landslip on the north side of the valley which had to be crossed by this watercourse and by two others of a smaller size which had been projected,—one of these was for the conveyance of pure water to Manchester, and the other for a portion of the compensation water to the river to be used at the lower end of the works for mill-power. The first mention of this slip is in a report to the Water Committee of 18th December, 1850, but it is referred to in various subsequent ones, and especially in one of 23rd April, 1851. It was known that this slip existed, the turnpike-road which crossed it at a higher level having moved about 3 feet in 13 years. It had, however, been long stationary, and it was believed it could be crossed with safety. As soon, however, as the excavation for the flood watercourse was made across it, it was again set in motion, and previous to the report of April, 1851, it had for some time been sliding down the hill at the rate of $\frac{3}{4}$ths of an inch per day. To obviate this tendency, a heavy retaining wall which was first thought of was given up,— a flat arch, which will be shortly described, and a great mass of earth-work was placed at the foot, within the site of the Rhodes Wood reservoir, which by its weight should counterbalance the force of movement. There was reason to suppose that the slip, though 800 feet in height, was superficial only, and that where the flood watercourse crossed it, it was not more than 18 feet in depth.

The two smaller watercourses had to be abandoned, but it was absolutely necessary to construct the flood watercourse for the purpose of securing immunity from floods. On the line of this watercourse and for about 80 yards in length (the width of the slip at this point), a flat arch of large stones, 25 feet in span, was constructed under the superintendence of Mr. Elias Smethurst, my masonry inspector, the foundations being laid on the upper side in what appeared to be unmoved ground, and the lower side abutting against the material of the slip itself, which was prevented from further movement by a heavy mass of earth-work placed against it and resting on the flat of the valley. The erection of this arch was quite successful, but some idea of the force it had to resist may be formed when it is stated that, although there was a space of 3 feet in width at the back of the masonry, the slipping ground closed upon it twice during the operation of turning the first length of 15 feet of the arch, and had to be cut off. I do not recollect the time occupied, but during this operation the ground moved downward 9 feet, and was finally resisted by the strength of the arch. This arch now remains. It is heavily weighted both on the top and on the lower side, and it has never moved since the day it was erected.

On the 11th September, 1850, the late Mr. Alderman Pilling made various depreciatory remarks in a meeting of the Town Council, which caused the following report to be written:—

"Manchester, 18th September, 1850.

"*Manchester Corporation Waterworks.*

"To the Water Committee.

"Gentlemen,—Feeling perfectly satisfied that you, as a Committee, are convinced of the accuracy of all the information and statements which I have from time to time laid before you, I think it scarcely necessary to make any remarks in reply to the observations of Mr. Alderman Pilling at the Council meeting on the 11th instant, and should not now do so except for the purpose of correcting, through you, any misconception out of doors.

"It may, however, be of service to bring before your notice, in a condensed form, the leading facts and features of the water scheme, that you may have yourselves the ready means of refuting any misrepresentations.

"In a work extending over many years, and embracing a great variety of operations, it is not unlikely that the various steps by which the whole of the projected undertaking is at length being carried out may escape the recollection of the members of the Committee, whose attention is necessarily distracted by other duties. I therefore propose to give, in as brief a manner as possible, the general outline of the scheme, as it has been gradually brought to maturity,—the views which have guided the Committee in determining at various times what portion of the work it was desirable to carry out, and the estimates of the cost of the works thus successively decided upon.

"I shall refer for the accuracy of my statements to printed and other documents in your own possession.

"The scheme of 1846, for which Parliamentary sanction was obtained in 1847, was laid out with a view of obtaining 20,000,000 gallons of water per day for the service of the town. The Parliamentary estimate for the whole of the work laid down upon the plans was £255,000. This included the Pendleton and Broughton service reservoirs, and the piping necessary to conduct to them the water through the town from Ardwick. The estimate for bringing the water to Ardwick was £210,000 (*vide* printed minutes of evidence before surveying officers, 1847, pages 21-137). This estimate was subsequently raised to £215,000., by adding £5,000. for the Mottram tunnel (*vide* report of Committee to Council, 5th July, 1848—Minutes of proceedings, 1847-48, page 161). Two other sums—one of £7,000. for enlarging the Woodhead reservoir, and another of £5,000. for an auxiliary reservoir for the millowners, although also added to the estimate as the Bill passed through Parliament, were subsequently included in the Parliamentary estimate for the Act of 1848.

"In the estimate of £215,000. was included £40,000. for the purchase of land and water privileges, leaving £175,000. as the estimated cost of engineering works; adding to this amount the two sums of £7,000. and £5,000. above alluded to, there is a total of £187,000. In the report of the Committee to the Council on the 5th July, 1848, the total engineering cost is stated to be £182,562., the difference being accounted for by the omission of the catchwater drains on the moors, and the millowners' gauge weir, together £4,070., and the accidental transposition of a figure making a further error of £200. These corrections bring the two estimates within £168. of each other, one being an estimate stated in round numbers, and the other in detail.

"In the progress of the Bill of 1847 through Parliament, it was arranged that the scheme should be materially enlarged and another Act applied for in the following Session. This arrangement is fully described in my report to the Committee dated 27th July, 1847, and included in your report to the Council on the 5th August following (*vide* proceedings of Council, 1846-47, page 184). In this report I stated that the Act of 1847, as it stood, would secure 15,000,000 gallons of water per day in the driest seasons, besides affording a supply of 60 feet per second for 12 hours per day to the mills,— that the new scheme would afford 75 feet per second to the mills, and 30,000,000 gallons per day to the town, and that by a re-arrangement of the works the same quantity of water to the town per day as was secured by the Act of 1847 (viz., 15,000,000 gallons, and 75 feet per second to the mills instead of 60), could be obtained for the same cost as would be required to carry out the works of the Act of 1847 (viz., £215,000., or with the additions alluded to, £227,000.).

"The second Act was applied for and obtained in the Session of 1848. The Parliamentary estimate for the works included in this Act was £145,000. (*vide* report of surveying officers, 1848—Minutes of proceedings of Council, 1847-48, page 169), making the total cost of completing the whole scheme to Ardwick £360,000. (£215,000 + £145,000.), to which must be added £100,000., the then estimate for piping the borough, making a total of £460,000. From this has to be deducted some abandoned works, which were rendered unnecessary by the second Act, amounting to about £19,000.; and to be added, £10,000. for increasing the size of the main pipes from Godley to Denton, leaving a nett estimate of £451,000.

"For this sum it was estimated that the whole scheme could be carried out down to Denton and Gorton, to which places all the water, viz.: 30,000,000 gallons per day, could be brought. From thence the pipes included in the Parliamentary estimate, together with those already laid from the Gorton reservoir, were only capable of conveying the quantity originally intended of 20,000,000 gallons per day. It required the enlargement of the intended new main from 32 to 36 inches, to place that part of the work on the same footing as the rest. The estimated cost of this was £4,300. (*vide* report to Committee, November 12th, 1859). This sum added makes the original estimates for supplying 30,000,000 gallons of water per day £455,300.

"The figures here given nearly correspond with those in Mr. Walker's report to the Exchequer Loan Commissioners, which appears in the report of the Committee to the Council, 5th July, 1848 (*vide* minutes of proceedings, 1847-48, page 167).

"The estimate given in his report, arranged in the same manner as I have adopted above, gives a total of £472,795. This, however, includes the Pendleton service reservoir and the pipes connected therewith, but is exclusive of the main between Denton and Ardwick. His estimate is shortly:—

"To complete the works for 20,000,000 gallons............£322,785
"Postponed works 50,000
                                                    ———————
                                                    372,785
"Piping borough..................................... 100,000
                                                    ———————
                                                    £472,785

"Mr. Walker assumes £350,000. as the smallest amount for making a complete work to bring 20,000,000 gallons to Ardwick.

"Immediately after the passing of the Act of 1848, it was determined to carry out so much of the works for which powers had been obtained as would enable the Corporation to guarantee the quantity of water secured to the mill-owners, and also to bring for the supplying of the inhabitants daily from 15 to 20 million gallons of water (*vide* report of Committee to Council, 5th July, 1848—Minutes of proceedings, 1847-48, page 170).

"Reference is made in this report to that which I presented to the Committee in July, 1847, to which I have already alluded, and in which a supply of 15,000,000 gallons per day is estimated to cost £227,000., including land, and £187,000. for engineering works only,—both sums, exclusive of the addition of £10,000. for the main between Godley and Denton.

"Subsequently to this, in November, 1848, a detailed estimate of the probable cost (according to the Parliamentary figures) of the engineering portion of so much of the scheme as was then contemplated, was furnished to the

Sub-Committee, in the progress of the arrangement with me for the superintendence of the work, in which the amount of engineering cost is estimated at £207,861., exclusive of the addition of £10,000. for the main. This is the document to which Mr. Alderman Pilling referred in his observations on the 11th instant.

"The difference between the two estimates is £20,761. Of this about £10,000. or £12,000. are due to the intended partial construction of the Torside reservoir, which it was found expedient to carry to some height, at the same time that the Rhodes Wood reservoir was being made. The remainder is the difference between a rough estimate in July, 1847, and a more careful one when the plans were prepared and the details more maturely considered in 1848.

"In compliance with your instructions, and with the resolutions referred to, the works were at first laid out and contracted for with a view to the execution of such portions as would secure the supply of 20,000,000 gallons of water per day;—works to the extent of about £34,000. in estimated engineering cost being postponed, amongst which was a portion of the Torside reservoir. A greater amount would have been postponed, but it was deemed expedient to construct all those portions of the works which could not be afterwards conveniently altered, of capacity sufficient to convey the largest ultimate supply.

"Difficulties having occurred in the construction of the Woodhead reservoir which at one time rendered it doubtful whether it could be completed within a period to enable the Corporation to supply the stipulated quantity to the mills, and more mature consideration upon the advantages of constructing the whole scheme at once, induced the Committee to complete the postponed portions of the undertaking. In October, 1849, arrangements were consequently made for the completion of the Torside reservoir; and in December, 1849, it was determined to enlarge the main from Denton to Ardwick to a size sufficient to convey the whole quantity of water. The anticipated cost of these works was about £21,000. (*vide* my reports, October 2nd and November 21st, 1849, and resolutions of Committee of same period). The completion of the remaining postponed portions necessary to insure the supply of 30,000,000 gallons, of course follows these resolutions, and the scheme is now being carried out in its entirety.

"I will now compare the probable cost at which it will be so completed with original estimates :—

"The gross amount of the original estimates, as I have already shown (including £14,300. for enlarged sizes of mains), for bringing the water to the town, and completing the piping within the borough, was £455,000

"The probable cost will be :—

"For the works between Woodhead and Manchester (see my report of 6th June, 1850)..........................£282,652
"Accommodation works and compensation to millowners, estimated at £11,257., but will probably cost 15,000
"Land (estimate £92,900.), say........................ 93,000
"Piping the borough 70,000

"Total.....................£460,652

being an excess of about £5,000., or a trifle over 1 per cent.; but which of course may yet, and probably will, be increased by unforeseen contingencies. If the damage by flood be added, the excess will still be under 2 per cent. In this amount is included the cost of constructing weirs and watercourses for the purpose of creating water-power equal to about 1,000 horse-power, in the valley of Longdendale; the estimated cost of which is about £9,400.

"The costs of obtaining the Acts of Parliament, and interest upon borrowed money, with other expenses, formed no part of the original estimates.

"I think it unnecessary to go further into an investigation of the various items of excess and saving. Fortunate circumstances on one hand have enabled us to meet unfortuate ones on the other. It is true that the works outside the borough have exceeded the estimated cost; but the saving within the borough balances the account.

"A material saving on the first contract which was made, enabled me to lay out and include in subsequent contracts many improvements which suggested themselves as the details of the various works were progressively designed and matured. These are alluded to and explained in my report of the 6th June, as well as the additional cost which has been incurred in providing for much heavier floods than had been anticipated.

"I cannot help congratulating the Committee, and feeling thankful myself for this opportunity of analyzing the whole cost, and in placing before the world in what I hope is a clear and distinct manner, a faithful account of the real facts of the case. It is rare that the expense of so large and intricate an undertaking can bear looking at so strictly in the face.

"I have the honour to remain,

"Your very obedient Servant,

(Signed)   "J. F. BATEMAN."

Allusion has been made to the separation of pure water from that which is occasionally turbid. Before the works were commenced observations were made upon the relative quantities of uncoloured and coloured water, as it was intended from the first to convey the pure uncoloured water to Manchester, and to store separately the turbid water for compensation to the river, or for delivery to Manchester when it had become sufficiently clarified by subsidence or exposure. It was known that exposure very materially improved the colour of water originally brown by the bleaching action of the sun and air. About one-half of all the water was uncoloured and the other half coloured. How the separation was to be accomplished remained to be decided.

In dry weather, when the streams and springs were unswollen by rain, the water was beautifully clear and absolutely unexceptionable, but as soon as the volume was increased by sudden rain the water was stained by peat, and unfit in that condition for dietetic purposes. Taking advantage of these circumstances an arrangement was suggested by one of my assistants, Mr. Alfred Moore, which has been carried out on all streams and with uniform success. It consists of a narrow slot in front of a weir into which the water falls when small in quantity, and is conveyed away by a watercourse beneath the top of the weir, to be delivered to Manchester; or, if more than sufficient for the wants of the town, it is stored in reservoirs set apart for the storage of pure water. When the springs and streams fall below the quantity required the deficiency is made up by drawing from these reservoirs. When rain falls and the streams are consequently swollen the water is generally discoloured—and then the water, increased in volume, jumps or passes over the narrow slot—passes down the weir and is stored in separate reservoirs, from whence it is given as compensation, or, when sufficiently clarified, is decanted off into the pure water reservoirs at lower levels. This principle has been applied to every stream whether large or small. It is self-acting and never gets out of order. The length and breadth of the slot have of course to be proportioned to the quantity of the water in the stream. Examples of the manner in which this arrangement has been carried out are given;—one, the Crowden weir, where a large stream receiving the drainage of about 3,300 acres is so treated, and another where a small stream is intercepted by a pure watercourse.

The pleasantness of water to drink depends principally upon temperature and aëration. Many soft waters are short of air and vapid to the taste, and are, therefore, disagreeable to those who have been accustomed to hard water highly aërated. The water, however, issuing from many geological formations are free from this objection, and those which, like those of the Manchester Waterworks, flow from the millstone grit are always pleasant to drink. Considering, however, that this pleasantness is due principally to the amount of air which the water contains, that which was intended for Manchester was in many instances broken by stepped weirs, so as to expose it as much as possible to the air; and the water from reservoirs was discharged by means of fountains which threw the water high up into the air in sprays, to be received again in basins from which it was conveyed to the town.

Another arrangement for securing the purity of the water has been to draw it from reservoirs for the service of the town always within a few feet of the surface. This arrangement has been carried out at Torside reservoir and Rhodes Wood reservoir, and the mode in which it is accomplished is shown on the sections of these reservoirs.

With all these precautions filtration was considered unnecessary, but the water, before being admitted to the pipes for delivery to the inhabitants, is strained through fine copper wire gauze which can be removed and cleansed when required. This gauze was originally 60 strands to the inch, then 40, but both were found too fine, and the gauze now used is 27 strands to the inch, which leaves 1-40th of an inch clear opening. The frames in which this gauze is fixed and the general arrangement are shown in drawing.

It was only necessary to introduce these arrangements at the service reservoirs. These reservoirs are at Godley and Denton, and are so deep that no vegetation will grow in them;—to prevent this, the water, if clear, must exceed 15 feet in depth, or the rays of the sun will strike to the bottom and produce a fungoid growth. The Denton reservoirs when full are 20 feet deep, that at Godley deeper. They have now been 30 years in use and no vegetation has ever occurred.

Torside and Rhodes Wood Reservoirs.

The construction of these reservoirs, together with other works, was let to Mr. Merritt, and managed by his agent, Mr. Golden. In consequence of the delay which seemed likely to attend the completion of the Woodhead reservoir, owing to the difficulties of the puddle trench there, the Torside reservoir, which it was at first intended to be only partially constructed, was arranged to be completed. The embankment of this reservoir was 100 feet in height; the puddle trench passed through 6 to 10 feet of river gravel resting on 8 or 10 feet of hard clay, which again rested on watertight rock, with an intervening bed of gravel 2 or 3 feet thick, and into this rock the trench was sunk several feet. One end of the bank was in watertight material, but the other had to be formed against alternate beds of shale and sandstone, so that it was requisite to bring an arm or puddle trench for some distance up the valley, on the northerly side, until watertight material was met with. This branch puddle trench was near the foot of the hill, and from thence to top water level, the surface was covered with a thick stratum of clay, technically called puddle lining, and pitched with stone on the top. This lining has been the cause of a great deal of trouble, as it frequently gives way and has to be renewed or replaced, which is now generally done by concrete, for experience has taught us that little reliance is to be placed in clay.

This, however, was not the only trouble which the bank created. Nothing could apparently be a better foundation than from 6 to 10 feet in thickness of river gravel; but when the bank was carried to its full height, 100 feet, and the reservoir filled with water, the bank stretched upon its base and broke the discharge pipes.

This circumstance will perhaps be best described by a report to the Water Committee made at the time, and dated in January, 1855:—

"The Torside reservoir having been completed, with the exception of the soiling of the outside slope of the embankment and the formation of a road on the top, the reservoir was gradually being filled in October and November, and about the middle of the latter month was within about 9 feet of being full, the depth of the water being then about 80 feet. On the 17th November, a fracture occurred in both ranges of the discharge pipes, and a considerable quantity of water escaped near the foot of the outside slope. The south range, which appeared to be the worst, was immediately closed by means of the valve on the inner end of the pipe, and examined, the water in the meantime being discharged as rapidly as the north range of pipes, with valves wide open, would permit. On examining the south range, it was found that the pipes had been torn asunder near the centre of the bank, and for a length of about 15 feet below the centre they were much crushed and broken. Through these fractures the water had escaped in considerable quantity. As soon as the reservoir was sufficiently lowered the north range was similarly examined; and though the injury was less serious than in the other range, yet it had also been torn asunder, several joints being opened which allowed the escape of water into the bank at a short distance below the centre.

"On careful measurement and investigation, it appears that the embankment has stretched itself upon its base both up and down the valley, carrying the pipes with it and tearing them asunder near the centre, as already described. In which direction the movement has been greatest I am not yet able to determine, but the total amount of elongation in the south range of pipes, since they were first laid, appears to be from 3 feet 6 inches to 5 feet; in the north range not so much. I believe every precaution which human foresight could conceive was taken to prevent such an occurrence. The pipes were sunk a considerable depth into the solid ground below the base of the bank, and imbedded in a great mass of concrete (except at the centre, where they were supported on stone pillars and surrounded by puddle), and each end abutted against substantial ashlar stone buttresses, which were carried deep into the solid ground.

"The embankment is constructed with a special view to prevent slipping, by being formed in layers, and the foot and outer part of each slope of rock and stony material, the centre mass of the bank on both sides of the puddle wall, being composed of the most clayey and adhesive material which the cuttings afforded. The probable cause of the movement is the existence of a bed of hard clay of from 5 to 8 feet thick, which underlies the gravel which forms the bed of the valley. The clay rests on a few feet of gravel, beneath which there is a close water-tight rock, into which the puddle of the bank has been securely tied. It is not unlikely that this bed of clay—partly in consequence of the weight on it and partly from being softened by the water—has yielded a little, or allowed the superincumbent mass to slide upon its surface. The immense quantity of rain which has fallen since the occurrence of the accident (18 inches in the last six weeks of the year, sufficient to fill all the reservoirs twice over) has kept the north range of pipes constantly engaged in passing the water, and it was not until this week that the reservoir could be emptied. The embankment appears to have sustained no material injury, notwithstanding some settlement which has occurred over the spots at which the water escaped into the bank, and where necessarily some material would be carried away. The requisite repairs to the pipes, to render them fit for temporary use, are being made with as much rapidity as possible. In order to prevent the recurrence of a similar accident —as it is evidently uncertain whether the embankment has yet come to a state of rest or whether it may not still extend itself to a wider base (in which case another fracture of the pipe is inevitable),—it has been considered desirable to abandon the permanent use of the pipes, and to adopt a new mode of discharge by means of a tunnel through the rock on the north end of the bank. This rock is very open, and as no masonry lining could be made sufficiently water-tight to prevent the escape of water, it is intended to introduce, as may hereafter be determined, one or more lines of pipes of large size through which the water will be discharged. Instructions for the commencement of the works have been given, and they may be expected to be completed in five or six months, at a cost probably of about £6,000.

"When the pipes are repaired water may be impounded in the reservoir 40 or 50 feet in depth without interfering with the various operations referred to, and the reservoir may then be partially used for the supply of the mills on the river until the time at which it must be again emptied for the completion of the inner end of the tunnel and pipes."

A new puddle trench was sunk into the clay near the foot of the inner slope, and the upper part lined over with puddle clay, 5 or 6 feet in thickness. The water was discharged by means of a tunnel in which two pipes are introduced—one of 48 inches in diameter, which draws off the water to within about 20 feet of the bottom, and another of 24 inches in diameter, which, as a syphon, will draw off the water to the bottom, the outer end being introduced into the Rhodes Wood reservoir, immediately below, at a level low enough for the purpose.

At the Rhodes Wood reservoir the pipes were laid in the same manner as at Torside, the most southerly one, however, being laid in a chase cut out of the solid rock and surrounded by concrete. The outer ends of the two discharge pipes were closed by 3 feet valves, and no trouble of any kind has been experienced here. Owing, however, to imperfect workmanship in the puddle wall of this embankment, some time after the reservoir was filled, water was observed to escape. The bank was cut open to the defective spot, and a layer of sandy material was discovered to have passed through from one side of the puddle wall to the other, and through this the water had escaped. This was cut out, the puddle restored, and the embankment raised to its full height.

A small reservoir was constructed below this embankment, and at the foot a gauge basin introduced for the purpose of ascertaining accurately the quantity of water which was discharged to the mills. This gauge basin was subsequently removed in consequence of an Act of Parliament being obtained in the year 1865 for the construction of two other reservoirs, called the Vale House and Bottoms reservoirs, for the supply of water to the mills, and for impounding flood water which would otherwise run to waste.

Vale House and Bottoms Reservoirs.

These two reservoirs are at a level too low for the supply of Manchester, and they are employed exclusively for the supply of compensation water to the river, the gauge or test basin being removed to the foot of the embankment of the lowest or Bottoms reservoir, at which point the water is delivered into the river. This will be described, and a drawing given of it in connection with the description of these two lower reservoirs, which have been the last constructed in the Longdendale valley.

Arnfield and Hollingworth Reservoirs.

The embankments of these reservoirs (which are formed on the Arnfield and Hollingworth brooks respectively) had to be composed entirely of clay, as no other material was to be found in the immediate neighbourhood. The Hollingworth reservoir is a little higher than that at Arnfield, and the pure water of the Hollingworth stream was carried past the reservoir on that brook and above the top-water level of the Arnfield reservoir to the Arnfield brook, where the two were united, and then carried by a watercourse round the foot of the embankment of the Arnfield reservoir to the conduit which conveyed the water from the Rhodes Wood reservoir and from the springs in the valley of Longdendale.

The outer slope of a portion of the Arnfield bank slipped, and part of the open watercourse had to be covered in and turned into a culvert, so as to flatten the slope of these slipped portions. The embankment was ultimately raised to its full height, and the reservoir filled with water.

At the embankment of the Hollingworth reservoir, the discharge pipes were sunk to a depth of 30 or 40 feet in the solid clay, and were supposed to be perfectly secure at this level—but not only did the embankment itself slide down the valley, but the clay beneath the base also moved down to such a depth as to dislocate the pipes, into which cast-iron cylinders had to be introduced for the purpose of restoring their continuity. These pipes were 24 inches in diameter. The introduction of the cylinders was successfully accomplished. This reservoir, as well as that at Arnfield, is perfectly watertight, and no other trouble has been experienced.

Both these reservoirs are used for the storage of pure water only, the turbid water being discharged over waste weirs into a reservoir below them, called the "waste lodge reservoir," which has been constructed for the supply of a mill on the Hollingworth stream. This waste lodge reservoir is formed by an embankment across which the pure water for the supply of Manchester is conveyed in an open watercourse. The waste water is carried beneath this watercourse into the brook below.

In the excavations for the formation of these embankments, various shells, both univalves and bivalves, apparently similar to existing species on the Lancashire shore, were met with, although the elevation of the ground in which they were discovered was 550 feet above the level of the sea, and at least 40 miles distant. From this it may be inferred that the clay of the district was at one time beneath or on the level of the sea, and that it has been (geologically speaking) only recently elevated.[*]

The united waters, namely those from Longdendale—from the Arnfield brook—and from the Hollingworth brook, were conveyed by a watercourse, partly open and partly covered, to the Mottram tunnel next described, and subsequently to the Godley reservoir.

Mottram Tunnel.

This tunnel pierces the ridge which lies between the valley of the Etherow and the valley of the Tame. No water could be conveyed to Manchester till it was completed. It is about 3,100 yards in length, and like most of the watercourses in connection with it, it has a fall of 5 feet in a mile. It was at first intended to be 5 feet in diameter and equal to the passage of 36,500,000 gallons of water per day. It was constructed 6 feet in diameter, and is capable of passing upwards of 50,000,000 gallons per day of 24 hours. This ridge had never previously been pierced, but it was well-known that between one end and the other a great fault or dislocation existed. Before the work commenced borings were made along the line of tunnel to ascertain the character of the material through which it would have to be driven. These borings disclosed the existence of a bed of quick-sand and silt upwards of 80 feet in depth, and extending for about 700 yards over about the centre of the tunnel. Beneath this quick-sand there lay a bed of black shale from 50 to 80 feet in thickness to the bottom of the tunnel. When this shale was reached by the preliminary borings a large

---

[*] The shells discovered were named at the British Museum as follows:—*Tallina Solidula—Cyprina Islandica—Cardium Aculeatum ?—Turritella Communis.*

quantity of water rose to the surface. Pipes of 2 inches in diameter were reared perpendicularly above the surface of the ground, being together 18 feet in length, and from the top of these the water poured, throwing up stones as large as pigeon-eggs, and some so large and angular that you wondered how they could rise from such a depth through a 2-inch bore-hole and be thrown out by the pressure of the water on to the surface of the ground.

It was, therefore, apprehended that in this quick-sand a large quantity of water would be met with, and the positions of the shafts were arranged so as to avoid it. The work was let in August, 1848, to Mr. Graham; but before the end of the year he had made so little progress and was evidently so incapable of completing the work in time, that it was taken out of his hands and executed by the Corporation themselves under my immediate superintendence. Mr. John J. Mawson was appointed resident engineer, John Molyneux, mining superintendent, and Robert Taylor, inspector of masonry and lining. Owing to the great quantity of water met with and the consequent slow progress made, it was found necessary to sink a shaft through the quick-sand, which had in the first instance been avoided. A place was found, by boring, in which there was as much silt as sand, and here a shaft was successfully sunk. Ten shafts in all were sunk, and the quantity of water yielded by these shafts and the tunnel was so large that for months upwards of 2,000,000 gallons on the average were raised per day. All the water contained in the quick-sand was at length drained out, and the gross produce of the tunnel, some years after it was completed, was but 68,000 gallons per day. At one of the shafts (No. 5 on the Section), 205 feet in depth, a serious accident befell my two inspectors, Molyneux and Taylor. They were going down together in a tub, when the engine-driver started at so great a speed that Molyneux called to him not to go so fast, when he checked his engine too suddenly and stripped the teeth of the cogwheel attached to the drum round which the rope was wound. Thus set at liberty beyond all control, the tub, with the two men in it, descended the shaft as rapidly as it could unwind the rope from the drum. There was a sumph-well at the bottom covered by 3 inch planks, and such was the impetus of the fall that the tub went through these planks. One man (Molyneux) had a compound fracture of one leg, and the other man had his ribs broken. Both were greatly bruised and shaken in other ways, but they both recovered. They both remained in my service for several years, and one (Robert Taylor) is still one of my inspectors. It was a wonder they were not both killed, but luckily for them the rope and head stocks did not follow; had they done so they could not have escaped destruction.

The tunnel was lined for the greater part with stone 9 inches in thickness set in Ardwick lime mortar—a lime which, though slow in setting, eventually sets hard under water. When the work was partly finished there was a threatened turn-out of masons. There was clay in the immediate neighbourhood above the tunnel, and on hearing of what was going to happen, I immediately made contracts for making it into bricks, and before the men knew what I was about I had about two millions of bricks stacked ready to be used in case of a "turn-out." The appearance of the bricks, however, was sufficient to keep the masons at work, and the bricks were all used in lining the tunnel before it was completed.

The work and the watercourses in connection with it were completed by October, 1850, in little more than two years from their commencement, and water passed through on the 17th of that month.

The cost was about £12. per lineal yard, including shafts, lining, and pumping water.

Godley and Denton Service Reservoirs.

On emerging from the Mottram tunnel the water is carried across a small brook for a short distance by an inverted syphon pipe, and then, for a short distance also, by a covered culvert to the Godley reservoir. This reservoir is on the slope of the hills and is the last point at which a reservoir of suitable elevation could be constructed. It is formed partly by excavation and partly by embankments, out of the drift or boulder clay, which here, as in other places, rests upon a bed of fine sand. This sand made its appearance in various places within the basin of the reservoir, and had to be covered by clay tied into the surrounding retentive material.

The elevation of this reservoir when full is 328 feet above Piccadilly, in Manchester, from which it is distant about 8 or 9 miles, and 155 feet above the service reservoirs at Denton.

The embankment of this reservoir at the deepest place is about 27 feet, and from this point the water, after being strained through copper-wire gauze, is conveyed by pipes of 40 inches diameter to the service reservoirs at Denton, which are distant about 4 or 5 miles. The water is also conveyed from the end of the culvert which supplies the Godley reservoir, by an independent line of pipes of 30 inches diameter laid since the first construction of the reservoir, and so laid as to avoid a small coalfield near Hyde, to a reservoir on a high point at Prestwich, from which the higher and more distant points of the district are supplied with water.

All the water which is admitted into the Godley reservoir may be measured through gauge-plates erected in the side of a small basin at the end of the culvert which conveys the water from Longdendale.

The embankments are made almost entirely of clay, with slopes inside of 3 horizontal to 1 vertical, and outside of 2 to 1. No inconvenience was experienced in the construction of the banks.

The water from the culvert or gauge-basin is conveyed beneath the bottom of the Godley reservoir to the pipes which carry the water to Denton, so that the supply may be continued although the reservoir should be empty for examination or repair.

The capacity of the reservoir is 9,800,000 cubic feet.

The reservoirs at Denton are two in number, being divided by an intermediate embankment. They are placed upon the highest ground in that district, and are formed by embankments raised above the surface of the ground. One contains 4,800,000 cubic feet, and the other 3,700,000 cubic feet. The slopes of the embankments inside and outside are 2 horizontal to 1 vertical.

The pipes from Godley reservoir are carried under the intermediate embankment to the further end, and there discharge the water into a basin, from which it flows into one or other reservoir over a gauge-plate so that the quantity can be accurately ascertained.

At these reservoirs, also, the water is strained through copper-wire gauze, and the inside slopes and bottoms of the reservoirs are lined with brick made from the clay upon the spot. On the bottom the bricks are laid flat, on the slopes on edge.

Either reservoir can be shut off for cleansing or repair, and the bottom is traversed by 6-inch pipes upon which fire-cocks are placed, so that in case of necessity they can be thoroughly washed from the main pipe by the pressure from Godley.

The brick lining, after nearly 30 years' exposure, had to some extent failed betwixt wind and water, and it has been recently replaced by stone pitching.

Water can be drawn from these reservoirs by 24 inch pipes, commanded by valves at the foot of the inside slopes, into a basin from which a covered culvert conveys the water to the Gorton reservoirs. Into this basin also a branch pipe of 24 inches diameter from the 40 inch main pipe is carried, so that not only are the Godley reservoir and the two Denton reservoirs supplied with water from Longdendale but the Gorton reservoirs also.

The supply to the town is divided into three zones, the highest and more distant parts from the Prestwich reservoir by the pressure from Godley, the middle, and by far the greatest part, by the pressure from Denton, and the lower parts of Manchester by that from Gorton.

Collecting Ground. The extent of ground from which water can be collected in Longdendale is about 19,300 acres, and this includes the drainage area to the Vale House and Bottoms reservoirs, which have been constructed at a level below that at which the water can be conveyed to Manchester. These reservoirs can only be used, therefore, for the supply of compensation water to the river, and into them the turbid water of the district is, so far as possible, conveyed.

Compensation to River. The compensation to the river at first given by the Act of 1848 was 75 cubic feet per second for 12 hours of each working day, equal to 14¼ inches in depth of rain upon the drainage ground. This was found to be more than could be usefully employed, and by a subsequent Act (1854) 20 cubic feet of this quantity were purchased, leaving the quantity 55 cubic feet per second for 12 hours of working days, equal to about 10¼ inches of the depth of rain from the drainage ground.

Pipe Laying.

The water was conveyed from the Godley reservoir to Denton by a line of 40 inch pipes, and from thence into the existing Gorton reservoirs by pipes of 24 inches in diameter and by a covered culvert.

The elevation of these reservoirs above the sea is as follows:—

Godley reservoir...............................	478 feet.
Denton ditto	323 "
Gorton upper ditto...........................	259 "
Ditto lower ditto.............................	245 "

The elevation of Piccadilly in Manchester, a high point, is 150 feet, and therefore 173 feet below the Denton reservoirs.

The lowest part of Manchester is 100 feet, and the highest part about 300 feet above ordnance datum.

From the Denton reservoirs the water was conveyed to Manchester by a pipe of 36 inches in diameter. The mode in which the water was distributed in the borough will be described hereafter.

While the main pipes were being laid, and before that operation was completed, various novelties were introduced.

The pipes, and consequently the valves which commanded them, were at that time (more than 30 years ago) of unusual size, and with a view of economizing labour and providing for sudden emergencies, I determined that there should be no valve, no matter what the size and pressure, which could not be opened and closed by one man. This was accomplished by gearing and by dividing the valves into compartments of unequal size, the smaller being equal in area to a small valve which could be worked by a single man. The velocity through this smaller opening was such that the larger compartment could then be opened with ease, or, if this still remained too much for one man's strength, he only had to wait until the pipe was filled and the larger part of the valve placed under back-pressure when it could be raised with facility. Drawings of these valves are given. Behind each large valve a momentum valve was placed, because it was conceived that the motion or pressure of a column of water several miles in length could not be arrested in the time in which it was necessary or desirable that a valve should be closed. The momentum valves were simply weighted apertures kept down by helical springs, and which were raised by increased pressure and then allowed the water to escape. They worked by pulsations, because the area exposed to the pressure of the water when the valve was closed was less than when the valve was open, but they answered the purpose perfectly and were frequently brought into play. At Broomstair bridge, where the pipes cross the river Tame, near Hyde, the action can be seen. There, there is a large valve, on the 40 inch main, with a momentum valve behind it, enclosed in a building and all open to view.

The large valves for discharging water from the Woodhead and Torside reservoirs are divided into three nearly equal compartments, any one of which can be raised by one man, and so the three successively.

The large valves were principally constructed by Messrs. Armstrong and Co., to whom, or perhaps to Mr. (now Sir W. G.) Armstrong, I am indebted for an ingenious arrangement for shutting off the water of a reservoir in case of a burst in the pipes below, which has been called a "self-acting closing valve." This valve closes if the velocity exceeds a limit to which it is adjusted. It consists of a large flat fish-shaped valve, placed horizontally in a swelled portion of the pipe, so that there shall exist at the valve and around it the same area for the passage of the water as in the general pipe. A diaphragm hangs suspended in advance of the valve crosswise of the pipe. This diaphragm is hung to a rod working through a stuffing-box and attached to a catch outside the pipe. The diaphragm is so adjusted that it will not move with the ordinary velocity of the water in the pipe; but if the velocity is increased, which it would be in the event of a burst, it moves and disengages the catch which sets at liberty a quadrant motion, actuated by a weight which slowly works the closing horizontal valve (through stuffing-boxes at the sides), the rapidity of the closing being checked by a small cataract through which water is gradually forced. The valve fits against facings, and stops further discharge of water, until the valve is again replaced in its original position and the diaphragm properly adjusted and attached to the catch of the quadrant. The opening of the valve is accomplished by a small hand force-pump.

Three of these valves were originally put down, two on the 40-inch main—one of which was at the entrance of the town of Hyde, about a mile from the Godley reservoir, and under 100 feet of pressure; and the other on the top of Broomstair brow, at the commencement of a long flat district in which there were many buildings; and the third immediately below the Denton reservoir, in a building by itself where its action may conveniently be seen. Here, in case the valve goes off, an alarum bell is rung in the keeper's house, set in motion by the action of closing. The reservoir-keeper, if at night, is aroused from his slumbers and informed that an accident has occurred which he must attend to.

That on Broomstair brow, for want, I suppose, of being properly adjusted, closed unexpectedly one day and burst a pipe behind it,—the concussion or the increased pressure due to the long column of water being too quickly arrested. This showed the danger of such a valve being placed in an improper position, and it was accordingly removed.

The other at the entrance to the town of Hyde was brought into action soon after it was placed, and proved of great advantage.

The usefulness of this invention will perhaps be best described in the following extract from a report dated 19th February, 1851:—

"The water was first turned through the Mottram tunnel, the watercourses at each end, and a portion of the 40-inch main, on the 17th October. On the 20th December it was passed through the whole length into the Gorton reservoirs, which were then considerably below their proper level, and allowed to flow regularly, with one day's exception, until the 14th January, when the reservoirs were both full and overflowing.

"On that day an accident occurred to the main in the town of Hyde, to which it may be desirable to refer more particularly. The great probability that some accident would occur in a main of so great a size, and extending four miles in length, when the water was first turned into it with full pressure, notwithstanding every care to prevent it, always rendered this portion of the work one of anxiety. No means had been discovered by which the flow of the water, in the event of a burst, could be spontaneously arrested; and the only precaution which it at first appeared possible to adopt, was the fixing of stop valves at sufficiently short intervals, which could be closed by hand, as rapidly as was consistent with safety, as soon after an accident occurred as a man could arrive at the place. Even then, the closing of a 40-inch valve, under a pressure varying from 100 to 200 feet, was a work of no slight difficulty; and the utmost vigilance and the most prompt attention would be requisite to lessen the evil effects of a sudden fracture of a pipe. Stop valves, of very improved construction, and arranged to close or open by manual labour, as early as possible, were placed at intervals of about a mile and a quarter, and the subject of self-acting means of closing, by the increased velocity of the water which would be consequent upon a burst, was kept constantly under consideration.

"The result was, that after due deliberation and many conferences upon this subject with Mr. Armstrong, of Newcastle, he ultimately suggested an arrangement for effecting this, which I determined to recommend for the adoption of the Committee in June, 1850. The character of the valve adopted is that of a huge "throttle valve," so arranged and adjusted that, with the ordinary or any fixed velocity of the water in the pipe, it remains immovable in a horizontal position, without obstructing the flow of the water. Should the velocity increase (by burst or otherwise) beyond the speed to which the machine may be adjusted, the catches by which the valve is maintained in a horizontal position are disengaged, and the valve closes and thus prevents any further flow of water. Several of these valves (three), which we have denominated 'self-acting closing valves,' have been constructed by Mr. Armstrong. By well considered arrangement and good workmanship, he has been able to bring them at once to a state of great perfection, and they act with the utmost delicacy and certainty. They have been placed in such situations as will best protect the country from injury in the event of an accident. For the protection of the town of Hyde, through the centre of which the 40-inch main is laid, one is fixed upon the pipe at its first entrance into the town.

"In the ordinary working of this main, there will be little pressure upon this portion of the pipe; but by the closing of the valves at Denton, or at Broomstair bridge, it would be subject to a dead pressure, when the water is at rest, of about 150 feet in the centre of the town.

"After the water was once delivered into the Gorton reservoirs, and the deep valley of the river Tame passed in safety, it was not considered desirable to submit the pipe to its utmost test until the reservoirs were full, that there might be no scarcity of water should an accident occur. As soon, however, as the reservoirs were full, the portion of the pipe between Broomstair bridge and Godley was subjected to the whole dead pressure of the water. On the 13th the water was thus on for several hours, without the occurrence of any accident. On the 14th the pipes were again tried, the water again remaining on for a considerable period without accident; when, after the pipes had been thoroughly examined, and every imperfect place supposed to have been discovered, and just as the water was turned on at Gorton, a burst occurred near the centre of the town of Hyde, about 400 or 500 yards below the self-acting closing valve. A piece six feet in length was blown out of the side of a pipe which at the time would probably be bearing about 130 feet of pressure. The volume of water discharged through such a fracture was of course at first immense; but the increased current acted back immediately upon the safety valve, which speedily closed, stopping at once the further flow, and cutting off the pressure of 100 feet of water. Nothing remained but the water in the pipe, between the valve and the fracture, to be discharged, and in a few minutes the rush of water ceased. Fortunately my assistants happened to be upon the spot, who further facilitated the escape of the water by opening valves and discharging it into the canal and river. The street was torn up at the point of fracture, and some £30. or £40. worth of damage done. It would be impossible to have had a better proof of the great value of the precautions adopted, or of the novel and peculiar valve which has been constructed. The accident occurred in a place in which, without such a spontaneous means of prevention, the greatest damage might have been done. The damage has been repaired and the pipe restored, and water again delivered to Gorton. When the reservoirs there are again filled, it is intended to try the whole length of main from Denton to Godley under full pressure, and to repeat the trial from time to time until all weak places and bad pipes (if any) have been discovered.

"It is right to mention that all the pipes were subjected to proof in a proving press before being laid, with a pressure equal to a 800 feet column of water; and that where actual pressure, when laid, exceeds 180 feet, the pipes are constructed of additional strength.

"It is impossible, however, to guard against all contingencies of subsequent damage in the carriage, laying, and jointing.

"To prevent the injury and possible fracture of a pipe which would follow from the momentum or shock which takes place on the rapid closing of a valve, and the sudden stoppage of the column of water, other safety valves for the free escape of the water under such accumulated pressure, called "momentum valves," have been attached to the pipe. These work as freely and as certainly as the self-acting closing valves."

The discharge pipes for the various reservoirs were made partly by Mr. Mahon, of Manchester, and partly by Messrs. Fox, Henderson, & Co., of Birmingham. Those made by the latter firm were cast at Renfrew, vertically with their sockets downwards. These were such superior castings, and the socket which had to bear the strain of "caulking up" was so much more solid than pipes cast in what was then the ordinary way, with the socket upwards, that I determined upon having the 36-inch main from Denton to Manchester and the pipes there cast in this way; and with the approval of the committee, arrangements for this purpose were made with Messrs. Cochrane & Co., of the Woodside Ironworks, near Dudley, who were the contractors for the 36-inch main, and for half the city piping.

Since that time I have always insisted on pipes being made in this manner, and it is the mode *now* almost universally adopted.

A very important novelty was introduced almost at the commencement of the work, and before any pipes were made.

This was a system of coating the pipes, inside and outside, according to a process patented by Dr. R. Angus Smith, which has been very generally followed, and, where properly performed, has added some 20 years to the life of a pipe.

The process consisted of immersing the pipes, when hot, in a bath or cauldron of boiling coalpitch, after the naptha and napthaline were distilled from the coaltar. The residuum was then hard, insoluble, and tastleless, and required an admixture of mineral oil to enable it to acquire, when boiled, proper fluidity for the operation.

It was not recommended for adoption until it had been sufficiently tested; and, as it was a new process, it was performed under my direct supervision, at first at Hyde (in a wharf rented for the purpose), and afterwards in a wharf in Store-street, in Manchester (the property of the Corporation).

It was well known that *soft water*, such as it was proposed to supply from Longdendale to Manchester, had a powerful corrosive action on cast and wrought-iron; and I was apprehensive that the water would be delivered in Manchester in a brown state, highly charged with iron.

The only mode which had up to this time been adopted by engineers, was to wash or paint the inside of the pipe with lime, which, however, was soon worn off, and corrosion of the iron took place.

The desirableness of discovering some cheap mode of protecting the pipe from such corrosion was constantly kept in view, and especially commended to the consideration of my chemical friends. It was, therefore, with no little pleasure that I was able to report favourably of Dr. Smith's proposal.

It was found that if rust, however slight, had taken place on the surface of the pipe, the coalpitch coating peeled off and was of no use.

The pipe-makers were therefore required to "pay over" or paint the pipe with linseed oil, both inside and outside, as soon as the sand was cleaned off, and while the pipe was yet warm.

In this condition the pipes were delivered to the Corporation, and subsequently proved and coated.

All rust or corrosion was prevented by the oil, and the pipes might lie exposed to the weather for a long time without injury.

In order to drive off any rust or dampness, and to allow the coalpitch to penetrate the pores of the iron—which to some extent were opened by the heating,—the pipes were first heated in a vertical pan, and then immersed in another containing the boiling liquid. They were sufficiently coated by being slowly let down by a travelling crane on a "gantry," and drawn up again. They had previously been subjected to hydraulic pressure in a proving press equal to a column of water 300 feet in height.

The smooth surface which resulted from the coating not only preserved *Increased discharge of pipes by coating.* the pipes for many years, but added materially to the volume of water which was discharged. When freshly done, the increase over the ordinary formulæ for calculating the quantity which a pipe would deliver, was equal to 40 or 50 per cent. Of course this increase was diminished when, after a time, corrosion inside took place; but pipes which had been laid for 18 years exhibited, when taken up, scarcely any signs of corrosion inside, and none whatever outside.

A recent examination of some of the 36-inch pipes, which were coated and have been laid for upwards of 30 years, showed that no corrosion had taken place inside in that time, but that the pipes were still as clean as when first laid down.

An interesting circumstance attended the introduction of soft water. *Mussels inside pipes. Effect of hard water.* The city was formerly supplied by water of great hardness,—that which was raised from the well at Gorton exceeded 20° according to Dr. Clark's scale. The stone pitching on the slopes of the Gorton reservoir, into which the water was admitted, was incrusted with myriads of small mussels *(Dreissena polymorpha)*, and the pipes which conveyed and delivered the water in Manchester were incrusted inside in the same way, thus practically diminishing the size of the pipe and retarding the flow of the water. The mussels no doubt derived the substance of which their shells were composed from the lime in the water, and it was matter of speculation what would become of them when water containing no lime was introduced from Longdendale and passed through the pipes. After a time, the mussels, no longer able to form shells, died, and were disengaged from the pipe, being carried by the current to the lower parts of the town and the ends of pipes. Pipes in such situations—and especially the smaller ones—were frequently found choked with dead mussels, and the water delivered varied in hardness from $1\frac{1}{2}$° to 7°. The harder water was no doubt attributable to the gradual absorption by the water of the shells of the mussels. This variation has long since disappeared, and the water delivered now is uniformly from 1° to 2° of hardness.

Dr. Smith subsequently sold his patent for coating pipes to various *Coating pipes.* ironfounders, who undertook to apply the process. It was, however, generally so imperfectly performed—the oiling having been neglected, and the varnish employed not always what it should be—that pipes professed to be coated for other works had frequently to be discarded, and subsequent experience has taught me to insist on the oiling previous to the coating.

The two operations of oiling and coating add from 5s. to 7s. 6d. per ton to the cost of the pipe, and the coating is of no use in the case of hard water, that is, in water of more than 4° or 5° of hardness, as hard water precipitates on the surface of the pipe an incrustation of lime, which eventually chokes up the pipe, and which takes place both on coated and uncoated pipes.

Turned and bored joints. Pipes up to 18 inches in diameter were chiefly united by what are known as "turned and bored joints." The first specifications for pipes described the ordinary joint of this description, which had at that time been used; but after the 40-inch main to Denton had been laid, and before the laying of the 36-inch from Denton to Manchester was commenced, the late Mr. Cochrane, of the Woodside ironworks, brought under my notice a joint which I at once adopted. Previous to this time, the "turned and bored joint" was faced for the whole depth of the socket, varying, according to the size of the pipe, from about 3 or $3\frac{1}{4}$ inches to 6 inches in depth. The joint, recommended by Mr. Cochrane, was faced for only $1\frac{1}{2}$ or 2 inches, on projecting parts both of the spigot and the socket; a space of about $2\frac{1}{2}$ or 3 inches in depth and $\frac{3}{8}$ of an inch in width being left for lead, in case the turned and bored joint should fail to be water-tight. The faced parts of the joint were generally smeared over with strong, quick-setting Roman cement; and the space to be subsequently filled with lead, in case of failure, was also filled with Roman cement. This joint has since then been generally adopted; but not only has the expense of the turning and boring been incurred, but the joint has also frequently been run with lead in the first instance, thus doing away with the economy of the turning and boring, and making the joint more expensive than need be.

Turned and bored joints—although the usual system for small pipes, which generally prevailed in the North of England—at the time of the commencement of the Manchester Waterworks had not been applied to pipes of large diameter, and I was considered a bold man to employ them for 18-inch pipes. Since then, the late Mr. Duncan used them for 30-inch pipes at Liverpool, and Mr. Gale, of Glasgow, to pipes of 48 inches diameter, with perfect success.

One great advantage of the system, besides its economy, is the greater rapidity with which pipes may be laid. This is frequently—especially in the crowded streets of a town—a matter of great importance. *Economy of turned and bored joints.*

There is a limit, however, to the economy of the turned and bored joint, the economy being principally experienced in pipes of small diameter. Take, for instance, a pipe of 6 inches diameter and 9 feet long. The ordinary weight of a pipe of this size is $2\frac{1}{4}$ cwt. The charge for turning and boring is generally about 5s. per ton. The cost per joint, therefore, for turning and boring, is $7\frac{1}{2}$d. If a wide socket for lead be used there is first introduced about $1\frac{1}{4}$ inches in depth of spun yarn. This is followed by lead for about $1\frac{3}{4}$ or 2 inches in depth, the weight of which, for a 6-inch pipe, will be 6 lbs., which, at 2d. per lb., amounts to 1s. The cost of the spun yarn will equal the cost of the cement, and the labour of "caulking" the lead will be much greater than the cost of filling the wide part of the joint with cement. Take again a pipe of 48 inches diameter. The ordinary weight of such a pipe 9 feet long and $1\frac{3}{8}$ inches thick is 3 tons. The cost of turning and boring, at 5s. per ton, will be 15s. per pipe; add the labour, and the joint will probably cost 16s. The cost of the yarn, lead, and labour for such a pipe with wide sockets will be not less than 20s. Therefore, though there is still an economy in large pipes, it is less in proportion than in smaller ones.

To get round corners or over undulating ground, "wide sockets" have to be employed, but these generally form a small proportion of the whole.

Another mode of joining the pipes was by an india-rubber ring,—the pipes being prepared for this purpose according to the sketch in the Appendix. *India-rubber joints.*

This plan was first tried and found successful at the Chorley waterworks; it was subsequently used to a small extent at the Manchester waterworks, and again at Glasgow and Wolverhampton,—at the former place in crossing some unstable bog land, with 36-inch pipes, and at the latter in crossing a coal field, where frequent subsidence of the ground took place,—in each place with great success.

Before the size of the piping for the city was determined, experiments were made upon an improved fire-cock. At the time of which I write, the old wooden plug, which was used for extracting water from the pipes for the extinction of fires, was a disgrace to the mechanical invention of the *Fire-cocks.*

age. It consisted of an upright orifice, into which a wooden plug was driven. When it was required to be used, this wooden plug was loosened by moving it backwards and forwards till it was blown out by the pressure of the water. A stand-pipe was then introduced into the opening, the fixing of which was often attended with difficulty, and invariably drenched the man to the skin whose business it was to attach it. When once in the aperture, it was held fast by wedges, generally secured to the casing or box of the plug. It was sometimes commanded by a branch with a stop-cock upon it, which was not opened till the stand-pipe was fixed in its place; but this was an expensive arrangement and frequently omitted. It was also the custom, as it still is in some places, to supply water at comparatively low pressure and by what is called the "intermittent system," a certain number of pipes only, or none, being constantly charged with water. This system is now happily exploded. In the case of Manchester, it was determined from the first to adopt the "constant system," and to have *all* the pipes constantly charged with water at high pressure.

The necessity of inventing something better and cheaper for the extinction of fires than then existed was seriously considered, and many valve-makers of the day were consulted with that view, but without any satisfactory solution of the difficulty. At that time I was engaged in the construction of waterworks at Warrington and Kendal. At the former place Mr. Alfred Moore was the resident engineer, and, partly from a suggestion of his, improved and rendered cheap and marketable by myself, the ball-valve was introduced, and subsequently manufactured to a large extent by Guest & Chrimes, of Rotherham, who have made many thousands of them. It consists of a ball, first made of wood covered with india-rubber, and afterwards of guttapercha, which is contained in a swelled part of the outlet and forced against the aperture by the pressure of the water, the space round the ball being equal in area to that of the opening. Into the mouth of the opening a stand-pipe is introduced and screwed tight under two lugs or ears. The ball is then depressed by a rod passing through a stuffing box in the top of the stand-pipe, with a hollow cup at the lower end to suit the rotundity of the ball, and the water released. To outlets near the top of the hollow stand-pipe fire-hose is attached, and the water directed by a man holding a jet to the burning premises. The whole operation can be performed in less time than it has taken to describe.

There was a trifling loss of pressure by the water passing the ball, but it was very inconsiderable, and was least in the form of fire-cock ultimately adopted; but the pressure in the pipe was, for many years, sufficient to throw the water over the highest building in Manchester.

The efficiency of the invention was first tried in Warrington and Kendal, and then introduced in Manchester. The centre of the city is occupied principally by warehouses of great value, frequently containing goods of still greater intrinsic worth.

It was, as already stated, wisely determined by the Corporation to adopt two rates within the borough to pay the interest of the outlay,—one called the "public rate," which was to be levied on *all* property, for the improvement which would attend the introduction of a good supply of water, constantly laid on at high pressure; and the other, called the "domestic rate," which was levied on houses only.

In hot climates it is probable that the ball-hydrant, as a fire-cock, will not answer, as the coating may be softened by heat, and indented by pressure against the iron orifice; but it possesses so many advantages, that wherever it can be used it should, in my opinion, be employed, and it may be that the covering of the ball, or the ball itself, may be made hard enough to resist all injury.

Air-valves. The ball-hydrant answers the purpose of an air-valve, as well as affording easy communication with the water in the pipe in the case of fire.

One of the most difficult operations in connection with the supply of water to a town is the safe discharge of the air which fills the pipes when empty. Every ball-hydrant acts as an air-valve, and when placed at the ends of pipes they act not only as air-valves but also as cleansing valves. As long as air only is discharged from the pipe, it will rush out at the various hydrants until it is followed by water, when the ball will rise and close the aperture against the further escape of either air or water.

In the case of what are commonly called "dead ends," that is, the end of a pipe beyond which water does not pass, there is frequently an accumulation of objectionable matter and of stagnant water, which may be discharged from the pipe by depressing the ball, in the same manner as when water is drawn for the extinction of fires.

By a modification of the principle of the ball-valve, a self-acting air-valve has been constructed, which, as far as I know, is the only self-acting air-valve in existence. Air accumulates in the upper bends of a pipe, which, if not discharged, will in many cases so fill the pipe as to obstruct the flow of water, and under such circumstances it becomes important to discharge the air. In a town this is of comparatively little importance, because every tap for the supply of domestic wants, or for other purposes, is in itself an air-valve; but in a long main, passing over an undulating country, where the pipe occasionally rises over the top of a hill which is not much below the level of the reservoir from which the water derives its pressure, it is important to discharge the air. Up to the time of the construction of the Manchester Waterworks, this had generally been accomplished by a cock placed on the summit of a pipe, opened by manual labour, and, of course, not always attended to.

By the introduction of the self-acting ball air-valve, all accumulations of air are at once discharged. The action is in this wise:—A very small opening for the discharge of the air under pressure is made in the top of a valve, in which is introduced a large ball which is heavier than air under pressure and lighter than water, so that, when air accumulates in the pipe, the ball will fall, and allow the air to escape, but will rise and close the opening when the water flows. Such valves have been introduced in every case where they appeared to be required, and they have always worked well and efficiently. (A drawing is given in the Appendix.)

In order to confer the greatest benefit on warehouses and other property subject to the "public rate," they were surrounded by hydrants for the extinction of fire, so arranged that should the water, from any reason, be shut off one pipe with which hydrants were connected, another would probably be in action, and one-half of the hydrants could be at once brought into play. Valuable blocks of buildings were ordinarily commanded by at least 50 hydrants in 100 yards. The great advantage which resulted from this ready and abundant supply of water for the extinction of fires is perhaps best attested by the change which has taken place in the destruction of property at risk.

The water was introduced into Manchester about the beginning of 1851, but it hardly got into full use till 1853. The old "intermittent" system had to be changed to the "constant system," and great care was taken in bringing this change about by dividing the city into districts, and seeing that each district was properly prepared for the change before it was actually made.

The percentage of property destroyed by fire from 1846 to 1850, before the introduction of the new water, was 21·3 per cent. of the value of property attacked; the amount saved was 78·6 per cent. From 1851 to 1855, the city having for about half the time the advantage of high pressure and constant supply, the percentage of property destroyed was 12·9 per cent., and of that saved, 87 per cent. Then came the full advantage of the constant supply and high pressure with a full water supply, and from 1856 to 1860 the percentage destroyed was only 7·7 per cent., being only one-third of the amount which was destroyed before the introduction of the new supply, and the amount of property saved was 92·2 per cent. From 1861 to 1865, the amount destroyed was 6·7 per cent., and the amount saved 93·2 per cent. From a recent return it appears that the percentage of property destroyed of that which was at risk was only 3·4 per cent., the years 1877 and 1878 being under 2 per cent.

The population of the city, and of the places dependent on the Manchester Corporation for a supply of water, is now about 900,000; and the pressure, which was at first abundant, became gradually diminished till new mains were laid, which restored it to full efficiency.

Streets which were formerly cottages, or small houses of two storys in height, have been converted into streets of warehouses, four or five times as high as the buildings destroyed.

In 1862, when the British Association met in Manchester, under the presidency of the late Sir William Fairbairn, experiments were made on the height to which water could be thrown from the street, with the following result:—Jets of ¾-inch diameter were attached to 75 feet of hose, of 3 inches diameter, which threw the water to heights varying from 52 feet to 104 feet, being generally from one-half to two-thirds of the height due to the pressure in the pipe from which the water was taken,— the pressure being indicated by a gauge at the point of experiment.

In February, 1852, the works in Longdendale were subjected to a severe trial, which is recorded in the following paper contributed at the time to the Manchester Literary and Philosophical Society, and published

Flood of February, 1852.

in the tenth volume of the Memoirs of that Society for the session 1851 and 1852:—

"Some account of the floods which occurred at the Manchester Waterworks in the month of February, 1852, by JOHN FREDERIC BATEMAN, F.G.S., Mem. Inst. C.E. (*Read March 23rd, 1852.*)

"In the year 1848, in giving to the Society a continuation of the periodical reports upon the fall of rain, the valley of Longdendale, from which the town of Manchester is to be supplied with water, was shortly described; and such observations as had at that time been made upon the rain in the district, and the quantity of water which flowed from the ground, also accompanied the paper.

"Since that period, most of the observations upon the fall of rain have been continued, and the vast works for the storage and conveyance of water, which were then only in contemplation, have been in great measure executed, and are now rapidly advancing towards completion.

"In the main valley of the Longdendale district, down which flows the river Etherow, three large reservoirs are now constructing, filling the valley for nearly five miles in length. These three reservoirs will contain, when finished, about 516,000,000 cubic feet of water, and will cover about 344 statute acres of ground. The Woodhead reservoir, which is the highest of the series, is formed by an embankment of 90 feet; it is about a mile and two-thirds in length, and receives the water naturally draining from about 7,500 acres of high mountain land. The Torside reservoir—the middle one and the largest of the three—with an embankment of 100 feet in height, and the Rhodes Wood reservoir, immediately below, with an 80 feet bank, have together an additional collecting ground of about 7,900 acres, making the total drainage to these three reservoirs 15,400 statute acres. The Torside reservoir is nearly two miles in length, and the Rhodes Wood reservoir about a mile.

"The following are some particulars of the reservoirs:—

Reservoir.	Embankment.		Reservoir.		
	Greatest height.	Contents.	Area.		Capacity.
	Feet.	Cubic yards.	A.	R. P.	Cubic feet.
Woodhead	90	152,707	134	8 18	198,725,698
Torside	100	399,129	160	0 6	236,659,578
Rhodes Wood	80	263,248	54	0 34	80,255,910
		815,084	349	0 18	515,641,176

"In the execution of works of this magnitude, placed across a valley down which the ordinary water and impetuous floods of so large a tract of mountain land are hurried with rapidity, it is very important to provide ample means for the safe passage of the water. Observations had accordingly been made with reference to this particular object for some years previous to the laying out of the works. From these observations it appeared that it was not likely that many floods would exceed 10 feet per second from every 100 acres of collecting ground, and that provision for 15 feet per second would be ample. The Woodhead reservoir was the first which was laid out for construction, and in designing the side channels or watercourses for carrying away the floods during the early progress of the embankment across the river, they were formed of such dimensions as would, with the assistance of a large discharge pipe under the embankment, pass off safely about 1,000 cubic feet of water per second, being at the rate of about 15 feet per second for every 100 acres.

"The ground was first broken for the construction of this reservoir in September, 1848; and in the following month, before much progress had been made, a very heavy flood occurred in the neighbourhood of Blackburn, which was the cause of a lamentable accident at Darwen, near that town, by the bursting of a private reservoir, and the consequent loss of twelve or thirteen lives. The volume of this flood I was enabled to determine with tolerable approximation to accuracy, by means of the reservoirs of the Blackburn waterworks, which were then just completed. It exceeded 25 feet per second for every 100 acres of collecting ground. Had a similar heavy fall of rain occurred in the upper part of the Longdendale district, it would have produced a flood of about 2,000 cubic feet per second at the Woodhead reservoir—nearly double the volume which had been provided for.

"Acting upon the experience and information thus acquired, an additional discharge pipe was immediately introduced, and the flood watercourse was enlarged as far as practicable, so that a flood of 1,500 feet per second could be passed with safety, with 16 feet of pressure upon the pipes. As the embankment gradually exceeded that height in the course of construction, the means of storage behind the bank would be increased; and by the greater pressure upon the pipes, more water also could be discharged, and in these ways provision would be made for the safe passage of a still larger quantity. On several occasions, in the course of the following eight or ten months, the floods amounted to 1,800 or 2,000 feet per second, showing the wisdom, and, indeed, the necessity of such a provision having been made.

"Early in October, 1849, just twelve months after the Blackburn flood, which had afforded such valuable information, the flood watercourse having been completed, the discharge pipes laid, and every arrangement made for proceeding with the embankment of the reservoir, the inner toe of that bank was raised to a height of about 16 feet, so as to give that amount of pressure on the discharge pipes in case of necessity. On the 7th, a very heavy fall of rain, accompanied by a hurricane from the north-east, occasioned a flood which set at nought all previous calculations; when at its highest, it amounted to upwards of 4,000 cubic feet per second, being at the rate of upwards of 50 feet per second for every 100 acres. After attaining this height, it flowed for the following three hours at an average of 1,800 feet per second. A weir on the watercourse across the Heyden brook, which was not quite finished, but which had been considered sufficiently so to secure the safe passage of the water, was absolutely beaten down by the force of wind and water; and a breach being made, through which the water passed, the watercourse was thus rendered useless. The water poured into the basin of the reservoir, and speedily overtopped the newly-formed piece of embankment. It had been raised to a height of 24 feet, and was raised 3 feet more during the progress of the flood, so that when the water reached the top it was 27 feet high. The bank was not long in being cut down, and a quantity of water, amounting to about 14,000,000 cubic feet, was at once set at liberty. For a short distance it carried all before it, and did more or less damage for four or five miles down the river. No serious mischief, however, was sustained, and happily no lives were lost. The quantity of water which was impounded at the time of the accident was about equal to that contained in the unfortunate Bilberry reservoir, near Holmfirth, which burst on the 5th of February, and did such fearful injury in the valley below. The difference in the circumstances of the two cases easily accounts for the difference in the two results. The depth of the water in the Bilberry reservoir was about 80 feet; at Woodhead it was 27 feet only. The embankment of the Bilberry reservoir, owing to its peculiar construction, gave way in a great mass at once, and the valley into which this mighty wall of waters was instantaneously hurled is a steep and narrow ravine, down which the water would continue to flow with impetuous velocity. The Woodhead valley, on the contrary, has a much more gentle slope, and is much wider throughout, occasionally expanding into level flats of considerable width; consequently the velocity of the water would be speedily diminished, and its volume absorbed by filling up the flat ground on each side. The damage was comparatively trifling, being all repaired or compensated for by the payment of little more than £2,000.

"The embankment was restored, and no further flood of any consequence occurred until the work was far advanced. The remaining reservoirs in the valley had been some time previously laid out and commenced, and abundant provision had been made at these new reservoirs for the passage of the floods.

"Of the various rain-gauges which are placed in the district, one only is registered daily, viz., that at Crowden Hall, the others being placed on the heights in somewhat inaccessible situations, and only observed weekly or monthly.

"The quantity of water which was received into the Woodhead reservoir, or passed by the flood watercourse, on the occasion of the flood alluded to, must have exceeded 3 inches in the 24 hours, or rather in the 17 or 18 hours during which the rain fell most heavily, and yet the depth registered at Crowden Hall was only $1\frac{4}{10}$ inch. Crowden Hall is about two-thirds of a mile below the Woodhead embankment, and the heaviest portion of the rain must, therefore, have been on the hills above the reservoir. At the Redmires reservoir of the Sheffield waterworks, on the same day, there were registered nearly $2\frac{1}{4}$ inches. The distance from Woodhead, in a direct line south-east, is $13\frac{1}{4}$ miles.

"The fall of rain in 1849 was about an average, there being at Crowden Hall $54\frac{4}{10}$ inches; 1850 was considerably below the average, the rain being only $44\frac{4}{10}$; and, singularly enough, almost the only heavy flood which occurred in the course of the year was on the 7th and 8th October, the anniversary of the destructive flood of the previous year, and (within a few days) of the Blackburn flood of 1848. The year 1851 was still more below the average, the rain at Crowden being only $40\frac{4}{10}$ inches. In this year the only heavy flood occurred about the 8th and 9th June.

"The fall of rain, as registered at the various rain gauges in the district since the end of 1847, up to which time they are recorded in my last paper to the society, is as follows:—

1848.	Brushes, 480 feet.	Windyate Edge, 1,700 feet.	Crowden Hall, 700 feet.	Rakes Moss, 1,620 feet.	Butterley Moss, 1,750 feet.	Mean of all the Observations.	Mean omitting Brushes.
	Inches.	Inches.	Inches.	Inches.	Inches.	Inches.	Inches.
January	2·0	1·7	1·1	...	1·6	1·6	1·5
February	8·0	9·2	8·2	...	10·1	8·9	9·2
March	4·7	4·4	5·5	...	4·9	4·9	4·9
April	1·5	2·1	2·6	...	2·9	2·3	2·5
May	1·2	1·8	1·0	2·1	1·0	1·4	1·5
June	5·3	6·1	6·8	7·0	6·2	6·3	6·5
July	4·2	4·2	4·6	4·4	2·4	4·0	3·9
August	5·8	7·5	7·0	7·8	5·8	6·8	7·0
September	4·2	5·4	4·3	5·1	3·4	4·5	4·5
October	5·8	8·3	8·0	6·0	7·5	7·1	7·5
November	2·6	3·2	3·1	4·0	2·3	3·0	3·1
December	3·6	3·8	3·7	2·8	3·7	3·5	3·5
Total	48·9	57·7	55·9	...	51·8	52·8	55·1

1849.	Brushes, 480 feet.	Windyate Edge, 1,700 feet.	Crowden Hall, 700 feet.	Black Clough, 1,700 feet.	Butterley Moss, 1,750 feet.	Mean of all the observations.	Mean omitting Brushes.
	Inches.	Inches.	Inches.	Inches.	Inches.	Inches.	Inches.
January	5·8	6·8	8·2	6·0	...	6·4	6·8
February	1·5	2·4	2·4	2·0	...	2·1	2·3
March	0·6	1·0	1·5	2·0	...	1·3	1·5
April	1·4	2·5	3·0	3·0	...	2·5	2·8
May	3·0	3·4	2·8	2·5	...	2·9	2·9
June	1·8	2·1	1·7	3·0	...	2·2	2·3
July	7·5	8·8	7·8	6·1	...	7·5	7·5
August	4·2	4·5	5·4	4·0	...	4·5	4·6
September	4·8	6·4	4·7	6·3	...	5·5	5·8
October	4·1	6·3	7·0	8·7	...	6·5	7·3
November	4·7	5·3	5·1	4·0	...	4·9	5·0
December	3·3	4·7	5·1	4·6	...	4·6	4·8
Total	42·7	54·2	54·7	52·2	...	50·9	53·6

1850.	Brushes, 480 feet.	Windyate Edge, 1,700 feet.	Crowden Hall, 700 feet.	Black Clough, 1,700 feet.	Butterley Moss, 1,750 feet.	Mean of all the observations.	Mean omitting Brushes.
	Inches.	Inches.	Inches.	Inches.	Inches.	Inches.	Inches.
January	2·9	4·5	3·3	4·2	2·3	3·6	3·3
February	3·4	5·0	4·4	4·6	2·8	4·0	4·2
March	0·6	0·8	1·1	3·5	0·7	1·3	1·5
April	2·4	3·5	4·0	4·0	3·0	3·4	3·6
May	1·5	2·1	2·0	1·5	1·2	1·7	1·7
June	1·5	2·9	3·4	3·5	2·8	2·7	3·0
July	3·7	5·5	4.8	7·9	4·1	5·2	5·6
August	4·0	6·6	3·2	5·9	3·0	4·5	4·7
September	1·5	2·6	1·3	0·7	1·2	1·6	1·6
October	3·6	6·4	6·5	5·5	4·0	5·2	5·6
November	4·3	7·7	7·3	7·5	3·0	6·1	6·5
December	2·4	2·9	1·3	4·0	3·4	2·8	2·9
Total	31·8	50·5	44·1	52·7	31·5	42·1	44·7

1851.	Brushes, 480 feet.	Windyate Edge, 1,700 feet.	Crowden Hall, 700 feet.	Black Clough, 1,700 feet.	Butterley Moss, 1,750 feet.	Mean of all the observations.	Mean omitting Brushes.
	Inches.	Inches.	Inches.	Inches.	Inches.	Inches.	Inches.
January	2·9	3·1	2·5	3·8	4·3	3·3	3·4
February	2·1	2·2	3·0	2·5	2·6	2·5	2·8
March	3·6	3·7	4·1	4·5	2·9	3·8	3·8
April	0·4	1·5	1·8	2·8	1·9	1·7	2·0
May	1·5	1·9	3·0	3·5	3·2	2·6	2·9
June	5·8	6·6	6·8	5·9	6·0	6·1	6·2
July	3·7	4·6	3·8	1·4	4·7	3·6	3·6
August	4·1	4·2	4·2	5·3	3·4	4·2	4·2
September	1·8	1·9	3·0	2·6	2·5	2·4	2·5
October	3·6	4·6	4·9	4·0	5·3	4·5	4·7
November	1·6	1·6	2·7	3·2	1·6	2·1	2·2
December	1·5	2·3	0·8	1·5	1·4	1·5	1·5
Total	32·6	38·2	40·1	41·0	39·8	38·3	39·8

"Many of the mountain gauges have been stolen, removed, or tampered with; and I am afraid that the only ones upon which much dependence can be placed are those at Brushes, Windyate Edge, and Crowden Hall. When the works are completed, the reservoirs themselves will be the best gauges.

"Before giving the particulars of the floods which occurred in the early part of last month, it will be well to describe the position of the reservoirs, and the means which they afforded of ascertaining with accuracy the quantity of water which was received. It has hitherto seldom or perhaps never happened, that a single heavy flood or fall of rain has been so accurately observed; this fact is my apology for endeavouring to place the particulars on record.

"In the early progress of the formation of the embankments, provision was made at each reservoir for the passage of the floods by the construction of a capacious cut or canal, called a flood-watercourse, above the level of the reservoirs, as already described. This provision was adopted and employed for the purpose intended both at the Woodhead and Torside reservoirs, until the embankments at each place were advanced to a height at which it was deemed safe to dispense with the aid of the watercourses, and to depend for safety upon the storage which the reservoirs afforded, and the means of discharge provided by the two lines of 4-feet pipes which had been introduced in all the embankments. It was necessary, also, as the work advanced, to cut across or destroy the watercourses for the purpose of completing what are technically called puddle trenches, which are deep trenches of retentive material, sunk for the reception of the clay or puddle employed to render the whole watertight. The permanent waste weirs of the reservoirs also had to be constructed on the site of the flood water-channels, for which purpose likewise they had to be dispensed with.

"The Rhodes Wood reservoir, the lowest of the three, would have been similarly provided with a bye-channel for the waste water, but delay had unavoidably arisen by the channel having to be formed over an ancient landslip. This landslip was well known, and had been long moving slowly. At the turnpike road on the north side of the valley it had moved about three feet in thirteen years; but the speed of its motion was materially increased on being cut into for the purpose of forming the watercourse. Means had to be resorted to for arresting its further progress, and the work was consequently so much delayed that this watercourse is not yet completed.

"Ample provision, however, for the passage of the floods at the Rhodes Wood reservoir was made by leaving a gap in the embankment, which remained open until the two higher reservoirs were so far advanced as to be able to hold all the water which could not be passed through the two pipes of the Rhodes Wood bank. The gap in this embankment was then closed, and the embankment raised as rapidly as possible.

"This step, however, was not taken—nor, indeed, any other which involved the necessity of subsequently depending upon the power of impounding in the reservoirs for security against damage by floods—without first considering what depth of rain could be safely stored in the reservoirs or passed through the pipes.

"Three inches of rain coming off the ground in 24 hours, with a considerable margin for its continuance, or for a heavier fall, was adopted as the base of our calculations, being considered as the maximum amount which need be provided for. This quantity the works were always in a condition to receive and pass with safety. It was thought from previous observation, that it was exceedingly unlikely that a larger fall of rain than this could occur over the whole district, and it was expected that should such a fall take place, the rain would then cease, and the reservoirs might be emptied for the reception of another flood.

"Such, then, being the provision which had been made, and the grounds for believing such provision to be sufficient, the position of the reservoirs at the commencement of the late floods was as follows:—

"The Woodhead embankment was raised to its full height, but it was not deemed prudent to fill the reservoir above a certain level, in consequence of operations which were going on to render the hill-side, into which the embankment had to be tied, perfectly water-tight.

"The Torside embankment was far advanced; but here also operations were being carried on to render the reservoir water-tight, which rendered it undesirable to impound water to a greater depth than about 30 feet.

"At Rhodes Wood reservoir, which, it will be remembered, is the lowest in the valley, the embankment was sufficiently advanced to allow water to be impounded 40 feet in depth. Through the pipes of this reservoir *all* the water had to be passed, and therefore, by calculating the quantity which could be discharged through them according as the pressure varied during the progress of the flood, the whole quantity could be precisely ascertained.

"It is well known that the velocity with which water is discharged through pipes, or through apertures, varies as the square root of the pressure or head of water above the opening.

"The proper co-efficient for finding the mean velocity of the water discharged, varies according to the character of the opening.

"The theoretical velocity due to the height, is the same as that of falling bodies, which is ascertained by multiplying the square root of the height by the co-efficient 8·0458.

"The co-efficient, however, for finding the actual velocity, varies from 5 to 7; that generally used for ordinary openings being from 5·1 to 5·4.

"Should the water approach the opening with any velocity, that must be taken into account, and a higher co-efficient employed.

"To determine the quantity which will be discharged through pipes, different formulæ have to be employed, for the friction along the sides of the pipe forms a material element in retarding the velocity of the water. Amongst many valuable rules deduced from the experiments of various eminent mathematicians and scientific observers, probably the simplest for calculating this velocity, and, perhaps, that most generally adopted, is one by Dr. Young, from Eytelwein's Hydraulics, and is as follows:—'Multiply 2,500 times the diameter of the pipe in feet by the height in feet, and divide the product by the length in feet, added to 50 times the diameter; then the square root of the quotient will be the velocity of discharge in feet per second.'

"This rule is a tolerably safe one in practice. I believe it to be under the truth for large pipes and high velocities; and it requires to be used with judgment in determining the discharge by small pipes where the system is complex.

"The circumstances under which the water was discharged from the Rhodes Wood reservoir were so far complicated as to render the determination of the proper co-efficient a question of some difficulty.

"Two pipes, each 4 feet in diameter and 803 and 870 feet respectively in length, were diminished at the outer end to 3 feet, the water being finally passed through a pipe of that diameter for about 20 feet in length, and through a 3-feet valve divided into two compartments. One pipe branched into two at the end, having a valve on each branch, and through both of which water was discharged. The pipe is too large and the circumstances too complex to admit of the application of the rule for calculating the discharge through pipes. The water would approach the opening with considerable velocity, acquired in its passage through the 4-feet pipe; and, therefore, rather a higher co-efficient than that usually employed for finding the velocity through openings should be adopted. From a consideration of all these circumstances, and from other observations upon the actual quantity of water discharged, the co-efficient adopted was 5·5; and this may be rather lower than it ought to be.

"With this co-efficient, however, the calculations came out, as will be shortly shown.

"The month of January had been marked by a considerable fall of rain, and at the end of the month the ground was thoroughly saturated, the streams and springs yielding considerably above their ordinary quantity of water. The heavy rain, which was the cause of so many serious and destructive floods, commenced on the morning of Wednesday, the 4th of February, and, with slight cessation on Friday and Saturday, continued with little intermission till the morning of Monday, the 9th.

"On the morning of the 4th, the Woodhead reservoir contained about 24,000,000 cubic feet of water, being about 34 feet deep and 47 feet below the top water level. The Torside and Rhodes Wood reservoirs were both empty. Early in the day the rain had so swollen the streams that the discharge pipes could no longer pass the water, and it began to impound rapidly in all the reservoirs. By Thursday night the water had attained its greatest height, the depth in the Woodhead reservoir being about 62 feet, and in the Torside and Rhodes Wood reservoirs about 30 feet. The quantity impounded was about 103,000,000 cubic feet in the Woodhead Reservoir, 14,000,000 in Torside, and 15,000,000 cubic feet in Rhodes Wood reservoir.

"From Thursday night the water gradually lowered till Saturday night, by which time the water had been drawn down about 9 feet in the Woodhead reservoir, and about 5 feet on the average in each of the others. The quantity discharged through the pipes of the Rhodes Wood reservoir during this period had averaged from 450 to 500 cubic feet per second. For 24 hours together—from Wednesday morning to Thursday morning—the flood had averaged 1,520 cubic feet per second, being, when at its highest, from 3,600 to 4,000 feet per second. This was from a tract of country, it will be remembered, of 15,400 statute acres, and amounts to about 25 cubic feet per second from every 100 acres of ground. The ordinary flow of the stream varies from 15 to 80 feet per second. The water which was passed through the pipes, or was impounded in the reservoirs during this period, was equal to a depth over the whole collecting ground of $2\frac{1}{5}$ inches.

"On Saturday night it again commenced raining heavily, and continued until two o'clock on Sunday afternoon. At this time the rain ceased for a couple of hours, but the streams were swollen to a volume of nearly 8,000 cubic feet per second, while the utmost that could be discharged through the pipes of the Rhodes Wood reservoir was under 600 feet per second. At four o'clock it again commenced raining with the same intensity as before, with every appearance of its continuing through the night. At this moment the prospect was one of great anxiety. Thousands of persons, alarmed by the dreadful catastrophe at Holmfirth, had passed up the valley in the course of the day, in all the pouring rain, to visit the scene of that calamity; or had assembled on the banks of the waterworks reservoirs, anxiously watching the progress of the flood, and waiting to see the final burst which the majority anticipated. Towards the evening, vehicles of all kinds, and horsemen at full gallop, despatched by anxious parties below to make inquiries, were constantly arriving; and, indeed, to the Engineer,—confident in the stability of his work, and in the provision which had been made for the safe passage of the waters,—it was matter of no light concern or slight responsibility. There remained only six or seven hours safe storage for such rain as was at that moment falling; after the expiration of which time, the valves of the Woodhead reservoir must have been opened to prevent the further rise of water in that reservoir, and the water allowed to pass over the puddle of the Torside bank, through a mass of rock which had been heaped together in the formation of the bank with a view to such a contingency, and over the top of the Rhodes Wood bank, through a large timber shoot, which had been hastily but substantially prepared during the progress of the flood, for the purpose of safely passing the water to the river below.

"In all probability these preparations would have been sufficient to have sustained a flood of one or two days longer continuance; but they must have been put to the test in the middle of the night, in extreme darkness, when it would have been impossible to have seen what was going on, or how to meet or remedy any defect which might have occurred. The work of destruction, at the worst, would have been very slow and gradual, from the excellent manner in which the embankment had been formed, and the retentive and coherent character of the great bulk of the material. Happily, there was no occasion for the trial. The sun went down red and glowing with a murky grandeur, dimly seen beneath the clouds, which, though breaking and clearing to the west, were then pouring down their contents in torrents at the place at which we stood. The rain gradually abated, and nearly ceased before six o'clock, and I was satisfied that the worst was over, and that all imminent danger was passed.

"Heavy flying showers continued through the night; but at daybreak the following morning it appeared to be again setting in for continued rain. The wind up to this time, during the whole storm, had been blowing steadily from the south-west, but it now gradually veered round to the north, and I then felt perfect confidence that the weather was taking up, notwithstanding the lowering and gloomy appearance of the morning. The rain subsequently ceased before noon, and by the end of the week the weather was quite settled and fine, the barometer gradually rising, and then remaining steadily fixed at an unusual height.

"The water which was impounded in the reservoirs when the rain ceased on the morning of Monday, the 9th, was about 160,000,000 cubic feet, of which nearly 140,000,000 were due to the rains of the previous week. By noon of the 13th the whole of this water had been discharged, and the reservoirs brought down to the same condition in which they were on the morning of the 3rd, when the rain commenced. The quantity discharged through the pipes of the Rhodes Wood reservoir, through which, as has been before observed, the whole had to be passed, was as follows:—

	Cubic feet.
"From 9-0 o'clock on the morning of the 4th, to 2-0 p.m. same day, 5 hours, at 300 feet per second	5,400,000
"From 2 0 p.m. to 12 0 p.m., 400 feet per second for 10 hours	14,002,000
"From 12-0 p.m., 4th, to 9-0 a.m., 5th, 450 per second for 9 hours	14,580,000
"From 9-0 a.m., 5th, to 7-0 p.m., 7th, 58 hours, at 450 feet per second	93,960,000
"From 7-0 p.m., 7th, to 7-0 p.m., 8th, mean discharge 500 feet per second, 24 hours	21,600,000
"From 7-0 p.m., 8th, to noon, 12th, 89 hours, at 550 feet per second	176,220,000
"From noon, 12th, to noon, 13th, 24 hours, at 450 feet per second	38,880,000
Total	365,472,000

"The quantity of water discharged was equal to a depth of $6\frac{1}{4}$ inches over the whole surface of the collecting ground, averaging nearly $1\frac{1}{4}$ inch per day for the $5\frac{1}{2}$ days during which the rain lasted.

"The rain at Crowden Hall, from the evening of the 3rd to noon on the 9th,—subsequently to which no material fall of rain occurred during the period that the reservoirs were being emptied,—was $5\frac{1}{10}$ inches. To determine the precise quantity of water due to the fall of rain, something must be deducted for the yield of the streams, supposing no rain had fallen. Their average volume, swollen as they were by previous rain, would have been about 60 cubic feet per second, which, for 9 days and 8 hours, would have amounted to 59,804,000 cubic feet, equal to about an inch in depth over the collecting ground, leaving the nett quantity of water due to the rain $5\frac{1}{4}$ inches, being $\frac{1}{10}$ of an inch more than the rain shown by the Crowden Hall rain gauge.

"The results just given from calculations upon the discharge through the pipes, I believe to be very near the truth—rather under than over; but the Woodhead reservoir afforded means for still more accurate observation. Here nearly all the water which reached the reservoir was impounded; and, as the capacity of each reservoir had been previously ascertained by careful survey and measurement, for every foot in depth, there can be no doubt as to the quantity of water received.

"From eleven o'clock on the morning of the 4th, till twelve o'clock at midnight on the 5th—a period of 37 hours—the quantity of water impounded in the reservoir was 75,720,000 cubic feet, and the quantity discharged 12,168,000; making the total quantity received 87,888,000 cubic feet,— $3\frac{1}{4}$ inches of rain over the drainage ground of the reservoir.

"From eleven o'clock on the morning of the 4th, to the same hour on the morning of the 5th, the quantity impounded was 62,000,000 cubic feet, and the quantity discharged 3,528,000, making the total quantity received in 24 hours, from 7,500 acres of ground, 65,528,000 cubic feet, being equal to $2\frac{4}{10}$ inches of rain. The rain at Crowden during this period appears to have been $2\frac{1}{10}$. To allow for the water which still remained to flow off the ground before the streams would regain their usual volume, we must add $\frac{1}{10}$ of an inch (after allowing for the natural flow), making the total quantity of rain which fell in 24 hours, as measured by the Woodhead reservoir, $2\frac{4}{10}$ inches.

"The rain which was discharged at Rhodes Wood, or impounded in that reservoir and Torside in the same time, exclusive of what was received from Woodhead, amounted to about 66,000,000 cubic feet of water from 7,900 acres, being as nearly as may be, the same quantity per acre as that received at Woodhead. The calculations may, therefore, be taken to show accurately the quantity of water which flowed down the river during this extraordinary rain; showing also, that the average rain over the district, taking the whole period, must have been 9 or 10 per cent. greater than the quantity received by the Crowden Hall rain-gauge.

"The rain in the district from the commencement of the year to the 9th of February, as indicated by the several rain-gauges, is as follows:—

	January.	February, to 9th.
At Crowden Hall	5 inches.	$6\frac{1}{4}$ inches.
" Butterley Moss	$5\frac{1}{10}$ "	$6\frac{1}{10}$ "
		$= 11\frac{1}{4}$ inches.
" Black Clough	$10\frac{1}{10}$ inches.	
" Brushes	$8\frac{1}{10}$ "	to 8th February.
" Windyate Edge	$8\frac{6}{10}$ "	"

"The following table will exhibit the daily quantities during the first nine days of February:—

	Inches.
Sunday, 1st	0·5
Monday, 2nd	0·4
Tuesday, 3rd	0·5
Wednesday, 4th	1·1
Thursday, 5th	1·2
Friday, 6th	0·8
Saturday, 7th	0·2
Sunday, 8th *	1·3
Monday, 9th †	0·5
	6·5

On the night of Thursday, the 5th, between 4·0 p.m. and 8·0 a.m. of the 6th, there fell 0·7 of an inch of rain.

"The quantity of water which flowed from the whole collecting ground of the waterworks—about 18,900 acres in extent—between the 1st of January and the 9th of February, exceeded 800,000,000 cubic feet; being nearly 200,000,000 cubic feet more than sufficient to fill all the waterworks reservoirs had they been empty on New Year's Day, although their capacity is equal to 32,400 cubic feet for every acre of collecting ground.

"No damage of any consequence was sustained by any portion of the works from the effect of the flood. Their efficiency was well tested and satisfactorily proved; but the heavy rain, penetrating into some ancient landslips on the north side of the valley, near the Rhodes Wood embankment, but above its level, set a mass of about 40 acres in extent in motion, which disturbed a quantity of masonry, and otherwise deranged the scheme at the spot at which it occurred. The security of the reservoir is not affected; but it will be a work of time and skill to arrest or obviate the effects of this sliding mass."

---

* This was between 4·0 p.m. on Saturday and 4·0 p.m. on Sunday.
† This was from 4·0 p.m. on Sunday to 12·0 at noon on Monday.

Some remarks of the Editor of the "Manchester Guardian" newspaper, who published an account of these floods, may be interesting:—

"'The reservoirs of the Manchester Corporation Waterworks in the valley of Longdendale, which stood admirably the great floods of Wednesday and Thursday in last week, had a yet severer test in the continued heavy rains of the three following days, till on Sunday some of the reservoirs were within seven hours (supposing the rain had continued to fall in equal quantity during the whole of that time) of being brim-full; and there was consequently considerable anxiety on the subject, especially amongst the millowners and other inhabitants of the valley within a little distance of and below the three great reservoirs of these works. This anxiety was of course greater than would otherwise have been the case, from the vivid remembrance of the recent horrors attending the bursting of the Bilbury reservoir, near Holmfirth, in Yorkshire; though there is no analogy in the nature and character of the works to warrant any apprehension of the one because the other had failed, as for years past all conversant with it had expected it to do. In order to enable our more distant readers to comprehend the general character and vast extent of the Manchester Corporation Waterworks, and the circumstances which led to their position on Sunday last, we must enter a little into detail.

"'Though in two instances, perhaps,—one in Scotland and one in Ireland,—there are single reservoirs larger than any of those of the Corporation waterworks, yet, taken as a connected series or chain of artificial lakes, constructed for the storage of water, those in the Longdendale valley have the largest aggregate capacity of any artificial sheets of water in the world. The great Croton waterworks, which supply the city of New York with water, give a daily supply of 35,000,000 gallons. The Manchester Corporation waterworks, including the 17,000,000 gallons with which they are bound by their Act to supply the millowners on the streams, before they can send a gallon to Manchester, will yield a daily supply of 45,000,000 gallons, or 10,000,000 gallons daily more than the Croton waterworks. This will give some idea of the extent of the Corporation waterworks, which collect the rain from a drainage area of some 18,900 statute acres, or $29\frac{1}{2}$ square miles of high ground, amidst the moors and mosses of the Pennine hills.'"

"We learn that on Wednesday and Thursday, the 4th and 5th instant" (February, 1852), "flood water to the extent of 2·4 inches in the 24 hours was safely passed or impounded in the reservoirs, with a considerable space still remaining for storing additional water. But before the stored water could be discharged from the reservoirs, a succession of other floods—especially during Saturday night and Sunday last—nearly exhausted the storage powers of the reservoirs; and on the evening of Sunday, the 8th, there remained provision only for the safe passage of heavy rain (which had then been continuing for some time) for a further period of six or seven hours. With some amount of risk, though probably not very great, the continuance of rain for even 24 hours might have been provided for. Under these circumstances, however, the excitement of the millowners and residents in the valley below the reservoirs, became very great during Sunday, stimulated, of course, by the recent catastrophe at Holmfirth; so that the whole valley was thronged by persons, many of whom came from some distance, notwithstanding the heavy, continuous, and beating rains, to see the reservoirs, examine into their state, and speculate as to the possibility of some of their embankments giving way. A little inn, which, from its usual quietness and loneliness, has for its sign "The Quiet Shepherd," was thronged from morning till night with people seeking shelter and refreshment; its stable and outbuildings were filled with guests, and the utmost excitement prevailed. On Sunday morning the rain continued to fall heavily from an early hour till about 2-0 o'clock p.m., without intermission. There was then a lull for nearly two hours, when it again commenced raining as heavily as ever, with a prospect of continuing during the night. Under these circumstances, Mr. Bateman, who had been on the spot almost constantly from the morning of Thursday last, feeling the very great and solemn responsibility that would attach to him in case of any accident, even of a trifling nature, occurring to an embankment, without any notice to the inhabitants below, thought it prudent, about half-past three o'clock on Sunday afternoon, to dispatch messengers to the parties immediately on the river, for some distance below the reservoirs, stating that, should it continue to rain heavily all night, some danger might be apprehended after the lapse of six or seven hours, and that it would therefore be prudent for them to prepare for the possibility of such a contingency. Of course this intimation spread great alarm throughout the valley, and the most vigorous efforts were made by some of the millowners and others to remove valuable property without delay; the occupants of cottages and other dwellings along the stream also hastily removed their furniture to the houses of relatives and friends at some distance from the course of the stream. Throughout the little village of Valehouse, the inhabitants were thrown into a state of the utmost consternation; for in the event of the bursting of the embankment, a large number of the houses must have been swept away. Some houses at Bottom's mill would also have been in imminent danger, as would others occupied by operatives employed by Messrs. Sidebottom, at Waterside mill; all these removed their furniture. Mr. H. Lees, who resides between five and six miles below Torside, had several carts and wagons constantly engaged for several hours in removing his household and other property. At Glossop the alarm was very general, and much damage was done to furniture during its hasty removal.

"Fortunately, however, for all concerned, in the course of rather more than an hour after this intimation had been given by Mr. Bateman, the weather cleared up; and as it promised well for the remainder of the night, and as the heavy flow of water during this interval had materially abated, he felt so confident of the perfect security of the works, that he dispatched other messengers, about half-past five p.m., to reassure the inhabitants, and to prevent or allay all unnecessary apprehension and alarm. The weather continued fine; the streams abated; and on Monday afternoon, the water within the reservoirs had been considerably diminished in quantity by the action of the discharge pipes.

"From what we have stated, we think it will be understood that an occasional flood of three inches or more in the 24 hours would be a matter of very little consequence, inasmuch as it could always be passed off in perfect safety. But a rapid succession of floods—one occurring before the effects of the previous one had ceased—must occasion such an accumulation of water in the reservoirs, that after a certain period they would no longer be able to hold any additional water, without running some risk, in the present unfinished state of the embankments and other works. The rains of last week and of Sunday were of this description, and the result was a constant succession of heavy floods, such as no previous calculation could have provided for; but the result has been most satisfactory, as showing that even that quantity might have been passed with perfect security."

This unusual fall of rain in so short a time was followed by one of the longest droughts which has occurred in that locality. It lasted 110 days; and, making allowance for occasional rain during that period, amounting altogether to about 5 days, the net duration of dry weather was 105 days. Thus the records of the year 1852 are of great value to the hydraulic engineer; for though the total fall of rain in the Longdendale district was only an average, there occurred in it one of the largest floods and one of the longest droughts with which we were at that time acquainted. The first showed the necessity for ample provision for floods; and the second the period for which storage should be provided. Since that time—now more than 30 years ago—other experience has been gained; and, though there have, perhaps, been no larger floods, provision for droughts of 120 days in districts of similar rainfall is the least that should be made. Where the

Landslip at Rhodes Wood Embankment.

rain is less, or the country less hilly, the provision should be greatly increased—in some cases even up to 300 days.

The excessive rain of February, 1852, set in motion an ancient landslip of about 40 acres in extent, lower down the valley than the one already described. On this ground, which exhibited no indication of moving, a contractor's village, called New Yarmouth, had been erected. This village was moved downwards about 8 inches during the night of the 6th February; and the masonry of the waste weir and waste watercourse of the Rhodes Wood reservoir was crushed and disturbed. The completion of the embankment, which formed, when finished, a buttress to the sides of the valley, and the addition of weight to the toe of the moving mass, arrested the movement.

The late Mr. R. Stephenson and the late Mr. J. K. Brunel called in.

On the occurrence of these landslips, and the consequent derangement of many features of the original design, I recommended the Council to ask the late Mr. Robert Stephenson and the late Mr. J. K. Brunel to advise with me as to the course to be pursued to prevent further mischief. This was agreed to, and these gentlemen soon after visited the works,—" various shafts were sunk and driftways driven, for the purpose of ascertaining accurately the depth and character of the moving mass, the nature of the material on which it had moved, and the quantity of water contained in the hill."

The course proposed to be adopted was approved by Messrs. Stephenson and Brunel.

The watercourses intended to be constructed across the slips, except that for the conveyance of flood-waters, were abandoned; the pure water of the streams and springs from the higher part of the valley was conveyed under the slips by cast-iron pipes, and a large supply of pure spring-water drawn from the base of the slipping ground by the various driftways, and conveyed direct to Manchester by the watercourse commencing below the Rhodes Wood reservoir.

Discharging Apparatus.

The mode of discharging the water from the Woodhead reservoir has already been described (see ante, p. 119). A brief description of the modes employed at other reservoirs will show the plans adopted; but, notwithstanding all the experience I have had, and my willingness to learn by failure as well as by success, I am still far from having any decided view as to the best means of drawing water from a great reservoir. Each case must be considered with reference to its peculiar circumstances, and no uniform or universal mode can be recommended or adopted.

Torside Reservoir.—The water is discharged from this reservoir through two cast-iron pipes laid in a tunnel driven through the hillside. The pipes are 40 inches and 24 inches diameter. There are two valves on the 40-inch pipe of 48 inches diameter, and the valve-door of each valve is made to lift in three sections. The door of the 24-inch valve is made in two sections. The valves are worked by a small turbine wheel near to the bottom of the shaft, communicating with gearing placed in a chamber at the top of the valve shaft. The pressure on the valves is 72 feet.

Rhodes Wood Reservoir.—The water is discharged from this reservoir by means of two lines of pipes, each 48 inches diameter, laid under the base of the reservoir embankment, commanded by valves at the outer ends 36 inches in diameter. The door of each valve is made in two sections, and the valves are worked by hand-gearing. The pressure on the valve is 72 feet.

Vale House Reservoir.—The water from this reservoir is discharged by two lines of 36-inch pipes laid inside a discharge tunnel driven through the hillside. The valves, 36 inches diameter, are placed at the foot of a shaft on the line of the tunnel, and each valve-door is divided into two sections. These valves are worked by a turbine in the same manner as described for the Torside reservoir. The pressure on the valve is 43 feet.

Bottoms Reservoir.—The water from this reservoir is discharged by two lines of pipes 36 inches diameter, laid inside a discharge tunnel driven through the hillside. The valves, 36 inches diameter, are placed at the bottom of a shaft on the line of tunnel, and are under a pressure of 48 feet. In this instance the valves are each worked by means of water admitted under pressure into a cylinder with a piston working in it. The cylinder is placed directly over the valves, and the door of the valve is lifted by two rods, which are coupled together by a cross head in which the piston-rod is also fixed. The communication between the door of the valve and the piston-rod is thus direct. The piston-rod is carried from the cylinder to the top of the shaft, where it passes through a head-stock placed on the floor of the valve-house, the upper part of the rod worked through the head-stock being marked to show the height to which the valve is open. To increase the facility of working, the dead weight of the lifting apparatus is balanced by a counter weight attached to a small cast-iron beam in connection with the lifting-rod. It being important that the water supplying the cylinder should be free from floating matter and as clear as possible, the water is obtained from the spring-water culvert which passes close to the valve-shaft. The water after being withdrawn from the culvert goes into settling wells, and from these is conveyed by cast-iron pipes down the shaft to the cylinders.

This arrangement for working large valves is preferable to the turbine, but all the work connected with it requires to be very carefully executed, and the water for use in the cylinder must be free from all turbidity. The working is very smooth and noiseless, whereas by the turbine, the rattle of the wheel-work of the gearing is great.

Bottoms and Vale House Reservoirs.

The Act for the construction of these works, and for the tunnel from the Hollingworth and Arnfield brooks under the village of Tintwistle, to the Bottoms reservoir, was obtained in the year 1865. These works were recommended in a report dated 30th May, 1860. In this report the following observations occur, after speaking of the compensation water to the mills on the river :—

"The water, however, now employed at these mills, and a large additional quantity—amounting in all to a certain and uniform supply of 860 horse-power—may be brought down and concentrated in one spot very favourable for the erection of a large manufactory, immediately below the new embankment, and between it and the public road. The situation is so convenient and in the midst of population, and so near other works, that there can be little doubt of being able to use or let the water-power on very favourable terms. If it were let, however, at only £5 per horse-power per annum—not half the cost of steam,—it would produce £1,800 a year—equal to the interest, at 4 per cent., of £45,000. This water-power could be obtained by bringing two-fifths of the compensation water from Torside reservoir by a conduit to run from the top of the waste weir at Rhodes Wood, above the proposed new reservoir, to the village of Tintwistle, and then turned down the face of the hill with a fall of 180 feet. This arrangement would give 260 horse-power. The other three-fifths of the compensation water would be drawn from the new reservoir, which, being the lowest in the series, would be nearly always full. When full, it would give an additional power of 150 horses, if applied on a turbine wheel, making a total of 410; but allowing only 100 horse-power in consideration of the water being occasionally drawn down, it would make the total reliable power as above stated—360 horses."

The reservoirs were, as has already been stated, at too low a level for the supply of Manchester; but they were above all the mills to which compensation in water had to be given, and they were to be filled by the surplus water and flood water of the district above. A plan of these reservoirs, and a geological section of the embankments are given. Their construction led to material alterations in the general designs of the works in Longdendale. It was originally intended that the Woodhead reservoir and the one below, viz., the Torside reservoir, should be appropriated to the storage of flood or turbid waters, and that Rhodes Wood reservoir alone should be filled with the spring-water from the valley when more abundant than was required, or from water from the upper reservoir decanted off when it had become sufficiently clarified or purified by subsidence, exposure, and time. The flood-waters, also, of the Hollingworth and Arnfield brooks had been to a great extent, allowed to run to waste, because there were no means of storing them separately either upon these particular streams or elsewhere, for the supply of the mills.

After the construction of the two lower reservoirs, the flood-waters which supplied them, after filling the Woodhead reservoir, were mainly conveyed by the flood watercourse to the new reservoirs.

The Torside reservoir is now, as far as possible, devoted to the storage of pure water in addition to that at Rhodes Wood, so that now the city of Manchester has not only the spring water at all times, and the pure water contained in the Rhodes Wood reservoir, as was originally intended, but that in the Torside reservoir also, and by recent arrangements the water stored in the new reservoirs at Audenshaw. By means of the tunnel under Tintwistle the flood waters of the Hollingworth and Arnfield brooks are now conveyed to the Bottoms reservoir, and contribute to the supply of that reservoir. Below the embankment of this reservoir a large gauge-basin has been constructed for the purpose of measuring the water which has to be given as compensation to the mills below, large waste weirs on each side of the gauge-basin being erected for the discharge of the floods which may be flowing from the reservoirs above or from the hills.

There was no material difficulty in the construction of the Vale House reservoir, the embankment of which is, for about 20 feet in depth, washed by the waters of the Bottoms reservoir when full, but very heavy masonry was required at the northerly end of the embankment of the Bottoms reservoir for the foundation of the waste weir and the various works there, which had to be constructed upon a thick bed of clay which overlay the flagstone rock, and which it was apprehended might slip when disturbed. The works were, however, successfully carried out, although when partially completed a heavy flood carried away a portion of the embankment in consequence of the insufficiency of a temporary trough which had been constructed for the passage of flood-waters.

The embankment and waste weir of this reservoir were formed with a view to being ultimately completed to a height of 7 feet above the Parliamentary limit of the Act of 1865. Powers to complete the embankment and waste weir as thus intended were obtained by an Act in 1882.

The house which has been constructed over the valves which discharge the water from this reservoir is converted into an ornamental temple, which contains a slab within it bearing the names of all the members of the Corporation who have served on the Water Committee since its formation in 1847. On the outside the arms of the Corporation have been carved, and another slab records the names of the successive chairmen of the committee, the engineers, and town clerk.

Reservoirs at Audenshaw.

Notwithstanding the construction of the reservoirs last described and the larger capacity for the storage of water which they afforded, there was still a considerable quantity of good water annually running to waste. The desire to store this, and to have at the same time a large quantity at the command of the city within a few miles, led to the construction of additional reservoirs at Denton and Audenshaw, for which an Act of Parliament was obtained in the year 1875. This arrangement was one of great advantage to the city of Manchester, for it not only provided a large additional amount of storage, but the reservoirs when filled with water would allow ample time for the examination or repair of works betwixt Denton and Longdendale. Between that valley and Godley there was but one means of communication, namely, by conduit and by the Mottram tunnel. Between Godley and Denton there was also but one line of pipes, although a second line had been laid from Godley reservoir to Prestwich, which passed so near the additional reservoirs at Audenshaw that it could be employed for filling them with water.

The additional reservoirs at Audenshaw are five in number, three of which have been already constructed. They are all placed on high land closely adjoining the two original service reservoirs at Denton. The capacity of all the five is about 2,099,500,000 gallons,—of the three which have been constructed 1,413,488,434 gallons. These three are nearly at the same level as those already existing. The two not yet constructed are at a somewhat lower elevation, but between the upper reservoirs and those at Gorton. They will probably be ultimately employed for storing water brought from Thirlmere, and are high enough to supply both the middle and lower zones into which Manchester has been divided. It required the construction of these reservoirs—or, at all events, of those which have been completed—to store all the good water from Longdendale, and not until they are filled, and all the other reservoirs in Longdendale are also in the same condition, can the city rely upon obtaining a supply from Longdendale of $24\frac{1}{2}$ million gallons per day in dry seasons. Plans of these reservoirs, which will show their general arrangement, are given.

The works have been rather long in construction in consequence of the tendency to slip which was exhibited by the clay of which the embankments were composed. All, however, is now stable, the tendency to slip having been prevented by the erection of brick buttresses in suitable places, and the reservoirs are now (August, 1883) being filled with water from Longdendale, the means of conveyance from that valley to the reservoirs being large enough for that purpose as well as for maintaining the ordinary supply to the city during the filling of the new reservoirs. The embankments were formed in a similar manner to what has been already described for others, with slopes of three horizontal to one vertical on the inside, pitched upon the face with stone, and two to one on the outside.

The plans of these reservoirs will sufficiently explain their details.

Auxiliary Reservoir.—In connection with the original scheme it was alleged by some of the lower millowners that they would not derive the same benefit from the compensation reservoir as the owners of mills higher up the river, for whose accommodation the water was to be let out of the reservoir at an early hour in the morning. To meet this objection, and to put all persons interested in the supply of water as nearly as possible upon the same footing, an auxiliary reservoir was constructed near the junction of the river Etherow with the Glossop brook, about two miles below the Bottoms reservoir. This reservoir is interesting from the somewhat novel mode in which water is admitted into and discharged from it. Self-acting floodgates, turning upon a central pivot, admit the water from the river; and when the reservoir is full, the water flows over a waste weir constructed of cast-iron, in which the sluices are placed which regulate the supply of water. Drawings of this reservoir are appended.

City Piping.

A good deal of what it was originally intended to give under this head has already been embodied in the description which has preceded, as, for instance, the particular form of hydrant which was introduced, and the protection against fire which was the consequence; the manner in which valuable blocks of buildings were provided with fire hydrants; the mode in which the pipes were cast, and the particular system of turned and bored joints which was adopted.

At the time at which the works were laid out (1840) the population of the city of Manchester and the surrounding districts which had to be supplied with water was, as has already been stated, about 400,000 persons. Before the piping was commenced a plan was prepared, of which a reduced copy is given, showing the manner in which the water was to be distributed in the city, and the quantity of water which the various pipes, according to size, would deliver at the level of the street. The quantities were calculated according to the formula of Eytelwein, which is in words as follows:—. "Multiply 2,500 times the diameter of the pipes in feet by the height in feet, and divide the product by the length in feet added to 50 times the diameter; then the square root of the quotient will be the velocity of discharge in feet per second."

The calculated delivery of water according to this formula, where coated pipes have been used, has proved to be much below the truth, particularly in the case of large pipes, and a nearer approximation to truth are the calculations which would follow the use of Bazin's formula, which is as follows:—

$$R.I = A.V^2.$$

in which $V^2 = \frac{R.I}{A}.$

R = Hydraulic mean depth.
I = Sine of the inclination.
V = Mean velocity.
A = Co-efficient.

Values of A in feet = $0\cdot0000457 \left(1+\frac{0\cdot0984}{R}\right).$

In laying out the piping for the distribution of water in the city the dimensions of the pipes were in the first instance determined without reference to those which already existed, and then as many of the old pipes as could be employed were incorporated with the system and brought into useful action.

Several canals had to be crossed by pipes of considerable dimensions. In such cases the pipes were formed into arches over the canals with large flanges at the points of junction, and longitudinal fins or ribs for additional strength. These pipes have never, so far as I am aware, given any trouble, nor has the water flowing in them been at any time affected by frost. The arrangement is so simple that it is not necessary to give a drawing.

The pipes varied in diameter from 36 to 3 inches, and were cast according to the drawings which are introduced at the end of the work.

The population of the districts supplied with water, and the extent to which the supply has been carried, have so greatly increased since the works were first laid out, that, in addition to the extensions rendered necessary for the supply of the additional population, new mains have had to be introduced for the purpose of bringing a larger quantity from the reservoirs and for restoring the pressure which originally existed to the full efficiency which was at first experienced.

It has already been stated that in designing the original works for the supply of water to the city, which were at that time the largest in this country, and in many respects are still so, there was but little previous knowledge or experience at the command of the engineer, and he therefore had to consider almost every detail, and to adopt various processes which up to that time had certainly never been practised. In this way many novelties were introduced, all of which have now stood the experience of more than thirty years, and most of which have been adopted in the execution of other works.

Among the many improvements which have been introduced may be enumerated the following;—

    1. Automatic system for separating pure and turbid water.
    2. The ball-valve hydrant.
    3. The ball-valve air-valve.
    4. Large valves to be opened by one man.
    5. Self-acting closing valves.
    6. Coating cast-iron pipes.
    7. Casting pipes vertically with the socket downwards.
    8. Modification of the turned and bored joint.
    9. India-rubber joints.
    10. Straining tanks.
    11. Compulsory unlimited rates.
    12. Testing and stamping office.
    13. System of life assurance.

Some of these were tried before they were introduced on the Manchester Waterworks. For instance,—the ball-hydrants were tried first at Warrington and Kendal, and the india-rubber joints at Chorley; but the separating system, the coating, the large valves, the self-acting closing valves, the improved turned and bored joint, and the casting of pipes with the sockets downwards or at the bottom, were all first adopted for Manchester, as were also the stamping and testing office and the life assurance.

Hydraulic science had been so little cultivated in Great Britain at the time at which the Manchester Waterworks were designed, that the few rules of calculation which the engineer at that time possessed were due to foreigners, and they had for the most part been deduced from experiments on a comparatively small scale. It was felt that in such large works as those of the Manchester Waterworks the truth of the laws which had been deduced might be fully and fairly ascertained. In laying out the works, therefore, arrangements were made for testing calculations in every conceivable way. The larger reservoirs were carefully measured and their capacity determined for every foot in depth. The smaller or service reservoirs were calculated in like manner for every inch in depth, and the results tabulated and printed. The quantity of water conveyed by each watercourse might be determined by sluices of given dimensions, by taking the area of the openings by the difference in the level of the water on each side, checked by the velocity and depth of the stream in the watercourses and by the quantity actually drawn out of or poured into reservoirs of known capacity. At the entrance to the Godley reservoir a small basin was constructed with a gauge-plate through which all the water passed, and the quantity might be determined by noting that actually received by the reservoir, the capacity of which had been determined for every inch in depth. At the Denton reservoirs the water conveyed by pipe from Godley was carried to the furthest ends of the reservoirs, and there discharged into a basin, from which it flowed over a gauge-plate into each of the two reservoirs. Here, also, the quantity actually received could be accurately ascertained, and the proper co-efficient for the depth over the gauge-plate could be determined.

By the Acts of Parliament which authorized the construction of the works, a certain quantity of water had to be delivered to the river as compensation. In order to avoid any dispute as to the delivery of this water, a test-basin was constructed at the point at which the water had to be delivered, so that the parties interested in the supply could ascertain for themselves, with the utmost certainty and accuracy, whether the stipulated quantity was being discharged or not. This test-basin has been generally mentioned in connection with the Rhodes Wood reservoir. In order to ascertain the proper co-efficient for calculating the pressure upon openings in a gauge-plate through which the water had to be discharged, experiments were made at the Godley reservoir, through the openings of the gauge-plate there, the water discharged being received into a large wooden tank where the quantity could be accurately measured. In this plate there were three openings, each 6 feet long and 6 inches deep, all exactly at the same level, but with different shaped edges, through which the water passed, as under:—

Compensation Water Test-basin.

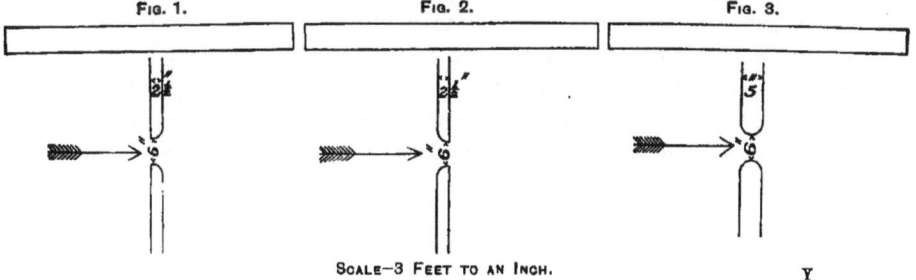

SCALE—3 FEET TO AN INCH.

The following was the result of the experiments:—

Head of water above centre of aperture. Inches.	Mean co-efficient of velocity (theoretical limit 8·04).		
	Aperture with curve outside. Fig. 1.	Aperture with curve inside. Fig. 2.	Aperture with double curve inside and outside Fig. 3.
48	5·78	7·04	7·60
42	5·66	7·04	7·60
36	5·67	7·04	7·60
30	5·60	7·04	7·80
24	5·60	7·04	7·80
18	5·50	7·04	7·78
12	5·60	6·89	7·30
6	5·30	6·00	6·55
Mean, omitting 6 inches experiment.........	5·63	7·02	7·64

Test-basin. In accordance with these results, the apertures in the gauge-basin and the pressure upon them for the delivery of the compensation water agreed to be given to the millowners were determined; but in order to enable the millowners or those interested in the supply of water to ascertain for themselves the actual quantity delivered, the water from the aperture of the gauge-basin was conducted in a trough over the top of the test-basin into the river below. This test-basin was square, with perpendicular sides, and its capacity could therefore be very easily ascertained. By the adoption of certain arrangements the water from the gauge-basin can be instantaneously turned into the test-basin, and can as instantaneously be arrested and allowed to flow in its accustomed manner in the trough over the top of the basin. The quantity which has been received, therefore, in a given time can be positively determined by taking the difference in level between what it was at the commencement of the experiment and what it was at its termination.

The test-basin is made large enough to occupy a minute-and-a-half in filling, if it were empty to start with, and it therefore affords ample time for accurate experiment.

Various other experiments than those above described were made,—amongst these were some for ascertaining the proper co-efficient for the discharge of water over a broad-topped weir. These experiments were made at the waste weirs of the original test-basin below the Rhodes Wood embankment. The coping of the weir was 3 feet wide, chamfered on each side so as to allow a flat surface on the top of 18 inches in width. After leaving the weir the water fell several feet in depth, and was received into the test-basin, where it was carefully and accurately measured. The results were, that the co-efficient for 7 inches going over the weir was 2·8, for 4 inches 2·7, and for $2\frac{3}{4}$ inches 2·63.

Experiments on discharge over broad-top weirs.

Another experiment of a very useful kind was to determine the quantity of water which would be discharged by a canal or river of uniform dimensions.

Du Buat gives the following rule for calculating the water which would be so discharged:—

"If we take unity from the square root of the superficial velocity, expressed in inches, the square of the remainder is the velocity at the bottom; and the mean velocity is the half-sum of these two. Thus, if the velocity in the middle of the stream be 25 inches per second, its square root is 5; from which, if we take unity, there remains 4. The square of this, or 16, is the velocity at the bottom and $\frac{25+16}{2}$, or $20\frac{1}{2}$ is the mean velocity."

Experiments on discharge in canals.

Various experiments proved that this rule was a very near approximation to truth, and could be safely depended upon; but for practical purposes, for determining the size of canal or conduit required for conveying given quantities of water, the following formula by Eytelwein may be taken:—

"The superficial velocity of a river is nearly a mean proportional between the hydraulic mean depth and the fall in two English miles; and the mean velocity of the whole water is still more nearly nine-tenths of this mean proportional."

Amongst the many novelties which have been introduced in the Manchester Waterworks I must not omit to describe the principle of Life Assurance, which was authorized by the Act of 1847, but which was not carried out till many years subsequently. The Corporation grant life

Life Assurance.

annuities on single and joint lives, and annuities for fixed terms of years secured on the borough rate of the city, the water rates, and rents levied under the authority of their various Acts, and the landed and other property of the waterworks. The assessable annual value of the rateable property in the city amounted in the year 1880 to £2,217,602. 10s.; and the Corporation are empowered to raise money for waterworks purposes to the extent of £6,175,000, the gross expenditure to the end of 1879 being £3,068,251. 16s. 3d. The security is, therefore, ample, and may be summed up as follows:—

    1st. The rateable value of property within the city amounting to upwards of £2,000,000 per annum.

    2nd. Cost of waterworks exceeding £3,000,000.

    3rd. Annual revenue exceeding £200,000.

    4th. Compulsory obligation to levy such annual rates as will meet all their engagements, of which the annuities form a part.

The public have largely availed themselves of the advantages thus offered.

Stamping Office. Another important feature in the distribution of the water has been the establishment of a testing and stamping office for internal fittings, and the appointment of authorized plumbers. Previous to these arrangements the public complained bitterly that the plumber was never out of the house; and the competition was such, that inferior work and inferior fittings were constantly introduced. Nothing is now allowed to be used that does not bear the mark of having been tested and approved at the Manchester Water Office. Each tap is weighed, so that the proper quantity of metal is insured, and the workmanship of every article has to be approved before it is stamped. The inhabitants, therefore, get good articles and good workmanship, and the only competition is for labour. Distant makers send their articles to be tested and stamped. The arrangements have been most successful in every way and have given universal satisfaction. The establishment of this system is due to Mr. Berrey, the very energetic manager of this department. The instructions to authorized plumbers have been well considered, and are printed in the appendix, that they may be copied and introduced wherever "constant supply," good fittings, and economy are desired.

In practice, notwithstanding the great additional demand which was made by the extension of population, the pipes within the city and its suburbs continued for a long time to deliver all the water which was required for the supply of the inhabitants and for the use of the mills and manufactories taking the water. Probably this is to a great extent accounted for by the pipes being made large enough to convey all the water which might be supposed to be required in seven or eight hours of each day, during which period the demand is always the greatest.

It has already been stated that the number of people supplied with water by the Manchester Corporation exceeds 800,000; and the following table will show the increase which has taken place in the city of Manchester and Salford and their immediate suburbs during the present century. It has been as follows at each decade, according to the public census tables:— *Population*

1801	90,399
1811	110,244
1821	154,807
1831	227,808
1841	296,183
1851	401,321
1861	727,312
1871	814,602
1881	997,226

Consumption.

The present consumption of water, exclusive of compensation water, is about 18,000,000 gallons per day, about one-third of which is taken for trade purposes. The number of persons supplied by the Corporation is, as stated, about 800,000, and the consumption is therefore about 22½ gallons per day each. Deducting one-third for the quantity supplied for trade purposes, leaves for domestic supply, general public demands, and waste, about 15 gallons per head per day.

Probably there is no large supply of water under constant supply and high pressure so economically distributed.

Depression in trade and wet seasons have kept the consumption down during the last two or three years; but in January, 1881, it was about

2,000,000 gallons a day more than it was three years before. The rate of annual increase since 1854—nearly thirty years ago—will be seen from the following table :—

Supply of Water from 1855 to 1882 inclusive.

Year.	Average quantity of Water supplied per day.	Year.	Average quantity of Water supplied per day.
	Gallons.		Gallons.
1855	8,078,152	1869	13,057,762
1856	8,277,156	1870	14,815,877
1857	9,708,468	1871	15,090,895
1858	10,808,184	1872	14,833,686
1859	10,558,952	1873	15,471,588
1860	10,907,183	1874	16,713,957
1861	10,716,228	1875	17,133,434
1862	10,864,489	1876	15,722,886
1863	10,801,923	1877	15,742,800
1864	10,828,645	1878	17,248,694
1865	11,156,433	1879	17,914,153
1866	11,281,923	1880	17,998,758
1867	13,250,000	1881	18,929,704
1868	12,059,333	1882	17,829,107

In a report to the Water Committee, dated March 18th, 1868, are the following observations, which may be of interest, as showing the irregularity in the supply of water to a town during the 24 hours of the day. I was anxious to obtain some accurate information upon the quantity of water which was consumed, with the view of ascertaining how far the means of supply would meet the demand. For this purpose I instructed the late Mr. Wilson, the then outdoor superintendent of the works, to take hourly observations upon the quantity of water consumed. This he was kind enough to do on three several occasions, and furnished me with the means of making the calculations required.

I report as follows:—

"The hourly gaugings were of special value for the purpose of determining whether there was any considerable amount of waste,—a fact which may be ascertained by comparing the quantity supplied in the busy hours of the day with that flowing out of the reservoirs in the dead hours of the night.

"The gross consumption on the average of the year 1867 was about 12,500,000 gallons per day, the maximum quantity at particular periods in the summer and autumn for a few days together reaching 14,000,000 or 15,000,000 gallons per day. Mr. Wilson is of opinion that the average of the year may now be taken at about 14,000,000 gallons per day, but that at certain seasons, for a week or a fortnight together, it will reach 15,000,000 or 16,000,000 gallons.

"I find that the hours of maximum draught from the Denton reservoirs, at which the hourly gaugings were instituted, are about double those of the minimum draught. For instance, on the day commencing at 11 a.m. on January 30th and ending at 11 a.m. on January 31st, 1868, the total quantity supplied from Denton was 7,911,328 gallons. From 10 a.m. to 5 p.m. the quantity scarcely varied,—it was equal to about 423,000 gallons per hour; from 5 p.m. to midnight it gradually fell to 267,000 gallons per hour; from midnight to 1 a.m. it was no more than 113,000 gallons per hour, and from that time it rose to 360,000 gallons per hour by 8 a.m. and to 422,000 gallons by 10 a.m. In the day, from 1 p.m. on the 24th February to the same hour on the 25th, the gross quantity supplied from Denton reservoir was 8,795,714 gallons; the hours of maximum draught were from 8 a.m. to 5 p.m., being generally a little under 500,000 gallons per hour. At midnight the quantity was reduced to 215,000 gallons in the hour, and from 9 p.m. to 6 a.m. the quantity never amounted to 300,000 gallons an hour. Now of this night quantity there can be no doubt but a considerable portion is wasted, and yet on the whole the consumption of water by the city and its suburbs is smaller per head than that of any other considerable town. The consumption of water is, however, increasing more rapidly than heretofore. Much of the increase is due to the better pressure upon the districts supplied from the Prestwich reservoir, and to the more abundant supply which that reservoir can afford to distant places."

Rainfall.

The following table will exhibit the rain which has fallen during the last 28 years at various places along the line of the Manchester Waterworks:—

Rainfall, 1855 to 1882 inclusive.

Year.	ELEVATION OF RAIN GAUGES ABOVE ORDNANCE DATUM.							
	Prestwich Reservoir, 347 feet.	Gorton Reservoir, 263 feet.	Denton Reservoir, 394 feet.	Godley Reservoir, 500 feet.	Arnfield Reservoir, 550 feet.	Rhodes Wood Reservoir, 590 feet.	Torside Reservoir, 680 feet.	Woodhead Reservoir, 660 feet.
	Inches.	Inches.	Inches.	Inches.	Inches.	Inches.	Inches.	Inches.
1855.........	...	25·55	24·19	24·54	30·63	34·49	...	40·43
1856.........	...	35·76	34·20	35·94	42·61	49·07	...	50·97
1857.........	...	31·41	29·16	30·81	36·59	40·04	...	46·06
1858.........	...	29·85	27·54	28·32	36·14	44·26	...	45·54
1859.........	...	34·18	34·26	32·60	40·20	47·26	...	53·85
1860.........	...	35·84	35·51	36·08	39·52	47·85	...	53·74
1861.........	...	29·78	28·28	31·11	32·48	40·22	...	44·24
1862.........	...	38·15	36·69	35·50	38·99	47·28	...	49·63
1863.........	...	37·30	35·81	36·14	38·19	48·04	...	53·77
1864.........	...	27·68	27·13	29·28	31·34	38·48	...	43·66
1865.........	...	28·17	28·28	26·49	29·37	37·15	35·08	40·85
1866.........	...	41·64	40·47	42·94	47·50	58·45	55·45	64·58
1867.........	...	34·17	34·11	36·57	39·46	49·55	47·98	55·96
1868.........	...	31·19	30·22	31·02	35·47	46·98	45·41	53·62
1869.........	...	33·75	33·24	35·66	40·05	49·16	50·98	59·12
1870.........	...	28·98	28·08	30·04	34·45	39·88	40·16	46·62
1871.........	...	29·58	29·10	31·45	35·38	38·99	38·27	45·75
1872.........	...	48·01	48·18	49·47	52·70	59·25	59·48	64·81
1873.........	33·05	27·99	27·30	29·28	35·58	37·66	38·62	41·14
1874.........	36·94	30·47	30·47	30·83	39·34	42·58	43·59	46·67
1875.........	40·10	32·58	31·41	32·17	38·85	40·78	43·87	45·89
1876.........	40·20	35·42	35·32	37·85	44·84	46·85	49·18	51·61
1877.........	47·39	44·14	43·64	43·48	54·07	57·05	60·85	63·44
1878.........	35·86	33·64	32·64	32·71	41·01	42·54	44·36	47·39
1879.........	34·82	30·66	31·55	31·18	39·57	41·91	43·14	46·62
1880.........	37·95	35·39	36·82	37·09	46·98	50·78	52·90	56·97
1881.........	40·99	34·92	36·44	36·17	42·34	45·59	44·90	50·85
1882.........	46·31	40·56	43·48	44·01	51·39	54·57	55·12	60·22
Average...	39·26	33·79	33·34	34·22	39·75	45·59	47·16	50·71

T. H. G. BERREY, Assoc. Inst. C. E.,
General Outdoor Superintendent.

The rain-gauge at Woodhead is about two miles higher up the valley than that at Torside, but placed at a lower level, being in the valley, while the other is on the hillside.

It will be observed that while the rain at the various places of observation near Manchester or on the plain which surrounds it, viz., at Gorton, Denton, and Godley, is nearly the same, it rapidly increases in the hills and as you ascend to higher elevations. Prestwich, which lies to the west of Manchester, gets more rain than the first three places named to the east. For some years rain gauges were kept on the high lands which form the summit of the drainage ground, and to obtain a correct, or nearly correct, account of the rain which falls on the ground from which the water is collected, about 10 per cent. must be added for the fall on the hills to the average of the three gauges in the valley of Longdendale, viz., Rhodes Wood, Torside, and Woodhead; but of the average rainfall recorded by the three gauges in Longdendale named, the quantity of water actually flowing from the ground and capable of being collected is 33 inches out of 42, so that the mean loss by evaporation or absorption is but 9 inches per annum. The total quantity available to Manchester, besides what is given as compensation to the river, will be between 24 and 25 million gallons per day when the reservoirs which have been constructed at Audenshaw are filled, and all the reservoirs in Longdendale can be filled to the brim.

The following Report, written in 1869, contains many useful observations from actual measurement upon the rainfall, the quantity of water flowing from the ground, and the loss by evaporation and absorption:—

"16, Great George-street, Westminster,
"July 30th, 1869.

"*Manchester Corporation Waterworks.*

"To the Waterworks Committee.

"Gentlemen,—The capabilities of your waterworks and the means you have of meeting the increasing demands for supplies which are constantly made upon you have been very fully brought before you in my reports of March 18th, October 7th, and October 28th of last year. The general results of the figures contained in these reports may be summarized as follows:—

"1st. When all the reservoirs now in hand are completed the quantity of water available for the city and its suburbs, after giving compensation to the stream, will be about 25,000,000 gallons per day; and secondly, the storage now available will enable you to deliver during such droughts as occurred in 1864, 1865, and 1868, about 15,000,000 gallons per day, which may be assumed to be about equal to the maximum demand at present.

"Subsequent to my report of October 28th, 1868, I received your instructions to work out accurately the past experience of the works, for the purpose of showing the actual quantity of water which the district has yielded and the proportion which has been delivered to the stream for the use of the mills. These calculations were all completed when your determination to withdraw a Bill which you had introduced into Parliament for the purpose of reducing the compensation, rendered it unnecessary to communicate immediately the information which had thus been obtained. A short summary, however, of the general results I gave in my report for the Council of the 2nd May last, and I now propose to give you the whole information in sufficient detail to enable you clearly to comprehend every phase of the question, and to base any further measures upon the knowledge which has thus been acquired.

"Referring to the table of general results which I gave in my report of May last, and which I repeat in the appendices, you will see that the two years of least rainfall were 1864 and 1865. In 1864 nearly 35 inches, and in 1865 32¼ inches in depth over the whole surface of your drainage area, flowed off the ground. On the average of these two years, therefore, the net produce of the district was equal to 33½ inches. With the amount of available storage which existed at that time, about 9 inches of water in each year ran to waste, and in 1866 no less than 30 inches. With the storage you will possess when Woodhead and Torside reservoirs are complete, as well as the reservoirs you are now constructing, probably no water in 1864 and 1865 would have run to waste if the discharge from the reservoirs had been equal to the quantity of water which the district would have supplied during these years, namely, 33½ inches per annum.

"The same storage would have enabled you to discharge throughout the drought of 1868, which was much more severe than 1864 and 1865, a quantity equal to about 31 or 32 inches in depth. It would require about 60,000,000 cubic feet of additional reservoir room in order to have carried through that drought at the rate of delivery equal to 33½ inches, which is equivalent to a town supply of 25,000,000 gallons per day, in addition to the river compensation.

"I give you in an Appendix (No. 1) the annual quantity of rain which has fallen during the last 14 years. It amounts on an average to 47·07 inches in the valley of Longdendale. The rain of the last five years, during which all the detailed particulars of fall and yield have been accurately calculated, is very nearly the same average, being 48·04 inches; and in these five years occur three periods of excessive drought. Taking whole years together they divide as follows:—One year of excessive rainfall, two years slightly above, and two years a good deal below, the average rain.

"You have, therefore, in the information which is afforded by the experience of these five years, almost every variety of extreme season which can occur. The average rainfall was $52\frac{1}{4}$ inches, the average produce from the ground was equal to $42\frac{1}{4}$ inches, the loss by evaporation and absorption, or the difference between the depth of water which flowed off the ground and the depth of water indicated by the rain-gauges being just 10 inches.

"Now of the difference between the minimum yield of $32\frac{1}{5}$ inches and the average of $42\frac{1}{4}$ inches a considerable quantity could be obtained by increased storage, and I have carefully considered this question. The ordinary mode of calculating the capability of a district is by taking the average available water resulting from two consecutive years of minimum rainfall added to what the capacity of the reservoirs would yield per day measured by the 730 days of the two years. This supposes the reservoirs to be full at the commencement and empty at the end of the period. It is not safe, however, to run the calculations so close, and I have ascertained by calculation that although in 1864 the storage which you would have, were all authorized works completed, would have been far more than sufficient had you even supplied water at the rate of 38 inches per annum, and would have been about sufficient for the supply at the same rate during the year 1865, yet in 1868 the great length of drought and the small amount of water which was yielded during that period of drought would only have permitted the supply of a quantity equal to about 32 inches of rain. To have supplied 38 inches during the year 1868, which was $8\frac{1}{2}$ inches less than the depth actually flowing off the ground, you would have required storage equal to about 900,000,000 cubic feet, or about 200,000,000 cubic feet more than you will possess when all the present reservoirs are completed. With such storage, however, you would be able to supply to the city nearly 31,000,000 gallons, or say, with perfect safety, 30,000,000 gallons per day through a season as severe as 1868. With the storage authorized, or being provided, we cannot calculate upon more than 23,000,000 gallons per day during such a drought as that of 1868.

"From this you will see that additional storage, to the extent of 200,000,000 cubic feet, would give you an extra 7,000,000 or 8,000,000 gallons a day in addition to what you will have when all your present works are completed. It must, however, be remembered that by impounding so large a quantity of the flood waters the *quality* of the supply will be deteriorated. At present the excellence of the water which is delivered in Manchester depends in a great measure upon so large a portion of it being derived directly from springs; and what is not pure spring water is selected water, separated from that which is turbid, and specially stored.

"In my report of the 7th October, 1868, I entered largely into the then position and the future prospects of the undertaking, and I endeavoured to show the necessity of immediately providing additional storage, remarking that if the increase in consumption went on as it was then doing, at the rate of 1,000,000 gallons per day in each successive year, the full quantity of water which the whole district would supply would be exhausted in eight or nine years. Of course, a reduction in the rate of increase, and such additional storage as I have now suggested, would prolong the period at which the supply would but just meet the demand. Many years, however, before this point of balance arrives, power should be obtained for getting supplies from other districts, as you cannot calculate upon carrying out any large scheme of extension in less than five or six years.

"Since my previous reports the Vale House reservoir has been completed, and the water has been held in Torside and Woodhead reservoirs at a higher level. The available storage may, therefore, now be taken at 500,000,000 cubic feet or 3,000,000,000 gallons. In about two years the Bottoms reservoir may be completed. This will add 65,000,000 cubic feet, making 565,000,000 cubic feet altogether. With your present storage you are able to supply about 15,000,000 gallons of water per day to the city. If the increase goes on at the rate of 1,000,000 gallons per day that increase requires additional storage of about 24,000,000 or 25,000,000 cubic feet each year. In 2½ years, therefore, all that even Bottoms reservoir will give you will be required; or should the increase be reduced or limited to 500,000 gallons per day, you will have the means of meeting the increased demand for five years from the present time.

"The Woodhead reservoir contains, at the height at which it is now generally held, about 120,000,000 cubic feet. It cannot be drawn off for repair until the completion of the Bottoms reservoir 2 or 2½ years hence, and then the supply to the city will be such that you cannot spare the water which the reservoir holds. The result is, therefore, that Woodhead reservoir must remain as it is, or other reservoirs to contain an equal quantity of water must be made before you can venture to repair this reservoir. It was estimated that the restoration of the Woodhead reservoir would cost £48,000. A portion of this outlay has already been incurred, and the sum still to be expended will probably amount to about £42,000, for which expenditure the reservoir will be rendered secure and about 80,000,000 cubic feet of water added to your storage.

"The appendices and diagrams accompanying this report are as follow :—

"*Appendices.*

" Appendix No. 1.—Table showing annual rainfall.
" No. 2.—Table showing capacity of reservoirs.
" No. 3.—Table showing average daily supply to city from 1855 to 1868 inclusive.
" No. 4.—Results of calculations of gaugings of water supplied from reservoirs during the five years ending 1868.
" No. 5.—Memorandum as to capabilities of Longdendale district, showing results of last five years.
" No. 6.—Particulars of draught of 1864.
" No. 7.—Particulars of draught of 1865.
" No. 8.—Particulars of draught of 1868.
" No. 9.—Summary of results of draughts of 1864, 1865, and 1868.
" No. 10.*

"*Diagrams.*

"No. 11.—Diagram of rainfall at Woodhead for six years from 1863 to 1868 inclusive.

"No. 12.—Diagram showing the probable flow of water in 1868 from the drainage ground, on the assumption that it corresponded with the ascertained results of similar streams in the Halifax waterworks.

"No. 13.—Diagram showing the quantity of water supplied to the river either as compensation or surplus water.

"I have the honour to be,
"Your very obedient Servant,
"J. F. BATEMAN."

---

* No. 10 is omitted, as it is only a volume of calculations which is too long and too uninteresting to print.

APPENDIX No. 1.—*Table showing Annual Rainfall in the Manchester Corporation Waterworks District.*

Date.	Gorton Reservoir. Elevation 263 feet.	Denton Reservoir. Elevation 324 feet.	Godley Reservoir. Elevation 500 feet.	Arnfield Reservoir. Elevation 575 feet.	Rhodes Wood Reservoir. Elevation 520 feet.	Torside Reservoir. Elevation 600 feet.	Woodhead Reservoir. Elevation 680 feet.
1854.—Totals	33·97	32·72	31·10	......	......	......	......
1855. "	25·55	24·19	24·54	29·91	34·49	......	40·38
1856. "	35·76	34·17	35·94	42·61	49·16	......	50·89
1857. "	31·41	29·16	30·81	30·59	40·04	......	46·03
1858. "	29·85	27·54	28·82	36·14	42·77	......	45·54
1859. "	34·18	34·26	32·60	40·20	46·84	......	53·85
1860. "	35·84	35·51	36·08	39·52	47·85	......	53·69
1861. "	29·76	28·28	30·11	32·48	40·22	......	44·24
1862. "	38·15	36·69	35·50	38·99	47·28	......	49·68
1863. "	37·80	35·81	36·14	38·19	48·04	......	53·77
1864. "	27·68	27·18	29·28	31·84	38·50	......	43·52
1865. "	28·17	28·28	26·49	29·37	37·25	35·08	40·85
1866. "	41·64	40·47	42·94	47·50	58·45	55·45	64·58
1867. "	34·17	34·11	36·57	39·46	49·55	47·98	55·96
1868. "	31·19	30·22	31·02	35·47	46·98	45·41	53·62
Averages	32·93	31·90	32·46	36·98	44·77	45·98	49·68

Mean of Woodhead and Rhodes Wood gauges for 14 years and Torside for 4 years, 47·07 inches.
Mean of Woodhead and Rhodes Wood gauges for last five years and Torside for last four years .... 48·04 inches.

APPENDIX No. 2.—*Table showing capacity of Reservoirs now authorized when completed and capable of being filled.*

Woodhead Reservoir	198,225,698 cubic feet.
Torside "	286,659,578 "
Rhodes Wood "	80,255,910 "
Vale House "	56,678,159 "
Bottoms "	64,148,167 "
Arnfield "	38,605,080 "
Hollingworth "	11,659,674 "
Gorton (Lower) "	16,160,000 "
Gorton (Upper) "	20,000,000 "
Godley "	9,815,805 "
Denton (No. 1) "	3,757,920 "
Denton (No. 2) "	4,775,989 "
Total capacity of Reservoirs now authorized..	785,736,870 "

Of the above storage, the quantity not yet available is as follows:—

Woodhead Reservoir,	upper 15 feet...............	77,285,787 cubic feet.
Torside "	upper 13 feet...............	78,606,672 "
Bottoms "	in course of construction.	64,148,167 "
		220,040,626 "

Leaving capacity of Reservoirs now available 515,695,744 "

APPENDIX No. 3.—*Table of average daily supply of water to the city for each month and each year from 1855 to 1868 inclusive.*

Month.	1855.	1856.	1857.	1858.	1859.	1860.	1861.	1862.	1863.	1864.	1865.	1866.	1867.	1868.
	Gallons.	Gallons.	Gallons.	Gallons.	Gallons.	Gallons.	Gallons.	Gallons.	Gallons.	Gallons.	Gallons.	Gallons.	Gallons.	Gallons.
January	8,295,940	8,104,994	9,190,309	10,968,239	10,807,840	10,580,909	13,904,596	10,560,741	9,837,385	10,940,786	10,167,594	9,967,090	11,090,906	12,465,713
February	8,941,761	8,068,490	8,942,846	10,867,265	10,360,069	11,216,164	11,676,874	10,903,108	10,437,198	10,139,876	10,167,210	9,908,604	12,577,926	12,470,043
March	8,133,175	8,759,643	8,900,526	10,639,600	10,998,219	11,288,107	10,696,947	10,210,787	10,393,097	10,161,048	10,704,389	11,098,589	11,687,959	11,769,239
April	7,450,625	7,586,459	8,989,748	10,385,951	9,980,450	11,493,977	9,903,505	9,900,595	9,777,864	11,139,144	10,676,300	11,463,988	11,199,013	13,968,395
May	7,908,946	7,840,194	9,642,459	10,925,741	10,746,986	10,988,685	10,573,139	9,281,946	9,968,445	10,447,417	10,689,699	11,944,488	10,943,085	12,929,890
June	5,840,348	7,869,430	10,570,647	10,761,497	10,883,508	10,710,989	10,269,437	10,390,932	9,915,630	10,598,256	11,615,698	11,889,610	10,596,377	14,440,190
July	7,801,179	8,645,919	10,831,870	10,758,425	8,963,060	10,988,949	10,804,777	10,710,209	10,696,930	11,069,669	11,340,489	11,845,488	10,467,170	14,807,452
August	9,404,398	8,430,969	9,747,540	10,674,484	9,815,898	10,716,977	10,856,987	10,389,154	10,696,528	11,396,473	10,930,857	10,895,401	11,536,478	9,368,969
September	8,104,896	7,736,796	9,977,826	10,635,280	11,150,441	10,198,446	10,063,459	10,623,236	9,935,948	9,949,960	11,900,206	10,489,447	11,684,846	8,040,118
October	7,946,572	8,493,196	9,783,446	10,893,306	12,047,462	10,460,578	10,098,475	5,234,926	11,064,458	10,510,422	10,067,541	11,316,996	9,968,561	8,447,699
November	8,477,599	7,596,114	9,590,590	10,728,204	10,998,705	9,614,131	8,279,330	9,998,397	10,017,389	10,067,924	10,854,550	11,829,905	11,626,949	12,997,809
December	8,735,896	8,559,280	9,594,042	10,730,885	11,000,999	10,118,094	9,961,075	10,156,394	9,946,986	9,795,187	11,160,087	10,196,381	11,475,023	14,150,702
	95,245,987	97,751,050	115,060,920	127,146,090	124,680,526	139,244,729	126,796,546	121,906,009	120,699,880	126,029,969	130,695,645	181,246,196	138,991,168	144,712,006
Average daily supply from Croton and Denton Reservoirs	7,937,246	8,344,304	9,586,910	10,595,741	10,405,026	10,770,384	10,478,045	10,150,500	10,949,110	10,507,744	10,838,579	10,937,099	11,332,594	12,059,333
Total average daily supply, including estimated supply from 40-inch main and 30-inch main	8,078,153	8,377,158	9,708,468	10,928,184	10,553,951	10,907,188	10,716,329	10,364,489	10,801,998	10,838,645	11,166,438	11,361,928	12,250,000	12,059,333

APPENDIX No. 4.—*Result of Gaugings.—Table showing total quantities of water run to waste.*

RIVER ETHEROW ONLY.

Date.	Total quantity run to waste in the year.	Average quantity run to waste daily.	Average quantity run to waste daily.
	Cubic feet.	Cubic feet.	Gallons.
1864	615,212,118	1,685,512	10,500,789
1865	479,698,195	1,314,241	8,187,721
1866	1,619,484,858	4,436,944	27,642,165
1867	1,243,952,410	3,408,089	21,232,394
1868	942,653,560	2,582,612	16,089,672
1864 and 1865, being the mean of 2 consecutive dry years	1,094,910,313	1,499,876	9,344,280
1864, 1865, 1866, 1867, and 1868,—5 years	4,898,583,083	2,684,154	16,780,588

River Etherow, with Arnfield and Hollingworth brooks added by approximation :—

Gallons run to waste daily—average.

1864	12,044,472
1865	9,896,646
1866	31,728,585
1867	24,854,504
1868	18,465,828
1864 and 1865, being the mean of 2 consecutive dry years	10,728,915
1864, 1865, 1866, 1867, and 1868,—5 years	19,196,907

Results of calculations of gaugings of Water supplied from the Reservoirs during the five years ending 1868.

The gaugings in question relate only to the water supplied from the works in the main valley of Longdendale. The quantity of water taken to the city from the main valley and the Hollingworth and Arnfield valleys is an assumption,—and it is also assumed that the produce of the Arnfield and Hollingworth valley is approximately the same as in the main valley.

YEAR 1864.

Total area draining to the lowest gauge, after deducting 845 acres for the Torside brook diversion, 14,900 acres.

	Cubic feet.
Total quantity discharged as compensation water	745,588,800
" " waste water	515,212,118
Total quantity discharged to the river	1,260,800,918

	Gallons per day.	
Average supply taken by the city and district	10,828,645	
It is assumed that the quantity taken from the Hollingworth and Arnfield districts would be about	2,000,000	
Leaving supply for city taken from main valley as	8,828,645	
8,828,645 gallons × 365 days ÷ 6¼ =		517,248,061

Water stored in Reservoirs :—	Cubic feet.	
In store, January 1st, 1864	355,555,049	
" " 1865	367,331,946	
Difference being stored		11,776,897
Total produce from 14,900 acres in the main valley of Longdendale		1,899,825,876

= 2·912 feet or 34·944 inches of rain out of a mean rainfall over the district for the year of 45·00 inches, showing the loss by evaporation and absorption to be in this year 10·056 inches.

Year 1865.

Total area draining to the lowest gauge—as in 1864—14,900 acres.

	Cubic feet.
Total quantity discharged as compensation water	741,308,000
" " waste water	479,698,195
Total quantity discharged to the river	1,221,006,195

	Gallons per day.	
Average supply taken by the city and district	11,156,433	
Of which quantity it is assumed that there would be taken from the Arnfield and Hollingworth district	2,000,000	
Leaving supply to city taken from the main valley	9,156,433	
9,156,433 × 365 days ÷ 6¼ =		536,452,334
		1,757,458,529

Deduct quantity taken out of store :—	Cubic feet.	
In store, January 1st, 1865	367,331,946	
" " 1866	356,736,617	
Taken out of store		10,595,329
Total produce from 14,900 acres in the main valley of Longdendale		1,746,863,200

= 2·691 feet or 32·292 inches of rain out of a mean rainfall over the district for the year of 41·316 inches, showing the loss by evaporation and absorption in this year to be 9·024 inches.

Year 1866.

Total area draining to the lowest gauge—as in 1864 and 1865—14,900 acres.

	Cubic feet.
Total quantity discharged as compensation water	748,688,000
" " waste water	1,618,484,858
Total quantity discharged to the river	2,362,172,858

	Gallons per day.	
Average supply taken by the city and district	11,281,928	
Of which quantity it is assumed that there would be taken from the Arnfield and Hollingworth district	2,000,000	
Leaving supply to the city taken from the main valley	9,281,928	
$9,281,928 \times 365 \div 6\tfrac{1}{4} =$		542,804,477

Add quantity stored:—

	Cubic feet.	
In store, January 1st, 1866	856,736,617	
" " 1867	878,349,320	
Taken out of store		21,612,703
Total produce from 14,900 acres in the main valley of Longdendale		2,927,590,088

= 4·511 feet or 54·132 inches of rain out of a mean rainfall over the district for the year of 65·439 inches, showing the loss by evaporation and absorption in this year to be 11·307 inches.

Year 1867.

Total area draining to the lowest gauge—as in 1864, 1865, and 1866—14,900 acres.

	Cubic feet.
Total quantity discharged as compensation water	788,936,000
" " waste water	1,239,122,294
Total quantity discharged to the river	1,978,058,294

	Gallons per day.	
Average supply taken by the city and district	13,250,000	
Of which quantity it is assumed that there would be taken from the Arnfield and Hollingworth district	2,000,000	
Leaving supply to the city taken from the main valley	11,250,000	
$11,250,000 \times 365 \div 6\tfrac{1}{4} =$		659,109,149

Add quantity stored:—

	Cubic feet.	
In store, January 1st, 1867	878,349,320	
" " 1868	887,471,678	
		9,122,358
Total produce from 14,900 acres in the main valley of Longdendale		2,646,289,801

= 4·077 feet or 48·924 inches of rain out of a mean rainfall over the district for the year of 56·496 inches, showing the loss by evaporation and absorption in this year to be 7·572 inches.

Year 1868.

The drainage area to the lowest gauge varied in this year as during a portion of the last half of the year the temporary gauge at Vale House was used. The mean area for the whole year has been taken at 653,181,538 square feet, or nearly 15,000 acres.

		Cubic feet.
Total quantity discharged as compensation water		685,405,246
" " waste water		942,653,560
Total quantity discharged to the river		1,628,058,806

	Gallons per day.	
Average supply taken by the city and district	12,059,333	
Of which quantity it is assumed that there would be taken from the Hollingworth and Arnfield district	2,000,000	
Leaving supply to the city taken from the main valley	10,059,333	
$10,059,333 \times 365 \div 6\frac{1}{4} =$		585,874,640

Add quantity stored :—	Cubic feet.	
In store, January 1st, 1868	387,471,678	
" " 1869	430,906,416	
		43,434,738

Total produce from 15,000 acres in the main valley of Longdendale 2,257,368,184

= 8·456 feet or 41·472 inches of rain out of a mean rainfall over the district for the year of 53·515 inches, showing the loss by evaporation and absorption in this year to be 12·043 inches.

APPENDIX No. 5.—*Memorandum as to capabilities of supply from Longdendale District, May 26th, 1869.*

SUMMARY OF RESULTS OF THE EXPERIENCE OF THE FIVE YEARS ENDING DECEMBER 31ST, 1868.

Years.	Mean Rainfall of the District, being mean of returns at Woodhead, Torside, and Rhodes Wood Gauges, +10 per cent.	Total quantity which flowed off ground, as registered by the Gauges, &c.	Loss by evaporation and absorption.	Quantity supplied to the City and to the Mills.	Quantity run to waste.
	Inches.	Inches.	Inches.	Inches.	Inches.
1864	45·0	34·944	10·056	23·556	11·388
1865	41·316	32·292	9·024	23·412	8·88
1866	65·439	54·132	11·307	24·132	30·00
1867	56·496	48·924	7·572	26·016	22·908
1868	53·515	41·472	12·043	24·156	17·316
Means	52·353	42·353	10·00	24·254	18·098

APPENDIX No. 6.—*Particulars of Drought of* 1864.

Drainage area, 18,000 acres.
Drought commenced May 24th, and ended October 11th—lasting 140 days.

	Gallons.
Quantity of water in store at commencement	1,779,000,000
" " end of drought	1,253,000,000
Quantity taken from store	526,000,000

Quantity supplied during this period:—   Gallons per day.
   To mills for compensation   12,728,568
   To town, *on average*   11,070,000

Total daily .... 23,798,568 × 140 days = 3,331,799,520

Balance supplied by rain and springs 2,805,799,520

The quantity supplied by rain and springs during this period is equal to 2·05 cubic feet per second from every 1,000 acres of drainage, and to 6·85 inches of rain flowing off the ground, out of 15 inches actual rainfall during this period.

APPENDIX No. 7.—*Particulars of Drought of* 1865.

Drainage area, 18,000 acres.
Drought commenced April 18th, and ended October 8th—lasting 172 days.

	Gallons.
Quantity of water in store at commencement	2,384,000,000
" " end of drought	912,000,000
Quantity taken from store	1,472,000,000

Quantity supplied during this period:—   Gallons per day.
   To mills for compensation   12,728,568
   To town, *on average*   11,833,000

Total daily .... 24,561,568 × 172 days = 4,224,589,696

Balance supplied by rain and springs 2,752,589,696

The quantity supplied by rain and springs during this period is equal to 1·6467 cubic feet per second from every 1,000 acres of drainage, and to 6·74 inches of rain flowing off the ground, out of 14½ inches actual rainfall during this period.

APPENDIX No. 8.—*Particulars of Drought of* 1868.

Drainage area, 18,000 acres.
Drought commenced 27th April, and ended 24th September—lasting 150 days.

	Gallons.
Quantity of water in store, April 27th	2,740,000,000
Pumped by the Gorton Engine between August 12th and October 3rd	27,000,000
	2,767,000,000
Quantity of water in store, 25th September	435,679,203
	2,331,320,787

Quantity supplied during the drought:—

	Gallons.	
To mills, full supply to 10th August—105 days, at 12,728,568 per day	1,336,499,640	
From 10th August to 24th September—45 days, at 6,364,284 per day	286,392,780	
Total to mills	1,622,892,420	
To city, unlimited constant supply to 3rd August	1,404,484,145	
From 3rd August to 24th September the water was shut off at night from 6·0 p.m. to 6·0 a.m.	435,136,407	
	1,839,620,552	
		3,462,512,972
Balance, being the quantity supplied by springs and rain		1,131,192,185

The yield of rain and springs is equal to 2·77 inches of rain flowing off the 18,000 acres of drainage ground, or to a flow of ·776 cubic foot per second from every 1,000 acres. The rain during this period was 9 inches; the loss, therefore, 6·23 inches.

APPENDIX No. 9.—*Summary of results of Droughts of* 1864, 1865, *and* 1868.

Year.	Length of Drought.	Storage available.		Rainfall during the Drought.	Mean flow from Drainage Ground.			Loss by absorption and evaporation, in inches.
		In cubic feet.	Cubic feet per acre of Collecting Ground.		In inches of Rainfall.	In cubic feet per second per 1,000 acres.	In gallons per day per 1,000 acres.	
	Days.			Inches.	Inches.			
1864	140	320,000,000	17,777	15·	6·85	2·05	1,107,000	8·15
1865	172	392,000,000	21,777	14·5	6·74	1·6467	889,218	7·76
1868	150	438,000,000	24,333	9·	2·77	·776	419,040	6·23

During driest period of drought of 1868 when rainfall was least—*i. e.*, from June 1st to August 3rd, or 63 days—the mean flow from the ground was only ·5114 cubic foot per second from every 1,000 acres, and the *minimum* flow during the whole drought was in the 7 days between July 27th and August 3rd, 1868, when it amounted to only ·329 cubic foot per second from every 1,000 acres.

In 1855 the consumption of water was in round numbers 8,000,000 gallons per day; in 1881, 18,900,000 gallons per day on the average of the year; but in dry seasons it is 19,000,000 or 20,000,000 gallons per day on the average of a month; while the daily consumption, especially in frost, frequently exceeds 20,000,000 gallons.

For the five months of May, June, July, August, and September in 1880 the average consumption was about 18,500,000 gallons per day. It is at such times that the capability of a waterworks has to be tested. This is only 6,000,000 per day less than the quantity which the Corporation can calculate upon obtaining from Longdendale; and as the ordinary increase may now be taken at about 800,000 gallons per day, the Longdendale supply will only last out about eight years, should the ensuing seasons be seasons of average rainfall,—a shorter period if the seasons be dry, longer if they should be wet.

I have given on page 151 the advantage which has accrued to the city of Manchester in the extinction of fires by the introduction of a good supply of water at high pressure, and I will now proceed to describe the advantages which have been derived from the supply of *soft* water.

It has been urged, and is sincerely believed by some parties—particularly by medical men—that hard water is necessary for the formation of bone. It might be sufficient to answer this objection against soft water by instancing that the largest men in Great Britain are those who cannot get hard water if they would, and that the smallest men are those who could not get soft water if they would.

Soft Water.

But a few words may probably be said upon what *is* soft water. The term has been long known, but the distinction in degrees may be said to be the invention of the late Dr. Clarke, of Aberdeen, who fixed one grain of lime or other soap-destroying ingredient in one gallon of water, or $\frac{1}{70,000}$ as one degree of hardness. Taking his test, water does not break or curdle soap under four degrees of hardness, but it does at five degrees and upwards. Four or five degrees, therefore, is the separating point,—and just as day fades into night and night into morning, so soft water and hard water die into each other.

The truth is, I believe, that both hard and soft waters are generally wholesome, though many painful diseases are common in districts of hard water which are scarcely known in those of soft water. Pleasantness to the palate is very much the result of habit, but much depends upon aëration, temperature, and colour.

The healthiness or unhealthiness of towns depends upon many other conditions than the state of the water.

When the soft water of Loch Katrine was introduced into Glasgow in place of the comparatively hard water of the river Clyde, which varied from 7 to 9 degrees of hardness—the population then being about 350,000 persons—the saving in soap and other articles of domestic consumption was about £40,000 a-year; and less than one-half of all the soap previously used by manufacturing establishments sufficed to produce better colours and better work than twice the quantity with Clyde water.

The population now supplied by the Glasgow Waterworks is upwards of 700,000, and the rates there have been reduced from sixteenpence in the pound to eightpence in the pound, the citizens of Glasgow justly priding themselves upon the advantages which they have derived both to health and comfort from the supply of the soft water.

It had been alleged that in towns with water of over 10 degrees of hardness (the average being 14·9) the mortality was only 22·2 per thousand of the population, while in those having water under 10 degrees (the average being 4·9) the mortality was 26·1, and in London, the water being 13 degrees of hardness, the mortality was 23·1 per thousand. From this statement it was inferred that the excessive mortality of towns using water under 10 degrees of hardness—a perfectly arbitrary division between hard and soft water—was due to the use of soft water.

Some years ago I had occasion to investigate this question.

On this investigation it appeared that the population of the towns using what was called hard water was 10·17 persons to the acre, while in those using soft water it was 21·474; so that in the towns of higher mortality the people were living more than twice as thickly upon the ground as in those places with which they were compared.

The population of Birmingham—a town supplied with water of $15\frac{1}{4}$ degrees of hardness, and, therefore, a hard-water town—was made up of those living in Birmingham, King's Norton, and Aston, the density of population being respectively 100, 1·27, and 2·7 persons to the acre, and the mortality being also respectively 26·5, 17·1, and 21 per thousand.

Liverpool is composed of Liverpool and West Derby, the two places being supplied with the same water of 9·6 degrees of hardness. The mortality in Liverpool was 33·29, and in West Derby 22·73 per thousand, the density of population being respectively 100 and 3·7 per acre,—sufficient, it may be thought, to account for the difference.

Manchester, Salford, and Chorlton-on-Medlock, all places supplied with the soft water of the Manchester Waterworks, exhibited a mortality at the same time of 31·48, 26, and 23·94 per thousand respectively. If the high death-rate in Manchester were due to the soft water, why did it not poison as many persons per thousand in Chorlton-on-Medlock and Salford?

While it is pretty clear from these statements that the high mortality of certain manufacturing towns is not due solely to the water the inhabitants drink, it is also evident, from previous statements, that very great economy is the result of its use, and therefore, I am, and always have been, a strong advocate for the introduction of soft water wherever it can be obtained. By proper management it may be delivered as colourless as the white water of a chalk district.

The saving in Manchester by the use of the water from Longdendale in place of that which they might possibly, but not probably, obtain from the new red sandstone beneath the city, cannot be estimated at less than eighty or a hundred thousand pounds per annum in domestic consumption alone, to say nothing of the saving which results from its use in trade.

It must, however, be admitted that in some cases soft water acts destructively upon lead pipes, through which it is ordinarily conveyed to dwelling houses, and carries with it so much lead as to be injurious to health. Such water must be avoided for domestic supplies; but it is generally the case that the effect of soft water upon lead is only transient, and the pipe through which it is conveyed becomes in a short time so coated by carbonate of lead that no danger need be apprehended.

It has been stated that a large portion of the water which supplies Manchester is spring water, either conveyed directly from the springs or separately stored in reservoirs set apart for the storage of pure water, and that before it was admitted to the pipes, which carry it to the city and there distribute it, the water was strained through copper wire gauze, no filtration being considered necessary. The water so delivered was for many years of excellent quality, but as the demand increased the springs and selected water did not furnish the quantity required, and the deficiency had to be made up by drawing from reservoirs in which water originally turbid had been stored, but which had apparently become so clarified and purified by subsidence and exposure as to be considered in all respects unexceptionable. Complaints, however, were occasionally made that the water was not what it formerly was, and as this was supposed to arise in part from the water stored in the Gorton reservoirs of the old company the supply from these reservoirs was discontinued. Some small settling reservoirs were constructed below the Arnfield reservoir for arresting any vegetable or other objectionable matter from the hills, and the watercourses were cleared out more frequently than formerly. These measures have been effective, and have put an end to all complaints. The water which is admitted to the pipes is as pure as it can be—no filtration could make it purer, but a certain amount of contamination arises in the pipes themselves which cannot be avoided. In the case of Manchester, too, it must be remembered that the pipes of the old water company, encrusted and lined with innumerable mussels, were incorporated in the system of general distribution, and they will no doubt contribute to the contamination.

On the 7th of February, 1877, I was able to report to the Water Committee as follows:—

"Gentlemen,—It is with unusual gratification that I now have to report an examination which I made of the works in Longdendale on the 31st ultimo.

"The whole of the works in that valley may be said to be now substantially completed.

"The Woodhead reservoir had, for the first time, run over the waste weir on the 14th January, and water was running over on the day of my visit. Thus was successfully brought to a termination the labour and anxiety of nearly a third of a century; for the works at the Woodhead reservoir commenced in August, 1848.

"On the completion of the embankment of this reservoir, and the attempted filling of it with water in 1851 or 1852, leakages appeared which created distrust in the soundness of the foundation on which the embankment rested. Various unsuccessful attempts were made to render the reservoir watertight. Eight years were subsequently spent in examining the valley on both sides of and below the river, in order to ascertain where a perfectly secure embankment could be constructed. Such a site having been discovered, it was determined to obtain an Act of Parliament for the construction of a new embankment. This Act was obtained in the year 1863, and the works were commenced shortly after. It is thus about thirteen years since the embankment which has now been so successfully completed was determined upon.

"In order that you may understand the difficulties which have been surmounted, I hand you in a geological section of the puddle-trench of the new embankment, from which you will see the various dislocated strata we had to contend with, and that the new puddle-trench has been sunk about 160 feet below the top of the old embankment, and for nearly the whole of this depth through solid rock. It was also sunk between 50 and 60 feet below the old river-course in the centre of the valley, and above 100 feet below the Manchester and Sheffield Railway.

"In order to gain a good foundation in the shale, on the northerly side of the valley, where the hill rises very rapidly, a tunnel 10 feet wide, of nearly 180 yards in length, was driven into the hillside, from the bottom of which the sinking was carried on until it reached a satisfactory foundation.

"No clay puddle, no matter how thick or how well made, could have stood the wasting or penetrating power of 160 feet pressure of water. The trench, therefore, was filled with hydraulic concrete wherever water could reach it through the fissures of the rock, or wherever the strata passed through were considered so pervious as to require the construction of an absolutely watertight wall to prevent escape from the reservoir.

"The greatest depth or height of concrete wall introduced in this manner is about 110 feet, varying in thickness from 6 feet at the bottom to upwards of 20 feet at the top. Concrete has also been introduced at the waste watercourse from the reservoir to the waste weir, and everything that could be thought of has been adopted for the purpose of making the work as sound and watertight as possible. The result is eminently satisfactory. No leakage whatever has been observed, the reservoir has been filled, and the water was running over the waste weir several inches on the day of my visit.

"The Torside reservoir has also given us much anxiety and trouble; but this also, I am happy to say, was full to within 9 inches on the occasion of my visit, and everything here also was in the most perfect and satisfactory condition.

"The Rhodes Wood reservoir and the Vale House reservoir were full of water, and running over.

"The Bottoms reservoir—the last of the series—was full to the level of the present height of the waste weir, which is 7 feet below that contemplated, and in anticipation of which, the bank across the valley and the arm puddle-trench on the south side have been constructed.

"I am thus able, for the first time, to report the completion of all the works in Longdendale, and I have to thank the Corporation for their continued confidence in me during the long period of their construction. I always felt that, if permitted, I could by time and judicious expenditure render every part of the work originally designed secure and satisfactory; but the confidence I might feel in myself I might not be able to impart to others, and it is therefore matter of special gratification to me that the Corporation have, without stint of means, entrusted every detail of the work to my judgment and control.

"The completion of the works forms a good opportunity for looking back to their origin and history.

"I laid out the first project for obtaining water from this district for the old Manchester and Salford Water Company in the year 1844. That project contemplated obtaining water from the Brushes Clough flowing to the Tame, and from the Hollingworth and Arnfield brooks flowing to the Etherow,—the works being laid out at such a level as would permit their subsequent extension into Longdendale.

"At that time the population of Manchester and Salford was about 320,000 persons. The works were in the hands of a company who durst not contemplate a large expenditure; and though my views extended far beyond the courage of the company, I had to project a scheme within what they considered would be the limits of prudent outlay.

"The Bill was introduced into Parliament, was violently opposed, but passed the Commons. The fears of the company then predominated, and the further progress of the measure was abandoned.

"Greatly disappointed, I resolved to work no more for the company.

"My inaction, however, nearly threw the future supply of water into the hands of a new company, bearing the imposing title of—'The Lancashire Water Company,' who introduced a Bill into Parliament in 1846, promoted principally by Mr. Hardcastle, of Bradshaw Brook, near Bolton, under the auspices of Mr. Hawksley.

"Acting on the advice of the Town Clerk, the Corporation wisely determined to take the supply into their own hands,—opposed the Bill of 'The Lancashire Water Company,' and on the promise of introducing a Bill of their own in the next session, defeated it.

"I had, while this opposition was proceeding, the honour of being consulted by the Corporation. Encouraged by the larger views which had in the meantime taken possession of all who had studied the water question, I laid out a much bolder scheme than that of 1844, abandoning the feeders of the river Tame and going at once into Longdendale, to which my views had always been directed. What I proposed was adopted by the Corporation, and successfully carried out by them in the session of 1847.

"Little was known at that time about gravitation water supply. Many of the few schemes which had then been executed had included a compensation reservoir for the millowners, to store flood waters in lieu of streams to be abstracted. I had, for several years previously, been engaged in similar undertakings at Bolton and elsewhere; and the first project for obtaining water from Longdendale contemplated the construction of the Woodhead reservoir for the exclusive use of the millowners, and the abstraction of various streams and the construction of other reservoirs for the use of the Corporation.

"In the course of the conduct of the Bill through Parliament these views were changed. It was deemed more to the interests of the Corporation to obtain the entire control of the water, subject to the delivery of a stipulated quantity of water to the river. Arrangements for this purpose were made with the opposing millowners, and a greatly enlarged scheme was introduced in the next session of Parliament, which virtually gave the Corporation the entire waters of Longdendale, subject to the delivery of a certain quantity to the river.

"This quantity was, from want of information at the time, and in ignorance of the real yield of the district, fixed at too high a figure, and was subsequently reduced by purchase.

"Various Acts have since been obtained for further extensions, chiefly with the object of increasing the storage; and now, almost every available site in the whole valley above the manufacturing population has been converted into a reservoir, and the utmost quantity of water which the district will yield has been obtained for Manchester.

"This quantity may be stated in round numbers at about 24,000,000 gallons per day; but it requires the completion of the storage reservoirs at Denton, now in progress, before it can be relied upon in dry seasons.

"At the time the works were first projected and in the hands of the old water company, the daily consumption was about 4,000,000 gallons. In 1855 it was about 8,000,000 gallons; and during the year just passed it has averaged 16,000,000 gallons. This, however, is less than the average of the preceding year, and must not be taken as the present normal quantity required in dry seasons. The smaller consumption during last year is due to several causes. It was a year of more than average rainfall; and the rain fell so as to do away to a great extent with street watering and garden watering, and to reduce the quantity taken for trade and domestic purposes. The town of Stockport, which is entitled, if it demands it, to 1,000,000 gallons, has taken very little; and much of the economy is due to the vigilance of Mr. Berrey, and house-to-house inspection for the purpose of reducing waste.

"The population now dependent on the Corporation is about 760,000 persons. In years of small rainfall the consumption is nearly 18,000,000 gallons per day; and the legitimate increase due to increasing population, their greater use of water, and extended trade demands, will approach, if it does not amount to, 1,000,000 gallons per day annually.

"You have at present a larger quantity in store than you ever had before; and when the Denton reservoirs are completed, you will be prepared for the greatest demand that can come upon you up to what the district will yield.

"You have now in your reservoirs 4,266,000,000 gallons; and the springs are at present so abundant, that nearly all the water which is to-day brought to Manchester is spring water which has never been impounded."

I have introduced this Report because it contains a short history of the works from their commencement to their completion, and gives in a brief form an account of what had been done in the 29 years which had then elapsed.

Up to the end of 1882, the cost of the works in Longdendale, the piping of the city, and the purchase of the old company's works, was £3,068,929. 8s. 7d., and the revenue for the year 1882 was £209,842. 10s. 8d.

Any history of the Manchester Waterworks would be incomplete which did not contain some account of what has been called the "Thirlmere Scheme." *Thirlmere Scheme.*

The works in Longdendale were laid out in 1846—37 years ago,—when the population to be supplied with water was not one-half of what it is at present.

A conviction that the prosperity—indeed the very existence—of a town depended on its supply of water, led me very frequently to consider where additional sources were to be obtained when those at the command of the Corporation were exhausted.

The prosperity of the cotton trade, and the growth of the various manufacturing towns in the neighbourhood of Manchester, had led to the extension of the waterworks of these various places; and, consequently, nearly all the good water which could be obtained from the hilly districts which lay to the north and east of Manchester had been appropriated, and sources to which I had looked forward for extensions of the supply to Manchester were no longer available. The population which the Corporation had undertaken to supply had increased from about 350,000 to nearly 1,000,000, and smaller places, less favourably circumstanced, were looking to the great cotton metropolis for assistance. Schemes which were too large in themselves to be profitably undertaken by small communities could be advantageously carried out by large towns, and as large supplies could generally be obtained more cheaply than small ones, I turned my attention to every district from which it was probable that an abundant supply could be obtained. I have, in the foregoing pages, described how the Longdendale project was gradually carried out, and shown how the demand for water was constantly on the increase.

I had long been of opinion that the vast quantity of water which was precipitated on the Cumberland and Westmorland hills and was running uselessly to waste, could be impounded and utilized for the manufacturing districts of Lancashire and Yorkshire.

I never could see the wisdom of the view which would confine the supply of water to the towns or places which lay within any particular watershed. Where the water was most abundant it was generally the least wanted; and towns had grown up where it was often difficult to find or obtain this essential contribution to life and prosperity. To my mind, the idea of confining such places to their own watersheds, and preventing their going for what they wanted where there was enough and to spare, was absurd. As well might it be urged that the coal which is produced in the neighbourhood of Newcastle should all be consumed in the valley of the Tyne, and none of it conveyed to London *or* the valley of the Thames.

The observations on rainfall of Dr. Miller, of Whitehaven, on the hills of Cumberland and Westmorland, had shown that the rain of average years varied according to locality from 80 to 200 inches, and most of it ran uselessly to sea. Here, at all events, was more than enough for the district in which it fell, or for the wants of the towns or mills on the rivers which conveyed it to the sea. Water was as much the natural produce of these hills as the artificial products of cotton and woollen in the towns on the plain.

The principle of "compensation" in water had shown from long experience that millers were benefitted by the storing of flood waters, which had the effect of equalizing the flow and mitigating the evils resulting from too much at one time and too little at another.

On these principles most of the great waterworks of the country had been carried out. Manchester is supplied from a stream which does not run through that city; Glasgow derives the bulk of its excellent and abundant supply from the valley of the river Forth; while Edinburgh, which lies on this river, obtains its water from streams which flow from other valleys. Liverpool helped itself from the Rivington hills, near Chorley, and is now obtaining a fresh supply from some of the sources of the Severn.

In all these cases, and in many others, water could not have been obtained had the towns been confined to their own districts and watersheds; and however taking may be the idea of dividing the kingdom into watersheds for the supply of water, the practice has wisely been to permit important places, to which water was a necessity, to go to other districts for what they wanted.

It was not enough, however, that there should be a large precipitation of rain, nor a sufficient extent of elevated ground. The water partook of the geological character of the district from which it flowed. The hard water of a limestone or new red sandstone district would not do. Soft water was essential to many processes of trade on which the employment of the inhabitants depended. It was equally desirable for all domestic and for most dietetic purposes, and it had therefore to be sought for in such localities among the hills as from their geological formation would ensure its production.

From a combination of all these circumstances, the Thirlmere scheme was adopted.

Pure soft water is obtained from some sands,—from the lower coal measures,—from the millstone grit,—from the silurian formation,—from granite, and from other primitive rocks. The hills which intervene between Lancashire and Yorkshire are, for the most part, millstone grit and the sandstones of the lower coal measures; and the towns which lie at the foot at each side owe their original existence, to a great extent, to the copious streams of soft water on which they were placed. These towns, from small beginnings, have increased in size and importance, and have appropriated nearly all the water which the neighbouring hills produce, so that towns which want large additional supplies must go to greater distances to obtain them. Hence the necessity of Manchester undertaking the construction of a work, the distance and cost of which have somewhat astonished those who are not well informed on the subject. Provision for the wants of the inhabitants and the trades they carried on was imperative; and it was necessary, above all things, to prevent any approach to a water famine. The gradual and regular increase in the daily consumption of water pointed to a no distant period at which the demand would equal or exceed the supply; and all who were interested in the future growth and prosperity of the district, and carefully considered its wants, saw the urgency of the case, and the desirableness of providing for all purposes and at all times an abundant supply of water.

Much, of course, depended on the seasons,—a succession of wet seasons might postpone the necessity for an additional supply for some years, but a succession of dry years might equally accelerate it; and as prudent men, the members of the Corporation of Manchester ought to provide for the latter. The total quantity of water which could be obtained from the Longdendale district was $24\frac{1}{2}$ million gallons per day on the average of the year. In the year 1878 the demand had reached nearly 18 million gallons per day on the average, and in dry weather and hard frost it was more; and it was increasing at the rate of nearly one million gallons per day per annum.

Any large scheme would take several years to complete from its first commencement, and therefore the demand might reasonably be expected to be equal to the supply before any fresh quantity could be obtained.

It was under these circumstances that the Act of 1879 for the construction of the Thirlmere Waterworks was obtained, but wet seasons, depression in trade, and a diminished surplus revenue, have contributed to induce the Corporation of Manchester to postpone the execution of the works; but the time has now arrived when any further postponement would be dangerous to the trade and prosperity of Manchester.

Before, however, describing the "Thirlmere Scheme," it will be desirable to show the various steps which led to its adoption in 1878, and to the Act which was obtained for its construction in 1879. These will be fully explained by what follows.

In the year 1868 I wrote an exhaustive Report, addressed to the Water Committee, showing how the consumption had increased since 1855, and referring to various reports in which I had calculated the quantity of water available for Manchester, and the recommendations which I had made from time to time for increasing the supply.

After showing the means at the disposal of the Corporation, and the gradual increase in the demand for water, I observe as follows:—

"It seems to me imperative that the question of extension beyond your present district should be immediately considered."

And I conclude with the following observation:—

"I have ventured to bring this subject before you from a sense of its great importance, and of the responsibility which rests upon me as your adviser, and upon yourselves as the Managing Committee, to look ahead and provide beforehand for the wants of the great community wholly dependent for their supply of water upon the waterworks under your charge."

In the spring of 1874 I had the honour of being consulted by the Water Committee of the borough of Liverpool, and for them I investigated all the available districts which had from time to time been previously proposed for extending their supplies. These districts included—

The Lancashire and Westmoreland lakes and rivers.

The Head Waters of the River Lune.

The Ulleswater and Haweswater Lakes.

The Hodder and the Ribble.

The Elwy and Alyd, tributaries of the River Clwyd.

The Ceiriog, a tributary of the River Dee.

Bala Lake.

The River Dee and its tributaries, and Windermere Lake.

These were all reported on by the late Mr. Duncan, the engineer of the Liverpool Waterworks, in the year 1866. He gave the preference to Bala Lake, which Mr. Rawlinson, C.B. (now Sir Robert Rawlinson), had also done in 1846 and again in 1866.

Nothing was done by the Liverpool Corporation after the Report of Mr. Duncan till 1873, when instructions were given to Mr. Jackson, C.E., of Bolton, to report his opinion on the best scheme for an additional supply of water.

Mr. Jackson reported in the early part of 1874, and it was after that that I was called in to examine into all the previously-named schemes, which had been successively abandoned as insufficient or as too costly by Mr. Jackson, who presented a new project for obtaining water from Bleasdale and Wyredale, between Preston and Lancaster.

It thus became my duty to examine all the districts which had at any time been proposed, including Mr. Jackson's new scheme, and therefore, both from this investigation and from the fact of my being, or having been, the engineer of most of the waterworks and canals which derived their supplies from the Pennine Chain of Hills, and of having, more or less, been consulted upon almost every work which had been projected or carried out by other engineers, I was intimately acquainted with every district from which water could be obtained.

I reported to the Waterworks Committee of the Corporation of Liverpool in August, 1874, and I concluded with recommending Ulleswater and Haweswater, to be carried out as a joint project with the city of Manchester for about three-fourths of the whole distance. Each Corporation to go for 40,000,000 gallons per day, or for a total of 80,000,000 gallons.

I recommended this scheme specially to their consideration on account of "the purity of the water, the inexhaustible supply, the simplicity of the "work, the non-interference with districts which may be reasonably claimed "by other towns, and the settlement of the question practically for ever."

I stated I was at that time, as engineer to the Manchester Corporation, looking out for a source from which Manchester might most cheaply and conveniently obtain additional supplies.

In May, 1875, I again reported to the Liverpool Corporation, answering various questions which had been submitted to me, and ending with an examination of the probable yield of wells in the New Red Sandstone (the prevailing geological formation in the neighbourhood of Liverpool, as it is also in Manchester), and the cost to be incurred (the Water Committee of Liverpool having determined that 20,000,000 or 25,000,000 gallons per day were as much as they would require in addition to their present source of supply), and I reported as follows :—

"The question of the probable yield of wells was thoroughly investigated by Mr. Robert Stephenson in 1850; and while his conclusions have, I think, never been questioned, experience has proved that they were substantially correct. The two important conclusions at which he arrived, as affecting the question now under consideration, were—That the sandstone is generally very pervious, admitting of deep wells drawing their supply from distances exceeding one mile; that there is little or no probability of obtaining more than 1,000,000 or 1,200,000 gallons a day from any one well, and this when not interfered with by other deep wells. We have been considering how best to obtain 20 or 25 million gallons of water per day by gravitation works, in addition to the present supply of 17 millions. Supposing that this quantity were to be obtained from the new red sandstone, it would require from 20 to 25 separate wells and pumping establishments, which, if they were placed two miles apart, would have to be scattered over 60 or 70 square miles of country. Mr. Stephenson estimated the cost of each well at £20,000, to which sum many things had to be added, making a total of £30,800 for each new station. Taking into account the rise in labour and materials since 1850, each well and pumping station may be put down as costing now at least £40,000.

"Twenty wells at £40,000 each £800,000

"The annual working expenses, exclusive of interest on capital, be estimated at about £1,600. These may now be taken at £2,000, which at 25 years' purchase, or 4 per cent., will be equal to £50,000 for each well.

"Twenty wells at £50,000 each........................... 1,000,000

£1,800,000

"To this sum must be added the cost of an Act of Parliament, interest on outlay during construction, legal and engineering expenses, and the cost of the necessary pipes and reservoirs for connecting all these twenty wells, and bringing their produce into a concentrated and workable system. All these items added, would make the cost greater than that of any of the schemes which have been recommended. Cost, however, is not the only point to be considered. All evidence goes to show that the supply from wells would be precarious, that it gradually diminishes by long-continued pumping, and that the water—hard to begin with—becomes harder by continuous pumping. From the analyses made for Mr. Stephenson's report, the hardness of the water from the public wells then existing was about 15°, according to Dr. Clarke's test. This must be compared with water from Bleasdale and Wyredale of probably 2° or 3° of hardness, and with Ulleswater of about 1°. The saving to the town from the softer water would go a long way towards paying the cost of the undertaking. I may also observe that if the water were derived from wells, they would, most probably, be much in the immediate neighbourhood of Liverpool; and as the water which supplied them would all come from the surface, it would carry down with it the pollution caused by the sewage of the town and the manure of the country, which might eventually deteriorate the quality of the water extracted."

On the 18th February, 1875, and again on the 23rd June, 1875, I reported to the Water Committee of the Corporation of Manchester, drawing their attention to the frequency of the occasions on which I had brought the subject of an extended water supply under their notice, especially requesting their attention to my report of the 6th October, 1874, in which I observe as follows:—

"It is of importance to observe that the quantity of water now required is constantly upon the increase. In 1855 the total quantity supplied was, in round numbers, 8,000,000 gallons a day. In 1865, ten years subsequently, it was upwards of 11,000,000, and during the summer of the present year it has been equal to nearly 18,000,000 gallons per day on the average, having in one week amounted to nearly 21,000,000 gallons per day. The quantity of water used per head, taking that as the unit of measurement for all purposes, is constantly upon the increase."

In the report of October, 1874, I also observe:—

"The domestic habits of the people are undergoing great changes by the freer use of water for the purposes of ablution, and by the introduction of water-closets and baths, while, at the same time, greater use is made of water by the residents in the suburbs, who not only use water for ordinary domestic purposes, but for stables, cattle, and gardens, all of which may be considered legitimate purposes, and for which the supply of water to a town should be employed.

"In a report dated the 7th October, 1868, I specially allude to the same subject. In that report the progressive increase was estimated, from the information then before me, at 1,000,000 gallons per day per annum; and I showed that at that rate of increase the quantity of water which the Longdendale district would afford, namely, 24 or 25 million gallons per day, would only last out eight or nine years from that date, or until about 1877.

"By the exercise of careful supervision, and well directed economy in the use of the water, the increased consumption which was then anticipated has been kept down, and the annual increase since that time has not amounted to what was then estimated. Care and economy, however, have, I think, produced the utmost beneficial effect which can be expected from them, and for the last five years the average annual increase appears to have been from 700,000 to 800,000 gallons of water per day, while during the last two years it has exceeded 1,200,000 gallons per day.

"The consumption to be provided for must not be taken upon the *average* daily amount of the year, but upon that which occurs during periods of drought, when the natural volume of the streams has to be supplemented by the water held in store. The consumption during such periods will be best seen from the following table:—

"*In Summer during Drought.*

	Gallons.
"The average daily consumption during the four months of June, July, August, and September, 1874, was	17,675,915
"Ditto for the month of June, 1874	18,768,758
"Ditto for the week ending June 22nd, 1874	19,636,229

"*In Winter during Frost.*

"Average daily consumption in the week ending December 28th, 1874	17,599,129
"Ditto January 4th, 1875	19,404,574
"Ditto January 11th, 1875	20,580,490

"The average daily consumption throughout the year 1874 was 16,713,957 gallons.

"As years pass away we are enabled by the continuous observations which are taken to calculate with more certainty the resources at your command.

"The utmost quantity which you can safely calculate upon obtaining in extreme dry seasons from the Longdendale district, even with the aid of the reservoirs you are proposing to construct at Denton (Audenshaw) is only from 24 to 25 million gallons per day. This is but 7,000,000 gallons per day more than is now delivered, and if the annual increase goes on as it has done, but six or seven years will elapse before the demand will exceed the means of supply.

"This is a serious matter for the future prosperity of Manchester and its neighbourhood, and I make, therefore, no apology for bringing the subject before you, and for urging your special attention to it. Your responsibility as the Water Committee of the Corporation, and mine as your professional adviser, are deeply involved in providing an ample supply of water for the important district which is under your charge."

Believing at that time that Liverpool would join with Manchester in getting the supply of water which the communities of both places required, I recommended to Manchester the adoption of Ulleswater and Haweswater in combination with Liverpool.

In my report of the 23rd June, 1875, I showed how the consumption per head was increasing and what was the increase, both within and without the city, both for domestic and trade supplies. In this report I observe:—

"The population of the districts immediately adjoining Manchester, and indeed for some distance all round, must be considered as inhabitants of

Manchester, probably carrying on their trade in the city and living beyond its precincts. They cannot be looked upon as aliens, nor should their interests be neglected, when it is seen that the increase in the domestic supply outside the city is nearly four times as great as it is within the city, and in the trade supply nearly three times as great.

"The rate of increase during the past five years in the domestic and trade supplies, both within and beyond the city, is as follows:—

"*Domestic supply from* 1869 *to* 1874.

"Within the city.............................. 14·2 per cent.
"Beyond the city.............................. 52·5 per cent.

"*Trade supply for the same period.*

"Within the city.............................. 15· per cent.
"Beyond the city.............................. 39·8 per cent."

In July, 1875, I was taken seriously ill, and did not attend to business till midsummer, 1876.

In the meantime, Liverpool had determined that "the carrying out "of a scheme in conjunction with Manchester might involve complicated "arrangements," and they had therefore resolved to seek for an independent supply without any combination with Manchester. It therefore became a question as to how and where Manchester, going independently, could best and most cheaply obtain the water it wanted.

Thirlmere had been suggested by Mr. Grave, the then Chairman of the Water Committee, who resided in the lake district; and during my illness, in the latter part of 1875, the question had been investigated by my then principal assistant and now my partner, Mr. Hill.

As soon as I was able, I examined the district myself, and reported to the Water Committee of the Corporation on the 22nd June, 1876.

I repeated an opinion which I had previously expressed,—that where a large outlay was contemplated in bringing water a distance of about 100 miles, a supply of not less than 40,000,000 gallons per day should be provided for; and I state as follows, what I believe is the experience of everyone connected with waterworks:—

"In spite of all precautions, and the exercise of every economy in the use and distribution of the water, increased consumption per head will invariably follow improved or altered domestic arrangements, and larger supplies will be demanded for trades on which the prosperity of the manufacturing districts depends."

I added, that the lake district was "the only one from which such a "supply of good and wholesome soft water could be procured."

The elevation of the three lakes which are high enough for the supply of Manchester by gravitation is as follows:—

    Haweswater .... 695 feet above ordnance datum.
    Thirlmere .... 533 " " "
    Ulleswater .... 477 " " "

Ulleswater being high enough for the supply by gravitation; Thirlmere, which was 56 feet higher, was obviously of sufficient elevation.

My investigation ended in an entire approval of Thirlmere as an independent source of supply for Manchester, as 40,000,000 or 50,000,000 gallons of water per day could be there procured.

The lake could be raised to any required height with little or no damage to, or interference with, any adjoining property. It was in the heart of the heaviest rainfall in the kingdom. The tunnel by which the water would have to be conveyed was only between two and three miles long in place of 8¼ miles, which would have been the length of the tunnel from Ulleswater, and the greatest depth of the tunnel below the surface of the ground was only 270 feet at Dunmail Raise, instead of 1,000 feet at Kirkstone Pass.

In a subsequent report I showed that insomuch as the aqueduct was determined to be constructed of a size large enough to convey 50,000,000 gallons per day, and that Thirlmere, with the addition of Millgill and Shoulthwaite Beck, would yield this quantity, there would be no room in the aqueduct for any water from Ulleswater, and that therefore it would be expedient to take advantage of the higher elevation of Thirlmere, and divide the extra fall equally over the whole length to Manchester. The works were accordingly so laid out, and great saving in cost was effected.

Thirlmere was consequently adopted by the Water Committee, as being apparently free from many of the objections which might be urged against Ulleswater. There was little residential injury, no lead workings,—the lake was little known. The lower half—by far the most beautiful—was never seen by ordinary tourists; and the first work towards Manchester was a tunnel of three miles in length, 270 feet below the summit, instead of one 8¼ miles in length, 1,000 feet below the summit, had Ulleswater been selected.

Moreover, the rain per annum at Thirlmere is 50 per cent. greater than at Ulleswater, Windermere, or Keswick, and the bulk of it runs away in useless floods.

I therefore received instructions in 1877 for preparing the necessary plans, and in 1878 a Bill was introduced into Parliament. It was submitted to a Committee (commonly called a "hybrid" Committee), consisting of five members elected in the usual way by the Committee of Selection, and five elected by the House of Commons generally. The Bill was violently opposed by interested parties, and from a sentimental idea that it was sacrilege to invade the precincts of the lakes for any such utilitarian purpose as giving a supply of water to famishing thousands of the manufacturing districts.

So far from the beautiful features of the country being injured by the operations of the Corporation, they will be preserved; for, in order to maintain the purity of the water to be collected in Thirlmere, the Corporation have purchased the whole drainage ground to the lake, and it is their interest to prevent the erection of buildings, of lead workings, or of anything which will tend to injure or contaminate the water.

The Committee, of which Dr. Lyon Playfair was the chairman, decided that Manchester being first supplied with 25 gallons per head per day according to its population, might be called upon to afford supplies of water to any place in the neighbourhood of the aqueduct between Thirlmere and Manchester.

This condition the Corporation of Manchester were quite willing to accept; but when the Bill was introduced into the House of Lords it was then ruled that it was a different Bill to that which had originally been introduced, and it was therefore thrown out on Standing Orders.

This objection was met in the following Session, and the Act for the construction of the works and the appropriation of Thirlmere was finally passed in the Session of 1879.

The execution of the works has been delayed from the causes which have been already mentioned, but a large portion of the property required has been already acquired, and the line of aqueduct from Thirlmere to near Bolton accurately set out.

It is proposed to raise the surface of the lake 50 feet $9\frac{1}{4}$ inches by an embankment at the outlet, which is never visited by any ordinary tourist.

A few fishermen may have been there; but there is no road to it, and it is in a rocky ravine, hidden from view by woods on each side.

By this raising, the lake will be greatly extended, and will be more in harmony with the surrounding scenery than the narrow river-like mere which now exists.

The higher the lake is raised, and the more water it is made to contain, the less will it be drawn down by the abstraction of water taken to Manchester. Less surface will be exposed at the upper end on the lowering of the water, and as the ground there consists of gravel and detritus from the hills, a fresh beach will be created which will rival the much-admired "silver strand" of Loch Katrine.

In place of a bad hilly road on the westerly side, now inaccessible to carriages, and rarely travelled except by a hardy pedestrian, the Corporation propose to substitute a good carriage road—following the sinuosities of the hills, and therefore free from the objections of straight lengths,—which will communicate with existing roads at each end and be thrown open to the public, thus affording to tourists, for the first time, the opportunity of seeing the lower lake.

The roads to be made by the Corporation will enable tourists to drive all round the lake; and tourists staying at Keswick or Grassmere may enjoy what will be one of the most beautiful drives in the lake district.

The aqueduct, after leaving Thirlmere, will enter a tunnel of three miles in length, emerging in the valley which leads to Grassmere. It will keep the high land above Grassmere, Rydal, and Windermere; it will be tunnelled under Chapel Green, Nab Scar, and Skelgill Wood; and where not tunnelled, will be cut out of the solid ground, so as to be free from all risk of leakage or bursting. The surface will be restored, and in two or three years after the work is completed no external trace will be visible. It will cross Troutbeck by an inverted iron syphon pipe buried in the ground, and be continued behind the residences of Hole Hird, St. Catherine's, and Elleray, by a tunnel nearly two miles in length, and nearly two miles to the east of the Windermere Railway Station.

The same mode of construction will be continued to near Bolton, the valleys of the Kent, the Lune, the Ribble, and a few others being crossed by inverted syphon pipes,—and at the bridges across rivers only, and at each end of the pipes, will any portion of the works be visible.

No residential injury will be inflicted, the surface will be restored, and no ground will be acquired except for bridges across rivers and a few manholes. Nothing more than an easement is necessary for the aqueduct.

The aqueduct, instead of being dreaded, should be looked upon as a blessing, being, in fact, a river of water where no water now exists.

From near Bolton the water will be conveyed in cast-iron pipes, mainly along public roads, to the various existing service reservoirs of the Manchester Corporation for distribution to the inhabitants.

The present area of the lake is 328¼ acres; and when raised as proposed (50 feet 9¼ inches) it will be 793 acres. The available capacity thus raised, when full, will be 1,300 million cubic feet, equal to upwards of 22,000,000 gallons per day for a whole year without rain, or to 32¼ inches in depth of water collected from the drainage area.

The drainage area is as follows:—

To the lake	7,400	acres
To Mill Gill	2,500	"
To Shoulthwaite Beck	1,020	"
Total	10,920	"

Say 11,000 acres.

		Gallons per day.
At 80 inches of rain collected in a year the produce will be		54,600,000
Compensation in respect of Thirlmere itself	4,126,425	
Compensation for the Mill Gill and Shoulthwaite Becks	1,394,062	
		5,520,487
		49,079,513

Return of Rainfall during 1877.

Month.	Helvellyn. Elevation, 1,900 feet.	Whiteside. Elevation, 2,100 feet.	Ullscarf. Elevation, 2,100 feet.	Armboth Fells. Elevation, 1,656 feet.	Wythburn. Elevation, 580 feet.	Armboth. Elevation, 550 feet.
	Inches.	Inches.	Inches.	Inches.	Inches.	Inches.
January	—	—	—	—	—	—
February	—	—	—	—	—	—
March ....*	3·3	2·4	4·5	2·9	4·0	3·5
April	4·8	5·0	4·9	3·6	3·8	3·5
May	7·5	7·8	9·6	6·7	6·8	6·0
June	6·8	6·0	10·2	7·1	6·7	6·5
July	12·0	10·3	14·2	9·7	10·8	8·5
August	10·9	10·1	13·1	9·4	9·8	9·0
September	5·5	5·4	8·4	6·4	5·6	5·1
October	14·9	15·1	22·1	17·3	16·7	14·8
November	17·1	22·2	28·9	20·0	22·0	20·3
December	7·8	7·3	14·6	10·3	10·2	8·7
	90·6	91·1	130·5	93·4	96·4	85·9

	Helvellyn.	Whiteside.	Ullscarf.	Armboth Fells.	Wythburn.	Armboth.
* March.	This month consists of 29 days.	This month consists of 13 days.	This month consists of 29 days.	This month consists of 29 days.	This month consists of 30 days.	This month consists of 27 days.

Estimate of cost of the whole scheme for 50,000,000 gallons per day .... £3,425,000.

Table showing Summary of Population.

	No.	1851.	1861.	1871.	1878.
Townships which Corporation are authorized by Acts of Parliament to supply *in detail*	37	429,120	512,317	587,652	649,107
Townships supplied under existing Acts with water in bulk	20	102,214*	127,915	149,805	168,788
	57	531,334	640,232	737,457	817,895
Townships within the powers of the Stockport District Water Company, partially supplied by the Manchester Corporation	23	81,105	87,092	91,368	94,599
Totals	80	612,439	727,324	828,825	912,494

* The populations of Atherton and Tyldesley are not given separately in census returns for 1851, and are excluded consequently in the number 102,214. The probable population of these places in 1851 would not exceed 10,000.

Table showing areas of Land exposed by drawing down Lake every 10 *feet, and capacity for each* 10 *feet in depth. Area of Lake when raised* 50 *feet* 9½ *inches,* 793 *acres—capacity* 8,130,686,693 *gallons or* 1,300,909,900 *cubic feet.*

	Upper 10ft. — Area of Lake raised 40ft. = 723½ acres.		Second 10ft. — Area of Lake raised 30ft. = 653¾ acres.		Third 10ft. — Area of Lake raised 20ft. = 565¾ acres.		Fourth 10ft. — Area of Lake raised 10ft. = 454½ acres.		Fifth 10ft. — Present area of Lake = 328¾ acres.	
	Area exposed.		Area exposed.		Area exposed.		Area exposed.		Area exposed.	
	By drawing down 10ft.	Total area exposed.	By drawing down 10ft.	Total area exposed.	By drawing down 10ft.	Total area exposed.	By drawing down 10ft.	Total area exposed.	By drawing down 10ft.	Total area exposed.
	Acres.	Acres.	Acres.	Acres.	Acres.	Acres.	Acres.	Acres.	Acres.	Acres.
Area uncovered between *a* and *b*	4¾	4¾	6⅛	11¼	6¼	17⅛	5¾	23¼	12⅛	35¾
" " *b* and *c*	4¾	4¾	5¾	10½	10⅛	21	8	29	7⅛	36⅛
" " *c* and *d*	2⅛	2⅛	2	4⅛	2¼	6¾	3	9¾	3	12¾
" " *d* and *e* (At Southerly end of existing Lake).	37⅛	37⅛	33⅛	71	36¾	107¾	45⅛	153¼	52¼	205⅛
Area uncovered between *e* and *f*	¾	¾	1	1⅞	1⅛	3	1¼	4¼	1⅛	5¾
" " *f* and *g* (At Deergarth and Hawes How).	9¾	9¾	9	18¾	12¼	31	24	55	17⅛	72⅛
Area uncovered between *g* and *h*	1	1	1⅞	2¾	3	5¾	2¾	8⅛	3	11⅛
" " *h* and *i* (At Armboth).	4½	4½	6¼	10¾	8¼	19	14	33	21	54
Area uncovered between *i* and *a*	4	4	4⅛	8⅛	7⅛	16	6⅛	22⅛	8	30⅛
Totals....................	69⅛	69⅛	70⅛	139⅞	88	227¾	110¾	338⅛	126⅛	464⅞
Capacity obtained by each 10 feet...... Gallons...	2,064,835,625		1,874,100,937		1,658,688,125		1,388,184,687		1,145,482,819	
Capacity obtained by each 10 feet...... Cubic feet	330,298,700		299,856,200		265,389,800		222,101,500		183,269,200	

The foregoing is a summary of the chief points which were prepared for, or given in evidence, in the Session of 1878. Since that time, the observations upon the rainfall have been continued, and the following tables will show the complete returns for the five years ending with 1882:—

1878.	Helvellyn. Elevation, 1,900 feet.	Whiteside. Elevation, 2,100 feet.	Ullscarf. Elevation, 2,100 feet.	Armboth Fells. Elevation, 1,650 feet.	Wythburn. Elevation, 580 feet.	Armboth. Elevation, 550 feet.
	Inches.	Inches.	Inches.	Inches.	Inches.	Inches.
January	6·8	5·6	13·3	10·0	9·6	8·5
February	6·0	5·4	8·9	6·7	6·6	5·5
March	3·0	2·3	5·9	3·9	4·1	3·9
April	3·6	2·8	4·5	3·1	3·4	2·9
May	8·5	9·0	10·3	7·9	7·8	7·3
June	4·6	4·9	5·5	4·7	4·5	3·9
July	1·2	1·3	2·1	1·7	1·3	1·5
August	8·0	8·1	9·9	6·8	6·9	6·7
September	9·3	7·8	14·1	12·6	10·1	10·0
October	11·0	10·2	17·1	13·7	12·1	11·7
November	2·9	3·0	3·2	3·1	3·4	3·2
December	3·0	3·4	4·2	4·1	4·3	4·2
Total	67·9	63·8	99·0	78·3	74·1	69·3

Mean of all the gauges, 75·4 inches.

1879.	Helvellyn. Elevation, 1,900 feet.	Whiteside. Elevation, 2,100 feet.	Ullscarf. Elevation, 2,100 feet.	Armboth Fells. Elevation, 1,650 feet.	Wythburn. Elevation, 580 feet.	Armboth. Elevation, 550 feet.
	Inches.	Inches.	Inches.	Inches.	Inches.	Inches.
January	1·5	1·8	2·8	1·9	2·1	1·9
February	4·1	4·2	7·7	4·6	5·7	4·5
March	5·1	4·5	10·7	7·1	6·9	6·2
April	3·5	4·0	4·3	3·3	3·4	3·3
May	2·0	1·9	3·0	2·1	2·0	1·9
June	9·9	9·6	14·4	9·5	9·2	8·5
July	10·3	8·8	14·4	9·5	9·4	8·2
August	9·0	8·1	13·0	9·2	9·7	8·9
September	10·1	9·4	15·0	10·5	10·4	9·6
October	3·6	2·8	6·1	4·5	4·1	3·5
November	1·8	1·6	2·8	2·2	1·9	2·0
December	6·4	5·9	11·3	8·1	7·4	7·2
Total	67·3	62·6	105·5	72·5	72·2	65·7

Mean of all the gauges, 74·8 inches.

1880.	Helvellyn. Elevation, 1,900 feet.	Whiteside. Elevation, 2,100 feet.	Ullscarf. Elevation, 2,100 feet.	Armboth Fells. Elevation, 1,650 feet.	Wythburn. Elevation, 580 feet.	Armboth. Elevation, 550 feet.
	Inches.	Inches.	Inches.	Inches.	Inches.	Inches.
January	3·1	2·4	5·3	3·8	3·2	2·7
February	10·4	11·7	14·6	11·1	11·9	10·6
March	3·1	3·4	4·7	3·7	3·8	3·7
April	5·7	5·8	8·9	5·8	7·0	5·7
May	3·2	2·7	5·5	3·8	3·4	3·1
June	5·4	4·3	7·8	5·2	6·7	4·2
July	8·2	7·6	10·1	8·4	9·6	8·5
August	2·9	2·0	3·8	3·1	2·7	2·8
September	8·5	8·3	10·1	8·2	8·4	7·5
October	2·3	2·5	2·9	2·7	3·6	4·0
November	10·9	8·8	20·1	15·4	14·3	12·9
December	5·6	4·4	9·2	6·9	7·0	7·1
Total	69·3	63·9	103·0	78·1	81·6	72·8

Mean of all the gauges, 78·0 inches.

1881.	Helvellyn. Elevation, 1,900 feet.	Whiteside. Elevation, 2,100 feet.	Ullscarf. Elevation, 2,100 feet.	Armboth Fells. Elevation, 1,650 feet.	Wythburn. Elevation, 580 feet.	Armboth. Elevation, 550 feet.
	Inches.	Inches.	Inches.	Inches.	Inches.	Inches.
January	1·0	0·8	1·5	1·2	1·1	0·9
February	5·8	5·1	8·3	5·9	7·4	6·7
March	7·2	5·3	10·0	7·5	9·2	7·5
April	1·8	2·0	2·9	1·9	2·1	1·8
May	7·4	5·9	10·8	7·4	8·7	6·6
June	9·2	7·6	14·7	10·1	9·6	8·3
July	7·4	5·7	11·6	8·0	7·7	6·4
August	9·1	7·9	12·8	10·3	8·8	8·1
September	4·3	3·4	5·6	3·7	4·0	3·5
October	4·1	3·6	6·8	4·9	4·8	4·5
November	15·6	13·5	20·8	13·8	16·0	14·1
December	8·3	6·9	10·6	8·1	10·1	9·2
Total	81·2	67·7	115·9	82·8	89·5	77·6

Mean of all the gauges, 85·8 inches.

1882.	Helvellyn. Elevation, 1,900 feet.	Whiteside. Elevation, 2,100 feet.	Ullscarf. Elevation, 2,100 feet.	Armboth Fells. Elevation, 1,650 feet.	Wythburn. Elevation, 580 feet.	Armboth. Elevation, 550 feet.
	Inches.	Inches.	Inches.	Inches.	Inches.	Inches.
January	7·3	5·1	11·4	8·2	8·6	7·6
February	9·8	7·5	15·4	11·1	10·4	9·3
March	6·4	4·8	11·6	8·3	8·2	7·3
April	6·9	7·2	8·9	6·6	7·1	6·7
May	6·4	5·7	7·4	5·2	5·9	4·4
June	8·7	6·7	10·6	8·2	8·9	7·2
July	14·3	11·9	19·3	13·9	14·8	13·5
August	7·3	5·2	8·5	5·7	6·4	5·1
September	5·8	4·7	7·0	5·1	5·3	4·6
October	6·8	5·9	9·8	6·8	6·9	6·4
November	11·9	9·6	16·7	12·0	13·2	13·1
December	6·2	4·9	10·6	7·1	7·8	6·7
Total	97·8	79·2	137·2	96·2	103·5	91·9

Mean of all the gauges, 101·3 inches.

As the scheme was presented to Parliament in 1878 and 1879, the estimated cost was divided into five increments of 10 million gallons per day each. Everything which could not be conveniently executed subsequently was estimated to be completed at first. Such for instance as tunnels, "cut and cover" watercourse, the embankment at Thirlmere, and the purchase of the drainage area and land required for the first 10 million gallons per day. The subsequent expense for each increased quantity of 10 million gallons per day consisted principally of cast-iron pipes and contingencies.

Estimated cost of obtaining *first* 10 million galls. per day was £1,740,437
Estimated cost of obtaining *second* 10 million galls. per day was 372,881
Estimated cost of obtaining *third* 10 million galls. per day was 375,081
Estimated cost of obtaining *fourth* 10 million galls. per day was 458,845
Estimated cost of obtaining *fifth* 10 million galls. per day was 477,286

Making a total of £3,424,530

as the gross cost of obtaining 50 million gallons per day, which was as much as it was assumed that Thirlmere would give.

These estimates included the whole cost of conveying the water, but did not include the cost of distribution within the limits of supply, engineering or legal expenses, nor interest of money during construction.

My task is now concluded. I have described briefly the history, the present position, and the future prospects of the Manchester Water-Supply, in the hope that the story may not prove uninteresting nor uninstructive to those who have benefitted by the wisdom, the forethought, and good management of the Manchester Corporation.

I have omitted many details which might probably be of interest to the scientific hydraulic student; but their introduction would have marred the continuity of the narrative, and would, perhaps, be more fitted for a purely scientific work than for a popular description of a great and important undertaking.

APPENDICES.

APPENDICES.

APPENDIX No. 1.—*Old Manchester—its Supply of Water.*

[Reprinted *from* the *Manchester Guardian* for November, 1850.]

THAT prime necessity of life—WATER—must always form an important and essential element in the consideration of those who settle in any hitherto uninhabited locality. It was the first thing regarded by our ancestors of old—whether Britons or Romans, Saxons or Danes—in selecting a hamlet or vill, a town or borh. We may therefore expect to find that old Manchester had such a supply of this element as largely contributed to its settlement and population; and though local annals as to its most ancient periods of existence do not survive to enable us to verify the fact, we think sufficient evidence may be adduced to throw some little light on this obscure subject.

The usual natural sources of supply are streams and springs; and to these, even in a very early period of civilisation, must be added the artificial means of supply derived from sinking wells. Ancient Manchester would have tolerably pure water in the rivers Irwell, Irk, Medlock, and Tib; and in Shooter's and Corn Brooks—"once on a time" pure and pellucid, and famous for their fish. In 1322, an "extent" or survey of the manor of Manchester was taken, which enumerates the lord's "several" and other fisheries upon the Irk, Medelake, (Medlock), the Irwell, and the Gorebrook. And even in 1440 the Irk was so celebrated for the flavour of its eels that the warden of Manchester rented the right of fishery, to supply the tables of the clergy during Lent. In these old times the river Tib was an open stream; now it is a covered and offensive sewer. As to natural springs, there was a very fine and copious one near the top of King-street, in what is now Fountain-street, which gave the name to that street; and the water from which, being conducted in pipes down Market-street, to a site now covered by Mr. William Tebbutt's grocery shop, No. 4, Victoria-street, was there collected and distributed to the inhabitants by means of what was called "The Conduit," which had several supply pipes, and which in later times was surrounded by iron palisades, and kept under lock and key. We shall have to revert to this conduit, but at present our business is with still more ancient works.

Perhaps the most ancient well in Manchester is one discovered in Castle Field, in the year 1820, and which seems to have been covered and lost before even the Romans made that locality the site of their station. In Aston's

Metrical Records of Manchester, under the date of 1820, we find this discovery thus celebrated:—

> "The next month, October, this History tells,
> Was discovered perhaps the most ancient of wells,
> In cutting down land, with a view on't to build,
> Near the banks of the Medlock, in famed Castle Field;
> Where the Romans have left such a proof they were here,
> That strangers, antiquaries, always go there;
> The well it was evident, formed of hewn plank,
> Had been made by the Britons for water, a tank;
> Ere Cæsar invaded, and long ere his towers
> Rose, mocking the natives, and their sylvan bowers." *

Our next record must be of a similar discovery of a well in the same neighbourhood about 1768-4, but which was, in all probability, a Roman and not a British work. Whitaker, in his "History of Manchester" (published in 1771),

---

* In the *Manchester Exchange Herald*, of October 17th, 1820, the following notice of the work of antiquity, above alluded to, was published by the author of this trifling production:—" Last week, in cutting and carrying away a part of Castle Field, to make the ground level near a new warehouse, lately erected on the banks of the canal, a very ancient well was discovered, about four yards below the level of the field which has been cut down for the above purpose. The well was square, and was formed of four upright posts, driven at the four angles into the bed of clay, and closed in by other logs of wood, placed one upon another, in the simplest manner, on the outside, so as to form a kind of chest, which was floored with the same rude materials. The logs were rudely hewn; they had evidently never been sawn either on the sides or ends; they were about five or six inches square, and, together, formed a hollow cube of four feet. The upper logs were level with the top surface of a bed of clay by which the well was surrounded, and into which the timber had been inserted. The wood, when first discovered, had little more consistency than paste, but on its exposure to the air became much harder, and more wood-like; it was perfectly black, and so much of a coal-like appearance as to favour the theory of such naturalists as suppose that pit coal was originally a vegetable substance. At the bottom of the well, a quantity of large stones, such as in this neighbourhood are called bowlers [boulders] were found; they were black and dirty, as though they had been taken from a sewer. The clay which adhered to the timber had also changed its colour by its proximity, from the rusty iron tinge of the native clay, to the appearance of the inferior potter's clay found in Dorsetshire. Over the well, unbroken, were various strata of sand and gravel, which, as the bank was broken down, gave proof that, except for about a yard and a half below the surface of the field, it had never been exposed to daylight since the strata was laid by the disposal of a flood. The part which the section discovered to have been acted upon by human industry was very visible to the depth of about a yard, and a few yards to the west of the part beneath which the well was discovered, the remains of a part of the foundation of the ancient fortification built by the Romans, afforded evidence, by contrast of colours, that the materials immediately above the well were already there, and that the well was lost—buried by the wreck of some great flood—before the Romans began to dig the foundations which are to this day so great an object of curiosity to antiquaries. In all human probability the well was the work of the ancient Britons (before they knew how to cut stone), so as to serve for the purpose of a well, and before saws were in their possession; and as the spring from which that well had been supplied turned out in another place in the same bank after the floods, the old well was soon forgotten. In all human probability the work now discovered is upwards of 2,000 years old, for it is 1,741 years since the Romans settled here; and the section of the foundation which intersects the line of strata above the well is a proof that they were not aware of its existence."

treating of its Roman period, when the military station covered Castle Field, and any town that might exist would be on the site of Aldport, says:—

"One or more wells would be sunk about the town for the necessary supply of water to the inhabitants, and one has been discovered, placed immediately on the outside of it, and sunk for several yards in the rock. It was found about eight or nine years ago, upon the erection of a little alehouse which stands opposite to the gate of Castle Field. On opening the ground a hole appeared in the rock about six feet square, and entirely filled up with rubbish. This was made so soft and sludgy by the spring below that a staff was easily thrust into it to the depth of four or five yards, and gave a temporary vent to the waters. And three coins of brass were found in it, and a piece of thick short gold wire. The latter had not the good fortune to meet with any man of taste, and was sold to an unknown person for 13s. And of the former, two appeared to be lost when an inquiry was first made concerning them, and the third was in great measure ruined by the rust. No inscription could be perceived upon it, and even no traces of one discerned, except such as fancy will perpetually suggest to the judgment on the examination of faded remains. Wells so squared as this was in the opening, and lined with hewn stones at the sides, as this with the native rock, have been discovered at Durnomagus or Caster, near Peterborough; at Procolitia, or Carrabrugh, in Cumberland; and Derventio, or Little Chester, near Derby. And the water of this and the other wells was probably raised either by the assistance of a pole playing upon a transverse beam, and loaded with a weight at the handle, by a common wheel or a little windmill. All these machines appear to have been early in use among the Romans, and they seem to have been simple and obvious in their construction."

In later times we find incidental notices of wells in the Court Leet records of the manor, one of which will suffice. In the entries of the Court Leet of April, 1628:—

"The jury having duly considered that there was in former time stairs down to the water at the wheat mill in the Milnegate, and that there were *two fair wells* for the use and benefit of the town, but now defaced and quite overthrown, by reason of leading or driving of horses or other cattle [down and up the said stairs], we order that no persons shall hereafter neither lead nor drive that way, under a penalty of 3s. 4d."

Then, in course of time, wells and springs would be enclosed within the curtilage of dwellings, and *pumps* would be put down. From the same Court Leet records we learn that in 1629 there was a pump in the Hanging Ditch, which in 1672 was declared to be on the lord's waste, and all right thereto was formally renounced by Henry Jackson, cloth worker, "over against" whose lands it stood. Passing over more than a century and a half, we find in Laurent's Plan of Manchester of 1793 delineations of the cross, the pillory, and the pump in the Market Place, opposite the Bull's Head Yard. Aston, in his Manchester Guide, published in 1804, says:—

"The water for culinary purposes is chiefly obtained from wells furnished with pumps. There is but one draw-well in the whole town, and that, very properly, is enclosed in a building which is always locked except the well is in actual use. Two springs in Castle Field [Were these the two old wells?] which issue from the side of the brow have the reputation of better water than any other wells, and are much resorted to for the tea table. The next in reputation is a pump in the College Yard. Whether either of the springs have been analysed or not does not come within the knowledge of the editor of this work. Almost every house of moderate size is furnished with a lead cistern, which serves as a reservoir for the rain which falls upon the building. By some this water is used not only for cleaning, but for brewing and even culinary purposes. Many of the old streets are supplied with soft water from the Infirmary pool, and the pits at Shudehill by the means of pipes brought from them. The reservoirs are kept full by means of an engine near Holt Town, which throws up water from the river Medlock above the level of Shudehill pits, into which it runs; and from thence in pipes under the pavement in Oldham-street into the Infirmary pool, from whence it descends into the lower parts of the town."

After all, the chief source of a water supply to the town was the spring in Fountain-street, the water from which was conveyed by pipes to the conduit in what was then part of the Market Place; but its site is now covered by the premises of Mr. William Tebbutt, grocer, Victoria-street. A brief historical notice of the conduit will be fitting here. In Baines's History of Manchester, vol. ii., p. 241, is a notice of it, to the effect that, in 1506, a species of waterworks was established, called—

"The public conduit (on the site of which in more modern times stood the Old Exchange) for the supply of the town with water from the spring at the top of King-street. The patroness of this valuable public work was Isabel Beck, widow and sole heir of Richard Bexwicke."

In searching for Baines's authorities, we find a passage in Hollingworth which shows that Isabel Beck was the daughter, and not the widow, of Richard Bexwicke. Of course her husband's name was Beck. The Bexwickes were amongst the oldest and most liberal benefactors of the town and its collegiate and parish church. Richard, the son of Roger Bexwicke, built the Jesus (now the Byrom) chapel on the south side of that church. It was given by Richard's daughter Isabel, the wife of one —— Becke (who, surviving both husband and father, was sole heir of the latter) to her daughter Cicely, who was married to Francis Pendleton; and his successor, Henry Pendleton, in August, 1658, gave this chapel to the town of Manchester. Hollingworth adds—"The said Isabel "Becke did also build the conduit in Manchester." And it appears that this benefactress of the community, not satisfied with erecting the conduit, left property for its repairs and maintenance for ever. Aston, in his Manchester Guide of 1804, says—

"It is a circumstance which ought not to be forgotten, that certain houses in Saint Mary's Gate were left by Isabella Beck (widow of the builder of the south side of the choir in the Old Church), who died in the reign of Elizabeth, to trustees for the perpetual upholding of the conduit. If the town has not received *for the last thirty years* the benefit from the legacy which the donor intended, perhaps in justice the boroughreeve and constables ought to have the rents arising from the land to apply to some other public purpose."

What has become of these rents? This is another subject fitting for the inquiry of the Charitable Trusts Committee of the Manchester Council. But our immediate purpose is to trace the existence of this conduit from its construction, about 1506, to its ceasing to give a supply of water in 1776,—a period of 270 years. The first notice of it we have discovered is in the Manchester Court Leet records of April, 1567, in which is an order to repair or fill up a hollow place in the ground near the "cundithe," of which two-thirds of the work or cost devolves on "Mistress Becke, or the heir of Robert Becke." In the same year it is referred to as "the conduit in the Market Place." The jury fix the 20th October as the day on which to repair it, and John Gee and George Pendelton are to declare "whom they think hath any money or lands for the same." So that in sixty years after the grant it had become doubtful who held the property charged with the maintenance of this conduit. In October, 1570, the jury appointed six gentlemen (and Mr. William Radclyffe, gentleman, consented to be their overseer) to "gather the charity of well-disposed persons, the which "they shall bestow for the mending and upholding of the conduit;" so that the houses in St. Mary's Gate had by that time been wholly lost as a source of maintenance. In September, 1573, the leet jury make the following order:—

> "That whereas the conduit of Manchester, a special ornament of the town, doth divers times lack water, the which, by the good furtherance of well-disposed persons, may be brought to such perfection that at all times hereafter there may be sufficient water to serve the town withal;—in consideration whereof the persons whose names follow are appointed by the said jury to gather and collect the charity of well-disposed persons for the amending the same, the which must be by bringing of other springs to the same, and not without great cost and charge:—William Radclyffe, Francis Penleton [the first time this name is spelled with an *e*], George Pendelton, Humphrey Haughton, Nicholas Becke."

This order is repeated in April, 1575, with the addition that no person is to wash any clothes or to scour any vessel at the conduit. In September, 1577, an order gives authority to the two constables to see to the amendment of the conduit, and that the keys should be kept by their appointment,—states that it is "now in decay "and ruin," and names four burgesses to help the constables in collecting money for its repairs. In October, 1578, the supply becoming inadequate, the leet jury order that no person shall take water from the conduit in any vessel "of greater "value [capacity] than one woman is able to bear full of water, and but one "of every house at one time, and to have their *cale* [call or turn] as hath been "accustomed." Officers were appointed to see this order enforced. In September, 1581, the conduit, an ornament to the town, is greatly decayed, "to the great "discommodity of the town," and the jury appoint eight gentlemen (including Nicholas and Thomas Becke) to be overseers of the conduit; and they are empowered, either by the voluntary "benevolence of well-disposed inhabitants" or by a mise, ley, or rate on the community to raise sufficient money to amend the conduit. This order also appoints the hours when the conduit shall be accessible, viz., from six a.m. to nine p.m. In April, 1586, a man is appointed to keep the keys, unlock the conduit at six a.m. and lock it at nine p.m. between Michaelmas Day and Lady Day, and the other part of the year to be open from six a.m. to nine a.m. and from three to six p.m., "according to an ancient order "made in 1586." In October, 1588, the key being withheld by some one, a new key is ordered to be made at the cost of the town, a keeper appointed, and no one to get water except when he is there. In October, 1590, the old locks are to be replaced by new ones, and the conduit overseers are empowered to make a collection or levy for repairs. In October, 1591, the boroughreeve is to keep both the keys of the head [or spring] and the conduit; he is to deliver these keys to the overseers, and when the repairs are completed the overseers are to return the keys to the boroughreeve. In April, 1612, the jury appoint five persons to gather a ley of the inhabitants, to be apportioned according to the use they conceive that every one hath or may have to fetch water from thence. In October, 1626, the jury prohibit the washing or cleansing of any calves' heads or meats, linen or woollen clothes, or any other noisome things at the conduit under a penalty of 12d. In October, 1629, John Hartley, draper, having claimed to be served with water at the common conduit of this town before any other, save Mr. William Radcliffe [the chief overseer thereof], the jury call on him to prove his right, and in the meantime that his claim should surcease. They order the overseers to pay him (out of £12. 15s. 1d., the balance of the ley in hand), what he may have disbursed for the use of the conduit or conduit heads. In October, 1630, is another order against washing noisome things at the conduit. In October, 1631, the following order was passed by the leet jury:—

"Whereas the common conduit, conduit heads, and pipes thereunto belonging, within this town, are in great want of repair, and whereas general summons hath been given unto all or most of the inhabitants to meet in the booths, and to advise together concerning the repairs of the said conduit and appurtenances, all which inhabitants, or most of them, did, in the place aforesaid, meet together, and accordingly did consider of the premises; and all or the greatest number of those that were present did freely and willingly consent and agree to have a general tax or ley, to be assessed towards the repairing of the said conduit and premises, upon the inhabitants who are housekeepers:—We therefore do order that the constables of our said town shall, within three weeks next ensuing, deliver unto the miselayers a paper book, ready made, and do further order that the miselayers shall, within one week after the receipt thereof, by and with the consent and advice of two honest and discreet persons of every street, tax the sum of £90 on the householders in general, and in particular shall reasonably tax and assess all and every of the housekeepers in such several sums of money as unto the said miselayers shall seem fitting for the repairing of the conduit; and shall make true and undelayed payment of all and every sum of money by them collected and gathered for the uses above said unto the overseers of the conduit for the time being. This order to be performed in every particular; subpœna, 20s. on every offender."

In October, 1634, only 36s. having been collected of the £20, the remainder is ordered to be collected within a month. Part of this ley of £18. 4s. being uncollected, the misegatherers in October, 1635, are strictly ordered to collect the remainder; defaulters in payment to be fined 10s. The jury also order the claim of John Hartley of second turn at the conduit, "as of right appertaining to the "house where his mother dwelleth," to be granted him as his due. In an enumeration of documents in the boroughreeve's chest in 1638, is "a deed of "feoffment for the ensuring of 40s. per annum for ever towards repairing the "conduit, conduit head, and pipes." By a subsequent entry we learn that the grantor of this rent was John Hartley. In October, 1638, the jury, after examining his accounts of disbursements for the conduit, order that he shall retain till needed a balance of 37s. in his hands. In October, 1648, the jury order that, in consideration of this 40s. per annum, Mr. John Hartley shall have the privilege of having water next to Major Radcliffe at all times, but only for the house then inhabited by Mr. William Byrom. In October, 1653, the jury being informed that John Hartley, of Strangeways, Esq., "hath revoked and kept in" the gift of 40s. a-year, order the conduit overseers to see it kept in repair at the public charge. In October, 1655, a keeper is appointed at a salary of 3s. 4d. a quarter. In October, 1656, a keeper is ordered "to take special notice of the abuses about "it, either by fighting of men's servants that come to fetch water or of those that "break off the lock. Every one to have his course [or turn] as they come, without "the disturbance one of another." In April, 1674, the jury order that—

"Whereas several persons water their horses at the cock of the conduit, and thereby take away the water that should serve the necessary use of the town, and there being a great scarcity of water some parts of the year, and likewise there being many persons that lie their horses and give them meat at the conduit, whereby dung and filth are left there, all persons are ordered to forbear, &c., under penalty of 2d. for every horse."

In April, 1679, we have Hartley's gift of 40s. a year renewed :—

"Whereas the deed of grant of 40s. yearly to be paid and chargeable upon the house of Caleb Somister, situate in the Market-street lane, formerly granted by John Hartley, late of Strangeways, Esq., deceased, for the repair of the conduit, is to be renewed and put into the hands and trust of new feoffees, we order that the constables shall pay for the drawing of the said re-feoffment and place it in their accounts."

We have from this point a large gap in the Court Leet records,—one volume containing the records of 45 years (1687-1732) being missing before they came into the possession of the Corporation; but at Michaelmas, 1737, we have the following order :—

"Whereas, for time immemorial, the inhabitants of this town (especially about both market places) have been supplied with water out of a large lead cistern, and by a common conduit pipe heretofore erected where the Exchange now stands; and forasmuch as the said cistern and common pipe were destroyed when the same Exchange was built, to the great complaints of the inhabitants of the town; and forasmuch as Sir Oswald Mosley, Bart. (lord of this manor), acknowledges to have in his hands £16. 8s. 4½d., which he received for the said lead cistern, and several other sums are in arrear and owing by persons who usually contributed towards the said common pipe;—now, for remedying the said complaints, we (the jury) order the four officers for taking care of the conduit to collect the said sum of £16. 8s. 4½d., and such other sums as are in arrear and owing, and to apply the same towards erecting and making another common water-pipe, to issue out of the same part of the said Exchange as shall be agreeable to the said lord of the manor and inhabitants of the town."

We suppose something was done to restore the cistern, &c., for we find no other record till Michaelmas, 1751, when the accounts of Edward Byrom, trustee for the conduit, were examined and approved.

This is the last record we can find in the archives respecting the conduit. We must just refer to the circumstance, that at the rejoicings for the coronation of Charles II., on the 23rd April, 1661, the conduit, instead of water, ran with "more generous liquor." In an old MS. letter from William Heawood, then steward of the Court Leet, copied into Aston's Guide, is an account of the Manchester festivities, from which we learn that after the authorities, inhabitants, troops, &c., had attended divine service at the Collegiate Church, where a sermon was preached by Warden Heyricke, from 2 Kings, xi., 12 :—

> "After sermon, from the church marched in order the boroughreeve, constables, and the rest of the burgesses of the town not then in arms, accompanied with Sir Ralph Assheton, knight and baronet, and divers neighbouring gentlemen of quality, together with the said warden and fellows of the said college and divers other ministers, with the town musick playing before them upon loud instruments, through the streets to the cross, and so forward to the conduit, officers and soldiers in their order, the gentlemen and officers drank his Majesty's health in claret, running forth at three streams at once of the said conduit, which was answered from the soldiers by a great volley of shot, and many great shouts, saying 'God save the King!' which being ended, the gentry and ministers went to dinner, attended with the officers and musick of the town, the auxiliaries dining at the same place. During the time of dinner, and until after sunset, the said conduit did run with pure claret, which was freely drunk by all that could, for the crowd came so near the same."

The period when the conduit ceased altogether to supply water appears to have been about 1775-6. We take the following from Aston's Manchester Guide:—

> "At the west end of the Exchange, which was taken down in 1792, was formerly a conduit which supplied that part of the town with good water. It was conveyed by pipes from the spring at the top of King-street, which ceased to flow when the sinking of wells in the neighbourhood had drained it. This was about 1775. Previous to the building of Norfolk-street, when known by the name of Marriott's Field, a kind of reservoir was kept up in the midst of it (filled by pipes from the same spring which supplied the conduit), from whence people fetched water, as well as from the conduit in the Market Place."

Some years ago, when Smithy Door was widened and part of it converted into Victoria-street, the writer of this article saw a portion of the foundations and some of the old piping of the ancient conduit, which were discovered in digging the foundations for the premises of Messrs. Southam and Son, grocers, now occupied by Mr. William Tebbutt.

We have already shown that a portion of the town was supplied with soft water, even in the earlier years of the present century, from the Medlock, the Infirmary Pond, and the Shudehill Pits by means of pipes. The pumping-engine for raising water from the Medlock for storage in Shudehill Pits was put down by Sir Oswald Mosley, lord of the manor. These and the wells and pumps continued to furnish the only supplies of water to Manchester for some time. It is difficult at this period to obtain any precise evidence as to the quality of that water. But we take the following remarks from an essay of Dr. Percival's, dated November, 1771, entitled "Experiments and Observations on Water, particularly on the Hard Pump Water of Manchester" (vol. iii. of his works, edition of 1807, page 173). After showing the injurious effect of impure and hard water in various complaints and disorders, Dr. Percival details chemical experiments on the nature and properties of the pump-water of Manchester, collected from nearly thirty pump-waters from pumps common to a whole neighbourhood, and then states that—

"From the foregoing experiments it is obvious that the pump-water of Manchester is, in general, very impure. It is impregnated with a large quantity of selenite—an earthy, astringent salt, composed of the vitriolic, nitrous, or marine acid, and calcareous earth; and at the same time contains no inconsiderable portion of alum, as may be reasonably inferred from the green colour which it strikes with syrup of violets. * * But what puts this conclusion beyond dispute is, that the earth of alum is frequently found in the wells of this town. I have now in my possession some of this earth, which, by the addition of oil of vitriol, has been converted into true alum. From the second experiment, it is evident that a quart of water contains upwards of 60 grains of adventitious matter; and supposing this quantity to be daily consumed in one way or other by every individual, which is a moderate computation, about 46 ounces, troy weight, of crude, earthy, indigestible, and by no means inactive salts, will in the course of twelve months be received into the body. * * One observation I cannot omit,— that the inhabitants of this place are peculiarly subject to glandular obstructions and scrophulous swellings; and that water loaded with stringent, earthy salts, hath a direct tendency to produce such complaints, has been already, I hope, evinced."

The following are such of Dr. Percival's conclusions as relate to the quality of the Manchester pump-water :—

"I. The Manchester pump-water is in general very bad and impure; it is impregnated with a large quantity of selenite, and contains also no inconsiderable proportion of alum.—II. The hardest water will become soft and miscible with soap, by the addition of salt of tartar; but such a quantity of the vegetable alkali is required to produce this effect on the Manchester pump-water as renders it offensive to the palate and unfit for common use. * * V. Mr. Boyle asserts that some pump-waters, by exposure to the sun and air for a few days, will become soft enough to be miscible with soap; but this is not the case with the hard-water of Manchester.—VI. Neither malt nor tea produce any softening effect on the hard-water in which they are infused; nor does fermentation improve or alter its nature; so that the wholesomeness of malt liquors must greatly depend upon the purity of the water which is employed in their preparation.—VII. Bricks harden the softest water, and give it an aluminous impregnation. The practice of lining wells with them, which is common in many places, is therefore very improper. Freestone communicates no pernicious qualities to water."

Under such circumstances, of an inadequate supply of water, and that of generally bad quality, it is not to be wondered at that some efforts should be made by the inhabitants to obtain a larger and purer supply. Two rival schemes being announced as seeking the sanction of Parliament, a public meeting of the inhabitants was held on the subject, at the Bull's Head, Market-place, on the 10th November, 1808, and again by adjournment on the 22nd December; Mr. Richard Rushforth, the boroughreeve, in the chair; when resolutions were passed to the following effect :—

"That it appears to this meeting that two schemes are intended to be brought before Parliament in the ensuing session for supplying the town of Manchester with water, to be taken chiefly from the Medlock and the Irk, or the springs and feeders which fall into them.

"That a committee be appointed at this meeting for taking these schemes into consideration; and that it be an instruction to such committee to inquire whether the object of supplying the town with water may not be effected in a way more eligible for the inhabitants at large, and less injurious to the private property of individuals, by drawing such supply from the river Irwell or other sources, and also to inquire whether it is worth while for the inhabitants of Manchester to take the management of such a concern into their own hands, and apply the profit arising from it to the improvement of the town or other public purposes; and, if so, by what means this can be best effected.

"That the committee for these purposes consist of the following gentlemen :—The boroughreeve and constables, Mr. G. Duckworth, Mr. Bateman, Mr. Thomas Entwisle, Mr. Robert Peel, jun., Mr. J. L. Philips, Mr. John Kennedy, Mr. R. Farrand, and Mr. C. M'Niven.

"That any five of such committee shall have power to act; and that they be requested to make an early report on the several matters here referred to them, and on such other matters connected therewith as they may think necessary for the information of the town.

"RICHARD RUSHFORTH, Chairman."

On the requisition of the committee above-named (of which Mr. James Bateman was chairman), the boroughreeve and constables (Messrs. Richard Rushforth, John Touchet, and John Lomax) convened a public meeting at the Bull's Head, to be held on the 2nd February, 1809, to receive and consider the report, and to pass resolutions thereon. This meeting is described as having been numerously and respectably attended. The chair was taken by the senior constable, John Touchet, Esq., and the committee's report was laid before the meeting and received. It was as follows :—

"Your committee have taken into consideration the two schemes proposed by individual adventurers to be brought into Parliament in the present session for supplying the town of Manchester with water; and they are of opinion that the sources from which such supply is intended to be taken are insufficient for that purpose, and that even if such sources were adequate, the application thereof would be highly injurious to private property, inasmuch as the same would cut off many of the springs and feeders which now supply large and extensive printing, bleaching, and dye works with water, and afford to numerous cotton factories and other works condensing water for their steam engines.

"Your committee are also of opinion that the supply of the town of Manchester with water ought to be under the direction of its own inhabitants, and that it would be contrary to sound policy to entrust the furnishing and control of this important article of food and cleanliness, on which the health and comfort of the inhabitants depend, to persons whose sole object will be the promotion of their own private interest, and who are induced to the undertaking from no other motive.

"Your committee are further of opinion that an ample supply of water for the use of the inhabitants of Manchester may be afforded from other sources than those mentioned by these undertakers, and in a manner which will not in the least degree injure or affect private property. One of these sources may be derived from the river Irwell, the water of which, below the town of Manchester, is more than sufficient to supply the mills and locks of the navigation on that river. The water may be advantageously taken in several places adjoining the town, and may be filtered through beds of gravel and sand, either natural or artificial, at a very small expense.

"The water may be raised to a proper height to supply every part of the town by means either of a steam-engine or a fall of the river Irwell not now occupied; and this may be effected either separately or in conjunction with a proposed plan to continue St. Mary's Gate by a regular descent to Chapel-street, in Salford, and from thence to Bolton, Bury, and other places north of Manchester; and to render the Irwell navigable to Hunt's Bank, and by means of warehouses and wharfs on each side of the new intended bridge, to place the termination of the navigable communication from Liverpool to Manchester in the centre of the latter town. The weir which would be required in that case to extend the navigation would produce a fall of the river more than sufficient in power to raise the requisite supply of water for the use of the town.

"Another source from which the town of Manchester may be adequately supplied with pure water, and which we think best, is through the Ashton canal. The water may be taken from the river Tame at the Dukinfield weir in times of flood only, and may be preserved in reservoirs to be made in lands of very little value near that weir.

"From these reservoirs it may be conveyed through the Ashton canal by regulated gauges to a reservoir near the town of Manchester, where it may be filtered and rendered pure for the use of the inhabitants. In its course it will supply the Ashton Canal Company with lockage water for the use of their navigation, and will be particularly valuable to them in dry seasons. The millowners will also be benefited by a diminution of the inconvenience they at present sustain from back-water in times of flood. The filtering reservoir may be made near Holt Town, where the water will be supplied at the height of twelve feet above the level of the street at New Cross, and may be made to flow into the highest apartments of every house in the town of Manchester.

"As the latter scheme will not require a steam-engine or any other expensive apparatus in its commencement or extension, it may be begun on a limited scale and extended in proportion to the funds which may be raised for its establishment. It may be commenced without even the expense of the proposed reservoir at Dukinfield weir, because the waste water which flows from the Ashton canal on the level of the Stockport branch, and at present is of no use, would be sufficient to supply a considerable part of the town of Manchester. If in the execution of the plan an intermediate resetvoir should be deemed necessary, an advantageous situation may be had in the lands of Mr. Green, in Clayton, from whence the water may be brought to the town of Manchester through either the Ashton canal or a separate tunnel.

"The means of raising money for carrying into effect this important plan, as well as the mode by which it may be effected more beneficially for the inhabitants of the town, have necessarily occupied the attention of your committee. The supply of the rich with good water will form but a small part of the object which the inhabitants of the town have in view. They will be anxious to communicate this gratuitous blessing of Providence to the poorest individuals. In this pursuit their interests and their inclinations will unite. They will, by preserving the health of the poor, prevent an increase of the rates for their relief, and by adding to their comforts and happiness procure for themselves the gratifying sensations of benevolence. This consideration ncessarily connects the scheme with the legal institution for the relief of the poor, and places the distribution of the profits in the hands of the churchwardens and overseers. When the funds are so applied, and the rates (which at present are so severely felt by the public) will be relieved by this new source of income, there can not be wanting a motive with any inhabitant of the town to prefer this supply of water to any other, which may be equally or more expensive and less eligible with respect to its purity.

"But although the distribution of the profits ought to rest with the churchwardens and overseers, there is another consideration which may render it more eligible to place the management of the waterworks in other hands. To effect these works it will be necessary to carry pipes under all the principal streets, and occasionally to interrupt the passage of carriages. That this interruption may be as small as possible—that the damages done to the streets may be effectually repaired,—that no disputes may arise respecting the amount of damages or the mode of repairs, and that the public may in this respect suffer the least inconvenience, it is advisable that the management of the works should be placed under the surveyors of the highways, and particularly so when the offices relating to the highways and the police are united.

"With respect to the means for raising money to carry the scheme into effect, your committee apprehend that a fund may be raised without any burthen upon either the landowners or the inhabitants. The churchwardens, in their corporate capacity, may be authorised by the new Police Act to issue transferable notes bearing interest payable yearly. These notes may either be made a perpetual loan or be payable at a stated period. In either case they will serve as a circulating medium, and will have this advantage over cash and bank notes that they will bear interest. The Legislature has already granted the privilege of issuing notes like these to many canal companies, and it cannot be supposed that the privilege would be refused to the first manufacturing and commercial town in the kingdom if the extent of that circulation were limited to a sum which is necessary to be raised for the preservation of the health and comfort of its inhabitants. The interest as well as the principal would necessarily in such a case be made a charge upon the poor rates raised in the town of Manchester. If this mode of raising money should be deemed ineligible by the inhabitants of the town other easy means may be readily suggested.

"It may be expected that your committee should state the probable profits or loss from the execution of this scheme. To do this accurately would require much more time than has been taken by your committee, and a considerable degree of information arising from practical knowledge. Your committee, however, have not been inattentive to this part of the subject. It is notorious that the profits of the New River Company in London have exceeded those of any other scheme ever instituted in this country. The two companies of proprietors of waterworks in Liverpool have had the goodness to communicate statements of their expenditures and incomes to your committee, from which it appears that although these are rival schemes and very expensive ones, they are likely to be productive of great advantage to the proprietors, and they afford indisputable evidence that if only one well-conducted plan should be adopted in Manchester, supported by the inhabitants at large and operating to the benefit of every individual, it must be crowned with ultimate and probably with immediate success.

"JAMES BATEMAN, Chairman of the Committee.

"Manchester, February 2nd, 1809."

The meeting then passed the following resolutions :—

"That it is the opinion of this meeting that the two schemes proposed by individuals to be brought into Parliament in the present session for supplying the towns of Manchester and Salford with water are ineligible; that the sources from which the supplies of water are intended to be taken are insufficient for that purpose; and that even if such sources were adequate, the application thereof would be highly injurious to private property, inasmuch as the same would cut off many of the springs and feeders which now supply large and extensive printing, bleaching, and dye-works with water, and afford to numerous cotton factories and other works condensing water for the steam engines.

"That it is the opinion of this meeting that the supply of the towns of Manchester and Salford with water ought to be under the direction of their own inhabitants; and that it would be contrary to sound policy to entrust the furnishing and control of this important article of food and cleanliness, on which the health and comfort of the inhabitants depend, to persons whose sole object will be the promotion of their own private interest, and who are induced to undertake their schemes from no other motive; and that the profits of such an undertaking ought in justice to be received by the inhabitants, to go in aid of the poor-rate or other public rates of the town.

"That a committee be appointed to oppose the above two schemes in Parliament, and that it consist of the following gentlemen, viz , the boroughreeve and constables, Messrs. J. L. Philips, George Duckworth, John Kennedy, Thomas Entwisle, James Bateman, Jonathan Beever, John Drinkwater, Thomas Belcher, William Myers, Otho Hulme, John Railton, Roger Farrand, Peter Ewart, Thomas Hoyle, jun , Charles M'Niven; and that any five of the committee be competent to act.

"That this meeting approves of the plan suggested by the committee for supplying the towns of Manchester and Salford with water, taken in times of flood only from the river Tame into large reservoirs, to be brought from thence through the Ashton canal to a proper situation near Manchester, where it may be filtered previous to its being conducted through pipes to the houses of the inhabitants; and that the committee be directed to communicate with the Ashton canal company for that purpose.

"That it be referred to the committee before appointed to employ proper engineers to digest a plan and form an estimate of the expenses attending the above undertaking, and of the probable profits to arise therefrom, and that the same be laid before a future town's meeting in time to enable them, in case they should approve thereof, to obtain powers in the intended police act for carrying the same into effect.

"That the expenses of the above opposition be paid from the police rates, and that a clause be inserted in the new police bill to authorise the payment thereof.

"That letters with copies of these resolutions and the report of the committee be sent to the following members of both Houses of Parliament [10 peers, and 16 members of the House of Commons] and to such other members as the committee may think necessary, requesting their attendance in Parliament to oppose the above schemes, and to support such plan as may be adopted by the inhabitants of Manchester and Salford for supplying themselves with water.

"That the thanks of this meeting be given to the committee for their zeal and attention in forming their able report."

Thanks being given to Mr. Touchet for his conduct in the chair, the proceedings then terminated.

The committee appointed at a meeting of February 2nd, 1809, subsequently made a long and formal report as to their proceedings in opposing the two water schemes—the one by Mr. Rennie, on behalf of the stone-pipe company; and the other by Mr. Dodd, the engineer, for supplying the towns of Manchester and Salford with water.

"On the 27th of January, 1809, the committee [appointed December 22nd, 1808] requested the boroughreeve and constables of Manchester to appoint a public meeting of the inhabitants to receive their report. In pursuance of this request, the boroughreeve and constables, by advertisements inserted in all the Manchester newspapers, appointed a public meeting of the inhabitants of the town of Manchester, to be held on the 2nd day of February then next, to receive the above report and to take the same into consideration, and to enter into such resolutions thereon as might appear expedient for the interests of the town. A public meeting of the inhabitants of Manchester was accordingly held on the 2nd of February following, when it was resolved, that the two schemes proposed by individuals to be brought into Parliament for supplying the towns of Manchester and Salford with water were ineligible; that the sources from which the supplies of water were intended to be taken were insufficient for the purpose; and that even if such sources were adequate, the application thereof would be highly injurious to private property. And it was further resolved, that the supply of the towns of Manchester and Salford with water ought to be under the direction of their own inhabitants, and that it would be contrary to sound policy to entrust the furnishing and control of that important article of food and cleanliness, on which the health and comfort of the inhabitants depended, to persons whose sole object would be the promotion of their own private interest, and who are induced to undertake their schemes from no other motive; and that the profits of such an undertaking ought, in justice, to be received by the inhabitants, to go in aid of the poor-rate or other public rates of the town. At this meeting your committee was appointed to oppose the above two schemes in Parliament, consisting of the following members, viz., the boroughreeve and constables, Mr. J. L. Philips, Mr. G. Duckworth, Mr. John Kennedy, Mr. Thomas Entwisle, Mr. James Bateman, Mr. Jonathan Beever, Mr. John Drinkwater, Mr. Thomas Belcher, Mr. William Myers, Mr. Otho Hulme, Mr. John Railton, Mr. Roger Farrand, Mr. Peter Ewart, Mr. Thomas Hoyle, jun., and Mr. Charles M'Niven.

"It was further resolved, that the said meeting approved of the plan suggested by the committee appointed on the 22nd December, 1808, for supplying the towns of Manchester and Salford with water, taken in times of flood only from the river Tame into large reservoirs, to be brought from thence through the Ashton canal to a proper situation near Manchester, where it would be filtered previous to its being conducted through pipes to the houses of the inhabitants; and the same committee were directed to communicate with the Ashton canal company for that purpose. It was further resolved, that it should be referred to the committee appointed on the 22nd Decmeber, 1808, to employ proper engineers to digest a plan and form an estimate of the expenses attending the above undertaking, and of the probable profits to arise therefrom; and that the same should be laid before a future town's meeting, in time to enable them, in case they should approve thereof, to obtain powers in the intended Police Act for carrying the same into effect. It was likewise resolved that the expenses of the above opposition should be paid from the police rates, and that a clause should be inserted in the new Police Bill to authorise the payment thereof.

"To these proceedings no opposition was even suggested; and an individual, since an active opponent to the payment of the expenses incurred, took upon him the advertisement of the resolutions in the London papers, and was among the first who received any money from the police funds on this account. The commissioners of police, who had thus far succeeded in communicating to the inhabitants at large the attempts of strangers to assume to themselves the right of supplying the town with water, and who found the inhabitants unanimous in resisting so unprecedented an interference, to which the undertakers had not been solicited by an individual inhabitant, or urged by any declared scarcity or want of water, deemed it their duty to comply with the resolutions of the inhabitants, unanimously expressed at their public meeting; and in conformity thereto, on the 15th February, 1809, made an order for the application of £300 towards opposing the Bills in Parliament for supplying the town with water. In consequence of the resolutions unanimously passed at the above meetings of the inhabitants and of the commissioners of police, active measures of opposition to the two schemes then before Parliament were immediately adopted. A solicitor and delegate, with witnesses, were sent to London; several hundred circular letters, with copies of the preceding resolutions of the inhabitants of the town, and the report of the committee, were distributed amongst the members of both Houses of Parliament. Personal applications were also daily made to such members as were thought most likely to give their support to the cause of the town; and on a representation of the facts, many were induced to engage zealously in the opposition of both the schemes. Amongst these, the town owes particular obligation to Sir Robert Peel, Colonel Patten, Mr. Coke (of Norfolk), Mr. Hibbert, Mr. Curwen, Mr. Horrocks, Mr. George Johnson, Mr. William Maxwell, Mr. William Clive, and Mr. Peel; Colonel Stanley was at this time confined by indisposition, and unable to attend the House, but he used every exertion in his power to promote the interests of the town; and Mr. Blackburne (though he had brought in the Stone-pipe Company's Bill) afterwards joined strenuously in the opposition to it. By the exertions that were used, objections were raised to Mr. Dodd's scheme, which afterwards ended in its defeat. The Stone-pipe Company's Bill, however, was supported by a variety of interests, and among others by persons who were under great obligations to the town of Manchester, from whom a different mode of conduct might reasonably have been expected. These different interests raised a force in support of this Bill, which carried it through the second reading in the House of Commons, by a considerable majority, notwithstanding, nearly 50 members attended as friends to the town, several of whom spoke with great force and ability against the principle of the Bill.

"Immediately after the second reading, the solicitor returned into the country and made a report to your committee of the circumstances that had taken place, and particularly that it had been asserted upon such second reading that a considerable part of the town was favourable to the Bill, and that such assertion had had great weight in preventing the Bill from being thrown out. Your committee then thought it their duty to obtain another public meeting of the inhabitants, to ascertain whether there was any truth or not in the assertion, and to submit all the circumstances to their consideration, and to take their further directions in the business. A meeting of the inhabitants of Manchester was accordingly, at the request of your Committee, called by the boroughreeve and constables, by public advertisement, and held on the 3rd day of April, 1809. At this meeting a report was made of the proceedings in Parliament relative to the above two Bills, and the representation which had been made in the House of Commons that a considerable part of the town was favourable to the Stone-pipe Company's Bill, and of the effect which such representation had had in preventing the Bill being thrown out; and the meeting resolved that it appeared highly important to the interests of the town of Manchester, that the Bill brought into Parliament by the Stone-pipe Company, for supplying the inhabitants with water, should not pass into a law; and that it should be an instruction to your committee to continue their opposition to such Bill with all possible diligence and effect. That it also appeared highly important to the interests of the town that the Bill brought, or proposed to be brought, into Parliament, under the direction of Mr. Dodd, for supplying the inhabitants with water, should not pass into a law, and that it should be also an instruction to your committee to continue their opposition to such last-mentioned Bill with all possible diligence and effect. These resolutions were carried with only five dissentient voices, and those of persons professedly interested in supporting the scheme of Mr. Dodd. In consequence of these last resolutions the solicitor returned to London, where the delegates and witnesses had remained, waiting the further directions of the town's meeting. In this interval fresh opposition had been raised against Dodd's scheme by the individuals whose private interests were likely to be affected by it, and this Bill was very soon afterwards abandoned by its promoters. The Stone-pipe Company's Bill, however, was supported with great strength; and as there did not seem much chance of getting it thrown out by the Commons, the course of the opposition (which had before been directed against the principle of the Bill) was now changed, and it was thought prudent to get the clauses made as favourable to the town as possible. For this purpose counsel were employed to attend the Committee of the Commons on behalf of the town, when the Bill was during several days debated, clause by clause, and many alterations made in it for the advantage of the town. The millowners upon the Medlock, who had carried on a separate opposition against the Stone-pipe Company's Bill at their own expense, had now obtained such protecting clauses as induced them to withdraw their opposition. The members, however, who had been prevailed upon to espouse their cause, continued to act steadily in support of the interests of the town. It was obvious that the Stone-pipe Company had omitted to comply with the Standing Orders of both Houses of Parliament, in the mode of giving their notices, lodging their plans, and in several other particulars; but it was deemed more prudent to reserve these objections till the Bill got into the House of Lords, where it was thought the town would have a better chance of success.

"On the 4th of May, 1809, the commissioners of police held a special meeting, convened by public advertisement inserted in all the Manchester papers of the 29th day of April preceding, for the sole purpose of taking into consideration the propriety of petitioning the House of Lords against the Bill promoted by the Stone-pipe Company for supplying the town with water, which Bill, if carried into a law, it was apprehended by the commissioners would be highly detrimental and injurious to the streets. The meeting was numerously attended, and it was resolved that the petition against the Bill then produced by Mr. Sergeant, the clerk to the commissioners, should be signed on behalf of the meeting and placed under the direction of your committee. On the 10th of August, 1809, the commissioners, in conformity with the resolutions of the town's meeting of the 2nd of February preceding, and in support of their own petition, made a further order for the application of £500 towards carrying on the opposition to the Stone-pipe Company's Bill, which sum was paid accordingly. Ten other petitions from different persons were also prepared and presented to the House of Lords against the Stone-pipe Company's Bill, and afterwards the opposition was carried on with the greatest possible exertion, both in the house and in the committee of lords, to whom the Bill was referred. Counsel, witnesses, and parties attended day by day for several weeks. During all this period the cause of the town received the most zealous and unremitting attention from the Earl of Wilton, on whose representation of the facts, some of the royal dukes and several other lords made a point of regularly attending the committees and supporting the just rights of the town. Lord Derby was confined by indisposition, but he paid all the attention to the business in his power. Lord Grosvenor, Lord Ducie, Lord Auckland, Lord Stanhope, Lord Radnor, Lord Bradford, and several other noble lords, took an interest in the cause of the town. It will appear from the following report of the lords' committee, not only that the objections raised by the petition were well founded, but that the delegates and solicitor of the town were justified in the hopes they had entertained of ultimately succeeding in their opposition.

"'Your committee beg leave to observe, that the first and second standing orders relative to canal bills have not been complied with, inasmuch as the parish of Manchester includes several townships, relative to none of which the notices have been given. Your committee beg leave to state that the third standing order has not been complied with, inasmuch as there has been no book of reference delivered in, in pursuance of the said order. Your committee also beg leave to state that the fourth standing order has not been complied with, inasmuch as it does not appear that previously to the Bill being brought to this house from the Commons, such application was made to all the owners or reputed owners, and also to all the occupiers of the lands through which the aqueduct was intended to be or may be carried, as by the said standing order is required. Your committee further beg leave to state that the fifth standing order has not been complied with, inasmuch as though the Bill contains a clause allowing a deviation from the line described in the map or plan deposited with the clerk of the Parliaments, no application appears to have been made to the owners or reputed owners and occupiers of the lands through which such aqueduct might pass, nor has a list of such owners or reputed owners and occupiers been deposited with the clerk of the Parliament.'

"Notwithstanding, however, these numerous breaches of the standing orders of the house (any one of which, it was understood from all former practice, would have been an absolute bar to the passing of the Bill) the house thought proper afterwards to decide that in the present instance the standing orders should be dispensed with. On this occasion, the Lord Chancellor, the Lord Chief Justice of England, Lord Redesdale, the late Chancellor of Ireland, and Lord Walsingham (chairman of the committee), all spoke forcibly against the measure; but, unfortunately for the cause of the town, they were in the minority, and the Bill was ultimately carried. Against this measure the following peers recorded their protest on the journals of the house, viz., the Lord Chancellor, the Lord Chief Justice of England, the Earl of Oxford, Earl Grosvenor, Lord Aylesford, the Bishop of Salisbury, Lord Harewood, Lord Redesdale, Lord Wilton, and Lord Walsingham."

The commissioners of police having ordered the balance of the expenses in opposing these Bills (£1,760) to be paid, part was paid, and the commissioners' law clerk was then served with two notices of appeal—one on behalf of Sir O. Mosley, who had contracted to sell his old waterworks to the Stone-pipe Company if they should obtain their Act; and the other on behalf of the Bridgewater Trust. These appeals were dismissed for informality; but new ones were entered by the same parties, and two additional ones, each by an individual in the service of Sir O. Mosley and of the Bridgewater Trust. The Court of Quarter Sessions, in May, 1810, again dismissed them, and then the Court of King's Bench granted *mandamuses* requiring the magistrates to hear them, and they were accordingly heard at the Salford Quarter Sessions of October, 1810, when a majority of the magistrates on the bench thinking that the police commissioners had no power to apply the police fund in a parliamentary defence of the rights of the inhabitants, though such defence be directed and carried on by the inhabitants at large, the orders of the commissioners for the payment were set aside. The committee mention incidentally that some of the Stone-pipe Company had sold their shares at a premium of 200 or 300 per cent.; and after detailing at great length the cicumstances attending the appeals, they conclude by thus pointing out the consequences of the decision of the quarter sessions:—

"The inhabitants of Manchester have no public rate or income expressly appropriated to the defraying the expenses of any application to Parliament, either to obtain or amend a Police Act or other Act for the improvement of the town: and it is to be regretted that they are equally destitute of any pecuniary fund for their protection in Parliament against any individual, or any set of individuals, who may apply for powers exceedingly injurious to its interests. For instance, a power to make waterworks and break up the streets (not either limiting the price or stipulating the quality of the water) has been already obtained, contrary to the wishes of the inhabitants. In some other towns (for want of opposition from the inhabitants) Acts have been obtained compelling the inhabitants to purchase the water. If the present waterworks in Manchester should prove unprofitable, or if the proprietors should not be satisfied with a profit of two or three hundred per cent., an application may be made for an Act to compel the inhabitants of Manchester to pay the proprietors such sums as may be satisfactory to the latter, and if the inhabitants are (by appeals like the present) deprived of the means of being heard in Parliament against such an application, Parliament may presume a tacit consent; and although none of the future proprietors of the waterworks may happen to be inhabitants of Manchester, it is possible that some one of them may have a tenant or servant, in whose name he can prosecute an appeal. Your committee, therefore, beg leave to submit to your consideration the high importance of immediately providing some adequate means for the support of your rights, your property, and your independence.—On behalf of the committee,

"J. LEIGH PHILIPS, Chairman."

We have now brought down our narrative of the water-supply for Manchester, to the time when a company was formed for the purpose of obtaining and supplying the inhabitants with a larger supply. In the "Picture of Manchester" it is stated that—

"About the year 1814 [1809] a public company, incorporated by Act of Parliament, purchased the water from the lord of the manor, and formed a reservoir about two miles from the town, into which water was conveyed by means of stone pipes, which so frequently burst that they were often a great nuisance, and swept off the profits on which the proprietors had calculated. Another Act of Parliament was afterwards obtained by the same company, and a very large reservoir was formed at Gorton, about four miles from the town; and iron pipes having been substituted for the stone ones, the inconvenience before complained of has been obviated, and the inhabitants are supplied with purer water."

We learn from another local record that the length of iron mains laid down in Manchester and Salford was, some years later, 70 miles, and the daily consumption about 1,400,000 gallons. Four reservoirs were made, viz., at Bradford, Beswick, Gorton, and Audenshaw. Under the date of 1822 (though the substitution of iron for stone pipes was some years earlier), we find the following doggrel lines in Aston's "Metrical Records of Manchester:"—

"The first month of the year it was settled by law,*
That as th' Waterworks Company profit do draw
From Manchester buildings, they also should pay
The rates of police and highways, and poor-ley,
The town had a triumph, for with love it dispenses
For folks who make profit by untrue pretences;
For th' obtrusive Act said, we perished of drought,
Nor for love water had, nor could it be bought;
That Manchester faces were covered with dirt,
And unknown was the luxury of a clean shirt.

---

* At the quarter sessions, where it was proved that the Waterworks Company held property in the town; and an order was, with great justice, made out for their paying rates commensurate with their interest.

> That anxious this stain from its 'scutcheon to wipe,
> Some folks had invented a curious stone pipe;
> Which, engrafted, would bring from the reservoir down,
> Water, sharplings, and tadpoles, through each street in town.
> But—mark the result!—it will not command praise!
> After breaking the pavement through streets and highways,
> And blocking up roads, when at work on their schemes,
> They found their stone pipes were no more than day-dreams;
> And as Midas, the miser, so famous of old,
> All he touched—'twas his punishment—turned into gold:
> So, as the stone pipes would not water inviron,
> Necessity touched them, and they became iron." *

The further history of the Water-Supply of Manchester, first by the Stone-pipe Company, and afterwards by the Manchester and Salford Waterworks Company (which two companies must not be confounded, for they were quite distinct and rival companies, and many years embroiled in chancery), all this we must leave to be noticed in a future article.

Water for Manchester—under the Stone-pipe Company and the Waterworks Company.

Having in a former article brought down our imperfect historical account of the Water-Supply of Manchester from the earliest times to the period when joint-stock companies were formed for furnishing a larger quantity than had hitherto been possessed, and when it became necessary to apply to Parliament for the requisite powers,—we now resume the subject with the year 1808, and may just premise, that for the facts about to be narrated we are mainly indebted to a printed document, but little known, entitled "A Narrative of the various Trans-"actions and Dealings and Matters in Controversy between the Company of "Proprietors of the Manchester and Salford Waterworks and Mr. Samuel Hill "and others, commonly called 'The Stone-pipe Company'":—

"In the year 1808, Sir George Wright, baronet, Messrs. William Mainwaring, "Samuel Hill, Henry Wright, and Richard Hill, carried on trade together as "co-partners in the business of stone-pipe manufacturers,—and with a view "of extending the sale of their pipes, they determined to form a waterworks "company, and to obtain an Act of Parliament for the purpose of supplying the "town of Manchester with water; and as a groundwork for the said intended "company to start upon, and to prevent competition, they applied to Sir Oswald "Mosley, baronet, the lord of the manor of Manchester, to purchase from him "his right, privilege, and property of supplying the said town with water."

---

* The stone pipes which the company at first laid down in the streets were found not to answer, and iron pipes were therefore substituted. The injury done to the pavement of the streets, and the inconvenience to the inhabitants, was beyond all calculation.

By articles of agreement dated July 4th, 1808, between these parties, Sir O. Mosley conveyed to the company all his estate, right, title, and interest, as lord of the manor, in the then existing waterworks, aqueducts, reservoirs, and all machinery, main pipes, &c., subject to the payment of a chief rent to Sir Oswald, in consideration of which, or of a sum of purchase money (to be determined by arbitration), he conveyed to the company a piece of land at Ancoats (3A. 2R. 19P. statute measure) with liberties to lay pipes, &c. As we have shown in a former article, after a protracted and severe parliamentary contest, the Stone-pipe Company got their Bill,—and we now give a brief sketch of its chief provisions.

The Act of 49th Geo. III., cap. 192 (passed 20th June, 1809), entitled "An "Act for more effectually supplying with water the inhabitants of the towns of "Manchester and Salford," &c., has a long preamble, setting forth that Sir O. Mosley, as lord of the manor, was possessed of waterworks and reservoirs, anciently constructed to supply Manchester with water from the Medlock at Holt Town in Ancoats; that Manchester and Salford had of late years become very populous, and the number of their buildings greatly increased, so that the waterworks were incapable of affording a sufficient supply, without considerable addition and alteration; and that the works would have been better constructed and carried on by a company of proprietors. It then enacts that various parties named shall be a body politic and corporate, by the name of "The Company of "Proprietors of the Manchester and Salford Waterworks." The original proprietors included Sir George Wright and four other gentlemen, named Wright, Samuel Hill, the Rev. Rowland Hill, and Richard Hill, Sir Henry Mainwaring Mainwaring, baronet, the Rev. Sir John Head, baronet, &c. The Act, after giving the company power to raise £60,000 by the creation of shares, and an additional sum of £50,000 in like manner, gives power to raise the latter sum on mortgage. Passing over the clauses for the internal government of the company by a board of directors, we come to the 32nd clause, which gives the company power to complete the waterworks for supplying water from the Medlock at Holt Town not higher up the river than where the Ashton canal crosses it near Holt Town. The clause gives power to erect machines, engines, and buildings, to dig up the soil of the streets, &c., and to lay pipes, &c. By the 29th clause, every engine they erect is to consume its own smoke. By the 41st, the company were not to enter the private streets of Henry Atherton, Esq., Ann, his wife, and Eleonora Byrom, without consent, viz., Camp, Charles, St. John, Byrom, Great and Little John, and Atherton streets; nor (42) to break up the soil of the wastes in the manors of Salford or Penhulton without consent. The 43rd recites, that for some time past Sir O. Mosley had taken from the Medlock 120,000 ale gallons per day, for the use of the waterworks; that to take a greater quantity might be to the loss of the Bridgewater Trust, and to the injury of the public, by stopping the canal navigation,—therefore the company is not to take more than 120,000 ale gallons daily, unless the water in the Bridgewater canal is running over the waste weirs. The 46th provides that gauges were to be so constructed as not to permit more than one-fourth of the whole current of the river to flow to the waterworks, so that in dry seasons the company might not take more than one-fourth. The 47th entitles the company to take the flood-water out of the Medlock. Engineers were to protect the mills and factories on the Medlock from the consequences of too much water being taken by the company. The 50th imposes a penalty on the company of £50 in various cases of violation of the Act. The 51st gives the option of special damages; and the 52nd empowers the mill-owners to prevent the company from diverting more than 120,000 gallons daily from the Medlock. By the 55th, the owners and inhabitants of houses may lay service pipes to the company's mains. There are penalties for fouling the water,— not to apply to water taken from and returned to the river for the purposes of trade; a penalty of £10 for supplying water to anyone not paying for it, except in cases of fire, repair of the pipes, &c. The 61st gives the company's servants power to enter premises to see that there is no waste of water. The 62nd requires every person taking water to provide a proper cistern, of "lead, stone, brick, "wood, or other materials," to receive the supply requisite for consumption, with a ball and stop-cock, to prevent waste. The remainder of the clauses relate to the recovery of water rent or rate, appeals, &c.

The narrative states that, pending the treaty of the parties with Sir O. Mosley, it was frequently mentioned that an Act was to be applied for, and a company incorporated to supply the two towns with water; and Sir O. Mosley always understood the parties were treating with him on behalf of such company. "The "first general assembly under the Act, was held on Wednesday the 12th July, "1809, at the Royal Oak in Manchester, at which the whole of the members of "the Stone-pipe Company contrived to get appointed officers for executing the "Act, and with a view, as the Waterworks Company contend, of taking unfair "advantages of the other proprietors of the Waterworks Company, and applying "the funds of that company to their own use. At this meeting, Sir George "Wright, Samuel Hill, and Richard Hill, and also George Bolton Mainwaring, "were appointed directors, and William Mainwaring was appointed treasurer, "and Henry Wright solicitor of the company, and the other directors were the "relatives and friends of the Stone-pipe Company. At this meeting it was also "resolved, that £60,000 should be raised by shares of £100 each; and that the "directors, or any three of them, should be empowered to draw on the treasurer, "at any time for such sums as they might find necessary; and the treasurer was "authorised to pay the same. The assembly was adjourned to the 4th January, "1810, not to be then held in Manchester, but in London, where all the members

" of the Stone-pipe Company then resided. The said Sir George Wright died in
" the month of December, 1809." A report as to an award was read at this
meeting, and also that Sir George Wright, chairman of the directors, was dead.
Four directors were required by the Act to go out of office at this meeting, and
this death causing another vacancy, " the Stone-pipe Company contrived, by the
" assistance of their relatives and friends, to have the same four directors re-
" appointed (one of whom was the brother of the said Samuel Hill, and another
" of them the son of the said William Mainwaring), and a friend appointed to fill
" the vacancy caused by the death of Sir George, in order to give a preponderating
" influence to the Stone-pipe Company over the funds of the Manchester and
" Salford Waterworks Company. At this meeting, Mr. Henry Wright (one of the
" Stone-pipe Company, and who had at the last meeting been appointed solicitor
" to the Waterworks Company), was appointed chief clerk of the undertaking;
" and at the same meeting, by the means aforesaid, the Stone-pipe Company
" contrived to get a resolution passed," committing the care and custody of the
common seal to the chief clerk. " The Stone-pipe Company having, by the
" means aforesaid, got one of their members (Mr. William Mainwaring) appointed
" treasurer of the funds of the Waterworks Company,—another of them (Mr.
" Henry Wright), appointed solicitor and chief clerk, with the custody of the
" common seal, and the remainder of the partners in the Stone-pipe Company
" appointed directors, they were enabled to dispose of and apply the funds and
" property of the Waterworks Company in any manner they thought proper; and,
" as a pretext for doing so, they caused, by their influence, the following most
" extraordinary minute and resolution to be entered at this meeting :—

> 'And it appearing to this assembly that it would be highly desirable to prevent any other persons from carrying on any other waterworks for supplying the towns of Manchester and Salford with water; and it also appearing that the Stone-pipe Company are now the owners of the waterworks and reservoirs anciently constructed for supplying the inhabitants of the town of Manchester and the neighbourhood thereof with water; and that the Stone-pipe Company have the power of erecting and making such additions, alterations, and improvements, and other works to the said ancient waterworks, aqueducts, and reservoirs, the better to enable them to supply the inhabitants of the town of Manchester aforesaid with water,—It was moved, seconded, and resolved unanimously,—That it be and it is hereby referred to the Court of Directors to purchase of and from the said company of proprietors of the stone-pipe manufactory the whole of their right, title, and interest of, in, and to the said waterworks, aqueducts, and reservoirs now belonging to them in the said town of Manchester, at the most reasonable price at which the same can be had and obtained.'

" It may be proper here to remark, that at every general assembly of the company,
" and at every court of directors, we find the members of the Stone-pipe Company
" always acting in the treble capacity of proprietors and directors of the Water-
" works Company and as partners in the Stone-pipe Company, and always
" contriving to have their friends and relatives attending to vote and to act
" upon every occasion when any arrangement was to be made between the

" Waterworks Company and the Stone-pipe Company. This will account for the
" above resolution, and what passes afterwards upon the subject. This meeting
" was adjourned to the 5th July, 1810. It appears by the Waterworks Company's
" books, that previously to the above-mentioned general assembly, held on the
" 4th January, 1810, Mr. Mainwaring, the treasurer, had actually paid to the
" Stone-pipe Company (his partners) out of the funds of the Waterworks Company
" [various sums, in all £4,500] on account of his and his said partners' alleged
" interest in the agreement made with Sir Oswald Mosley." " On the 5th July,
" 1810, a general assembly of the proprietors was held, at which fourteen pro-
" prietors only were present, two of whom were the said Henry Wright and
" Richard Hill, members of the Stone-pipe Company, and five others were
" directors interested in the Stone-pipe Company (one of whom was appointed
" chairman of this meeting), when a report, purporting to be a report of the
" directors, signed by the said Henry Wright as chief clerk, was presented, from
" which the following is an extract:—

> ' Your directors have to state to you that, in pursuance of the instructions given to them at the last general assembly, they have purchased from the Stone-pipe Company the whole of their right, title and interest in and to the ancient waterworks at Manchester; for these they have given the sum of £14,000, which has been paid by instalments to the said company.'

" No part of this sum of £14,000 was ever paid or mentioned to Sir Oswald
" Mosley. The agreement of the 4th July, 1808, was made for a nominal
" consideration. Sir Oswald Mosley would at that time have made an absolute
" conveyance of the whole of the property comprised in the agreement, free from
" any rent whatever, for a much less sum than £14,000; indeed, the rent reserved
" was a full consideration for the property. The Stone-pipe Company never paid
" to Sir Oswald Mosley the rent mentioned in the agreement; the Waterworks
" Company have paid the rent to Sir Oswald Mosley from the commencement.
" It appears that long before the said report was presented by Mr. Henry Wright
" to the last-mentioned meeting, Mr. Mainwaring, the treasurer, had paid the
" whole £14,000 to his partners, as appears from extracts from the company's
" books." Then the conveyance of the land, &c., of Sir Oswald Mosley is set
forth, reserving thereout a clear yearly rent to Alexander Radcliffe Sidebottom,
in trust for Sir Oswald Mosley, his heirs, &c., of £624. 10s. 1d.,—the conveyance
being " to the use of the said company of proprietors of the Manchester and
" Salford Waterworks, their successors and assigns, for ever." " No notice what-
" ever is taken in the above recited conveyance of the £14,000 which had been
" paid by Mainwaring, the treasurer of the Waterworks Company, to the Stone-
" pipe Company, as a consideration for the purchase of their alleged interest in
" the agreement made with Sir Oswald Mosley, or of any interest they had or
" claimed to have had under that agreement. The agreement is recited, and it is

"very natural to suppose that if the parties who made that agreement with Sir
"Oswald Mosley had had any interest separate from the Waterworks Company
"in the premises, Mr. Sidebottom, who prepared the conveyance, would have
"made them to join in the conveyance as conveying parties; and the reason he
"did not do so was his ignorance of any such claim. It is evident he considered
"them as mere agents of the Waterworks Company, and prepared the conveyance
"accordingly. No part of the £14,000 was, of course, paid to Sir Oswald Mosley.
"On his being made acquainted with the circumstances (which were communicated
"to him a short time ago) he was much astonished, as he, from the commencement
"of the treaty for the sale of the ancient waterworks, understood that an Act was
"to be applied for to incorporate a water company, and he promised to the parties
"contracting with him to assist them, and did assist them with all his interest in
"obtaining the Act. Had the Act not been obtained, the agreement would have
"been cancelled; and, indeed, a great part of it was materially altered by substi-
"tuting other lands, &c., in lieu of the premises contracted for, and changing the
"quantum of rent, as appears by the conveyance above recited. The directors'
"report shows that the £14,000 was paid to Messrs. Samuel Hill, Henry Wright,
"and Richard Hill, in their characters as partners in the Stone-pipe Company."

At the general assembly of the 5th July, 1810, the directors reported that it appeared from admeasurement of the streets and squares in Manchester that 15 miles of main and 45 miles of service pipes would be requisite for the full supply of the town, and that they had contracted with the Stone-pipe Company for the necessary pipes, which were in course of delivery. By the agreement with this company, an engineer of the Waterworks Company was, prior to any delivery of stone pipes from the manufactory, to prove them at Gloucester or Tewkesbury; the Waterworks Company to pay for the pipes within two months after delivery. By the schedule to this agreement, 36,200 yards of stone pipe were to be provided; those of 18-inch bore, at 45s. per yard; 15-inch, 35s.; 12-inch, 30s. 9d.; 9-inch, 18s. 8d.; 8-inch, 16s.; 7-inch, 13s. 9d.; 6-inch, 11s. 6d.; 4-inch, 7s. 8d.; and 3-inch bore, at 4s. 11d. per yard. "At the time of making this agreement, the
"Stone-pipe Company were well aware of the elevation of the reservoirs con-
"structed for supplying Manchester and Salford with water, and the pressure the
"stone pipes would have to sustain, and could not but have known (had they tried
"the pipes before delivery, agreeable to the terms of the contract) that the pipes
"delivered would not bear the requisite pressure; and that, instead of their
"proving to be good, proper, and serviceable stone pipes, they were not proper
"pipes, and would not be serviceable to the Waterworks Company: in fact,
"they all turned out to be useless, as will be made to appear below. What
"became of the above agreement (which we suppose was the one laid before Mr.
"Preston) we know not; it is not to be found, and, possibly, it was never executed;

"we suppose the Stone-pipe Company destroyed it for some reason or other, "and aftewards submitted another in its stead." [This agreement omits the power to the company's engineer to prove the pipes; it is signed by the four survivors of the Stone-pipe Company, and the counterpart has the seal of the Waterworks Company appended.] Pipes to the amount of £23,049 were delivered at Gloucester or Tewkesbury, for the Waterworks Company, between March, 1811, and December, 1812, "but none of them were ever proved before they were so "delivered." "There are many circumstances which convince us that the Stone-"pipe Company, at the time they executed the agreement with the Waterworks "Company, were aware that the stone pipes (which were bored out of blocks "of soft rotten stone) would not bear any pressure of water, and would prove "unserviceable; and, for the purpose of preventing the discovery of these circum-"stances, Mr. Samuel Hill, being a director in the Manchester and Salford "Waterworks Company, proposed to superintend the laying down the pipes in "the Manchester streets himself, and his proposal was, as a matter of course, "accepted by his brother directors; and in May, 1810, he proceeded with full "power to Manchester for that purpose." "The stone pipes were laid in the "streets of Manchester as soon as delivered there, under the immediate superin-"tendence of the said Samuel Hill, and his brother, Richard Hill (another of the "directors of the Waterworks Company); and they so contrived to lay the pipes "in the different streets, and placed apart from each other, that no trial of them "could be made with the water in the reservoir until long after the Stone-pipe "Company had obtained payment of the following sums from the Waterworks "Company, viz." [in all, £36,984.] Various doubts arising as to the sufficiency of the stone pipes to carry the water, a motion was made that no more pipes be paid for till it could be ascertained whether they would bear the pressure of the water, but it was negatived. It was the 10th or 11th July, 1812, that the sub-engineer, Mr. Freemantle, turned some water into a part of the 18-inch stone-pipe main, laid down near the reservoir, "and the main burst, although a little pressure "had been laid on it. The breakage had been repaired, and another trial made;" but Freemantle was "much concerned to state that the main pipes had failed in "no less than six places." He had also "tried some 9-inch pipes with the "forcing pump, part of which would not sustain the pressure put upon them by "the pump." Another attempt to bring the matter under the notice of the proprietors was overborne by such directors as were members of the Stone-pipe Company; and instructions were sent to Freemantle to "make the trial of every "pipe, from the Ashton canal only before you cover them." A further trial of the pipes previously laid showed them to be very defective. At a special general assembly in September, 1812, a report was read from Mr. Rennie, to the effect that the stone pipes should be used only in the parts of Manchester where the pressure does not exceed 30 or 40 feet, and that in the lower parts of the town iron pipes should be substituted; for unless a stone of a superior strength and quality were found, it would not answer. He recommended that all the stone pipes laid should be joined to the main and thoroughly tried before any more pipes were sent to Manchester. This advice seems to have been neglected, and various things done by the stone-pipe members of the Waterworks Company's board; till, at a special general assembly on the 15th September, 1812, it was resolved that no more pipes be sent to Manchester without the orders of a general meeting. Mr. Freemantle was directed to furnish an account of all the stone pipes burst or deficient after being laid, but this was obviously impossible. "Nearly the whole of the pipes had been laid underground, and had never been "proved, and were then out of sight. The fact was, the whole were defective, "unsound, improper pipes, and not suitable or serviceable. The water had never "been put into any of them, excepting a length of main of about 400 yards, which "burst as often as the water was laid on. The first thing the Stone-pipe Company "now did was to make Mr. Freemantle their friend, which they effectually did; "and as they had the complete control of the directory, they determined on "placing out of sight the remainder of the stone pipes included in the above "invoices, preparatory to the junctions so frequently above alluded to. We "therefore find all the strength now employed by Mr. Freemantle in laying down "stone pipes in the streets without joining them, and in a short time he had put "the whole of them out of sight. There were a great many pipes, however, "which were so very bad, that the Stone-pipe Company (a short time previously "to the next general meeting of the Waterworks Company) had a large pit "excavated in Beswick, and these bad pipes (all of which were included in "the above-mentioned invoices) thrown into it and covered up, to prevent their "being seen by the proprietors, who were about to assemble at Manchester. "This could not have been done without the knowledge of Freemantle. The "fact was communicated to the Manchester proprietors many years after it had "taken place, and the pipes were found in the pit before mentioned."

We might fill columns with the further history of this extraordinary management, by means of which the Stone-pipe Company ordered pipes to a great extent, notwithstanding prohibitions, and had them laid, and got paid for them,—knowing all the time that they could not resist the pressure of the water. But in order to postpone the evil day, the pipes were laid disjointedly, and were not attached to the mains, so that the water could not be turned through them when laid. They made a proposal to substitute iron for stone pipes, in certain cases, which was accepted. Some most extraordinary payments were made to the Sone-pipe Company,—the clerk being authorised to accept drafts, and to use the common seal of the company for various purposes. At length, at a special meeting in London, on the 26th November, 1813 (held, as several previous ones, without regular requisition or notice), the directors reported that the company were in great pecuniary difficulties, and a committee of inquiry was appointed of seven proprietors, who, on the 17th December, presented their report. This report states that, "it was fully understood the pipes were to be equal to a "pressure of 150 feet, as stated in the estimate of iron pipes, the reservoir being "nearly 100 feet higher than parts of the service of the streets, which was con- "sidered the great desideratum of the company. Under this engagement, the "Stone-pipe Company have supplied a large quantity of pipes, including all the "large mains that will be required above 9-inch bore, which have been, in part, "laid to the length of 16,732 yards; and there are now remaining in your wharf, "unlaid, 4,027 yards of service pipes. When the junction of the pipes was com- "pleted to the reservoir, the proprietors learned, by statements from all quarters, "as well as from the reports of your resident engineer, the inadequacy of the "pipes to bear the necessary force of water from the reservoir that had been built "professedly and intentionally with the specific purpose of supplying the highest "parts of Manchester." "Your committee regret to state, that notwithstanding "the pressure is reduced under 25 feet, yet the pipes prove defective, and, if "suffered to remain, the great object which the works have been erected to effect "will be defeated, and a constant additional charge, in raising the water from "the lower reservoir to the upper, entailed on the proprietors, which is rendered "useless by the several cisterns placed for to lower the pressure to the level of "each cistern, although it was first raised as stated, and still continued at a heavy "expense. This circumstance your committee feel it their duty to point out to "the proprietors, as their plans and intentions are entirely frustrated by the stone "pipes not having been good, sound, and proper, or tried by the Stone-pipe "Company before their being sent from their works, according to their engage- "ment; for which failure your committee are of opinion this company are entitled "to redress from the Stone-pipe Company." The job becomes more and more manifest. Another passage in the report shows that in January, 1810, stone pipes, instead of being cheaper than iron (which would have borne the heaviest pressure), cost 30 per cent more than iron pipes; and subsequently their price became "full 70 per cent. more than iron, exclusive of defective or damaged "pipes." The committee add that "the pipes can never be rendered equal to "the pressure they were intended to receive, nor can they be depended upon "even at their present reduced force." And, in conclusion, they state "their "complete and unanimous conviction that, unless the stone-pipe system be aban- "doned, the inevitable ruin of the concern must be the consequence. Yet, in the "face of this report, and of the reappointment of the reporting committee on the one "hand, and of the constant breaking and leaking of the stone pipes on the other, "the directors continued to urge the laying of stone pipes with all expedition." On the 7th February Mr. Freemantle died, without having made any return of defective pipes; a relative of one of the stone-pipe directors then acted as engineer, and extended the laying of the stone pipes. "For the last twelve "months the Waterworks Company had been labouring under great pecuniary "difficulties, and the acting directors being composed of the Stone-pipe Com- "pany, were carrying on the concern by means of accommodation paper, and by "misapplying the common seal of the Waterworks Company. They had run the "company into debt at this time, by these means, upwards of £40,000, and the "concern was on the eve of bankruptcy." Yet, on the 15th September, 1814, at a meeting in Manchester, only eleven proprietors present (the majority being connected with the Stone-pipe Company), the directors speak of an "amicable "arrangement;" and after referring to "the incontestible proofs which your "directors have of the *efficacy* of stone pipes," they order as many stone pipes of different bores "as can be laid with expedition." At length, the Stone-pipe Company having obtained all the money they could from the Waterworks Company, at a special Meeting in London, on the 13th December, 1814 (thirteen proprietors present), it was resolved that the Stone-pipe Company agree that their contract with the Waterworks Company should cease to all intents and purposes from this day, 13th December, and that mutual releases be given. No releases were ever given or prepared, nor was the contract with the Stone-pipe Company ever given up or cancelled; and the Stone-pipe Company soon after became embarrassed. This Stone-pipe Company is stated to have consisted of four persons only,—Samuel and Richard Hill, Henry Wright, and G. B. Mainwaring.

We purposely pass over a number of bonds and bill transactions which resulted from the fatal influence of members of the Stone-pipe Company in the councils of the Waterworks Company. These bonds gave rise to long litigation in the law courts. As early as 1813 the latter company had to go to Parliament for further powers to raise more money; and the Act 57 Geo. III. cap. 20 (passed 1st April, 1813), empowered the company of proprietors to raise amongst themselves any sum not exceeding £100,000. Power was given to borrow the money on mortgage, or by granting annuities, or by bonds or promissory notes; and this last power was much abused by certain individuals in the management. A trust-deed, stated to have been agreed to at an illegal meeting, dated the 17th April, 1815, did not much improve the company's position; and at length "the affairs of the Waterworks Company had, by the improper management of "the directors, set forth in this narrative, been brought into a lamentable state. "No person would sell the company anything upon credit. The trustees men- "tioned in the deed of 17th April, 1815, were in the receipt of the water rates.

"Sir Oswald Mosley had made a distress for his rent. The taxes were much in
"arrear, and there was not one penny even to pay labourers' wages. The Stone-
"pipe Company were represented to be insolvent. Under these circumstances,
"there appeared no means of extricating the company from its difficulties;
"however, the proprietors, being aware of the situation of the company, deter-
"mined to change the management of the company's affairs, and to appoint
"directors residing at Manchester, where, in future, they should hold their courts,
"and where the entire management of their affairs should be carried on. This
"gave some confidence to the people of Manchester, and several gentlemen
"residing in Manchester consented to become directors. The directors at Man-
"chester held their first court in Manchester in the month of August, 1816, but
"it was found impossible to investigate the former accounts, or to obtain any
"satisfactory information as to the company's affairs, until they were in possession
"of the books, documents, and papers then in the possession of the London
"directors and Stone-pipe Company, some of which (with much reluctance, and
"after many repeated applications for them), were sent to Manchester in the
"month of March, 1817. Although the directors at Manchester were unaware
"of the illegal transactions of the Stone-pipe Company before referred to, yet
"the unsound state of the stone pipes, and the claims of the Stone-pipe Company
"to a sum of £2,511. 2s. 2d. drew the attention of the directors to them, and they
"were determined to resist the payment, and informed the trustees named in the
"deed of trust of such their determination. In the month of May, 1817, Mr.
"Ruddock being then engineer to the Waterworks Company, gave it as his
"decisive opinion that the stone pipes could not longer be used with effect; and
"he was instructed to make an estimate of what it would cost to replace them
"with iron pipes. He made an estimate accordingly, and presented it to a
"general assembly of proprietors held on the 14th May, 1817, at Manchester."
"Mr. Ruddock's estimate amounts to £21,920. 6s. 2d. for substituting iron pipes
"for stone pipes. The Manchester directors being of opinion that the company
"could not flourish until the numerous debts due to their *bonâ fide* creditors were
"satisfied, suggested that money should be raised for that purpose by the creation
"of an additional number of shares, which suggestion was carried into effect, and
"by the proceeds thereof, with a sum of £20,000 borrowed from the commissioners
"for the issue of exchange bills, the *bonâ fide* creditors of the company were paid;
"and in August, 1819, the directors were in the receipt of the water rates, and
"the trustees named in the deed of the 17th April, 1815, never afterwards inter-
"fered." "In 1823, it had cost the Waterworks Company upwards of £16,000 in
"replacing defective stone pipes with iron."—Here ends this "strange, eventful
"narrative," which has scarcely ever been surpassed as a history of the way in
which the company for some seven years could be continually fleeced by the

vendors of a useless article, just because these vendors had the address to keep the reins of the company's government in their own hands. The proprietors at large were very great pecuniary sufferers; but all this time the inhabitants of Manchester and Salford were also suffering from the greatly inadequate supply of water, which was not remarkably good or pure at the best.

In 1816, it became necessary to take further powers to raise money, and accordingly the Act of the 56th Geo. III. cap. 12 (11th April, 1816), was obtained; the preamble of which recites, amongst other things, that under the Act of 1813, the company had borrowed £29,230 on bonds, and that yet the money was inadequate to complete and carry on the works. The Act then empowers them to raise money by borrowing on mortgage, or by grant of annuities. It also makes various provisions to protect the company against a repetition of the evils under which they had so long suffered. The 11th clause requires the company to make fire-plugs in every street, &c., supplied with water from their mains, the keys of the plugs to be deposited where the fire engines are kept. The company was also to deliver keys of the plugs to the fire insurance offices.

The next legislation was in 1821,—the statute of 1st and 2nd Geo. IV. cap. 47, being passed on the 7th May that year. Its preamble recites the three previous Acts; that the inhabitants of Manchester and Salford, and also of Hulme, Chorlton Row, Ardwick, Newton, Cheetham, Broughton, and Pendleton, had of late increased, and were still increasing, and that it was necessary the company should adequately supply all these with water. Power is then given to raise £50,000 by new shares, and the usual powers are given to borrow on mortgage, &c. No waste or surplus water to be taken from the Rochdale or Ashton canals. Clause 14 limits the rates to be paid for water,—the maximum rate on any inhabitant not to exceed £10, and the company not to supply any inhabitant for less than 12s. yearly unless they think fit. Persons requiring an extra quantity for baths, closets, washing carriages or horses, or for trade purposes, to contract with the company. The scale of rates was, under £20 rental, not more than £7. 10s. per cent.; under £40, 7 per cent.; under £60, 6½ per cent.; under £80, 6 per cent.; under £100 rental, 5½ per cent.; above £100, 5 per cent. on such rental.

Next came the Act of 4th George IV. cap. 115 (27th June, 1823), which, after reciting the former statutes, and the increase of population and buildings in the various townships, now including Beswick, Bradford, Droylsden, Openshaw, Gorton, and Denton, sets forth that the water of the river Medlock (whence the inhabitants of all these places were then supplied) was found to be insufficient adequately to supply them; and that it is expedient that the company should be enabled to supply water thereto from some more adequate source. Power is then given to purchase lands, and to lay out rental in extending the works; to raise £20,000 on bonds, if necessary, to complete the works, by making one or more reservoirs in that part of the valley in Gorton north-east of the Ashton and Oldham Canal, where it crosses the valley, and to make watercourses, &c., to convey the water thence to the existing reservoirs in Beswick; such conveyance to be made through a culvert or trunk formerly made by the Ashton Canal Company. Engineers to be appointed to fix gauges, to prevent the company from taking more than the flood water, but the company to take the flood water. Inhabitants may lay service pipes to the company's mains, on giving notice. The same water rates as in the Act of 1821, and the same regulations as to fouling the water, cisterns with ball and stopcock, &c., as in former acts. There are various clauses protecting the lands of individuals at Gorton, and others for securing the water-power supply to the millowners, by means of gauges, &c. Still the company were prohibited taking more than 120,000 gallons daily from the Medlock, except in floods, and then only one-fourth the flood current.

The Act of the 4th Vict. cap. 8 (6th April, 1841), was to enable the company to raise a further sum of money. Power is given to create new shares; to raise £100,000 by mortgage; the power given by the 58rd Geo. III. to borrow on promissory notes is repealed; an annual account to be made up, and a copy sent to the clerk of the peace; a penalty of £200 (and a further continuing penalty of £20 daily) is imposed on gas makers corrupting the water within the limits of the Act; the gas mains to be four feet distant from the water mains; and where they must cross, the gas pipe to be laid above the water pipe at the greatest practicable distance, to be at least nine feet long, and laid so that no gas-pipe joint should be within four feet of the water pipe. Penalty as to gas pipes laid otherwise, £5; and a power is given to examine the gas pipes whenever any contamination of the water arises from gas; penalties for contamination, £20, and £10 daily during its continuance after notice. There is also power to indict gas makers for nuisance.

The last of the series of Acts of the company was that of the 9th Vict. cap. 10 (14th May, 1846), "to raise a further sum of money." Power is given to raise £200,000 by the creation of shares, or by mortgage, to re-borrow money, and to raise money by subscription, to pay off mortgages.

The Old Works.

The existing works of the Manchester and Salford Waterworks Company, which become the property of the Corporation on the 1st of January next, are the following:—Three reservoirs at Beswick, about one mile and a half from Manchester, estimated to contain 5,404,811 cubic feet of water, and two reservoirs at Gorton, about four miles distant, estimated to contain 85,678,241 cubic feet. "Two "of the reservoirs at Beswick are upon a level with the river Medlock, which, "when there is flood water in that river, receives such water, which sometime "afterwards is pumped from them by a steam engine of 60 horses' power into an "adjoining service reservoir of about seven acres, at an elevation of 100 feet "above the town. The Gorton works consist of a store and service reservoir, "being about 143 feet above the town, into which the water is received from about "1,500 acres of drainage ground. From the service reservoirs at these works main "pipes are laid, which convey the water into the town; 1,750 yards of a main "of 18 inches diameter are laid from Beswick to Manchester, and 7,057 yards of "a 24-inch main from Gorton to Manchester. There are also 5,300 yards of an "18-inch main laid from the Gorton works to those at Beswick, with a view of "supplying the latter when there are no floods in the river Medlock. From "these mains, other pipes, of diameters varying from 15 inches down to 2 inches, "besides lead mains from 1 to 1½ inches in diameter, are branched off for the "supply of the various districts, and the main pipes now laid extend 120 miles, "or thereabouts. The present quantity of water distributed by the company is "not 3,000,000 gallons per diem. On the mains and service mains a number of "cocks are placed, so that the water in any district may be turned on or off at a "short notice. With respect to the height of service, that varies from 40 to 140 "feet, according to what draught may be in the district supplying; but when the "stop-cocks before-mentioned are worked, the force of the water is concentrated "to any given point, and can be applied to extinguish fires, without the aid of "fire engines, at an average height of 90 feet." The Company supplied sixteen townships and places with water, the aggregate population of which, in 1841, was 329,020. Their income for 1846 was £30,065—derived from the supply of water to dwelling houses, trading places, warehouses and factories, and public institutions, £28,463, and sundry other receipts, £1,602. The following was in 1847 and is still the Company's scale of charges :—

DWELLING HOUSES.					
Rates per Annum.	£. s.	Rates per Annum.	£. s.	Rates per Annum.	£. s.
Cellar Dwellings	0 4	Houses of the rent of—		Houses of the rent of—	
Houses of the rent of—		£20	1 0	£120	3 15
£5 and under	0 6	" 25	1 4	" 130	3 18
" £6 and less than £7	0 7	" 30	1 8	" 140	4 0
" 7 " 8	0 8	" 35	1 12	" 150	4 2
" 8 " 9	0 9	" 40	1 16	" 160	4 4
" 9 and not exceed 10	0 10	" 45	1 19	" 170	4 7
" 11	0 11	" 50	2 2	" 180	4 10
" 12	0 12	" 55	2 5	" 190	4 15
" 13	0 13	" 60	2 8	" 200 to £210	5 0
" 14	0 14	" 65	2 10	" 220 " 230	5 5
" 15	0 15	" 70	2 12	" 240 " 250	5 10
" 16	0 16	" 80	2 18	" 260 " 270	5 15
" 17	0 17	" 90	3 3	" 280 " 290	6 0
" 18	0 18	" 100	3 7	" 300 and upwards, 2 per cent.	
" 19	0 19	" 110	3 11		

Water closets: For houses above £20 rental, 10s. per annum for one, and 5s. for each additional water closet after the first, where there are more than one.—For houses below £20 rental, 5s. per annum each closet.—For every ten houses farmed by the owner, using one closet supplied from a cistern, 2s. 6d. per annum per house, or 25s. per closet.—Private baths, 15s. per annum.—Carriages and horses, &c.: Four wheels, 5s. per annum; two wheels, 3s. per annum; horses, 4s. each.

Note.—Such of the above specified rates as respect dwellings, the rental of which does not exceed £12 per annum, are conditional on the supply to such dwellings being contracted for by the owners, and the remainder of the above rates are subject to the following discount, if contracted for:—20 per cent. for houses above £12 rent, and not exceeding £20; 15 per cent for houses above £20 rent.

The water rates are payable quarterly, in advance, on the 1st day of January, the 1st day of April, the 1st day of July, and the 1st day of October in each year.

In January, 1845, the Company supplied—

Dwellings.	Rental.	Dwellings.	Rental.
8,726	£5 and under.	695	£40 to £50.
17,174	£5 to £10.	149	£50 to £60.
3,608	£10 to £15.	75	£60 to £70.
2,225	£15 to £20.	53	£70 to £80.
869	£20 to £25.	81	£80 to £100.
404	£25 to £30.	110	above £100.
429	£30 to £35.		
162	£35 to £40.	29,760	

Besides these, amongst public institutions, &c., they supplied in 1845, 51 factories, 702 warehouses, lock-up shops and offices, 12 public-houses and lock-ups, 4 markets, 44 churches, chapels, and schools; in all, 836: and amongst establishments for trading purposes supplied were 263 retail brewers (exclusive of dwellings), 46 wholesale brewers, 207 stables (exclusive of those connected with inns, taverns, &c.), 48 wine and spirit vaults, 12 chemical works, 26 silk and woollen dyers, 14 hat dyers, 22 smithies, 25 letterpress printers, 13 stone, sand, and coal yards, 105 engine boilers; in all, 905 places of trade. Of public institutions, factories, and other buildings, not dwelling houses, in the district, there were, in 1845, the number of 8,456, of which 1,742 were supplied by the Company, and 6,714 unsupplied. The public baths and wash-houses consumed, in 1845, about 10,500 gallons daily. Various medical and other charitable institutions, soup kitchen, infants' schools, &c., were supplied with water gratuitously, and, in most cases, unlimitedly. The infirmary had in this way 755,550 gallons, and the house of recovery, or fever ward, 141,983 gallons. The following shows the average daily supply of water to the town in the four years specified:—

Year.	No. Tenants.	Estimated Population.	Gallons. Daily.	Each Person Gallons Daily.
1832	17,443	87,215	1,212,212	13.89
1841	29,202	146,010	1,432,741	9.81
1845	31,501	157,505	2,037,160	12.93
1847	34,806	174,030	3,001,264	17.24

The length of main pipes in December, 1846, was:—In Manchester, 55 miles; Salford, 17$\frac{5}{8}$; Hulme, 8$\frac{7}{8}$; Chorlton-upon-Medlock, 9$\frac{1}{8}$; Ardwick, 6$\frac{1}{3}$; Gorton, 5; Openshaw, three-quarters of a mile; Bradford, seven-eighths of a mile; Beswick, 1$\frac{3}{8}$; Newton, half a mile; and Cheetham, 4$\frac{1}{4}$ miles;—total, 109$\frac{7}{8}$ miles. We are informed that the present length of their mains [November, 1850] is about 120 miles. The water is generally on from four a.m. to five p.m. As to analyses of the quality, one sample sent to Mr. John Davies, by Mr. Paton, was between eight and nine degrees of hardness, by Dr. Clark's test; another from Dr. R. A. Smith's laboratory, was found by Mr. A. P. Halliday to be 7·6 degrees of hardness; and a third, only 4·38 degrees of hardness, being much superior to that from the red rock.

APPENDIX No. 2.—*Report of* PETER CLARE, *F.R.A.S., and* JOHN FREDERIC BATEMAN, *F.G.S., M. Inst. C.E., being the Committee appointed for superintending the Measurement of Rain falling along the Lines of the Rochdale, Ashton-under-Lyne, and Peak Forest Canals; with Observations upon the Returns, and other particulars, by* JOHN FREDERIC BATEMAN.

[Extracted from the "*Memoirs of the Literary and Philosophical Society of Manchester*."—
Read April 11th, 1848.]

THREE years have elapsed since the last Report on this subject was presented to the Society. During this period the observations have been regularly continued, and the results are as follow. It is almost unnecessary to remark, that the old rain gauges, called the Canal Company's gauges, are placed on the roofs of dwellings, and the Society's gauges on the ground, the observations being taken with a view of ascertaining the difference in the quantity registered in the two situations.

RAINFALL ALONG THE LINE OF THE ROCHDALE CANAL.

1845.	SLATTOCKS, near Middleton. 450 ft. above sea.		MOSS LOCK, near Rochdale, about 500 ft. above sea.		WHITE HOLME RESERVOIR, Blackstone Edge, about 1,200 ft. above sea.		TOLL BAR, Blackstone Edge, about 1,000 ft. above sea.		BLACK HOUSE, near Ripponden.		SOWERBY BRIDGE, 300 ft. above sea.	
	Canal Company's Gauge.	Society's Gauge.	Canal Company's Gauge.	Society's Gauge.	Canal Company's Gauge.	Society's Gauge.	Canal Company's Gauge.	Society's Gauge.	Canal Company's Gauge.	Society's Gauge.	Canal Company's Gauge.	Society's Gauge.
	In. Dec.	In. Dec.	In. Dec.	In. Dec.	In. Dec.	In. Dec.	In. Dec.	In. Dec.	In. Dec.	In. Dec.	In. Dec.	In. Dec.
January	1 47	..	1 80	..	2 05	3 8	2 09	4 0	1 80	2 5	1 26	1 9
February	1 27	..	1 05	..	0 90	1 2	0 80	1 3	0 51	1 1	0 00	0 5
March	2 10	..	1 60	..	2 09	5 0	2 80	5 1	3 00	4 9	1 91	2 5
April	1 85	..	1 40	..	2 30	3 0	1 99	3 0	2 00	3 0	1 17	1 9
May	1 30	..	1 08	..	1 90	3 8	1 86	4 0	1 80	2 7	1 81	2 1
June	2 75	..	2 55	..	3 80	5 0	3 36	5 0	3 60	3 7	2 01	2 5
July	3 25	..	2 85	..	3 80	4 3	3 70	4 5	3 91	4 7	3 17	4 0
August	4 75	..	5 00	..	5 00	8 3	4 60	8 2	4 80	8 0	4 93	5 5
September	3 17	..	2 55	..	3 60	4 7	3 30	4 6	3 40	6 3	2 91	2 3
October	3 85	..	3 45	..	4 36	8 9	4 20	8 8	4 20	7 0	3 02	3 5
November	2 20	..	2 15	..	2 90	4 3	2 12	4 2	2 70	5 1	1 81	2 2
December	4 25	..	3 95	..	7 15	..	6 70	12 0	7 70	12 8	4 03	5·4
	32 21	..	29 43	..	39 85	52 3 11 mo.	37 02	64 7	39 42	61 8	28 03	34 3

RAINFALL ALONG THE LINE OF THE ROCHDALE CANAL—*continued*.

	SLATTOCKS, near Middleton, 450 ft. above sea.		MOSS LOCK, near Rochdale, about 500 ft. above sea.		WHITE HOLME RESERVOIR, Blackstone Edge, about 1,200 ft. above sea.		TOLL BAR, Blackstone Edge, about 1,000 ft. above sea.		BLACK HOUSE, near Ripponden.		SOWERBY BRIDGE, 300 ft. above sea.	
1846.	Canal Company's Gauge.	Society's Gauge.	Canal Company's Gauge.	Society's Gauge.	Canal Company's Gauge.	Society's Gauge.	Canal Company's Gauge.	Society's Gauge.	Canal Company's Gauge.	Society's Gauge.	Canal Company's Gauge.	Society's Gauge.
	In. Dec.		In. Dec.	In. Dec.	In. Dec.	In. Dec.	In. Dec.	In. Dec.	In. Dec.	In. Dec.	In. Dec.	In. Dec.
January	3 15	..	4 50	4 5	5 00	5 7	4 85	6 1	4 15	5 0	2 79	3 4
February	0 95	..	6 65	1 0	1 80	2 0	1 74	2 0	2 00	4 5	0 61	1 2
March	1 50	..	1 35	2 1	2 70	4 0	2 08	3 9	2 60	3 5	1 95	2 5
April	2 88	..	2 40	3 8	4 18	5 4	4 55	5 1	4 20	5 2	5 19	5 4
May	1 00	..	0 80	1 1	1 00	0 9	1 15	1 0	1 20	1 8	0 00	0 0
June	2 00	..	1 70	3 0	2 60	3 1	2 72	3 5	2 68	4 0	1 84	2 6
July	3 30	..	2 75	3 0	3 20	4 1	2 80	4 0	3 40	5 2	1 31	2 9
August	3 97	..	2 45	3 8	5 50	3 4	5 20	3 8	4 00	2 8	1 25	2 1
September	1 20	..	0 85	1 4	1 06	2 6	1 00	2 5	0 90	1 0	0 79	0 9
October	3 91	..	2 50	4 2	5 20	5 7	4 50	5 6	5 00	5 5	3 95	4 4
November	1 70	..	1 76	2 1	3 70	4 3	3 50	4 4	3 60	3 0	1 62	2 0
December	0 20	..	1 05	1 7	1 20	2 0	1 00	2 0	1 07	1 0	0 18	0 5
	25 76	..	22 76	31 7	37 14	43 2	35 09	43 9	34 80	42 5	21 48	27 9
1847.												
January	1 00	..	1 10	1 4	1 90	3 2	1 70	3 1	1 80	3 0	1 55	1 6
February	2 50	..	1 41	1 9	2 90	3 8	2 63	3 4	2 70	3 0	1 32	2 2
March	0 90	..	0 84	dmgd.	1 40	2 3	1 00	2 5	1 20	no ret.	0 95	0 9
April	1 63	..	1 29	dmgd.	2 40	3 8	2 30	4 0	2 20	2 5	1 25	2 2
May	2 30	..	3 25	3 5	3 60	3 4	3 72	3 5	3 90	3 5	2 87	3 5
June	2 90	..	2 55	3 1	2 60	2 5	2 47	2 5	2 57	3 4	1 20	1 9
July	1 80	..	0 80	1 6	0 55	1 1	0 75	1 3	0 60	1 3	0 25	0 8
August	1 65	..	1 35	2 0	1 70	2 3	1 80	2 3	1 90	2 3	0 87	1 6
September	3 80	..	3 41	4 5	3 60	4 4	3 90	4 5	3 40	3 5	1 10	3 0
October	4 00	..	4 00	4 3	4 50	5 5	4 80	5 5	4 80	5 5	2 77	3 8
November	3 20	..	3 15	3 8	4 30	4 5	3 80	4 5	3 90	4 5	1 55	2 4
December	4 20	..	3 80	5 2	6 30	11 0	6 20	11 0	6 50	13 8	4 63	3 0
	29 38	..	26 95	31 3 10 mo.	35 75	47 8	34 57	48 1	34 97	46 3 11 mo.	20 31	26 9

On the Peak Forest and Ashton Canals, there are only two places where gauges remain on the tops of houses. These are at Marple and at Comb's Reservoir, both on the Peak Forest Canal.

The comparative results between the old gauges placed on the tops of the houses, and the Society's gauges placed on the ground, are as follow:—

| 1845. | Marple, 581 feet. || Comb's Reservoir, 850 feet. ||
	Old Gauge.	Society's Gauge.	Old Gauge.	Society's Gauge.
	In. Dec.	In. Dec.	In. Dec.	In. Dec.
January	1 04	2 20	1 68	3 70
February	0 48	2 50	0 79	1 80
March	1 01	1 70	2 00	3 60
April	1 36	3 00	1 68	3 00
May	0 71	1 45	1 85	2 70
June	2 82	4 25	3 57	5 00
July	3 50	4 75	3 97	5 10
August	5 81	8 25	7 52	9 10
September	1 92	2 75	4 00	5 00
October	1 94	2 70	2 75	4 10
November	1 20	1 75	2 36	4 00
December	2 28	3 50	4 73	8 00
Total	23 57	38 80	36 90	55 10

Mr. Wood, the Canal Company's engineer, in whose charge the gauges are placed, is of opinion that the Society's gauge at Comb's reservoir for this year (1845) indicates a greater quantity of rain than was received by the gauge, as he found it to be leaky on removing it to a more convenient position. The returns do not show, apparently, any greater discrepancy than is to be observed at other places where no leakage occurred.

| 1846 | Marple, 581 feet. || Comb's Reservoir, 850 feet. ||
	Old Gauge.	Society's Gauge.	Old Gauge.	Society's Guage.
	In. Dec.	In. Dec.	In. Dec.	In Dec.
January	2 81	4 15	3 23	5 50
February	0 54	0 80	1 20	2 00
March	1 16	1 60	1 91	2 60
April	3 46	5 00	4 10	4 60
May	0 60	0 85	1 49	2 20
June	1 80	2 45	2 62	2 70
July	2 87	3 25	2 48	2 80
August	2 52	3 85	4 45	5 80
September	0 94	1 45	1 02	1 20
October	5 11	6 35	4 86	5 10
November	1 28	1 70	1 89	2 50
December	1 03	1 40	1 18	2 10
Total	23 57	32 85	29 93	38 10

263

1847.	MARPLE, 531 feet.		COMB'S RESERVOIR, 850 feet.	
	Old Gauge.	Society's Gauge.	Old Gauge.	Society's Gauge.
	In. Dec.	In. Dec.	In. Dec.	In. Dec.
January	1 20	1 65	1 58	2 60
February	2 18	3 00	2 28	3 50
March	0 75	1 05	1 14	1 60
April	2 30	3 00 Part only.	2 35	4 00
May	1 23	2 80	4 15	5 30
June	2 57	4 10	2 88	3 90
July	1 33	1 80	0 93	1 00
August	2 50	3 80	3 48	3 40
September	4 22	7 90	5 74	8 20
October	2 71	5 50	3 62	5 40
November	2 22	4 10	3 18	4 50
December	3 16	7 00	4 24	7 90
TOTAL	26 37	45 70	35 57	51 30

Accompanying the above returns from the Peak Forest and Ashton Canals, there have also been received the returns of the rain which has fallen at other places on or near the lines of the canal, as indicated by gauges which have always been placed near the level of the ground. They are as follow:—

1845.	FAIRFIELD, 320 feet.		Waterhouses Lock, Ashton Canal, 360 feet above sea.	Inclined Plane, Chapel-le-Frith, 1,121 feet.
	Old Gauge, a few feet above Ground.	New Gauge, 1 foot above Ground.		
	In. Dec.	In. Dec.	In. Dec.	In. Dec.
January	2 20	1 80	1 90	2 60
February	1 60	1 70	2 00	2 00
March	3 60	3 00	3 20	2 20
April	1 90	2 20	2 40	2 80
May	1 30	1 10	1 50	2 30
June	4 20	3 70	3 90	4 00
July	3 60	3 40	3 80	3 90
August	7 30	6 70	6 40	7 60
September	3 00	2 80	2 70	3 60
October	3 70	3 70	4 00	3 10
November	3 00	2 80	3 00	3 10
December	7 10	6 00	8 00	6 00
TOTAL	42 50	38 90	42 80	43 20

1846.	FAIRFIELD, 320 feet.		Waterhouses Lock, Ashton Canal, 360 feet above sea.	Inclined Plane, Chapel-le-Frith, 1,121 feet.
	Old Gauge, a few feet, above Ground.	New Gauge, 1 foot above Ground.		
	In. Dec.	In. Dec.	In. Dec.	In. Dec.
January	3 60	3 30	3 90	4 40
February	1 80	1 80	1 40	1 60
March	1 70	1 70	1 80	2 60
April	3 00	3 00	3 50	5 80
May	0 90	0 90	0 80	1 90
June	2 90	2 40	2 80	4 00
July	3 90	3 90	4 20	2 90
August	3 60	3 60	3 80	5 00
September	0 80	0 80	0 70	1 80
October	5 80	4 70	4 90	5 40
November	3 70	3 10	2 40	2 40
December	2 10	1 50	1 60	2 00
TOTAL	32 80	30 20	31 80	38 80

For the year 1847, returns have been received of the rain which has fallen at various places within the district traversed by the Peak Forest and Macclesfield Canals, and the Manchester Sheffield and Lincolnshire Railway, in addition to those already alluded to. Many of these are of an experimental nature. Those which appear to bear upon the subject of this paper are introduced in the following table:—

1847.	FAIRFIELD, 320 feet above sea.		Waterhouses Lock, 360 feet.	Inclined Plane, Chapel-le-Frith, 1,121 feet.	Todd's Brook Reservoir, 620 feet.	Brink's Edge, 1,600 feet.	Comb's Moss, 1,670 feet.	Bosley Reservoir, Macclesfield Canal, about 600 feet.	Woodhead Station, Manchester & Sheffield Railway, 1,000 feet.
	Old Gauge.	New Gauge.							
	In. Dec.	In. Dec.	In. Dec.	In. Dec.	In. Dec.	In. Dec.	In. Dec.	In. Dec.	In. Dec.
January	1 50	1 50	1 20	2 80	1 78	1 14	2 60	..	2 20
February	2 90	3 00	2 00	3 90	2 33	1 68	1 78	..	2 64
March	0 80	0 80	1 20	1 80	0 88	0 77	0 79	1 05	1 84
April	2 20	3 30	2 80	3 90	3 08	1 93	2 45	2 58	3 21
May	4 95	5 10	5 30	4 50	4 17	3 95	4 50	3 91	3 16
June	3 20	3 30	3 10	3 20	3 70	1 05	3 44	3 18	2 62
July	1 00	0 95	0 80	1 50	0 97	0 95	1 53	1 43	1 29
August	4 00	3 70	3 30	2 90	2 95	2 40	2 96	4 77	1 57
September	5 50	5 50	5 50	6 40	6 17	4 40	4 17	6 85	2 98
October	4 90	4 80	4 70	4 30	3 71	2 77	4 48	2 97	4 72
November	3 50	3 50	3 80	3 60	3 04	3 85	2 52	2 84	2 45
December	5 20	5 30	4 60	5 70	5 60	5 05	4 63	3 95	4 44
TOTAL	39 65	40 75	38 30	44 00	38 39	29 44	35 85	33 03 10 months	33 12

The gauges employed at the five new places in the preceding table, viz., Todd's Brook Reservoir, Brink's Edge, Comb's Moss, Bosley Reservoir, and Woodhead, are all similar, and of a new construction. The results indicated by them vary so greatly from those of other gauges in their immediate neighbourhood, as to occasion great suspicion of their accuracy. For instance, the gauge at Woodhead, which is situated at the head of the Longdendale Valley, hereafter alluded to, shows only 33 inches of rain at an elevation of 1,000 feet above the sea. From this district it was ascertained by careful daily measurement, that $49\frac{1}{2}$ inches of water had actually flowed off the ground, and the rain indicated by two neighbouring gauges in the same district, within a distance of $2\frac{1}{2}$ miles, was respectively $50\frac{1}{2}$ inches and $62\frac{1}{10}$ inches—the latter being at an elevation of about 1,750 feet, and the former 700 feet above the sea.

It seems exceedingly probable, from an examination of this new gauge, that it is liable to be affected in a serious degree by evaporation, and the difference may perhaps be assigned to this cause. The whole apparatus is placed above the surface of the ground—the water is received by a metal funnel, and conducted from thence by a short pipe at the bottom, through the top of a wooden box, to a glass bottle of large area placed within the box and open at the top. The water is not covered by a float, and the surface is therefore in contact with the atmospheric air. It is not suggested that the evaporation would be as great as from the surface of an open pond; but that it does take place to a considerable degree seems to be evident.

As evaporation is greater in proportion to the altitude of the situation, the supposition that the discrepancy is to be assigned to this cause, will also account for the anomaly (as compared with the general result of all the other returns) at Todd's Brook and Comb's Moss, where it would appear, from the results furnished by these new gauges, that *less* rain falls on high land than on low. If the returns were properly corrected by a due allowance for evaporation according to the altitude, the true state of the case would probably be found to agree with the evidence from other places.

The rain gauge at the top of the inclined plane at Chapel-le-Frith is an exception to this rule, as it appears to show, pretty regularly, less rain than falls at Comb's reservoir at a lower elevation. This may probably arise from local causes, as it is at variance with the general testimony within the range of the same elevation.

All the society's gauges—those at Fairfield, and that at the top of the inclined plane at Chapel-le-Frith, put down by the canal company—are cylindrical gauges, with an upright graduated rod attached to a float covering the surface of the water, which indicates the depth of rain caught within the cylinder.

Objections have been made to this form of gauge from the effect alleged to be produced by the rod as it rises above the level of the top of the cylinder, exposing additional surface, and adding in that manner to the collecting surface of the gauge.

Experiments have been made for some years by Mr. Wood, the engineer to the Ashton and Peak Forest canals, to ascertain the effect produced by rods standing some height above the top of the gauge.

That a sensible effect is produced, increasing the quantity of water caught, appears to be clearly established from these experiments; but they do not afford any assistance in determining the height at which the rod begins to affect the accuracy of the register, nor do they furnish any data from which to calculate the proportionate increased quantity due to the elevation of the rod.

For instance, in one situation a rod of 1 inch in diameter, standing 24 inches above the top of the gauge, collected in twelve months 8·18 inches of rain; while in another place a rod of the same diameter, but only $18\frac{3}{4}$ inches long, collected in the same time 27·89 inches, the quantity of rain as indicated by the rain gauges being respectively 40·75 and 51·30.

Again, a staff or rod of 2 inches diameter, and $18\frac{3}{4}$ inches long, collected in twelve months 20·67 inches, the rain being apparently at that place 38·39. At another place, a rod of the same diameter and length, where the rain appears to have been 35·85, collected in the same period 58·99 inches.

These differences are enormous, and apparently unaccountable.

On consideration, it appears probable that the rod will produce no sensible effect until it rises to a height greater than half of the diameter of the gauge. This supposes that the rain will not often reach the ground at a more acute angle than 50°. If the rain descend at that angle, and the rod stand at a height equal to half the diameter of the gauge, any rain which would be intercepted by the rod would have fallen, had the rod not been there, within the area of the top of the gauge, as will be seen by the sketch in the margin.

If the rain come straight down, or nearly so, as it often does in heavy rain in summer, the rod might stand at a much greater height without producing any effect. If the rain be driven by strong wind nearly horizontally, which would be the case in very exposed situations, then of course a slight elevation of the rod will intercept rain which would otherwise pass entirely over the gauge. It may, however, be fairly assumed, that in the foregoing observations from the society's gauges, which are about 7 inches in diameter, the results may be taken as perfectly accurate till the rod rises more than $3\frac{1}{2}$ inches above the top. In taking the observations, the gauges have been regularly emptied at the end of every month; and there would only be some amount of error, therefore, in those months in which the rain exceeded 3¼ inches, the amount of error being probably proportionate to the greater depth of rain.

To remedy this objection for the future, instructions have been given either to tie down the rods or to detach them from the float, merely using them at the time an observation is taken. The latter method is the best, as the float rises on the surface of the water collected, thereby preventing evaporation; while by tying down the rod the water would rise above the float, and be subject, to some slight extent, to loss from so much evaporation as could take place on the surface of the water confined within the cylinder and covered by the funnel top, the hole at the bottom of which is almost entirely filled by the graduated rod. This could not be very much; but to whatever extent it did take place it would affect the result and show less than the real fall.

Notwithstanding the objections which may be made to the precise accuracy of the observations in consequence of the effect produced by the index rod having been allowed to rise in some months to a height greater than three or four inches, and that they may be supposed therefore to indicate a fall of rain something greater than the truth, they have fully served the purpose for which they were undertaken. They have clearly established the fact, that a gauge placed on the top of a house does not indicate the correct quantity of water falling on the ground. They also show that a large per centage must be added to such observations as have been made by means of gauges placed on buildings in order to form any correct estimate of the actual fall of rain at the place of observation, and they may in that way be made materially useful in correcting the results of many years of observations in such unfavourable positions.

They show also that within the range of the observations more rain falls on high ground than on low.

The observations which are now being made will, it is hoped, be free from all objections; and if future results confirm those of the past it would be desirable to recommend to all parties who have hitherto been at the trouble of keeping registers of the quantity of rain falling in different places, but whose gauges have been injudiciously placed, to continue them for the future in situations better calculated for obtaining accurate results.

The following observations upon the fall of rain and the quantity of water flowing off the ground are from measurements taken in the course of the inquiries made during the last few years with reference to the supply of Manchester with water from the hills beyond Stalybridge and Mottram, lying at a distance of from ten to twenty miles east of Manchester.

In the highest part of this range of hills, known by the name of the Penine Chain, the river Etherow and its various mountain tributaries take their rise.

Some of these uniting near Woodhead form there a deep romantic valley called Longdendale, running for several miles nearly due west between hills which rise abruptly on each side to a considerable height, reaching in some cases nearly 2,000 feet above the level of the sea.

The valley is hemmed in to the west by the high land at Mottram, which, however, is not high enough to intercept the clouds driven before the westerly winds.

In the upper part of the valley the tributary streams, falling from 1,000 to 1,200 feet in a few miles, join the main stream in the valley of Longdendale nearly at right angles, thus breaking the surface of the country into various cross valleys and deep ravines. The summit of this district is Holme Moss, nearly 2,000 feet above the sea. It is the highest eminence in the whole chain, though it rises but slightly above the surrounding table land, the elevation of which, from the crests of the valleys just described, varies from 1,500 to 1,900 feet. The millstone grit caps the summits in various parts, forming occasionally perpendicular precipices several hundred feet in height, and in other parts the sides of the valleys consist of beds of indurated shale. Some considerable portions of the tops of the hills are covered with peat and others with gravelly clay. The more easterly portion of the district consists of the lower coal measures.

For hills of this elevation it is scarcely possible to find any which, from their position and character, would be more likely to induce a large fall of rain, or to allow a larger proportion of that which falls to flow down the streams. It is from this district that the town of Manchester is to be supplied with water.

Measurements of the volume of all the various streams have been made daily since the end of 1846, and rain gauges have been placed at various elevations and at different parts of the district, from which the quantity of rain which has fallen has been ascertained.

In an adjoining valley, down which flows the Swineshaw Brook, a tributary of the river Tame, similar observations have been made since the end of 1844. This valley lies nearly east and west, and is completely land-locked, turning abruptly to the north through a narrow glen just before it joins the river Tame. The summit of the valley is at Windyate Edge, which is the summit also of two tributaries of the Etherow, the Hollingworth, and Arnfield brooks.

Rain gauges were placed at the bottom of the Swineshaw valley near the point at which the volume of the stream was measured, and on Windyate Edge near the summit. For some time also a gauge was kept about midway.

The brook was measured regularly twice a day. During the years 1846 and 1847, the index rod of the rain gauges was constantly tied down so as to prevent its rising above the top of the cylinder, and partially so during 1845. These observations, therefore, are free from objection on account of the additional surface exposed by the rod, though there may be some loss from evaporation.

In taking the rain-gauge observations in the Longdendale district the index rod was tied down from their commencement in November, 1846, to Midsummer, 1847, since which time the rod has been detached, and inserted only at the time an observation is being taken.

The streams were measured—one (the river Etherow) three times a day, some twice a day, and others once a day. But in the results, which are given in monthly amounts, it has been found necessary to omit many months, in consequence of the gauges being frequently injured and rendered unfit for use for some days, by the effects of violent and destructive floods.

SWINESHAW BROOK—RAIN, AND DEPTH OF WATER FLOWING OFF GROUND.

The extent of ground draining to the point at which the volume of the stream is measured is 1,250 statute acres.

1845.	Rain.				Flow.
	Brushes, 480 feet above the sea.	Windyate Edge, 1,700 feet.	Bower Flat, 1,400 feet.	Probable mean rain over district.	Depth in inches flowing off ground.
	In. Dec.	In. Dec.	In. Dec.	In. Dec.	In. Dec.
January................	..	3 1	..	3 0	1 668
February	..	1 8	1 5	1 8	1 764
March................	..	5 5	4 0	5 5	2 892
April	2 5	..	2 7	3 0	2 424
May	2 8	..	3 6	3 6	2 436
June	4 3	..	4 1	4 3	2 364
				21 2	13 548
July	4 2	4 7	5 0	4 7	3 048
August	8 3	14 8	9 6	10 0	7 236
September	3 3	4 1	3 2	3 7	2 736
October	4 9	5 9	..	5 5	4 608
November	3 4	4 0	..	3 7	2 904
December	10 3	11 0	..	11 0	6 624
				38 6	27 156

Depth of rain in first six months, 21·2 inches, of which there flowed off the ground 13·548, or nearly two-thirds.

Depth of rain in last six months, 38·6 inches, of which there flowed off the ground 27·156 inches, or nearly three-fourths.

Rain for the whole year, 59·8 inches, of which there passed down the brook 40·704, or upwards of two-thirds.

It is possible that in this year the fall of rain has been registered too high, in consequence of comparative inattention to the index rod. The fall of rain in other places was just an average.

SWINESHAW BROOK.—1846.

1846.	Rain.				Flow.
	Brushes, 480 feet above the sea.	Windyate Edge, 1,700 feet.	Probable Mean.		Depth in inches flowing off Ground
	In. Dec.	In. Dec.	In. Dec.		In. Dec.
January	3 8	6 8	5 3		4 908
February	2 0	2 2	2 1		3 180
March	2 1	2 2	2 2		1 944
April	5 9	4 8	5 3		4 894
May	1 4	..	1 5		1 452
June	4 0	5 8	5 0		1 176
			21 4		17 554
July .... ⎫					
August .... ⎬	10 0		11 0		
September .... ⎭					
October	5 3	5 6	5 4		3 636
November	2 4	2 4	2 4		2 184
December	2 1	2 7	2 4		2 863
			21 2		8 683
First six months			21 4		17 554
			42 6		26 242
Say for three months omitted					7 000
					33 242

In this year the index rod of the rain gauge was tied down. The measurement of the stream was suspended during July, August, and September; but it is probable that the 7 inches supposed to have flowed off the ground during this period is not far from the truth. This year was considerably below the average fall of rain, nearly one of the driest on record; and the above results may be taken as the fall and produce in such an extreme period.

SWINESHAW BROOK.—1847.

1847.	Rain.			Flow.
	Brushes.	Windyate Edge.	Probable Mean.	Depth in inches flowing off ground.
	In. Dec.	In. Dec.	In. Dec.	In. Dec.
January	1 7	1 8	1 75	2 1
February	4 4	3 9	4 15	4 8
March	1 7	1 4	1 55	1 7
April	4 0	5 1	4 55	3 2
May	6 8	8 0	7 40	4 4
June	3 5	3 7	3 60	2 0
	22 1	23 0	23 00	18 2
July	1 6	1 5	1 54	1 3
August	3 2	3 3	4 25	1 0
September	6 5	6 0	6 25	3 3
October	3 5	4 9	4 20	3 2
November	3 8	5 0	4 40	4 0
December	5 9	7 5	6 70	6 1
	24 5	28 2	26 35	18 9
Whole Year	46 6	52 1	49 35	37 1

The fall of rain during this year was about an average, in some places rather more. It fell, however, very unequally, the last three or four months making up for previous deficiency.

The proportion of the water flowing off the ground to that which fell was about three to four. The quantity of the rainfall which was lost to the river was about 12 inches,—that being apparently the annual amount required for evaporation, the supply of vegetation, and absorption by the ground in a year of average rain.

The springs in this valley are very copious, and though neither the fall of rain nor the average volume of the stream are equal to the Longdendale district, yet the supply of spring water in dry weather is greater in proportion to the extent of drainage ground.

In December, 1844, no rain fell, and yet the springs yielded a quantity of water equal to a depth of 1 inch over the whole drainage ground, the mean volume of the stream being the same as in August, 1847, in which month the fall of rain was $3\frac{1}{4}$ inches.

The following table shows the fall of rain for the year 1847 and for the two last months of 1846, at all the places in the district at which rain gauges have been put down:—

1846.	Brushes, 480 feet.		Windyate Edge, 1,700 feet.		Crowden Hall, 700 feet.		Rake's Moss, 1,620 feet.		Butterly Moss, 1,750 feet.		Mean of all the Observations.		Mean, omitting Brushes.	
	In.	Dec.	In.	Dec.	In.	Dec.	In.	Dec.	In.	Dec.	In.	Dec.	In.	Dec.
November	2	4	2	4	2	0	2	4	3	0	2	4	2	4
December	2	1	2	7	2	8	3	1	4	0	2	9	3	1
Two Months	4	5	5	1	4	8	5	5	7	0	5	3	5	5
1847.														
January	1	7	1	8	2	2	2	4	3	7	2	4	2	5
February	4	4	3	9	4	3	4	6	4	3	4	3	4	3
March	1	7	1	4	1	7	2	3	1	4	1	7	1	7
April	4	0	5	1	4	7	3	3	9	0	5	2	5	5
May	6	8	8	0	4	9	7	9	4	8	6	5	6	4
June	3	5	3	7	3	1	3	3	3	4	3	4	3	4
Six Months	22	1	23	9	20	9	23	8	26	6	23	5	23	8
July	1	6	1	5	1	4	2	0	1	1	1	5	1	5
August	3	2	3	3	3	5	5	1	6	5	4	3	4	6
September	6	5	6	0	7	5	8	7	8	2	7	4	7	6
October	3	5	4	9	5	1	4	4	5	4	4	7	4	9
November	3	8	5	0	6	0	4	3	8	3	5	5	5	9
December	5	9	7	5	6	1	8	2	6	0	6	7	6	9
Six Months	24	5	28	2	29	6	32	7	35	5	30	1	31	4
Whole Year	46	6	52	1	50	5	56	5	62	1	53	6	55	2

In the preceding table, the last column, which is the mean of all the rain observations, omitting Brushes on account of its being in another valley, may be taken as the mean fall of rain, for the year 1847, in the Longdendale district, so far at least as the gauges may be supposed to indicate the real quantity.

The measurements of the streams, however, lead to the belief that more rain has fallen than the rain gauges show. They are placed in the valleys, and at mean heights, none being quite on the tops of the hills; and it is probable that *there* heavy rain has fallen, and contributed to swell the streams, which has been beyond the range of the rain gauges.

The next table exhibits the depth of water flowing off the ground, as measured in various streams in the Longdendale valley. It shows also the drainage or collecting ground to the point of measurement on each stream, and the mean flow as deduced from all the observations.

LONGDENDALE VALLEY.—DEPTH OF WATER FLOWING OFF THE GROUND.

1847.	Hollinsworth Brook. Drainage Ground, 1,890 acres.	Arnfield Brook. Drainage Ground, 884 acres.	Hollins Brook. Drainage Ground, 470 acres.	Great Crowden Brook. Drainage Ground, 1,761 acres.	Little Crowden Brook. Drainage Ground, 1,436 acres.	River Etherow at Vale House. Drainage Ground, 15,676 acres.	Mean Flow.	Mean Rain.
	In. Dec.	In. Dec.	In. Dec.	In. Dec.	In. Dec.	In. Dec.	In. Dec.	In. Dec.
January	..	..	..	3 5	3 0	..	3 25	2 5
February	..	..	..	..	3 4	..	3 40	4 3
March	1 20	1 70	0 60	..	..	..	1 17	1 7
April	..	..	4 80	..	4 5	..	4 65	5 5
May	..	..	..	..	5 1	..	5 10	6 4
June	1 60	1 80	0 13	2 2	2 2	..	1 59	3 4
July	1 90	1 08	0 24	0 7	0 7	..	0 92	1 5
August	1 06	1 41	0 78	1 8	1 4	..	1 29	4 6
September	..	..	..	6 2	5 1	5 89	5 73	7 6
October	..	..	..	6 9	7 8	4 80	6 50	4 9
November	..	10 40	4 90	5 6	5 7	6 90	6 70	5 9
December	..	9 24	8 60	..	10 4	8 40	9 16	6 9
	5 76	25 63	20 05	26 9	49 3	25 99	49 46	55 2
Rain during period of observations	9 95 / 4 Mos.	22 42 / 6 Mos.	25 80 / 7 Mos.	32 65 / 7 Mos.	54 7 / 11 Mos.	26 10 / 4 Mos.	/ 12 Mos.	/ 12 Mos.

By comparing this table with that of the Swineshaw Brook in the same year, it will be seen that in the Longdendale district the quantity of rain falling and that flowing off the ground are considerably greater.

In the Swineshaw Valley the mean rain was 49·35 inches, and the water flowing off the ground 37·1 inches.

In Longdendale the rain was $55\frac{2}{10}$ inches, the produce of which was $49\frac{1}{2}$ inches, i.e., the rain in the two districts is as 49 to 55, the produce as 37 to 49.

By uniting the Swineshaw observations with those in Longdendale the mean rain and flow would be as follows:—

1847.	Rain.	Flow.	1847.	Rain.	Flow.
	In. Dec.	In. Dec.		In. Dec.	In. Dec.
January	2 36	2 85	August	4 32	1 24
February	4 30	4 10	September	7 38	5 12
March	1 70	1 80	October	4 66	5 67
April	5 22	4 12	November	5 48	6 25
May	6 48	4 75	December	6 74	8 55
June	3 40	1 65			
July	1 52	0 99		53 56	46 59

On examining the last tables it will be found that in many months, particularly during October, November, and December, the quantity of water flowing off the ground appears to be larger than the rain which fell during the same period.

During months in which little rain fell this would be accounted for by the produce of the springs; but in periods of excessive rain, such as the last four months of 1847, in which the rain was 24¼ inches, and that which flowed off the ground 25¼ inches, although it is reasonable to suppose that the ground would be so saturated that very nearly all the rain would flow down the streams in torrents, yet we could scarcely calculate upon more. The produce of springs from water previously stored up would no doubt add something to the quantity, but not enough to account for the whole.

It is most likely, therefore, that either the streams have been over-estimated or the rain under-measured.

On a careful examination of all the returns from which the tables have been constructed, it seems probable that the latter supposition is the correct one. Every stream bears the same sort of evidence, although the measurements were necessarily taken at different periods of the day.

It is true that at all times, and in swollen states of brooks particularly, the measurement of streams by daily gaugings, although they are repeated several times a day, can only be considered as a tolerable approximation to the truth. According to the height of the flood at the time the measurement is taken, they may indicate rather more, or rather less, than the average quantity. Still, the observations regularly continued, will in the course of the year pretty well correct each other, and the result obtained by taking the mean of upwards of 700 measurements of the same stream, at equal intervals of time, cannot be far from the truth.

It is probable that had rain gauges been placed on the summits of the highest hills as well as in the valleys, and on elevated parts about midway of the whole rise, the returns would have shown a greater fall.

APPENDIX No. 3.—*Report by* GEORGE WINGROVE COOKE *and* JAMES MEADOWS RENDEL, *Esqrs., on the Manchester Sheffield and Lincolnshire Railway (Supply of Water) Bill.*

N.B.—The figures in the margin refer to the questions in the evidence.

To Her Majesty's Commissioners of Woods, Forests, Land Revenues, Works, and Buildings.

My Lord and Gentlemen,—We, the undersigned surveying officers appointed to hold a Court of Inquiry, and hear evidence in the matter of a Bill " to enable " the Manchester, Sheffield and Lincolnshire Railway Company to convey, by " means of reservoirs and aqueducts, the water not required for their canals, called " the Peak Forest Canal and Macclesfield Canal, to the boroughs of Manchester, " Salford, and Stockport, for the better supply of water;" and to make local survey of the districts affected by the provisions of the said Bill, having held an inquiry in the Town Hall, Manchester, at which evidence was adduced by all parties interested, and having made such local survey as aforesaid, have the honour to report to you the evidence so adduced and the result of our survey.

Position of the Promoters.

The promoters of the Bill are the Manchester Sheffield and Lincolnshire Railway Company.

This company, by purchase, authorized by Acts passed in the last Session of Parliament, are the proprietors of the Peak Forest and Macclesfield Canals. They have all the powers conferred upon the original Canal Companies by the Acts under which those canals were constructed. [9 and 10 Vict., c. 267, ss. 1 and 2.]

The Peak Forest Canal.

The Peak Forest Canal was constructed under the provisions of an Act of the 34th Geo. III. (28th March, 1794.)

By the first section of this Act the company are empowered to supply the canal "with water from all such brooks, springs, streams, &c., as shall flow or be "found in digging the said canal, or within the distance of two miles thereof," making compensation in manner thereinafter mentioned.

By the ninth section it is provided that the company shall not be authorized to take for the navigation, any rivulet or spring visible at the time of the commencement of the Act, flowing to the supply of any mill, except in times of flood and wet seasons, and when there shall be a surplus of water for the supply of the mills.

It is then, by the same section, provided, that for the purpose of taking such flood-waters, the company shall erect on each brook, along the side of each of their reservoirs, a gauge weir and a tumbling bay. This gauge weir is to be so constructed, that the natural stream of the brook may pass through its former channel.

The dimensions of the gauges are then specified.

The Todds Brook gauge is to be 4½ inches in depth by 10 feet in length.

The Combs Brook gauge, 3¼ inches by 10 feet.

The Hockham Brook gauge, 3 inches by 10 feet.

By the tenth section it is provided, that if the gauges be not sufficient for the full and ample supply of the mills and works, then the company shall enlarge them to the extent necessary to secure to the mills the natural streams of the said rivers in common seasons.

On the Todds Brook and the Combs Brook the gauges have been duly erected, and reservoirs have been constructed for storing the flood-waters.

On the Hockham Brook a gauge was erected, but no reservoir was made.

Under this Act no time was limited within which the powers to erect gauges and make reservoirs must be exercised.

It was not suggested in the course of the inquiry that the existing gauges do not allow the natural streams of the brooks to pass.

The Macclesfield Canal.

This canal was made under the powers granted by an Act of the 7th Geo. IV. (11th April, 1826.)

By the second section of this Act the company are empowered to construct five reservoirs for the supply of water to the canal:—(1) The Pit Shrigley; (2) The Upper Sutton; (3) The Lower Sutton; (4) The Upper Bosley; (5) The Lower Bosley reservoirs. They are further empowered to make feeders to the reservoirs, and to supply them with the flood-waters as may be necessary for the purposes of the navigation.

The third section provides that the company shall take no waters of any brook flowing to the supply of any mill, &c., except in times of flood and wet seasons, as in the Peak Forest Canal Act.

The fourth section directs, that for the purpose of ascertaining the surplus water, two engineers therein named, shall gauge and award what shall be a sufficient and ample supply of water for the said mills respectively, and that such award shall be for ever binding upon the parties and their heirs and assigns.

By the seventh section, the gauges determined by the award of the engineers are to be erected and kept in repair by the company.

Section 188 enacts, that at the end of seven years all the powers given by the Act shall cease as to all such works as shall not have been completed by that time.

Within the period limited by the Act the engineers made their award, the Sutton and Bosley reservoirs were constructed, and gauges were placed upon the Radcliffe Brook, the Shell Brook, the Flas Brook, the Furnival's Coppice Brook, and the Bosley Brook, which feed the Bosley reservoir, and upon the Rosendale Brook, which feeds the Sutton reservoir; a gauge was also placed upon the Ridicar Brook, which overfalls directly into the Macclesfield Canal.

Object of the Promoters.

The Railway Company is, therefore, at present in the possession of powers authorizing them to take into their reservoirs, and to store for the purposes of the Peak Forest and the Macclesfield Canals, all such waters of the brooks above-mentioned, as the gauges fixed upon these brooks will not take.

These flood-waters have been found to be more than sufficient for the purposes of the navigation, and they exceed the capacity of their present reservoirs. The company now seek powers to extend their present storage-room, and to bring the surplus, over the requirements of their canals, to Stockport, Manchester, and Salford. To increase their storage-room they propose to construct a new reservoir upon the Hockham Brook, where the gauge has hitherto been inoperative, to enlarge the area of the Todds Brook and Sutton reservoirs, and to increase the capacity by raising the banks of the Combs and Bosley reservoirs. The gauges on all the brooks they propose to leave unaltered.

Opposition from Parties locally interested.

The opposition from parties locally interested was raised:—

1st. By the owner of land proposed to be taken for the enlargement of one of the reservoirs, who however did not suggest that any special injury would be caused to his estate, and insisted only that there was no public necessity for the scheme.

2nd. By the town of Macclesfield, which objected that the Rosendale Brook is an important tributary to the Bollin, which passes through that town; and—

3rd. By the millowners upon the streams.

With respect to the objection raised by the town of Macclesfield, we would observe that the river Bollin is formed by a junction of the Rosendale and the Langley Brooks;—that during the time that the Rosendale Brook flows in its ordinary volume, the scheme in question will not affect the Bollin, for the whole of that volume will pass through the gauge; and that in times of high flood, when water from the Rosendale Brook would be taken, a large quantity of flood-water comes down the channel of Langley Brook and increases the Bollin to an extent quite sufficient for all purposes of sewerage. The statement in the evidence that in dry seasons the Bollin is nearly dry, is, we submit, quite beside the question, inasmuch as the proposal is to take water from its tributary only in times of flood.

Q. 1727 et seq.

The millowners' opposition is of a nature which calls for no observation from us, inasmuch as its force depends upon the decision of the question, whether they have any property in the flood-water which may remain after the exigencies of the canals have been supplied. As the result of the evidence, we may, however, state, that it does not appear that any of the millowners who appeared before us to oppose, have ever made use of this water, or that they have ever found it necessary for the purposes of their works to impound the whole of the night-water which runs to waste, even when the brooks are flowing in a volume far below that which the gauges are capable of taking.

Q. 1584.
1664.

As to interference with bleaching or paper works, the facts stated in Mr. Joseph Hughes's evidence are, we submit, quite insufficient to establish any case. Mr. Hughes is accustomed to bring spring-water from a distance for his paper works; the floods that would feed the Waterworks reservoir occur upon an average during 50 days in a year; and that flood-water is not very generally necessary for his purposes is sufficiently shown by the fact that he has only storage room for an hour's supply.

See table at Q. 2040.

1698, 1680, 1681.

District proposed to be supplied.

Such being the title of the company to their water, we come now to remark upon the district within which they propose to sell it.

This district is, by clause 4, defined to consist of the boroughs of Manchester, Salford, and Stockport; and the company propose that the word "borough" shall mean the Parliamentary, and not the Municipal borough.

See table (A) after Q. 6.

These boroughs, with the addition of the places along the line of main service-pipes, contain 98,277 houses and 457,529 inhabitants.

Of these the municipal borough of Manchester has 46,577 houses, exclusive of 6,105 dwelling cellars which are generally enumerated as separate houses, and 295,277 inhabitants.

Salford Parliamentary borough has 18,782 houses and a population of 93,513. Stockport Parliamentary borough has 16,721 houses and a population of 66,997.*

---

* We have taken the total from the statement of the promoters of this Bill, but for the items we have been compelled to have recourse to the statement of the Corporations of Manchester, Salford, and Stockport. The total population tallies within 2,000, but there is a large discrepancy between the promoters' gross estimate of houses and the number as stated by the Corporations' returns in boroughs and townships. Possibly the promoters have counted the dwelling-cellars as separate houses.

The population of Manchester and Salford (with certain out-townships which are not included in the Parliamentary boroughs, but which should not be excluded from any estimate of the population requiring supply) has been estimated in our report upon the Manchester Corporation Bill (No. 1) to be likely to amount, ten years after the works can be completed, to 567,000.

The population of Stockport, calculated at the same rate of increase, will then be 99,000.

The total population of these three boroughs and of the out-townships, calculated at an increase of $2\frac{1}{2}$ per cent. per annum, will amount in ten years after the works can be completed to 660,000.

Present Supply.

These boroughs are at present supplied by the Manchester and Salford Water Company and by the Stockport Waterworks.

Upon the state of supply in Manchester and Salford we have already reported in our report upon the Manchester Corporation Waterworks Bill (No. 1).

Stockport is supplied by means of wells sunk in the red sandstone. This company (according to a newspaper report of proceedings held before the surveying officers in the matter of the Stockport Improvement Act, and which report was put in and verified before us by the town clerk of Stockport) state that they supply 958,464 gallons daily; their receipts are about £1,500 per annum, and they supply 4,007 houses out of 16,721, a proportion of scarcely one-fourth.

The Corporation of Stockport are anxious to purchase the present works, and to obtain a supply of water from the promoters of this Bill; the present supply has probably been much overstated, the water is of an undesirable hardness, and the duration of the supply is, upon an average, only two hours and a half a day.

If we could believe that the houses now supplied by the company consumed nearly 1,000,000 gallons daily, 4,000,000 would be required for the adequate supply of this town. The quantity at present supplied has probably been very much overstated; we believe, however, that for an ample supply for domestic and public purposes, and with a convenient supply for trading purposes, 3,000,000 gallons of water a day may be well consumed in Stockport.

We have already reported, as the result of the evidence in the Manchester Corporation case, that 10,000,000 of gallons a day is not more than an adequate supply for the domestic, public, and trading waterworks of that municipal borough.

Salford, and the out-townships (which last are not included in the district proposed to be supplied by this Bill, and which have consequently not gone into the total of its population), for a permanent and convenient supply, will require 5,000,000.

The district, therefore, which the promoters of this scheme propose to supply, requires a present supply of 18,000,000 daily.*

Quantity of Water to be Obtained.

See statement in Appendix.
Q. 22.

The engineer of this scheme calculates that he will obtain from his works a daily supply of about nine millions and a quarter of gallons.

The total acreage of the drainage ground is 15,848 acres. He estimates 36 inches as the depth of rain falling and 24 as the depth flowing from the ground. Nine inches of the 24 he considers to flow to the millowners and the remaining 15 to the reservoirs.

Q. 20.

This is a low estimate of the rainfall, and there appears to be little doubt that the quantity of rain so estimated does fall, even in dry years, in this district.

The quantity, however, which the reservoir will obtain cannot be determined without considering another element of the calculation.

Q. 598.

The capacity of the millowners' gauges, if they were running full night and day, would take a quantity of water equal to a fall of 20 or 21 inches over the whole of the drainage ground.

Q. 599.

If, therefore, the millowners' gauges were full throughout the year, only 3 or 4 inches in depth, instead of 15, would run into the reservoirs.

It follows that the quantity of water which these reservoirs will receive will depend not only upon the amount of the fall of rain, but also upon the manner in which the rain falls. Unequal falls, and successions of drought and floods, would give a large portion of water to the reservoirs; equal falls, and no drought, would carry the bulk of the water past the reservoirs and through the millowners' gauges.

---

* It will, perhaps, be remarked, that we have here assumed the necessity of a much larger quantity of water (30 gallons per head) than the minimum quantity of the Health of Towns Commissioners, which is 12 gallons per diem for each individual of the population (2nd report, p. 52). This estimate of 12 gallons is, however, expressly confined to domestic purposes. Domestic purposes hardly form the largest item in the consumption of water in a large manufacturing town. Every shopkeeper uses a large amount of water in his business, which is not understood to be included under domestic purposes. The supply of water-closets has been taken into this category since the report above-quoted was made; the washing of a horse or carriage it still not included. Manchester, Stockport, and Salford are crowded with factories, all of which are ill supplied with water for feeding their boilers. In such a district the water-want must be much greater for trading and other non-domestic purposes than in towns of an ordinary character. The town clerk of Manchester states that 20,000,000 of gallons daily could be well consumed by the borough alone (see report upon Manchester Corporation Bill No. 1); 4,000 houses in Stockport are said to be ill supplied by nearly a million. If we take the quantity at one-half, the supply is equal to that we have assumed, and by the returns of the present Salford and Manchester Company (see table in the evidence on Manchester and Salford Waterworks Bill), it appears that their supply to their customers has been 17 gallons per day per head, although the supply of this company is upon all hands admitted to be utterly insufficient. We believe that we have rather under than overstated the requirements of the district; but even if the absolute necessities should have been over-estimated, it is satisfactory to know that all parties agree that a still greater quantity would find profitable employment.

The additional risk of failure of water is illustrated in the evidence of Mr. Wood, the engineer to the canals. This witness had measured the flood-water which flowed to waste by the Todds Brook and Combs reservoirs, on account of the incapacity of those reservoirs to receive it.

In 1844, 2,500,000,000 of gallons flowed by. Q. 995.

In 1845, 3,286,000,000. Q. 1023.

In 1846, only 500,000,000 flowed by. Q. 1024.

In this year, however, 200,000,000 were taken to aid the Manchester and Salford Waterworks Company.

But, adding this 200,000,000, we find that in 1846 only 700,000,000 were rejected by the millowners' gauges and by the existing reservoirs. This quantity is not one-third of what was so rejected in 1844, nor one-fourth of what was so rejected in 1845.

The witness accounts for this great difference by saying, that the rain falling more frequently during that year had caused more to be taken by the millowners' gauges.

Here is a risk (from a cause quite independent of the amount of rain) of the supply to be obtained from this scheme falling to one-third of this ordinary quantity. The light floods all flow away through the millowners' gauges, and the heavy floods only give water to the reservoirs. Q. 1190, and Bateman, Q. 1449.

Q. 1271, Q. 1445.

In times of extreme floods, the whole of the surplus water cannot be taken by the reservoirs. The velocity with which the water comes down to the gauges will alone increase the quantity running through; but it appears doubtful whether, with the gauges as now fixed, the company can prevent a very large portion of the flood-water running to the millowner over the gauge, when the waters mount suddenly. Q. 1168.
Q. 1160.

Some deductions must be made from the estimate of the engineer to allow for these contingencies, and we are of opinion, upon a careful analysis of the evidence, that from 6,000,000 to 8,000,000 gallons is the only estimate which can be safely made of the quantity derivable for waterworks purposes from this scheme in unfavourable years. The engineers agree in placing the result higher than this; but Mr. Bateman arrives at his result by allowing to Mr. Homershaw what he has assumed for himself, that is to say, an amount of fall of rain which we consider to be an over-estimate. Q. 1580, et seq.

Quality of the Water.

The drainage grounds from which the water is by this scheme proposed to be collected are of a character extremely favourable to the purpose. The Todds Brook, the Hockham Brook, and the Combs Brook gathering grounds are of the millstone grit formation, very generally covered with clay; the surface is to a

2 M

considerable extent precipitous, and the waters run off the ground rapidly. There is no moss or peat ground except about 300 acres draining into the Combs.

These are the waters which it is proposed to convey along the Peak Forest Canal to the filtering beds at Marple.

We visited these grounds on the morrow of a day of incessant rain, and we found a flood running high over the millowners' gauges. We procured specimens of the waters of each, which accompany this report. Considering the swollen state of the streams at the time, they are particularly bright.

With respect to the degrees of hardness of these waters, the analysis put in by the promoters of the Manchester Corporation scheme shows that Hockham Brook is 1·3, Combs Brook 3·4, the reservoir in which its flood waters are impounded 1·9, Todds Brook 3·4, and its reservoir 1·85.

These waters, therefore, are of a high degree of softness in their reservoirs. In passing along the canals they appear to have lost a portion of that quality, for they were found to be at Disley, in the Peak Forest Canal, 6·2. This is doubtless occasioned by their very languid course over the soil of the canal, and by their mixture with the drainage of the cultivated land upon its banks. The water being originally of rather a higher degree of softness than is necessary, or perhaps desirable for domestic purposes, would probably be found not to exceed 3 or 3·5 degrees if the canal were pitched with stone and its current increased, both which measures are contemplated by the present scheme.*

The drainage ground of the Sutton and Bosley reservoirs are of a character somewhat inferior, being still clay upon millstone grit, but having portions of cultivated land among them. The brooks and reservoirs range from 2·8 to 3·8 degrees of hardness, and when brought along the Macclesfield Canal, which these reservoirs feed, they have at present a degree of hardness of 7·6.

This water, however, is proposed to be kept chiefly for the navigation purposes.

Of the Ridicar Brook water we have no analysis. It is stated to be a particularly fine stream, and it feeds the Macclesfield Canal. Its drainage land is very favourable.

Samples of water, obtained during a flood, accompany this report.

We submit, however, that the softness of water is but one of its qualifications for domestic use. Water may be very soft, and yet, being very much infected

* Dr. Clarke fixes four or five degrees as the point within which water is sufficiently soft for washing purposes—a high degree of softness, when we recollect that the average of the London pipe water is twelve, that some is sixteen, and some of the pumps eighty degrees of hardness. We submit that water may be too soft for domestic purposes. The softer water is the nearer it approaches to distilled water, and "it is well known," remarks Dr. Clarke, " that distilled water acts very readily upon lead."—*First Report of Health Towns Commissioners, p. 3, et seq.*

with vegetable impurities, may be very unfit for the purposes of a town. We have thought it necessary to submit the samples to Professor Graham for examination, and his report will be annexed to the Supplementary Report, which we shall have the honour to submit upon the comparative merits of the competing schemes.

Upon the result of the evidence, and of our personal survey, we beg to express an opinion that the drainage ground of this scheme is of a very superior character, and that the flood water obtained from it, if conveyed without any considerable deterioration, must be well qualified for domestic purposes.

Works and Estimates.

Upon the due adaptation of the proposed works and estimates to the efficient carrying out of the object proposed, Mr. Rendel alone of your two surveying officers is capable of forming a judgment from inspection of the plans and of the sites of the intended works. Upon this portion of the inquiry he begs to report that the works are perfectly practicable,—that they are exceedingly well adapted to secure the whole of the water which the engineer could deal with,—that the storage ground is ample and the sites of the reservoirs safe, and that no engineering difficulties appear to offer. The estimates seem to be in all respects fully sufficient. Observations upon this point have been already made in the report upon the Manchester Corporation Scheme.

Cost of Supply.

Beyond the sums included in the estimates, a certain portion of the capital already expended in the works is proposed by the company to be considered as capital invested in the waterworks, the cost of the Todds Brook reservoir, and a portion of the cost of the canals used as conduits.

This would raise the capital employed in bringing water to Blackfriars Bridge, connecting Salford with Manchester, to £300,000. *Q. 696, et seq., 910.*

The company propose to sell this water in bulk to existing companies, or to local administrative bodies, at prices to be fixed by arbitration, or at a maximum price of three-halfpence per thousand gallons delivered, filtered, at Marple; but they also take power to break up the streets, and lay down pipes in all three boroughs. *See MS. clause to amended Bill deposited with the appendix of the maps.*

They propose to use this power only for the purpose of compelling the existing water companies or local administrative bodies to buy their water in bulk. If, however, the possession of the power should not have this effect, they would doubtless put it in force, and become themselves distributors of water.

If they should sell in bulk, £300,000, added to the cost of the works by which Manchester, Salford, and Stockport are already supplied with water, and the cost of the extra piping required for an efficient service, would be the capital upon which a profit must be paid by the water consumers of Manchester, Salford, and Stockport. To this must be added the expenses of the management, and the total will be the cost of distributing a supply of from six to eight millions of gallons per day to a rapidly-increasing population of nearly half a million,—to the trade wants of the most energetic manufacturing district in the world, and to the public necessities of three large and densely-peopled boroughs.

We are sorry to be obliged to add, that neither the evidence adduced by the parties, nor our own inquiries, have enabled us to bring this total cost out in figures.

The amendment proposed in the Bill has, however, enabled us to estimate the cost of eight millions of gallons per day, delivered at Marple. This, at three-halfpence per thousand gallons, would amount to £18,250 per annum. To this must be added 10 per cent. upon the cost of the pipes which bring the water to Blackfriars Bridge from Marple.

The engineer's estimate for this portion of the works is £90,719. 11s. 2d. The total cost per annum of a daily supply of eight millions of gallons delivered at Blackfriars Bridge would be £27,820. The cost of distribution has still to be added.

If, on the other hand, the existing companies should refuse to take the water, a very large sum would be expended in piping; and there would be, for some time, a competition between this company and those which now exist. The probable ultimate effect would be, that the sum so expended would be added to the capital already stated as that upon which the consumers would pay a profit.

We humbly submit it for the consideration of Parliament, whether, if it should be decided to sanction this scheme, the power of competition, attended by so great an unnecessary outlay, is the most expedient form in which power can be given to this company to force a sale of their water.

Form of the Bill.

After the case as to the merits of the scheme had been closed, we went through the clauses of the Bill, inviting discussion, and requiring explanations as to its several provisions. The probability of Parliament sanctioning a general measure renders it inexpedient, we submit, that we should report at any length upon the particular clauses. We may remark, however, that the Bill recognizes the principle of constant supply under pressure (clauses 41 and 42); and requires the company, upon request of the house-owner, or of the occupier with the house-owner's consent, to fix pipes and apparatus, and to keep the same in repair. (Clauses 43 to 47.) It also provides (by clause 84), that the company shall be subject to the provisions of any future general Sanitary Act.

A copy of the Bill, containing the amendments to be proposed in committee, is annexed to this report, and we beg leave to refer to the short-hand writer's notes of the discussion upon the clauses, for a more particular exposition of the views of the promoters, and for the extent to which they appear willing that the obligations of the company may be increased and their powers abridged.

Conclusion.

In conclusion, we beg to report, that this scheme appears to have all the requisites for securing to Manchester, Salford, and Stockport, a daily supply of from six to eight millions of gallons of water well adapted to domestic purposes; but that this quantity is quite insufficient to supply the wants of the district which the Bill purposes to embrace.

We have the honour to be,

My Lord and Gentlemen,

Your very faithful servants,

GEO. WINGROVE COOKE,
JAMES MEADOWS RENDEL.

The Temple, 28th February, 1847.

Appendix No. 4.—*Manchester Corporation Waterworks—General Instructions to Authorized Plumbers.*

1. Persons requiring a supply of water must, in the first instance, obtain from the superintendent or other authorized officer of the Waterworks Committee, instructions as to the proper point for the introduction of the water on to the premises. Such persons must, at their own cost, provide, lay down, and maintain all service pipes and fittings which may be required within their premises, including one foot of lead service piping beyond the boundary thereof.

2. In case the service pipes are of lead, they are required to be of the following strength, viz.;—

$\frac{3}{8}$-inch diameter.................... 5lbs. per lineal yard.
$\frac{1}{2}$-inch   "   .... 6lbs.   "   "
$\frac{3}{4}$-inch   "   .... 9lbs.   "   "
1-inch   "   ....12lbs.   "   "
1$\frac{1}{4}$-inch   "   ....16lbs.   "   "

3. A stop-tap will be required to be affixed on the service pipe, inside the premises, and as near to the entrance as possible; and in all places where the stop-tap is fixed in the ground, authorized plumbers will be required to fix over the same a small cast-iron guard box, to indicate the situation of such stop-tap, which box must be inserted with cement into a flag 18 inches square and 3$\frac{1}{4}$ inches thick, in such a manner as to prevent its being removed without the flag. All stop-cock boxes must not be less than 14lbs. weight, with a proper orifice therein for stamping, as per pattern, which may also be seen at the stamping office.

4. Private service pipes are required to be laid *three feet below the surface of the ground*, and also to be brought out through the boundary of the private premises three feet below the street or roadway, and in default of this regulation being complied with, the pipes will not be connected by the Corporation.

5. Before the connection for the supply of water can be made, or before any additional fittings can be connected to an existing service pipe, the work must be inspected and approved, and authorized plumbers are especially warned not in any case to connect to a pipe laid for lime slaking, and thereby supply water to the premises without first receiving a written order from the proper officer of the Waterworks Committee.

6. Printed forms will, upon application, be furnished to authorized plumbers, which they will be required to fill up and deliver at the Waterworks Offices, as a

notice of the fittings being ready for inspection, and also of any alterations made in existing service pipes or fittings.

7. None but proper valve taps or self-closing taps are to be fixed, and of such a description as the Waterworks Committee may approve of.

8. "Plug" taps are only allowed to be fixed on descending pipes from cisterns.

9. Copper bit joints will not be allowed, but in all cases a proper wiped joint must be made.

10. No house or other premises will be allowed to have more than one supply pipe, either from the main or from any adjoining premises.

11. No steam-engine boiler, or any description of closed boiler, will be allowed to be supplied direct from the service pipe, but a cistern must be provided in every case, and the supply taken therefrom.

12. No tap for domestic purposes in dwelling-houses, or for drinking purposes in warehouses, will be allowed to be supplied from a cistern, but in all such cases drawing-off taps must be fixed on the service pipe before it enters the cistern; baths, water-closets, urinals, and wash-basins only are allowed to be supplied from a cistern.

13. Dwelling-houses must be supplied by service pipes of the diameter stated below, which rule all authorized plumbers are hereby instructed to carry out, viz.:—

$\frac{3}{8}$-inch—One house above £10, and not exceeding £20 per annum rent, or not more than two cottages not exceeding £10 per annum each.

$\frac{1}{2}$-inch—One house above £20 per annum rent, but not exceeding £70 per annum. Six houses in one block may be supplied by this size of pipe, but the rents must not exceed £14 per annum each.

$\frac{3}{4}$-inch—One house from £70 to £200 per annum, but not more than four houses together at £50 per annum each. Seventeen houses in one block may be supplied from this size of pipe, if the rents do not exceed £12 per annum each.

N.B.—The *full diameter of pipe* must be continued through the whole of the houses supplied together.

Where dwelling-houses are situated beyond the limits of the city, and in which no trade is carried on, and are supplied together from one service pipe, the owner will be liable to the payment of the water rent. The city comprises the following townships:—Manchester, Hulme, Chorlton-on-Medlock, Cheetham, Ardwick, and Beswick.

14. Urinals may either be supplied by a self-closing tap from the service pipe of approved description, or by a urinal cistern of approved pattern.

15. No water-closet will be allowed to be supplied direct from the service pipe, but must be supplied from a cistern of the description mentioned in clause 16. Samples of these cisterns may be seen in work at the Waterworks Stamping Office, in the basement of the Town Hall (entrance Lloyd-street).

16. Cisterns for water-closets must be of the principle known as 73 x *for common hopper closets, and of* 73 N T *for the usual pan closets,* of Guest and Chrime's make, or of other approved makers, containing two alternating valves on the same principle, and constructed not to deliver more than 1½ gallons of water at a flush, the pulls of which cisterns must be so constructed as to prevent their being fixed in any position to allow the water to be left running to waste.

Descending Pipes to Water-closets from Regulation Cisterns.

17. These pipes must be the same diameter as the union pipe attached to the cistern.

18. The overflow pipes of all cisterns hereafter fixed must act as warning pipes, and must be brought through the external wall of the premises supplied with water at such a conspicuous point below the level of the bottom of the cistern as may be directed, and there properly maintained,—which pipe must be of sufficient diameter to deliver any water wasting from the different diameters of ball taps when out of order, and such pipes must be of lead.

19. Every cistern which shall be used for the storage or reception of water supplied by the Corporation shall be made, and at all times maintained, absolutely water-tight, and shall be provided with a ball tap, *which must be branched into the inlet pipe thereof,* and the latter made secure to the side of the cistern, as a connection to the *end* of such pipe will not be allowed. The ball tap shall be so fixed as not to become submerged when the cistern is full, the level of the water at which time shall always be maintained at two inches below the overflow or warning pipe; *and every such cistern shall be made capable of inspection.*

20. Every overflow or waste pipe which shall be attached to any cistern in use previous to the 1st of January, 1871, shall be altered in accordance with regulation No. 18, after the Corporation shall have given to or left at the last known place of abode of the person liable to pay for the water supplied to such cistern, 24 hours' notice in writing, requiring such overflow or waste pipe to be so altered in accordance with the regulation referred to.

21. Every bath to which water is supplied by the Corporation shall be provided with a well-fitted and perfectly water-tight ground *outlet plug,* with chain complete, or such tap as shall be approved and stamped.

22. No overflow pipes other than such as are made to act as detective or warning pipes, previously referred to in regulation No. 18, shall be made or attached to any bath in which water supplied by the Corporation shall be used; and every overflow pipe which is now attached to any such bath shall be permanently altered to the satisfaction of the Corporation, after they shall have given to or left at the last known place of abode of the person liable to pay for the water supplied to such bath, 24 hours' notice, in writing, requiring such overflow pipe to be so altered.

Resolution of the Waterworks Committee of March 12th, 1878.

28. LEAD CISTERNS IN DWELLING-HOUSES.—*Resolved*, "That after the com-"pletion of the plumbing work in dwelling-houses now in course of erection, no "cisterns in which Corporation water is intended to be stored be allowed, unless "constructed of slate, stone, or iron."

By order of the Waterworks Committee,

JOSEPH HERON, Town Clerk.

Waterworks Offices, Town Hall, Manchester,
February 21st, 1874.

24. The Waterworks Committee will provide and fix all water meters, and will also lay the service pipes from the boundary of the premises to the inlet of the meters and fix the stop-cocks thereon, at the expense of the occupier of the premises; and each inlet pipe and stop-tap must not be interfered with by authorized plumbers or any other persons, without the sanction of the superintendent or other authorized officer of the Waterworks Committee.

25. The Waterworks Committee will not sanction any fire-cocks or hydrants being fixed inside private premises, either from the main or from any cistern supplied with water by the Corporation; at the same time they will consider any application for permission to attach any private stand-pipe and hose to the street hydrants, to be used in case of fire only.

26. Information from authorized plumbers or other parties as to any infringements of the preceding instructions will receive the immediate attention of the Corporation.

27. Authorized plumbers will be struck off the list if found lending their names to unauthorized persons.

Testing and Stamping Arrangements.—Testing and Stamping Internal Water Fittings.

The following regulations must be complied with:—

28. All taps and other water fittings must be tested and stamped by the proper officer of the Corporation.

29. No taps or apparatus will be stamped but those of the best quality of each maker, samples of which will be kept for inspection at the stamping office.

30. The taps must be on the screw-down principle, with loose valves and stuffing boxes; the diameter of all orifices in the seat on which the valves work in the stop-taps to be the same size as the taps themselves; and all taps must be capable of resisting a pressure of 300lbs. to the square inch, to which they will be subjected in testing.

81. The bib and stop taps must be of the following average weights, viz.:—

    1-inch .... $32\frac{1}{4}$ ounces.
    $\frac{3}{4}$-inch .... 21 "
    $\frac{1}{2}$-inch .... $11\frac{1}{2}$ "
    $\frac{3}{8}$-inch .... $8\frac{1}{4}$ "

Double-valve bib taps—

    $\frac{3}{4}$-inch .... $22\frac{3}{4}$ "
    $\frac{1}{2}$-inch .... $13\frac{1}{4}$ "
    $\frac{3}{8}$-inch .... $10\frac{1}{4}$ "

82. Ball taps must be of the best quality, and the diameter of the tap and ball as under:—

    1-inch diameter of tap not less than 6 inches diameter of ball.
    $\frac{3}{4}$-inch "   " $5\frac{1}{2}$ inches "
    $\frac{1}{2}$-inch "   " $4\frac{1}{2}$ inches "
    $\frac{3}{8}$-inch "   " $4\frac{1}{2}$ inches "

83. The rods or spindles from the balls to the taps must not be less than the following lengths:—

    1-inch diameter of tap .... 13 inches long.
    $\frac{3}{4}$-inch "   .... 13 inches "
    $\frac{1}{2}$-inch "   .... 11 inches "
    $\frac{3}{8}$-inch "   .... 11 inches "

84. The strength of such rods or spindles must not be less than as follows:—

    End next the tap.   End next the ball.
    1-inch $\frac{1}{4}$ by $\frac{3}{16}$-inch........................ $\frac{1}{2}$ by $\frac{3}{16}$-inch.
    $\frac{3}{4}$-inch $\frac{1}{4}$ " $\frac{3}{16}$-inch....................... "   "
    $\frac{1}{2}$-inch $\frac{1}{4}$ " $\frac{3}{16}$-inch....................... $\frac{1}{2}$ " $\frac{3}{16}$-inch.
    $\frac{3}{8}$-inch $\frac{1}{4}$ " $\frac{3}{16}$-inch....................... "   "

The rods or spindles referred to above may be of the following strength, in lieu of those stated, viz.:—$\frac{5}{16}$ by $\frac{3}{16}$ inch.

85. Such taps without balls or spindles must not be less than the following weights:—

    1-inch .... $22\frac{1}{2}$ ounces.
    $\frac{3}{4}$-inch .... $10\frac{3}{4}$ "
    $\frac{1}{2}$-inch .... $7\frac{3}{4}$ "

Ferrule Taps for Baths.

86. The weight required in future by the Waterworks Committee for the above taps without the handle will be 20 ounces, and no taps of this nature will be passed and stamped of lighter weight.

37. Makers of or dealers in taps are requested to put their names on such as are of the best quality, as none others will be stamped.

38. The following fees will be charged for testing and stamping:—

    Bib and stop taps .... 2d. each.
    Ball taps .... 3d. "
    Water-closets .... 6d. "
    Closet cisterns............................... 3d. "
    Stop-cock boxes.............................. 2d. "

Note.—Any authorized plumber who shall change his address is directed to send particulars of such change to Mr. Berrey, at these offices, or his name will be omitted from the list subsequently printed.

Further Notice to Authorized Plumbers.

1. The Waterworks Committee have decided that all persons who are now or may hereafter be supplied with water by meter may dispense with the 73 N.T. or other regulation cisterns to water-closets if they think proper, and fix any closets that will pass the testing office without such cisterns in future.

2. On and after the 1st of January next all stop-cocks to be fixed on service pipes must be of larger diameter than such pipes:—for instance, ⅜-inch pipes must have ½-inch stop-cocks; ½-inch pipes, ¾-inch stop-cocks; ¾-inch pipes, 1-inch stop-cocks; and 1-inch pipes, 1¼inch stop-cocks.

3. Authorized plumbers can, therefore, inform any of their customers as to these amended regulations.

                          By order,
                                T. H. G. BERREY.

Waterworks Offices, Town Hall, Manchester,
       November 11th, 1878.

INDEX.

PART I.—HISTORICAL.

PAGE
1 Early remains.
2 Original "Fountain" and Fountain Street.
2 Rejoicings on Coronation of Charles II. when "Fountain" yielded claret.
3 Waterworks of Sir Oswald Mosley.
3 Analysis of water by Dr. Percival, 1771.
4 Rival water schemes, 1808.
5 Report of Committee on these schemes, 1809.
8 Resolutions thereon.
9 Manchester and Salford Waterworks Company, commonly called the "Stone-pipe Company," 20th June, 1809.
10–14 Proceedings of this Company.
16 Change in management, 1816.
16 Iron pipes substituted for stone ones.
17 *Manchester Guardian* newspaper account of "Old Manchester and its Supply of Water," November, 1850, and Appendix No. 1.
17 Application to Parliament for additional powers, 1821.
18 Again, in 1823, power obtained to construct reservoirs at Gorton.
19 Works at Gorton completed in 1825 or 1826.
19 Mr. Nicholas Brown, Engineer.
20 Company first paid a dividend in 1831, 22 years after first Act obtained.
20 Called in Mr. Simpson, Engineer, 1841.
21 Quantity of water supplied from year 1836 to 1841 inclusive.
21 Estimated quantity required.
22 Mr. Simpson recommended a well at Gorton.
23 Well commenced in autumn, 1845.
23, 24 Particulars of well.
25 Health of Towns Commission, 1844.
25, 26 Character of hills between Lancashire and Yorkshire.
26 Many Waterworks established, 1825.
27–35, 36 Observations of Mr. Thom, of Rothesay.
27, 28 Shaw's Waterworks, near Greenock.
28 Turton and Entwisle Reservoir and Bolton Waterworks.
28 Bann Reservoirs, Ireland, 1835.
29 Glossop Reservoir.
29, 30 Rain gauges and rain returns.
31 Oldham Waterworks, 1838.
31, 32 Rochdale Canal rain returns.
33, 34 Dr. Dalton, and Appendix No. 2.
37, 38 Results of experience at Turton and Entwisle Reservoir—Mr. Askworth.
38 Belmont Reservoir—Bolton Waterworks.
39–50 Report to Mr. Cooke and Mr. Murray on increased supply of water to Manchester, June, 1844.
50, 51 Bill introduced into Parliament and withdrawn by Company, 1845.

PAGE
51–54 Report to Chairman and Directors of Manchester and Salford Waterworks Company, May, 1845.
55 "The Lancashire Waterworks."
56 "Lyme Scheme" of Manchester and Salford Waterworks Company.
56 Opposition of Manchester Corporation.
57 Received instructions to suggest best mode of remedying deficiency.
59–67 Letter to Mr. Vaughan, of Stockport, July, 1846.—Description of works proposed by Corporation, 1847.
68 Preliminary Inquiries Act, 1846.
68–70 Etherow Reservoirs Bill
73 Observations on professional evidence.
76 Observations of Surveying Officers on insufficiency of supply.
76, 77 Dr. Smith's and Mr. Holland's analyses of water.
77, 78 Analyses by Professor Graham, of University College, London.
79, 80 Observations by Mr. Holland on saving by use of soft water.
80, 81 Proportion of coloured to uncoloured water.
81–84, and Appendix No. 3. Scheme of the Manchester Sheffield and Lincolnshire Railway Company, and Report of Surveying Officers thereon in Appendix No. 3.
84, 85 Statement of Town Clerk of Manchester.
85–89 General or supplementary Report of Surveying Officers on all schemes submitted to them.
89–91 Act of 1847.
91, 92 Arrangement with millowners for extension of scheme.
92, 93 Act of 1848.
94–96 Report of Surveying Officers on same.
96 By Acts of 1847 and 1848 the works, &c. of the Manchester and Salford Waterworks Company were transferred to Manchester Corporation.
97 Price agreed for.
97–105 Agreement.
106 Arrangement with landowners.
107 Corporation borrowed £250,000 from Commissioners for Loans to Public Works.

PART II.—DESCRIPTIVE.

110 Woodhead Reservoir.
113 Flood of July, 1848.—Increased means of discharge.
114–117 Still greater flood.—Embankment broken down.—Damage done.—Report to Water Committee.
118–120 Particulars of various floods.
121 Torside and Rhodes Wood Reservoirs.
122 Landslip at Rhodes Wood.
123–127 Report to Water Committee on works in general.—Answer to Alderman Pilling.
128 Mode of separating pure water from that discoloured described.
129 Fountains, strainers, syphons.
129 Torside and Rhodes Wood Reservoirs further described.
130–132 Slipping of base of Torside Bank.—Report to Committee.
133 Vale House and Bottoms Reservoirs.
133 Arnfield and Hollingworth Reservoirs.
134 Mottram Tunnel.
136, 137 Godley and Denton Service Reservoirs.
138 Drainage area.

PAGE
138 Compensation to river.
138–151 Pipe-laying.
141 Self-acting closing valve—usefulness.
143 Casting pipes with sockets downwards.
143–145 Coating pipes.—Dr. R. A. Smith's process.
145 Effects of soft water on mussels in old pipes and reservoirs.
146, 147 Turned and bored joints.
148 Indiarubber joints.
148, 149 Fire cocks or hydrants.
149, 150 Air valves.
150 Protection against fire.
151 Height of jets from streets.
151–167 Heavy rain of February, 1852, reprinted from account published by the Manchester Literary and Philosophical Society in their 10th volume, and remarks on same in *Manchester Guardian* newspaper.
167 Long drought after heavy rain.
168 Landslip at Rhodes Wood Reservoir Embankment.
168 Mr. Robert Stephenson and Mr. J. K. Brunel called in to advise.
168–170 Apparatus for discharging water from reservoirs.
170 Bottoms and Vale House Reservoirs.
171 Alterations in arrangements.
172 Reservoirs at Audenshaw.
174 Auxiliary Reservoir on river Etherow.
174 City piping.—Formulæ employed.
176 Novelties or improvements.
177 Experiments on discharge of water.
178, 179 Results of same.
179, 180 Life assurance.
180 Testing and stamping office.
181 Population.
181, 182 Consumption.
183 Irregularity in supply.
184 Rainfall.
185–198 Observations on rainfall, loss, &c., and particulars of droughts of 1864, 1865, and 1868.
198–201 Advantages of soft water.
201–205 Report on completion of works in Longdendale.
205–223 Thirlmere scheme.
225 Appendices.
227 Appendix No. 1.—" Old Manchester—its supply of water," reprinted from the *Manchester Guardian* newspaper of November, 1850.
244 Appendix No. 1.—Water for Manchester, under the Stone-pipe Company and the Waterworks Company.
256 Appendix No. 1.—The Old Works.
260 Appendix No. 2.—Report to Manchester Literary and Philosophical Society on measurement of rain.
275 Appendix No. 3.—Report of George Wingrove Cooke and James Meadows Rendel, Esqrs., on the Manchester Sheffield and Lincolnshire Railway (Supply of Water) Bill.
286 Appendix No. 4.—General instructions to authorized plumbers.

ERRATA.

PAGE
53 Three lines from bottom, for "classes" read "clauses."
67 Five lines from bottom, for "parliamentary" read "preliminary."
68 First line, for "contact" read "contest."
91 Four lines from top, at end of line, after the words "to be" insert the word "on."
107 Add end of Part I.—"Ferntower, near Crieff, N.B., January, 1859."
112 Sixteen lines from bottom, strike out comma after "door," end of line, and insert it in next line after "only."
129 Nine lines from bottom, after word "been" insert "upwards of."
138 Eleven lines from bottom, after "inches" introduce the words "per annum."
140 First line, after the words "large valves" introduce the words "on the city piping and the original ones at Woodhead, Torside, and Rhodes Wood reservoirs."
143 Eighteen lines from top, "for "Mahon" read "Mabon."

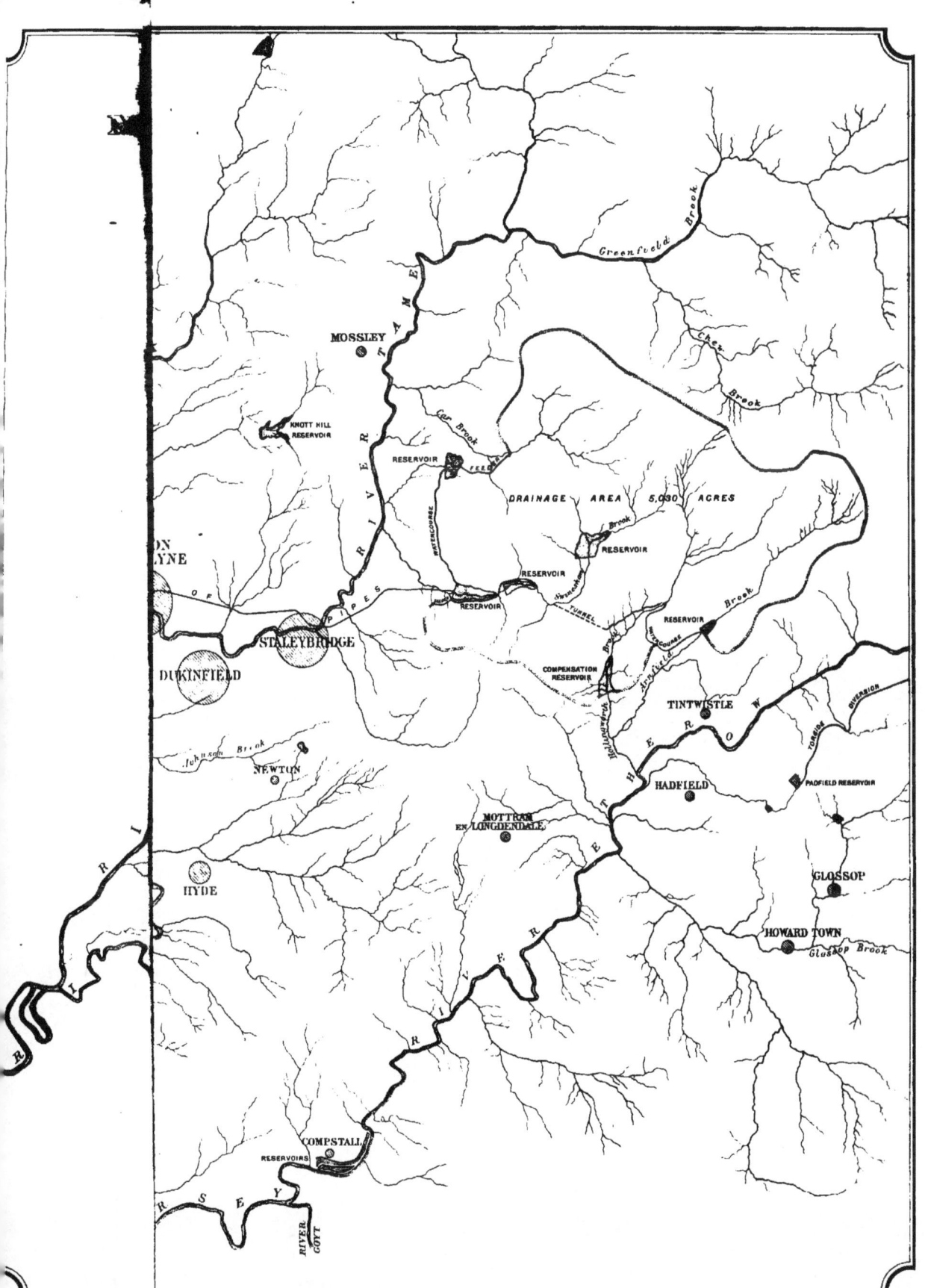

THE NEW YORK
PUBLIC LIBRARY

WOODHEAD

PLAN SHEWING OLD EMBANKMENT — NEW EMB

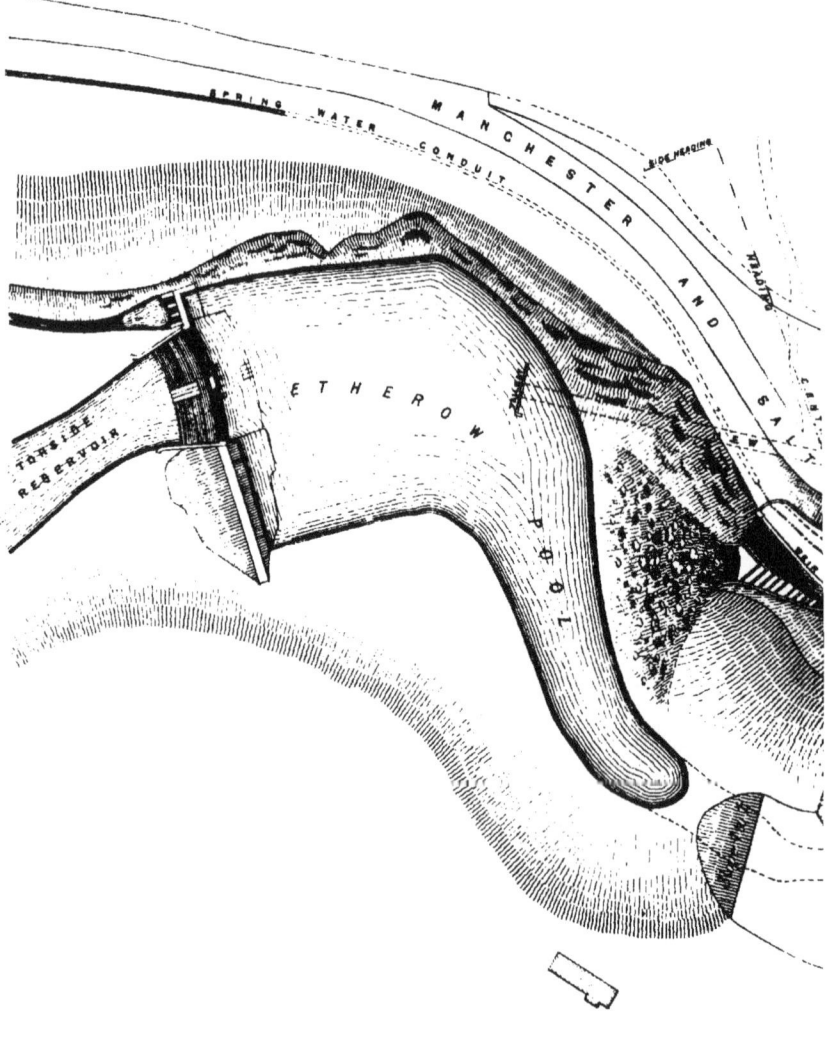

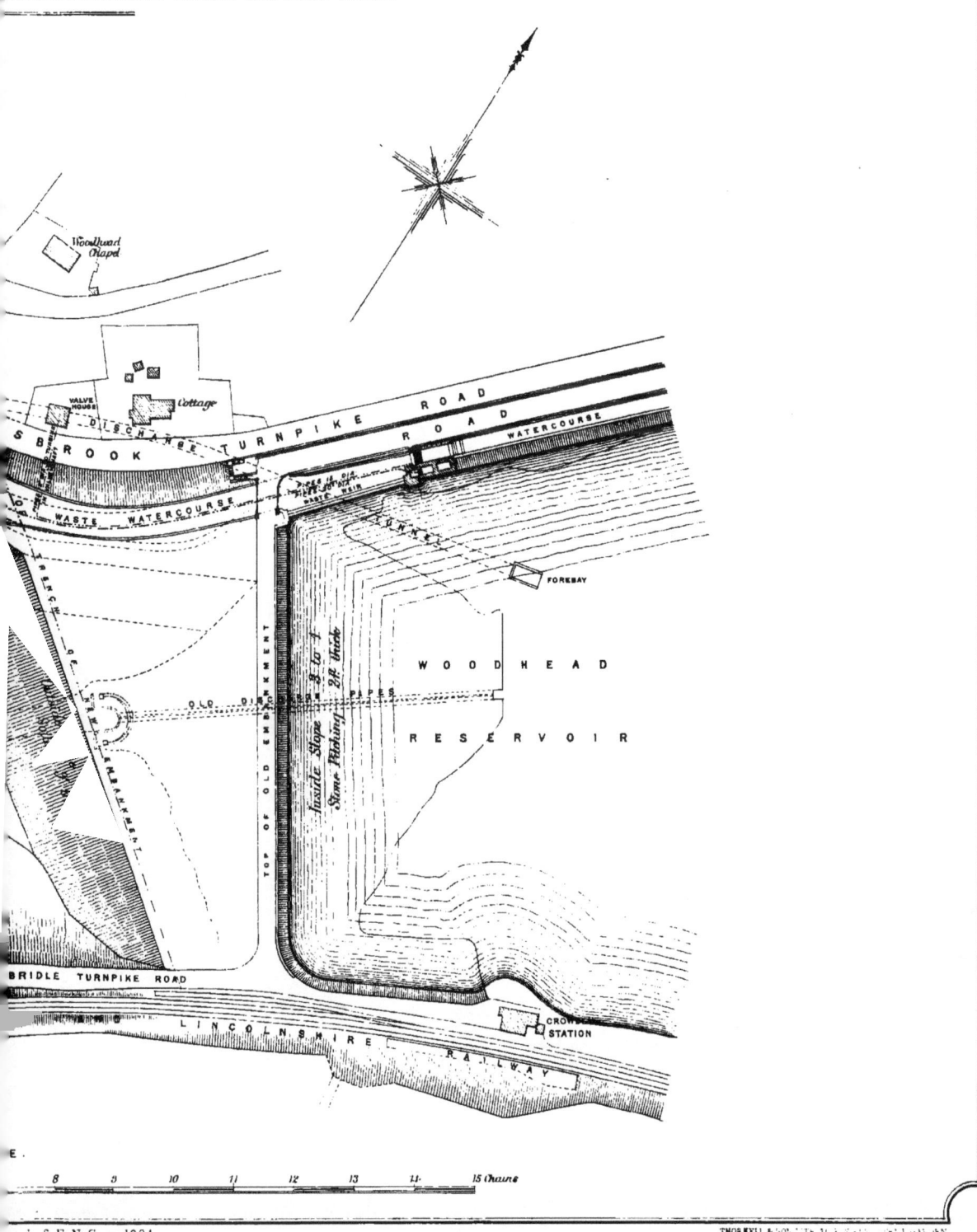

WOODHEAD R[ESERVOIR]

LONGITUDINAL SECTION OF PUDDLE TRENCH FOR THE SECON[D]

Road

Discharge Tunnel
Manchester & Saltersbrook
Turnpike Road

T.S. No 1

30" Pipe for Spring Water

T.S. No 2

HEADING 381 FEET LONG

WASTE WATERCOURSE

STRONG HEAVY ROCK OPEN JOINTED

SHALE

BOTTOM OF CONCRETE

Level of Etherow Weir

SHOREY OR SHALE

BROKEN UP
WITH BITS

No 1.
CONCRETE

No 2.

Level of Etherow Weir

Top Bank

Slope 2 to 1

NEW EMBANKMENT

PUDDLE

Slope 1 to 1

Original Surface

Level of Etherow Weir

CONCRETE

TRANS[VERSE]

SC[ALE]

Feet 10 0 50 100

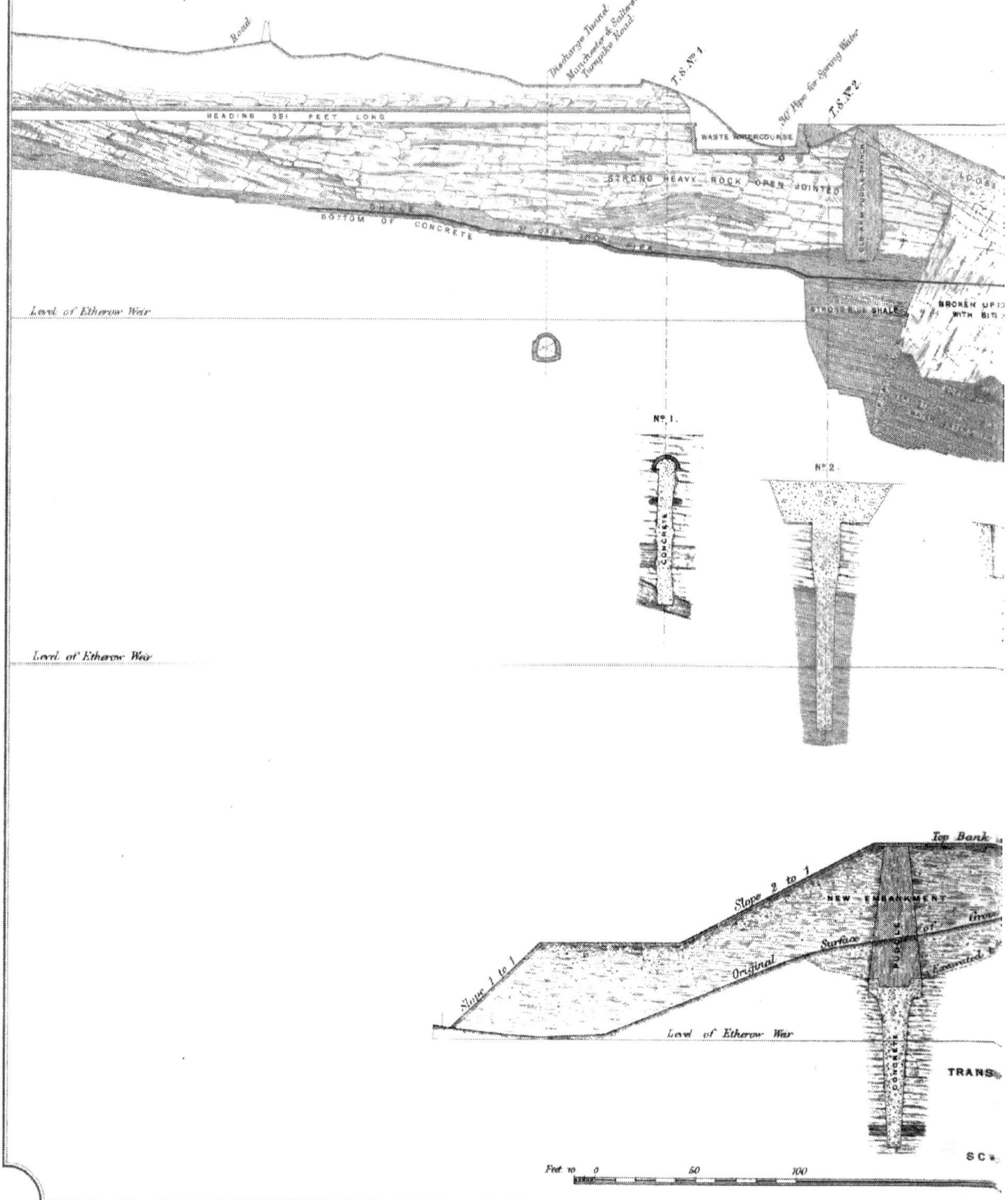

Manchester, T J Day — L[ith.]

RESERVOIR.
OND EMBANKMENT SHEWING THE GEOLOGICAL STRATA.

TRANSVERSE SECTIONS OF CONCRETE FILLING IN TRENCH.

No. 3.   No. 4.   No. 5.   No. 6.

OLD EMBANKMENT.

VERSE SECTION No. 3A

Scale: 200   300   400 Feet

London, E. & F. N. Spon, 1884.

WOODHEAD
DETAILS OF WASTE

PLAN

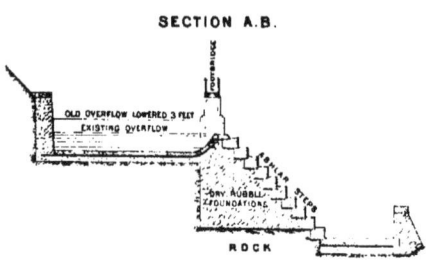

SECTION A.B.

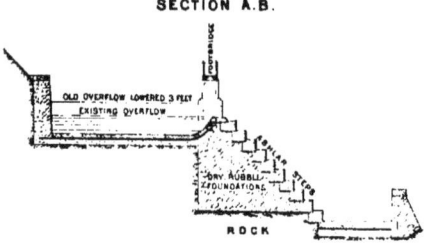

SECTION C.D.

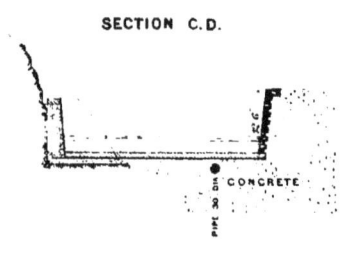

SECTION I.K.

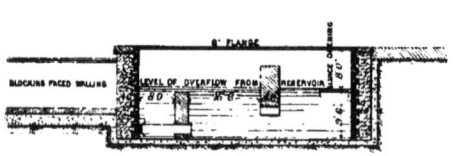

SECTION L.M.

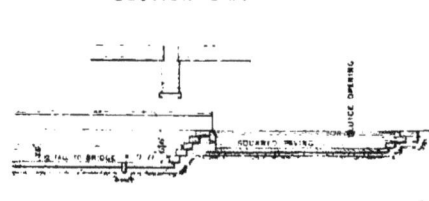

Manchester, T J Day

RESERVOIR.
WATERCOURSE.

SECTION E.F.

SECTION G.H.

SECTION N.O.

SECTION P.Q.

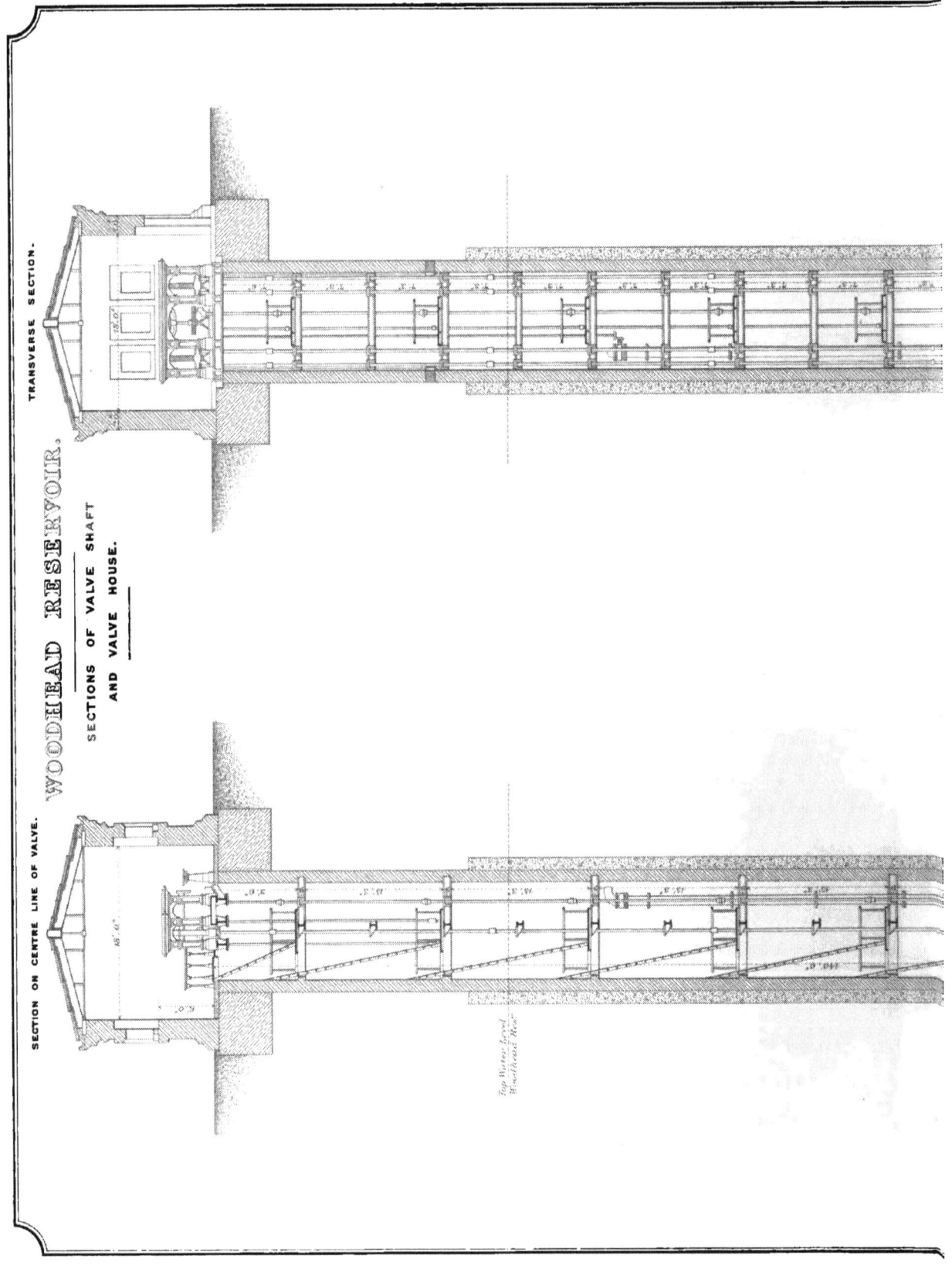

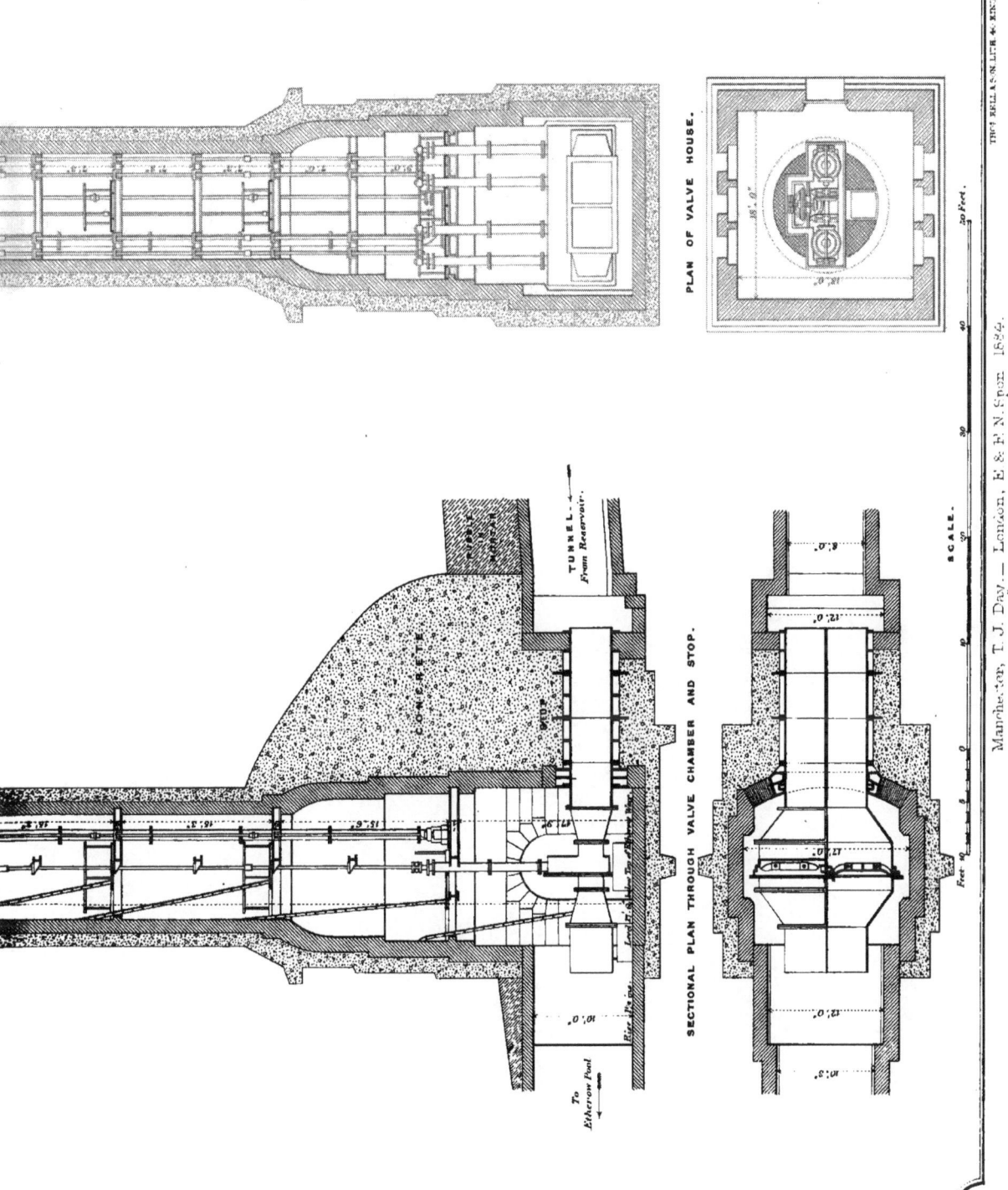

WOODHEAD RESERVOIR.

48 INCH SLUICE VALVE AND ORIGINAL GEARING.
(THREE SLIDES)

SECTIONAL ELEVATION.

VERTICAL SECTION.

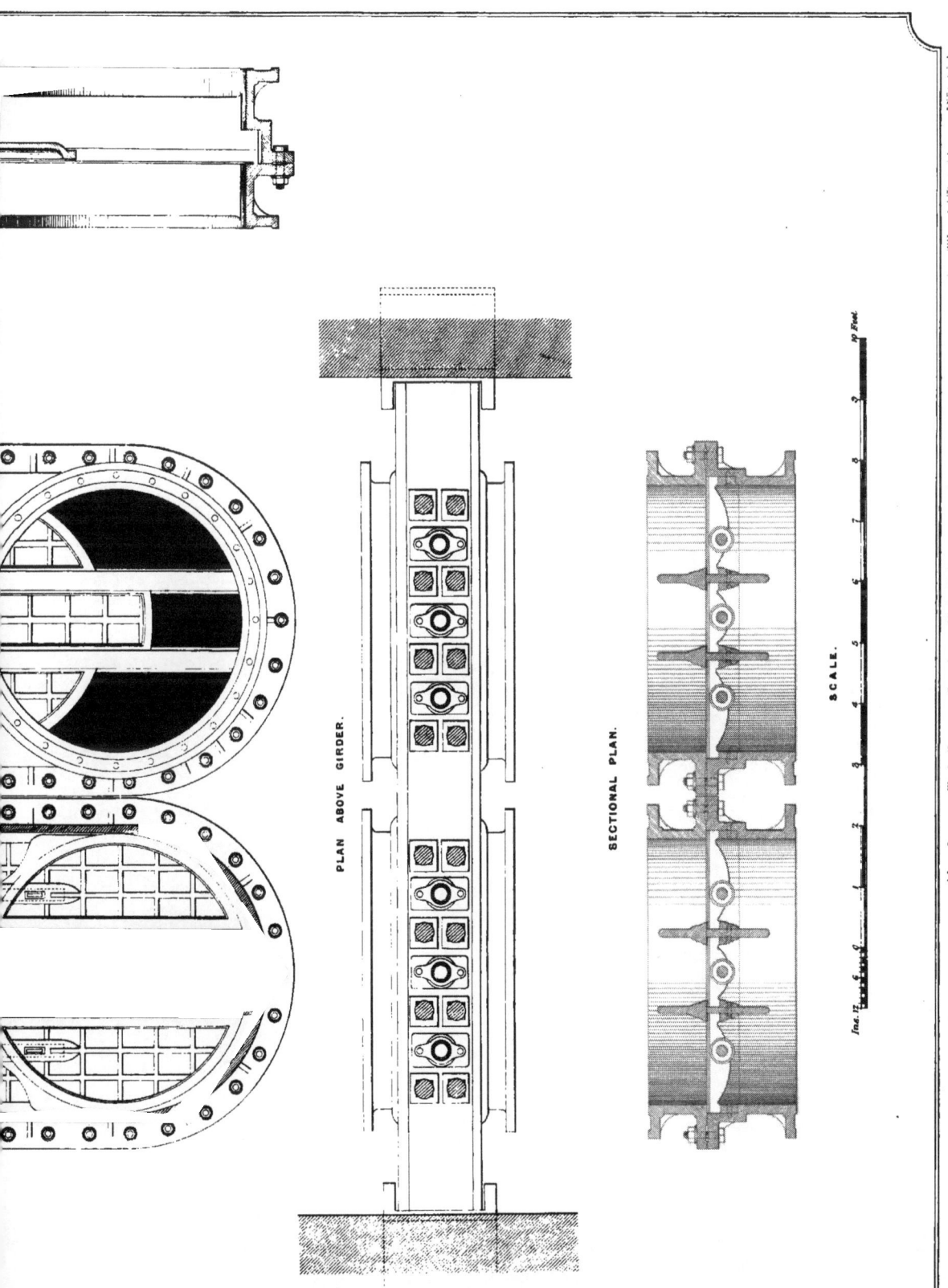

WOODHEA
DETAILS

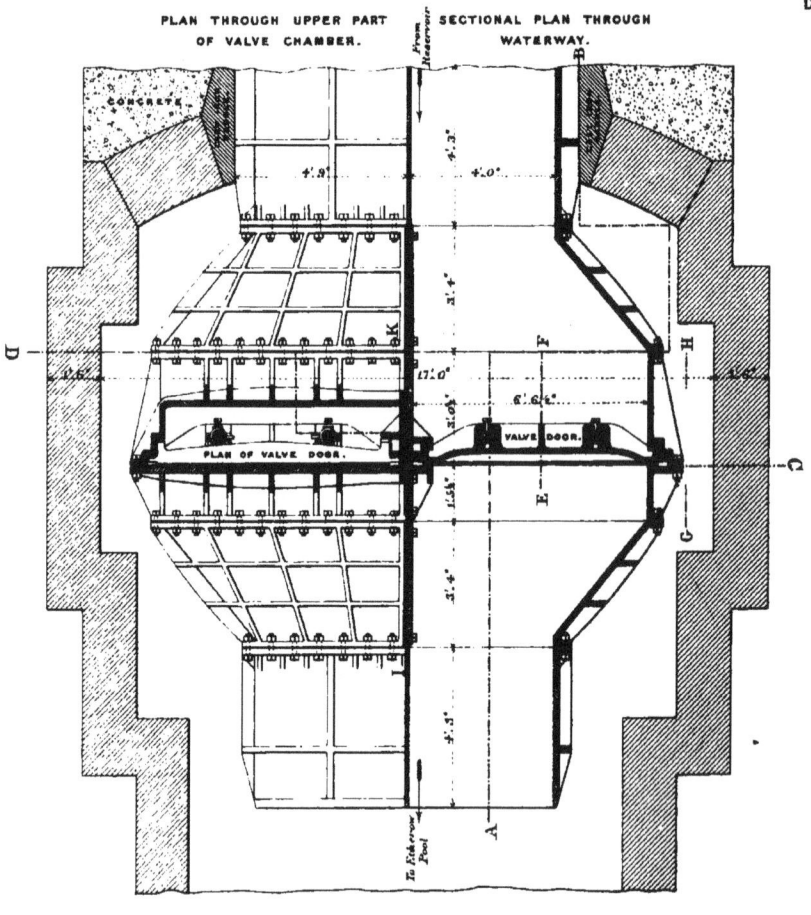

PLAN THROUGH UPPER PART OF VALVE CHAMBER. SECTIONAL PLAN THROUGH WATERWAY.

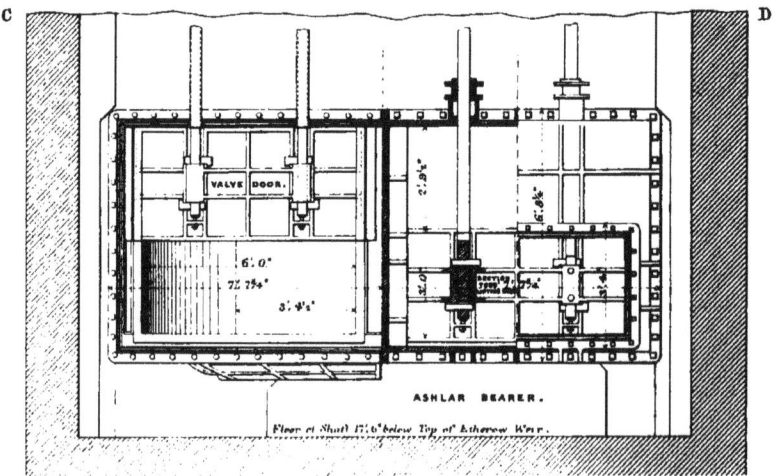

ELEVATION, WITH CHAMBER CASTING REMOVED, SHEWING VALVE FACE AND BACK OF VALVE DOOR.   PART SECTION THROUGH VALVE CHAMBER.   PART ELEVATION OF VALVE CHAMBER.

SECTION ON LINE C.D. TOWARDS RESERVOIR.

RESERVOIR.
LARGE VALVES.

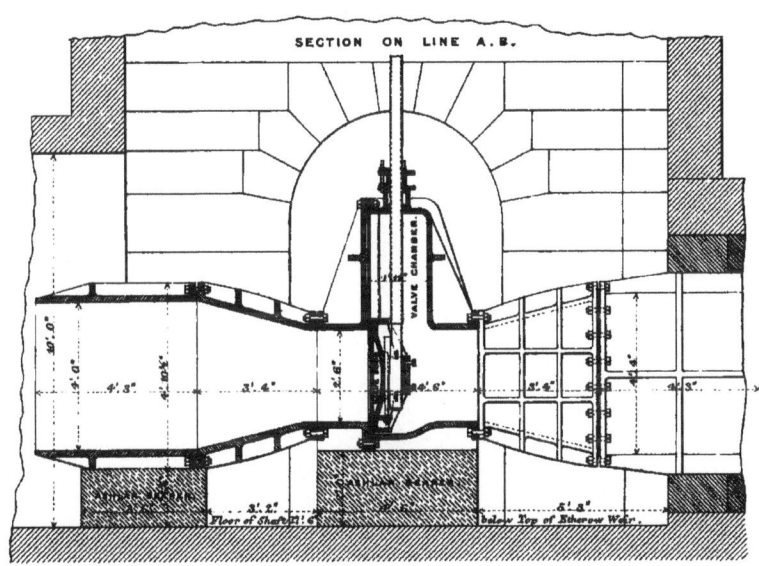

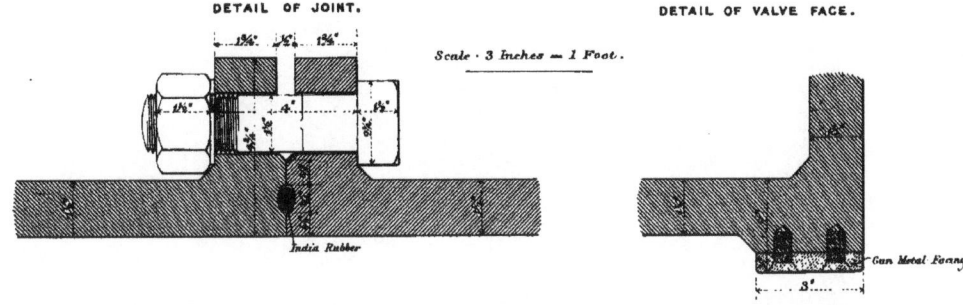

London. E & F N. Spon 1884

WOODHEAD RESERVOIR

GEARING FOR
GENERAL

PLAN.

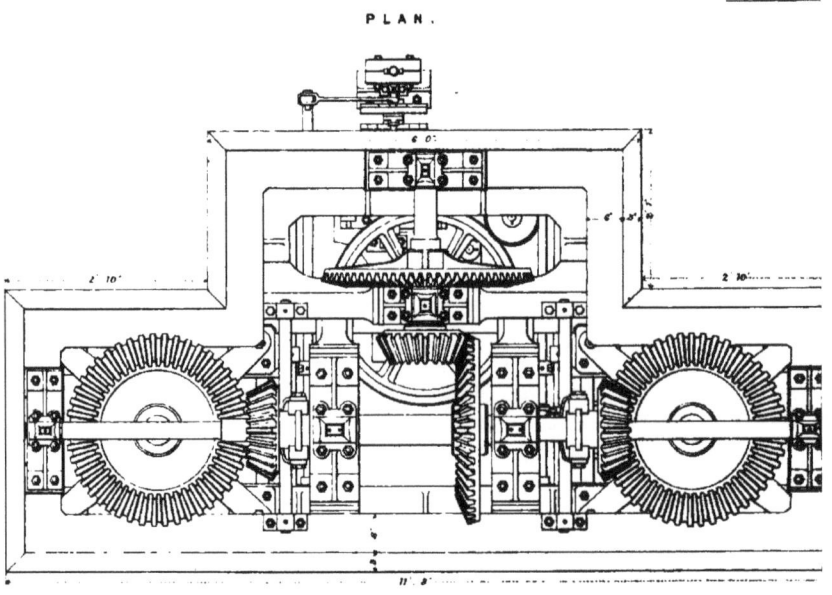

ELEVATION.

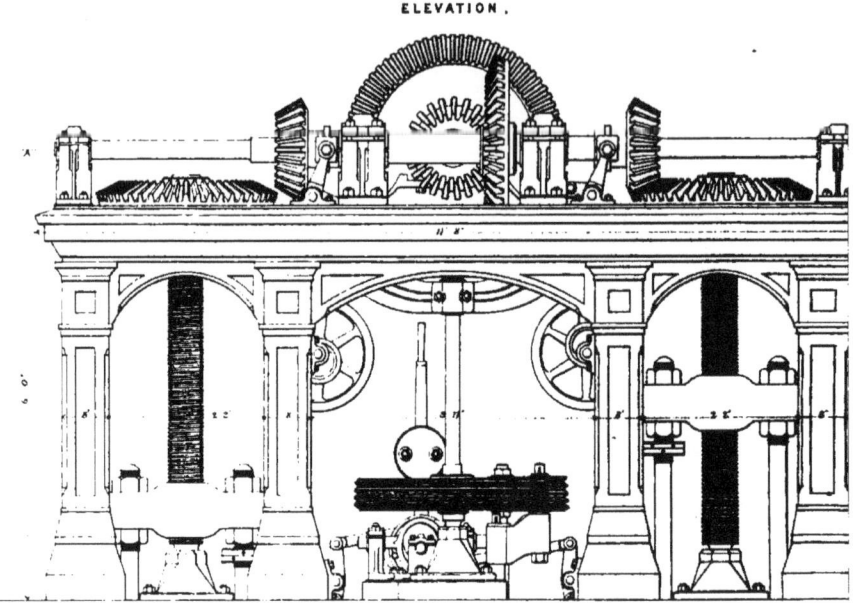

SCALE ½

Manchester, T J Day

- DISCHARGE TUNNEL.   SHEET. 1.

ARGE VALVES.

RAWING.

DETAIL OF FRICTION GEARING.
1/8ᴺᴰ FULL SIZE.

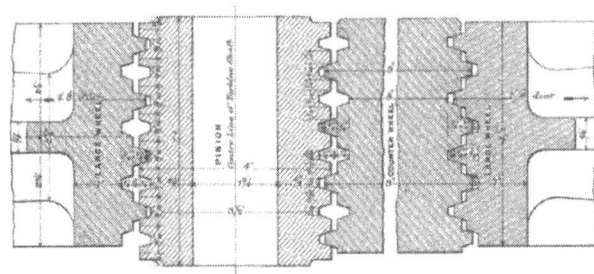

END VIEW.

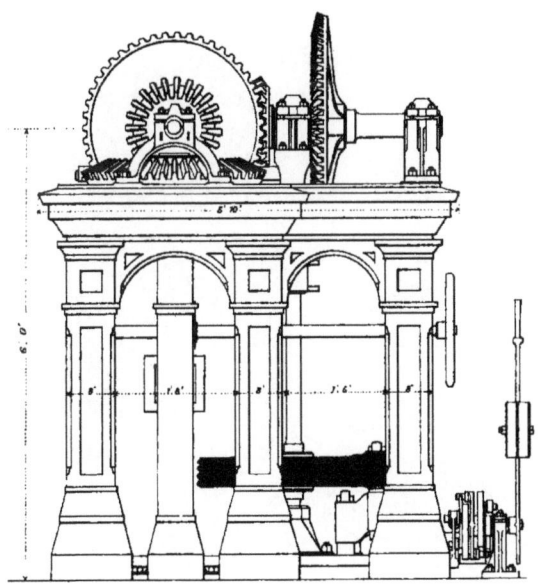

TO A FOOT.

E. & F. N. Spon, 1884.

WOODHEAD RESERVOIR

GEARING FO

DETAILS OF GEARING O

PLAN.

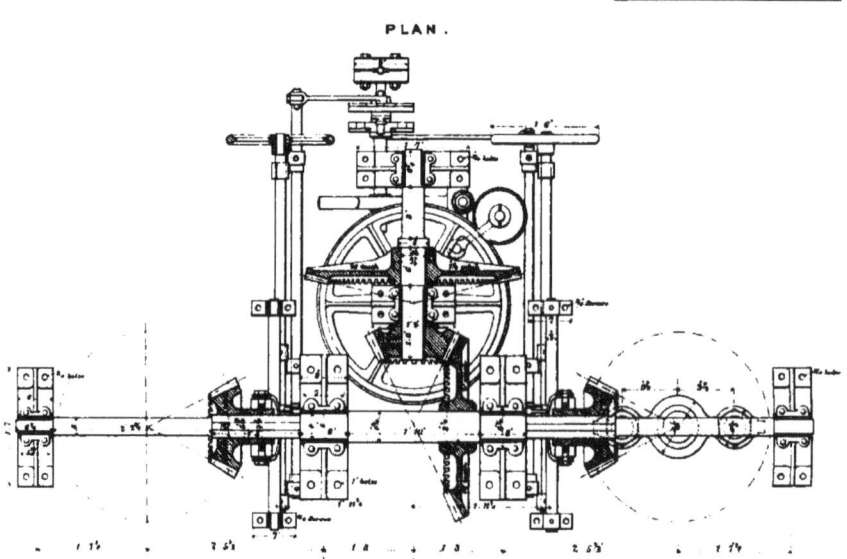

SECTIONAL ELEVATION.

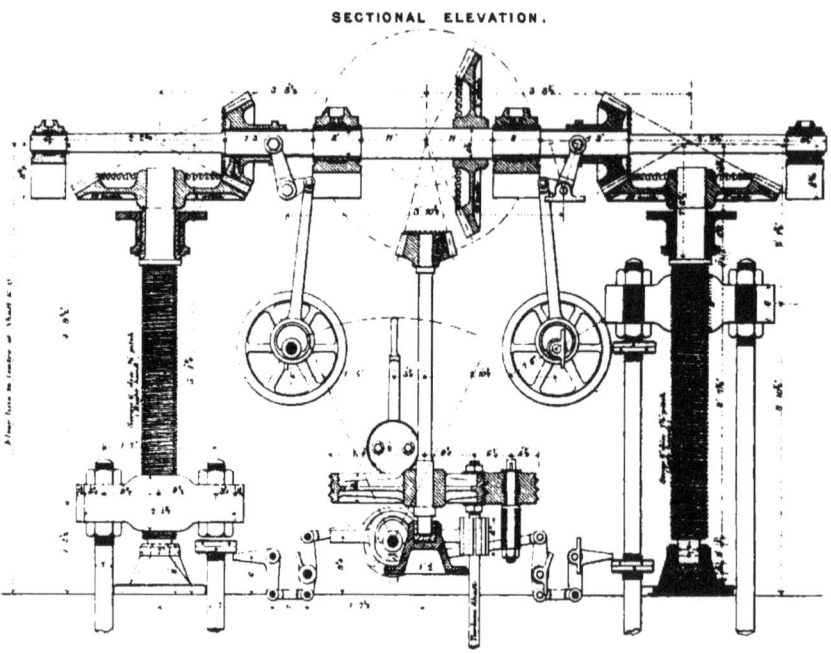

— DISCHARGE TUNNEL.

LARGE VALVES.

LY— ALL FRAMING OMITTED.

SHEET. 2.

DETAIL OF REVERSING MOTION.

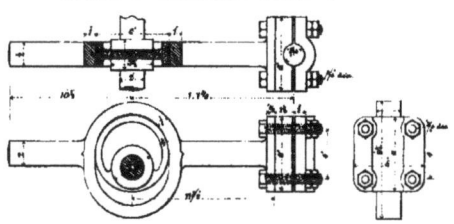

DETAIL OF DISCS FOR SELF-ACTING MOTION.

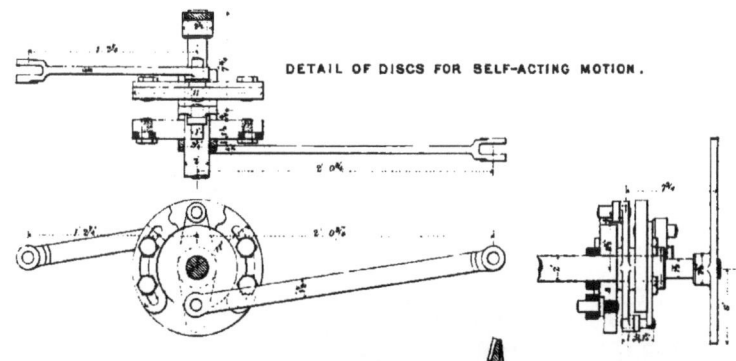

DETAIL OF CLUTCH MOTION.

CROSS SECTION.

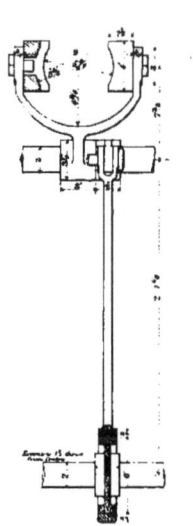
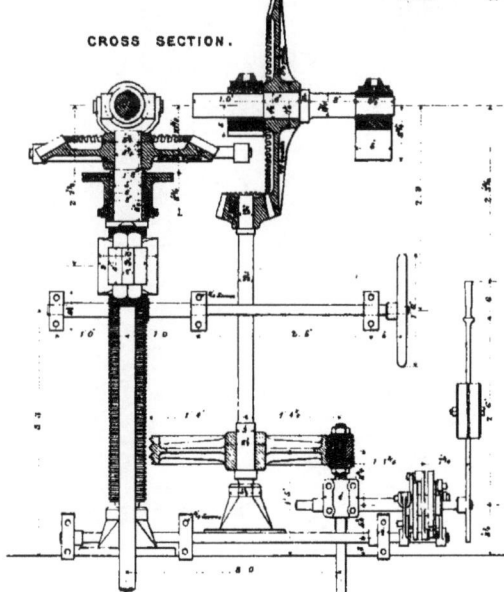

WOODHEAD RESERVOIR

GEARING FOR
DETAILS OF FRAMING —

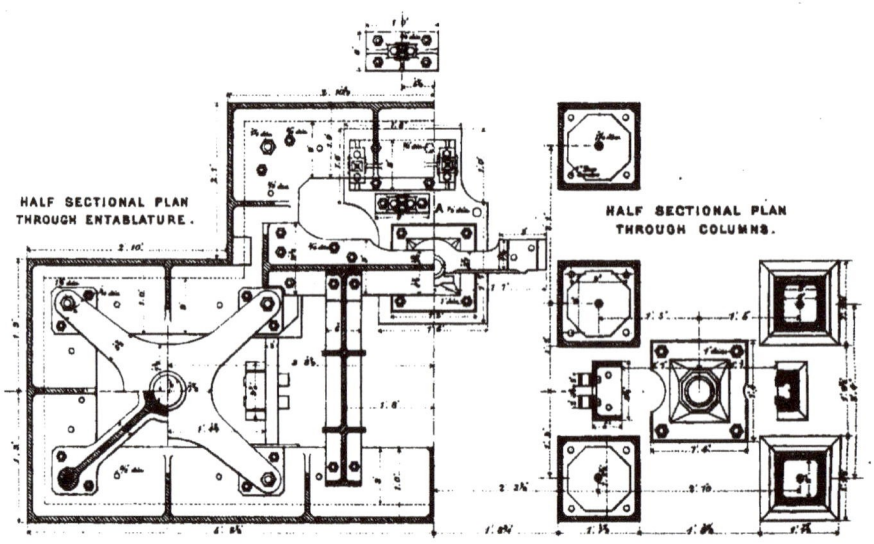

HALF SECTIONAL PLAN THROUGH ENTABLATURE.

HALF SECTIONAL PLAN THROUGH COLUMNS.

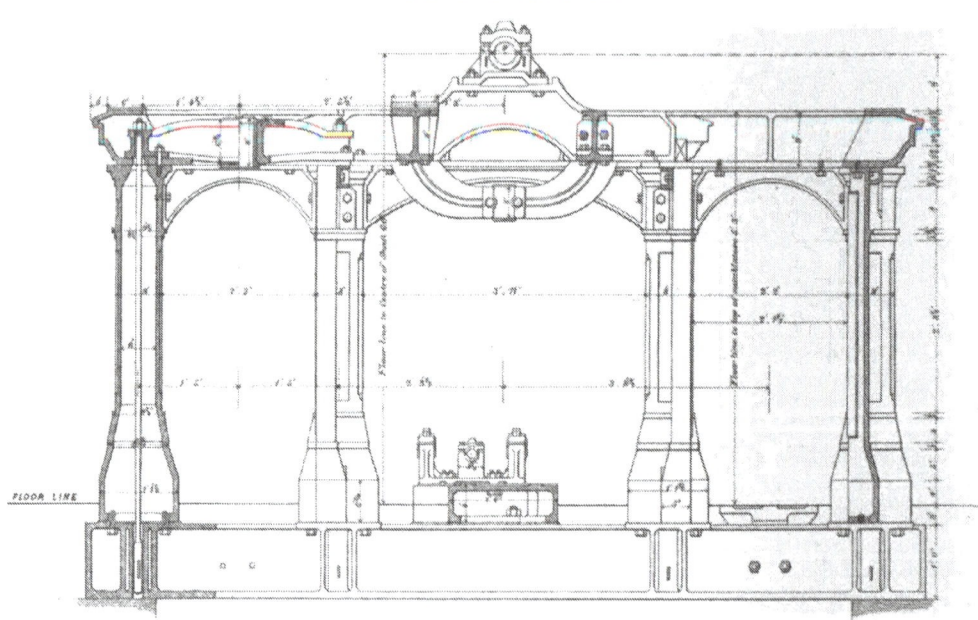

SECTIONAL ELEVATION.

SCALE

Manchester T. J. Day

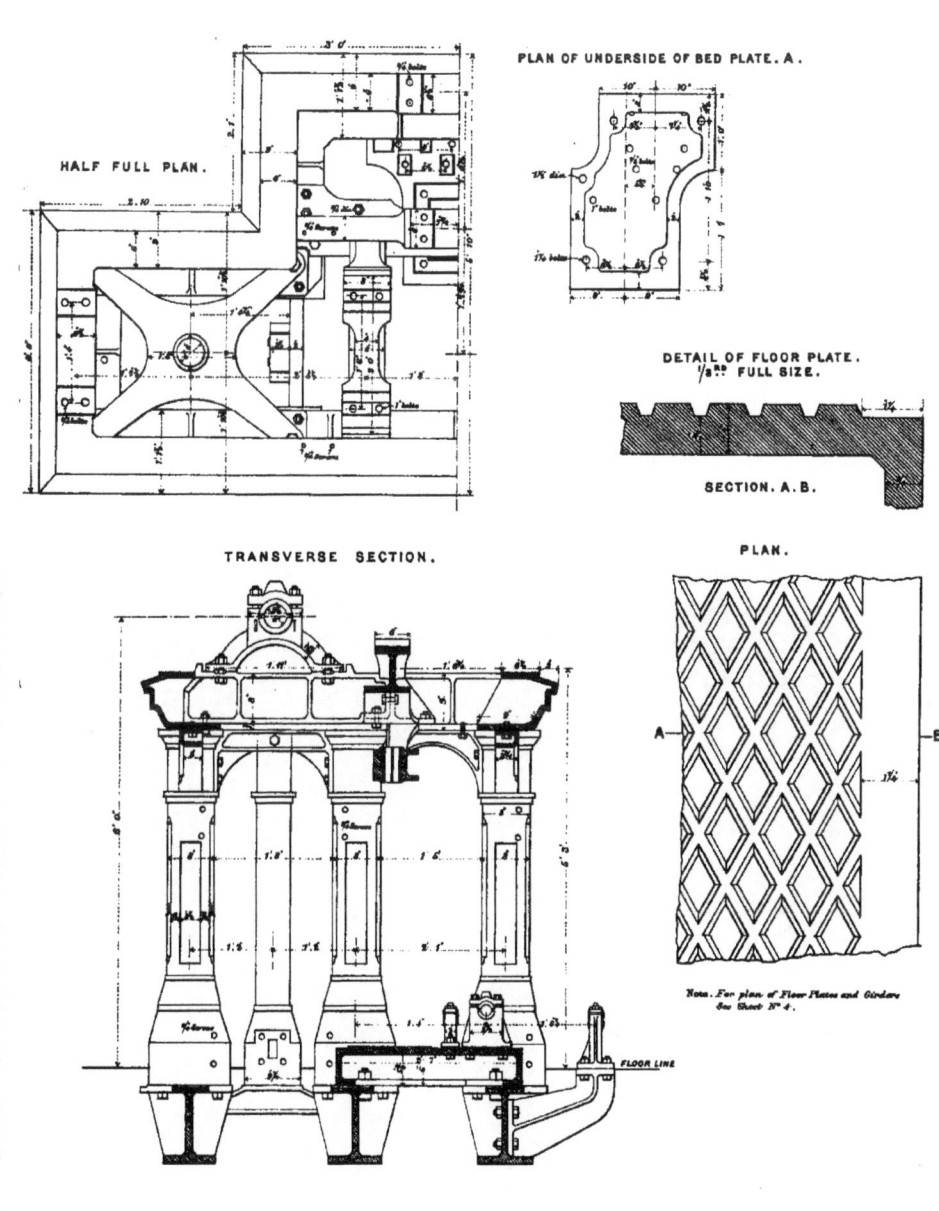

WOODHEAD RESERVOIR

GEARING FOR
DETAILS OF FLOOR

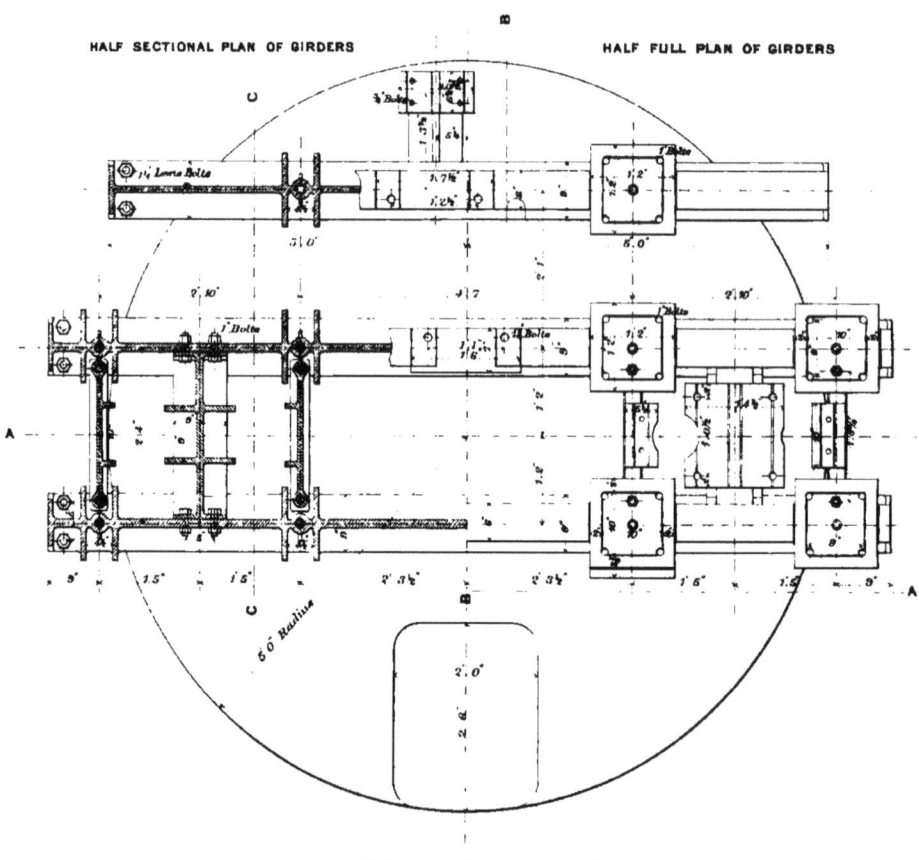

HALF SECTIONAL PLAN OF GIRDERS   HALF FULL PLAN OF GIRDERS

SECTION OF PLATES ON CENTRE LINE

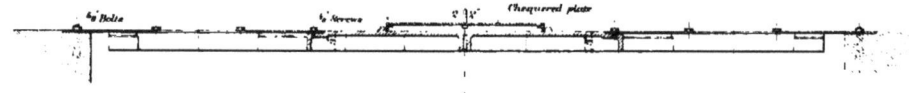

SECTION OF GIRDERS ON LINE A A.

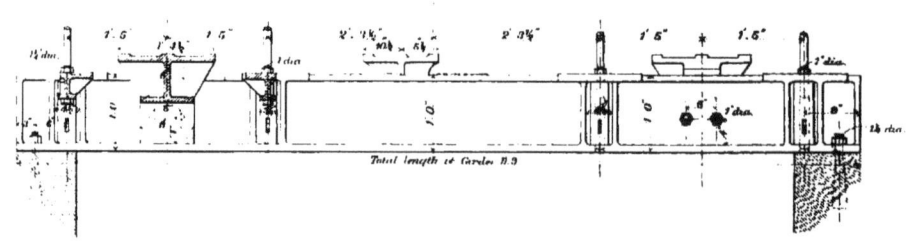

Manchester, T J Day

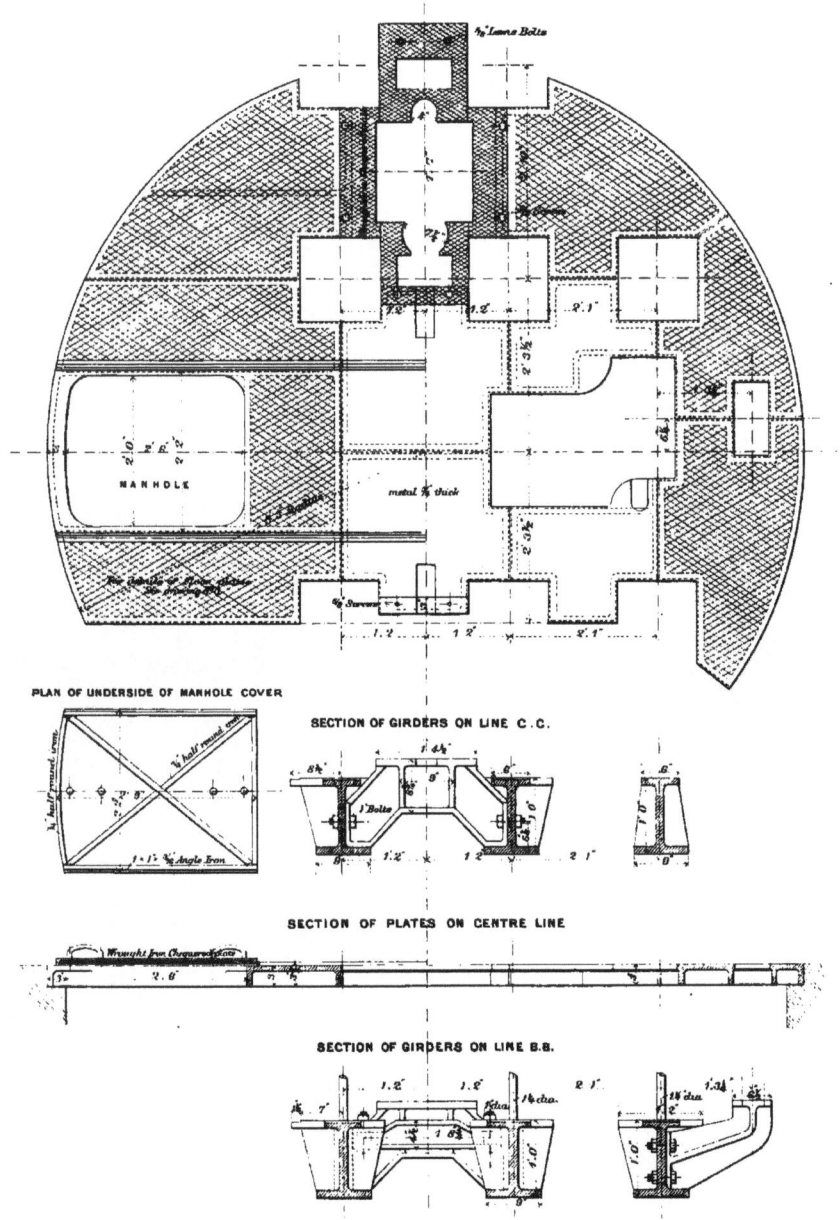

DIAGRAMS OF RAINFALL AT
FROM 1863 TO

18

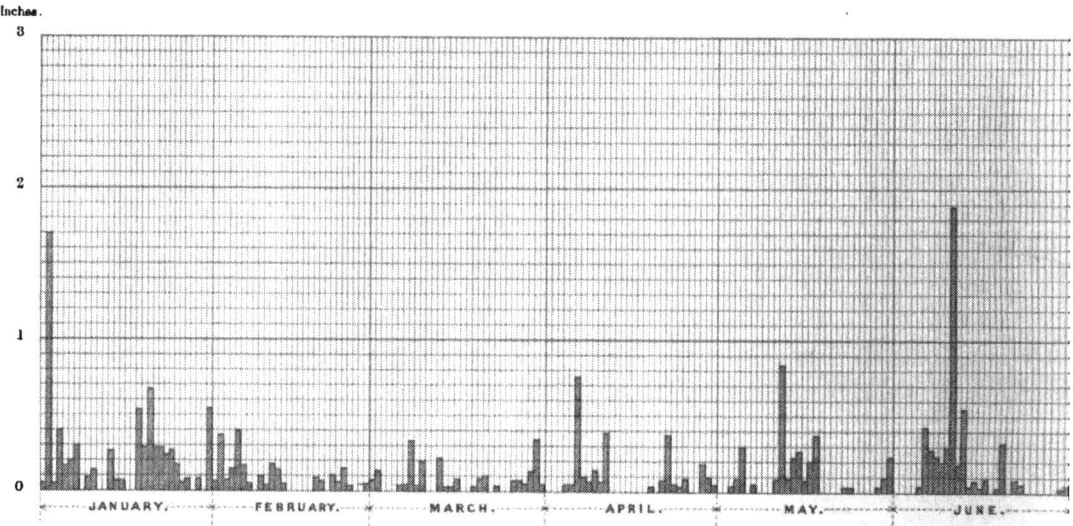

Total Rainf

18

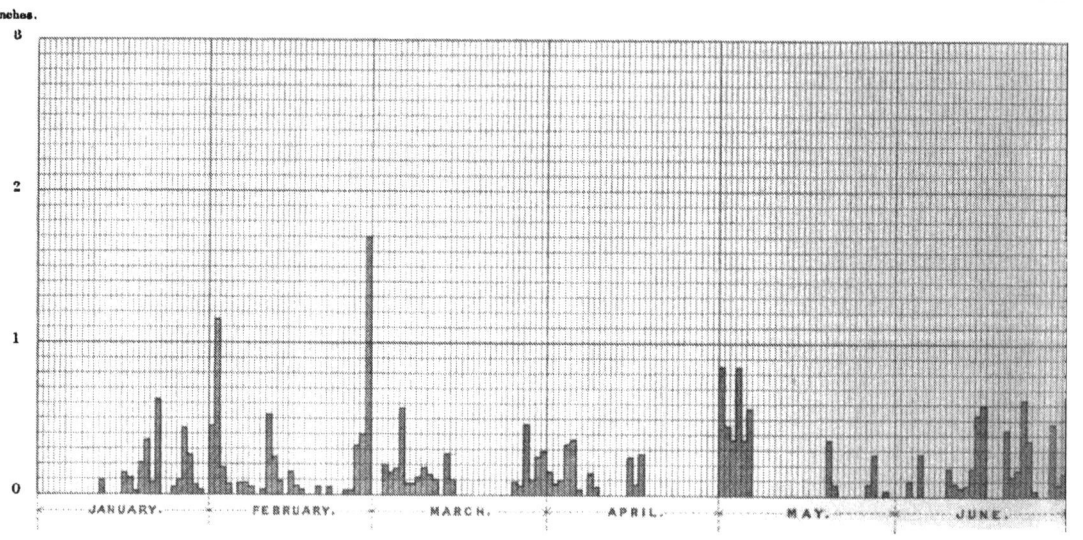

Total Rain
Dry Year. — The Rainf
being absorbed and t

Manchester, T. J. Day.

OODHEAD EMBANKMENT.

INCLUSIVE.

SHEET. 1.

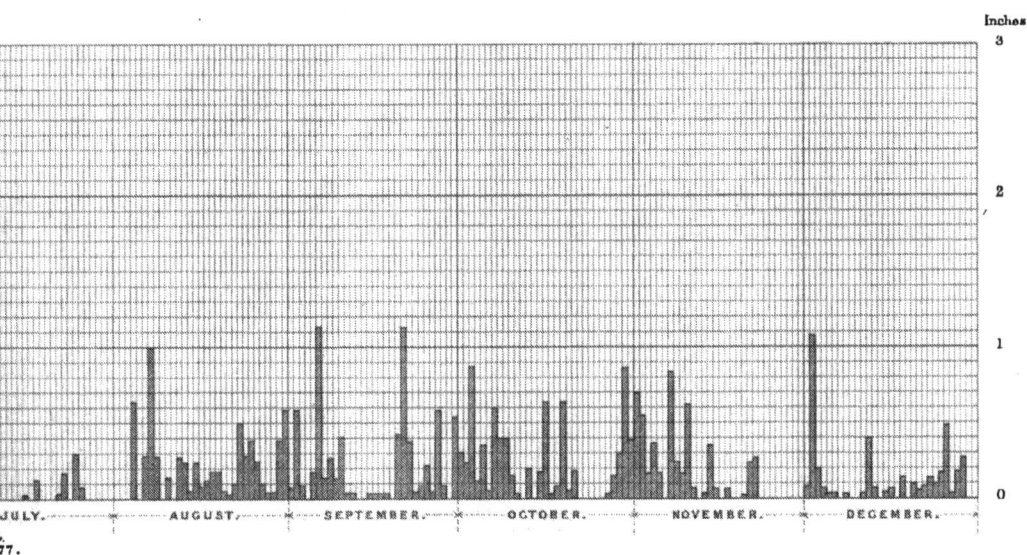

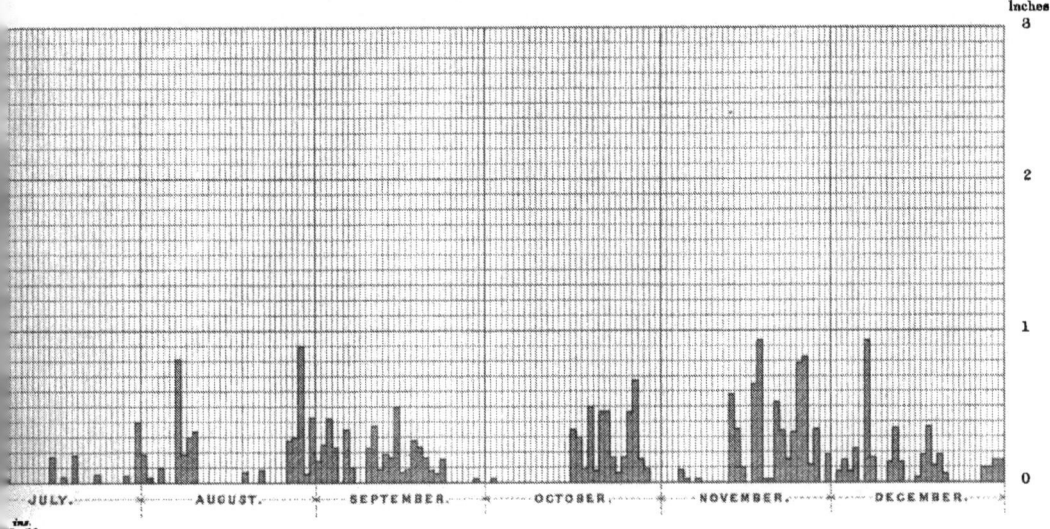

E. & F. N. Spon. 1884.

DIAGRAMS OF RAINFALL A[T]

FROM 1863 TO

18

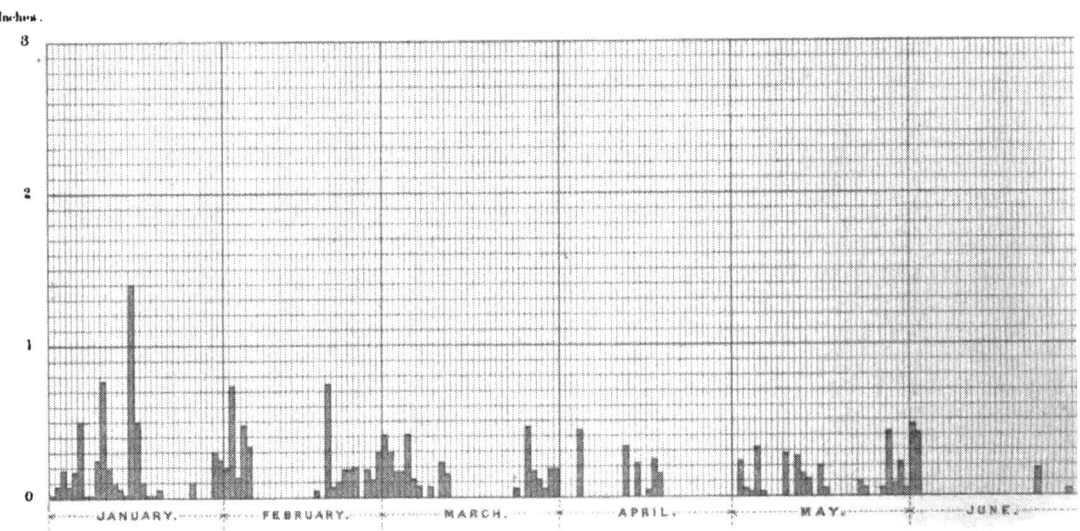

Total Rain
Very dry Year. — Springs and
after previous

18

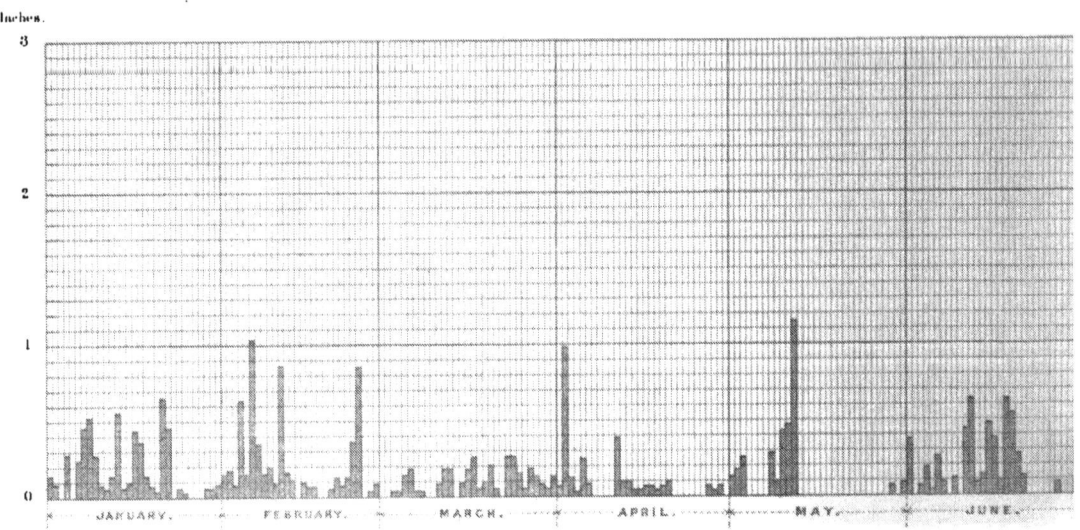

Total Rain
Very w

WOODHEAD EMBANKMENT.

SHEET. 2.

8 INCLUSIVE.

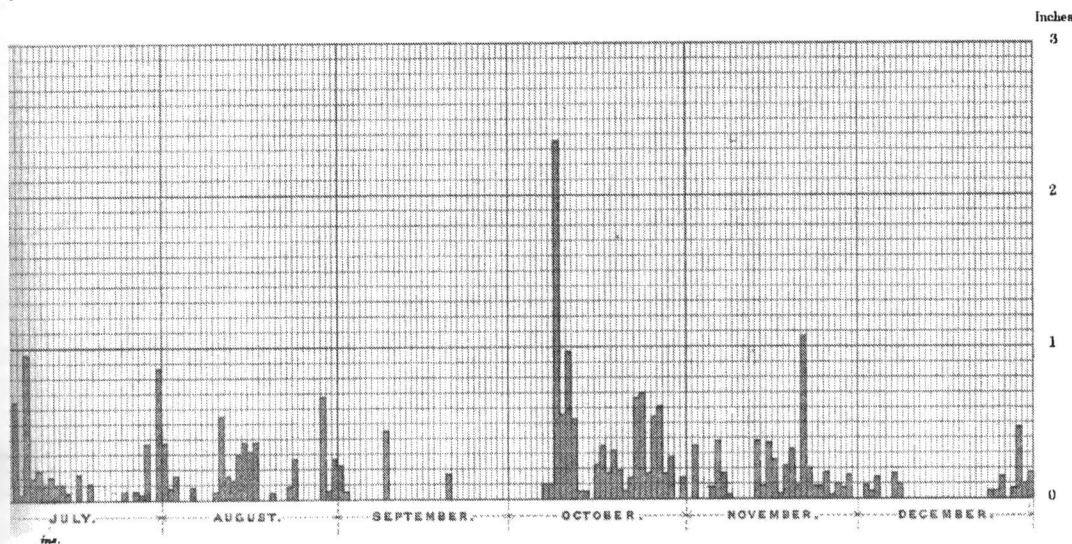

ins.
40·35.
sums not fully replenished,
ars' drought.

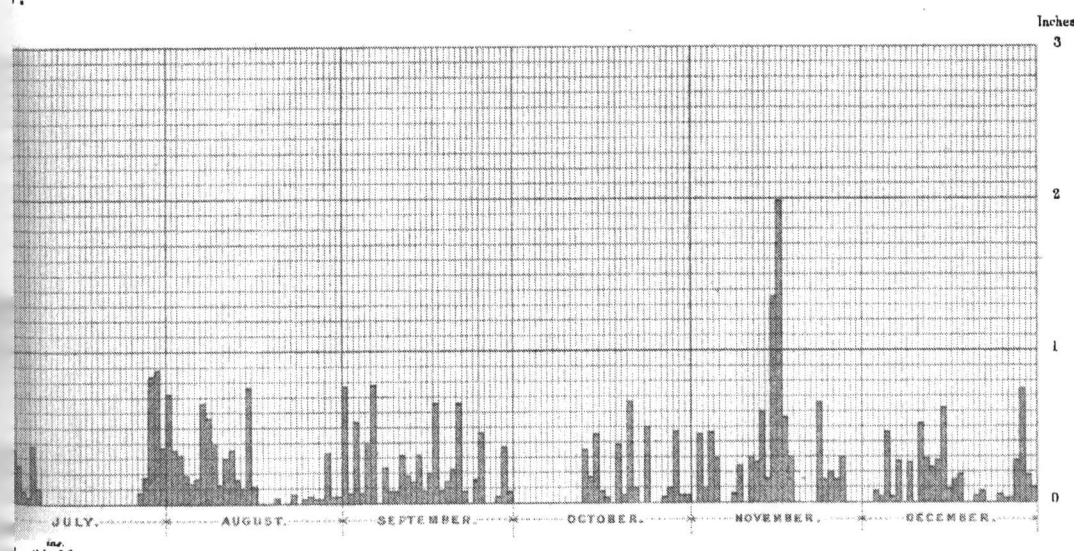

ins.
44·58.
Year.

DIAGRAMS OF RAINFALL AT

FROM 1863 TO 1

186

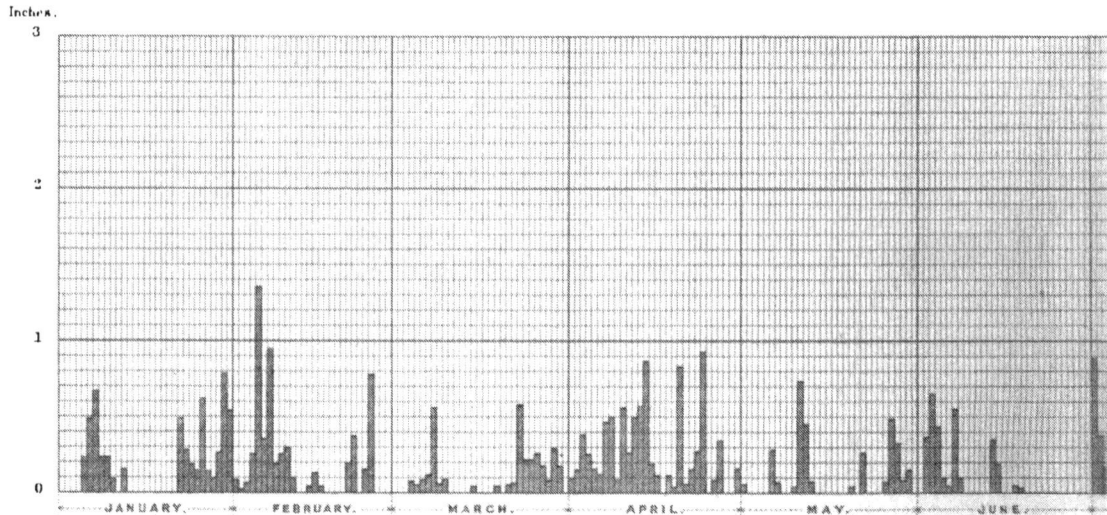

Total Rainfa

186

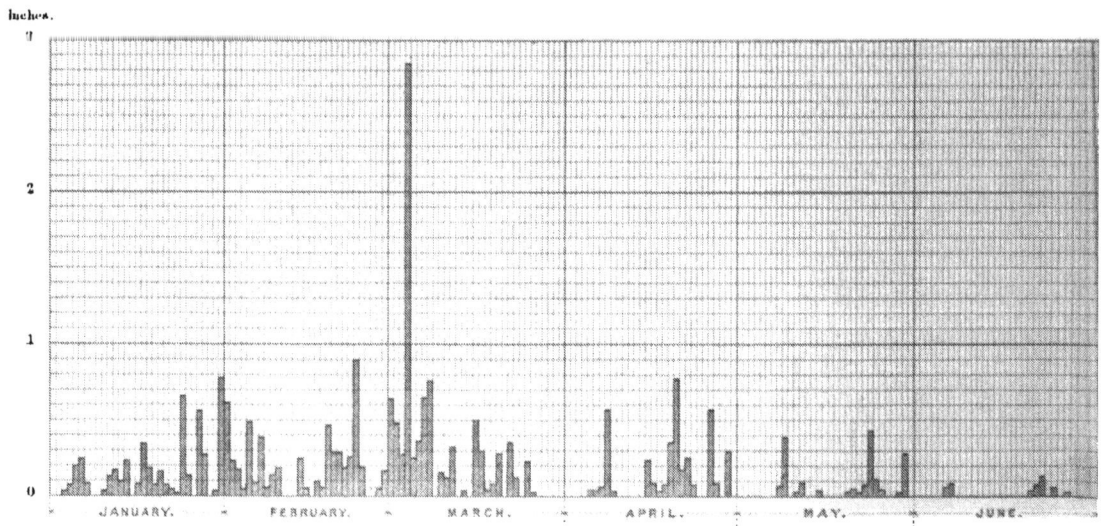

Total Rain

Extraordinary dry Summer. - Rain
being the unequal fall of R

Average Rainfall of the

WOODHEAD EMBANKMENT.

SHEET. 3.

 68 INCLUSIVE.

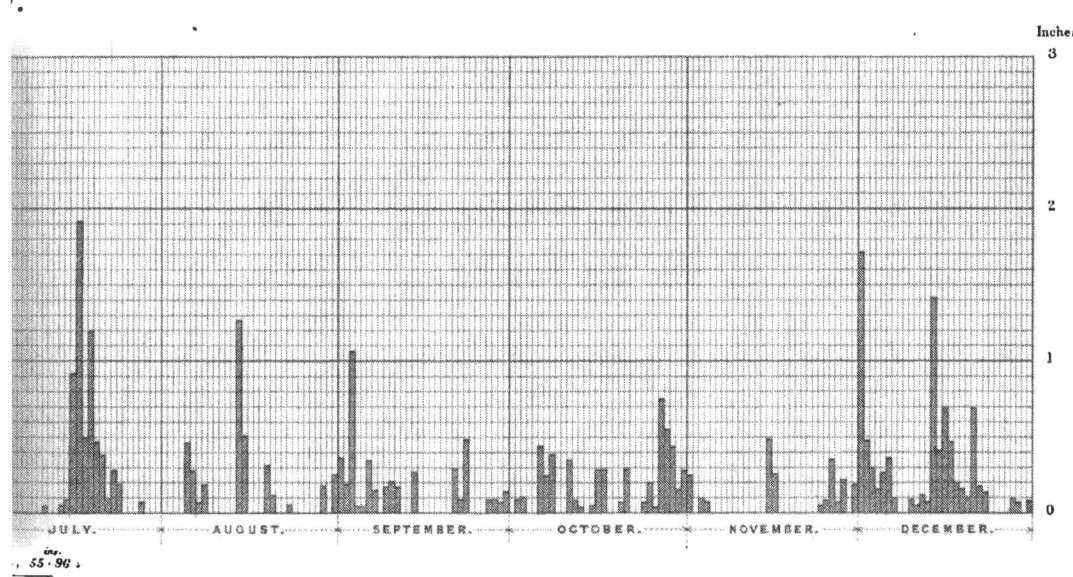

55·96

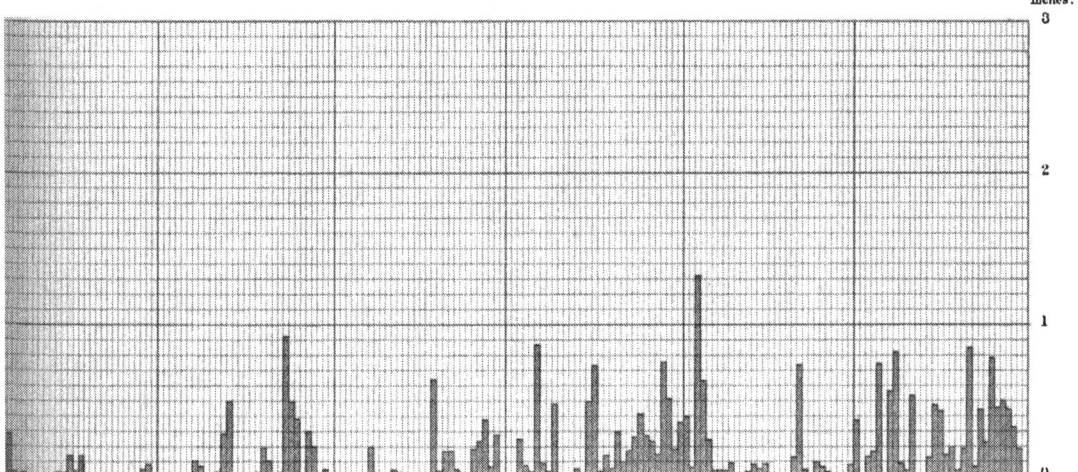

52·67

up to the average, the peculiarity
during the monthly periods.

years = 51·99 inches.

E & F N Spon 1884.

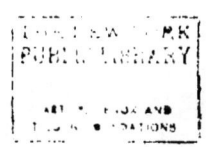

SEPARATING WEIR

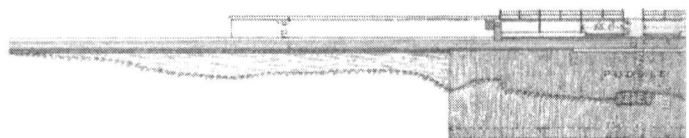
LONGITUDINAL SECTION ALONG C

SECTION A.B.

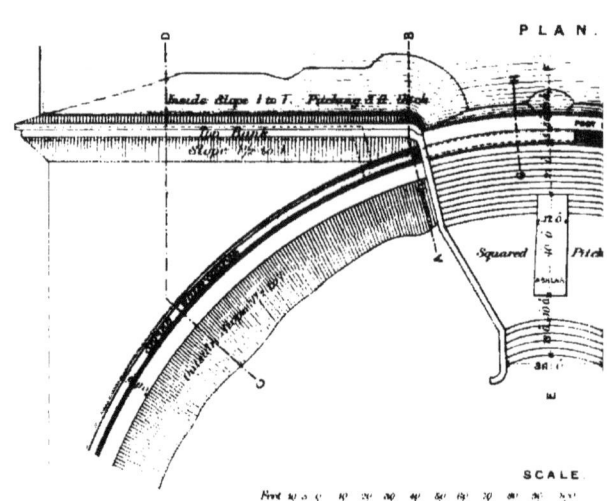
PLAN.

SCALE

SECTION E

SEPARATING ARRANGEMENT FOR SMALL STREAMS
SECTION.
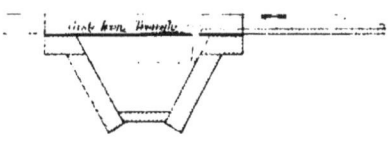

PLAN.
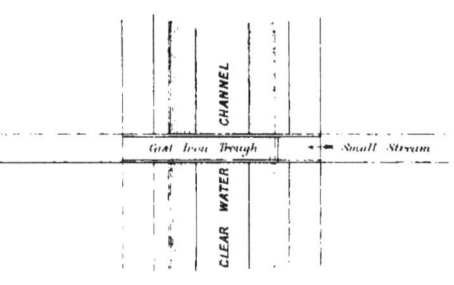

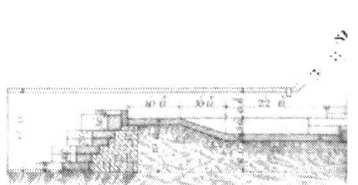
SECTIONAL P

SCALE
SCALE FOR

Manchester, T J Day

T CROWDEN BROOK.

ENTRE OF WATERCOURSE.

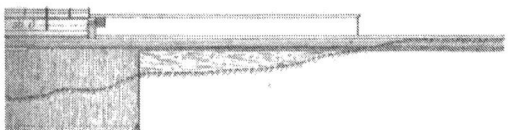

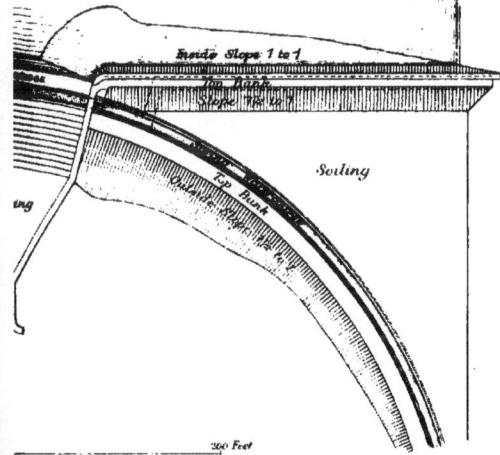

SECTION C.D.

ELEVATION SHEWING CULVERTS.

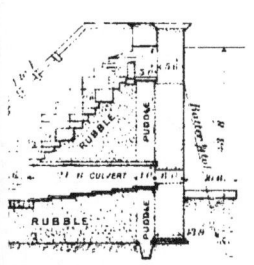

SECTION G.H.

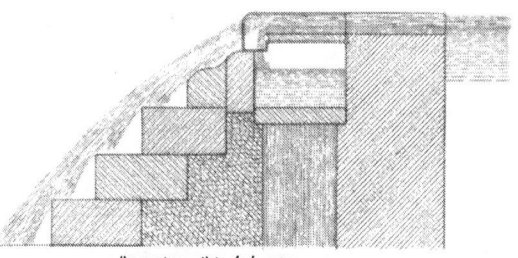

Separation of turbid water in Large streams (Pure water coloured blue)

N SHEWING CULVERTS.

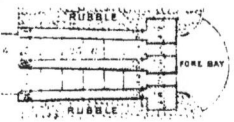

DETAILS

ARGED DETAILS

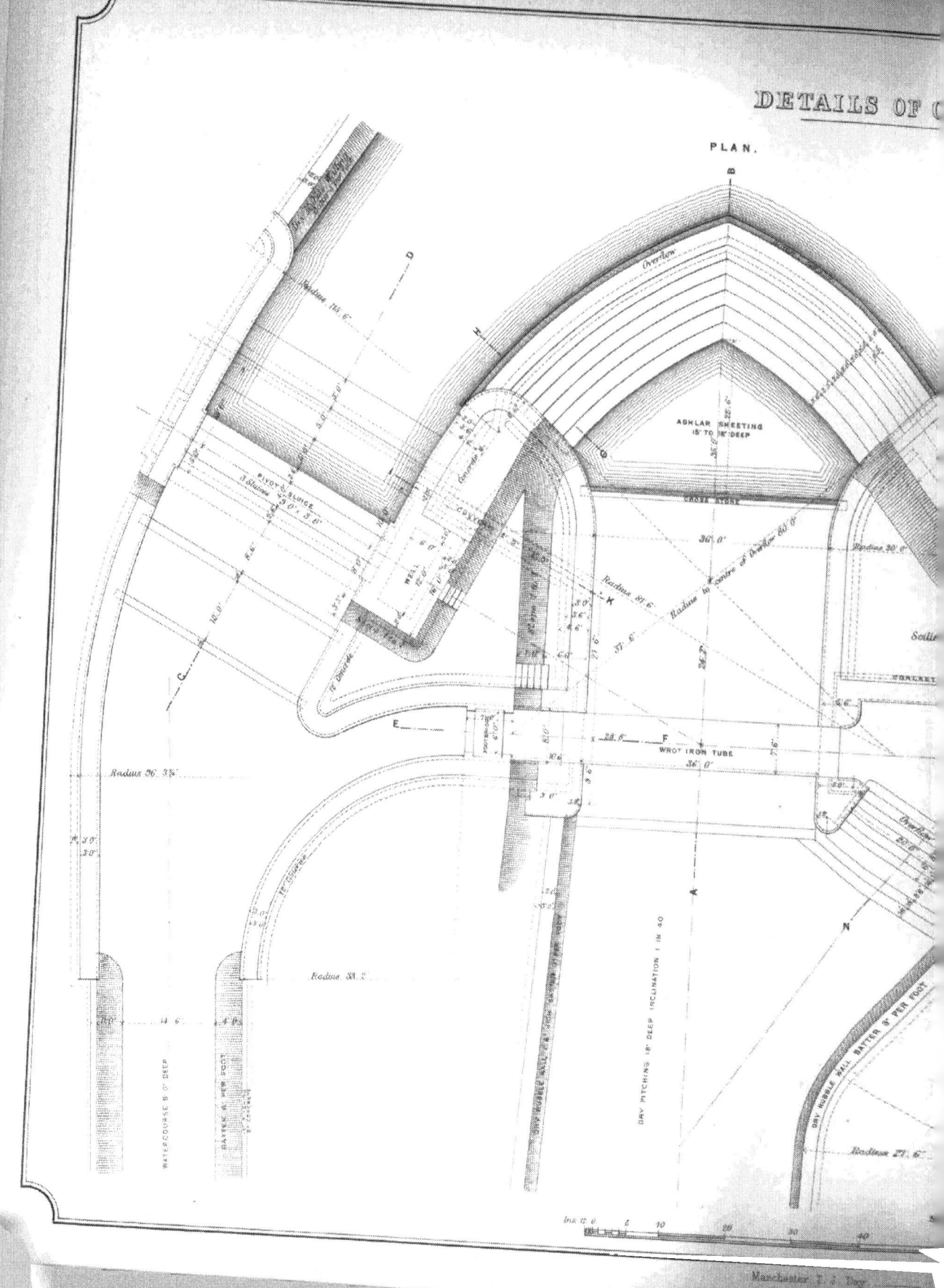

OWDEN WEIR.

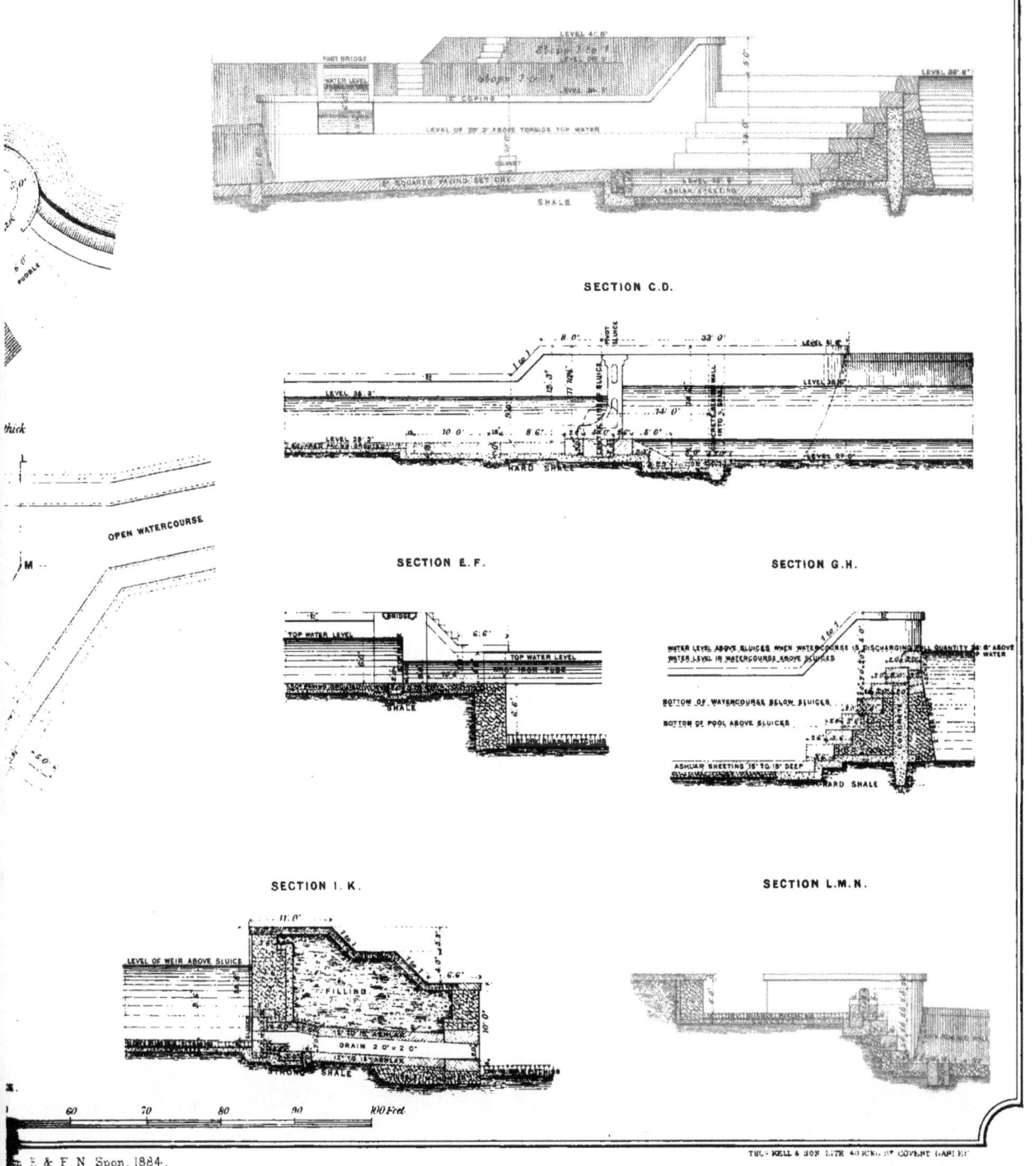

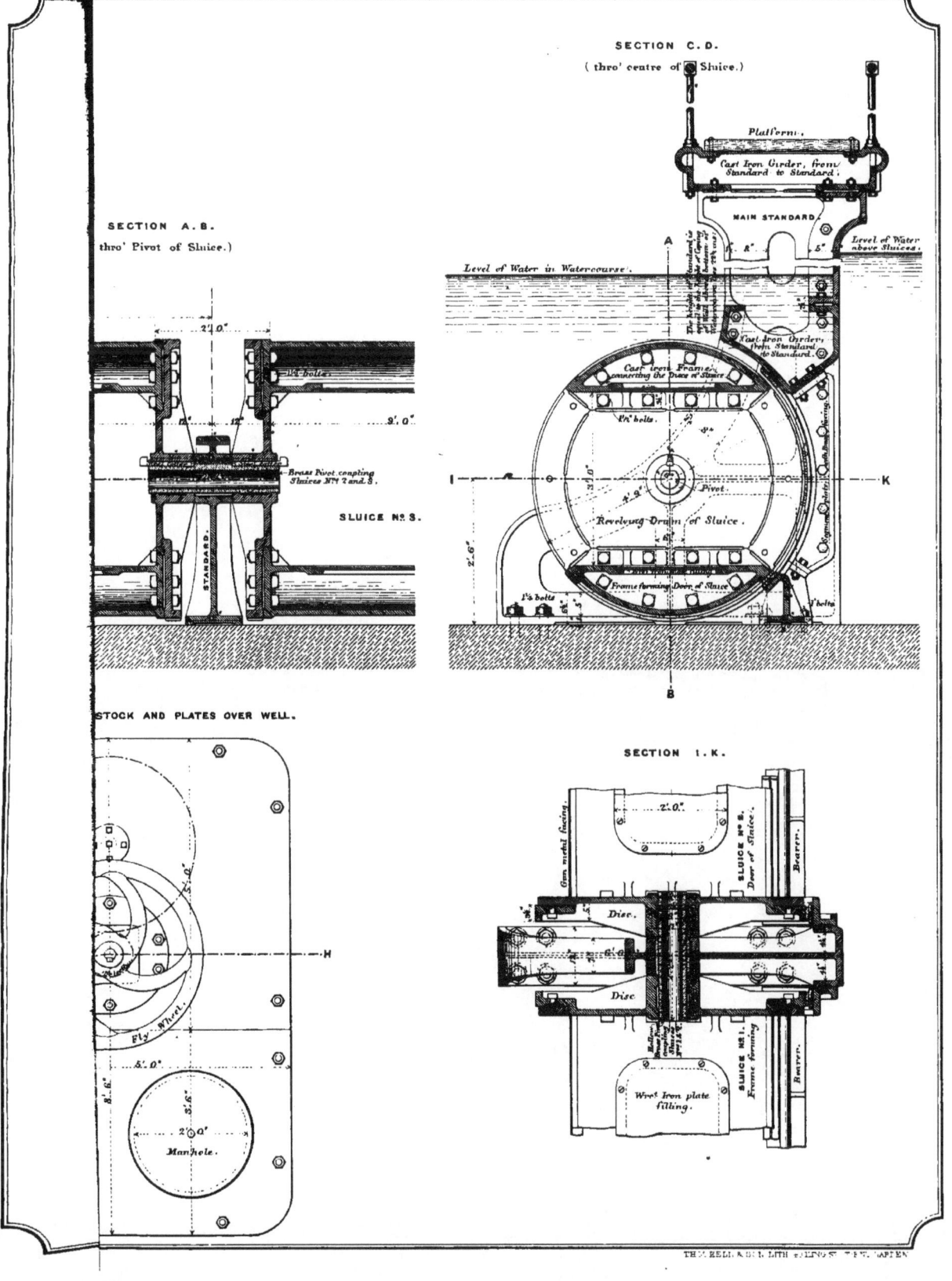

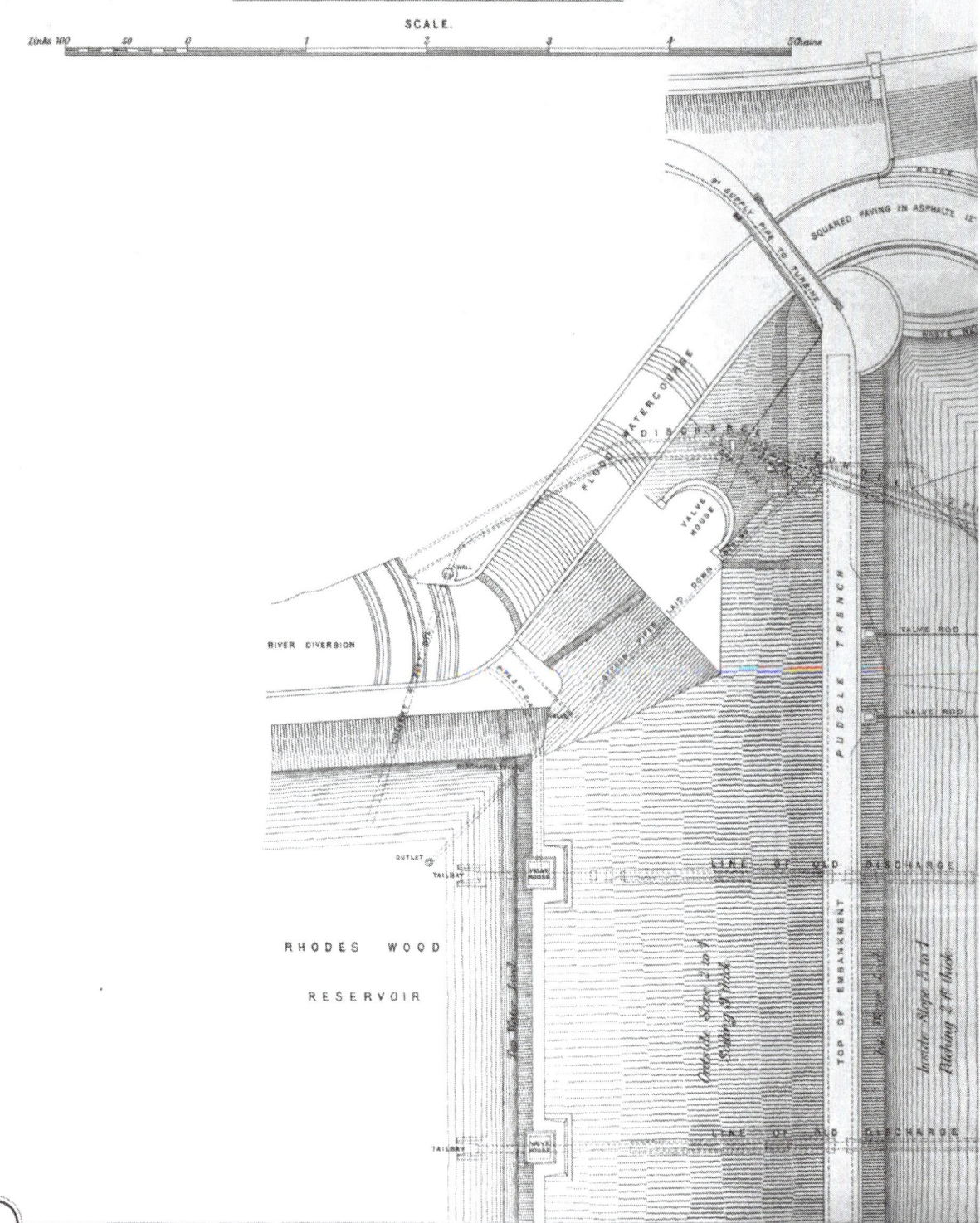

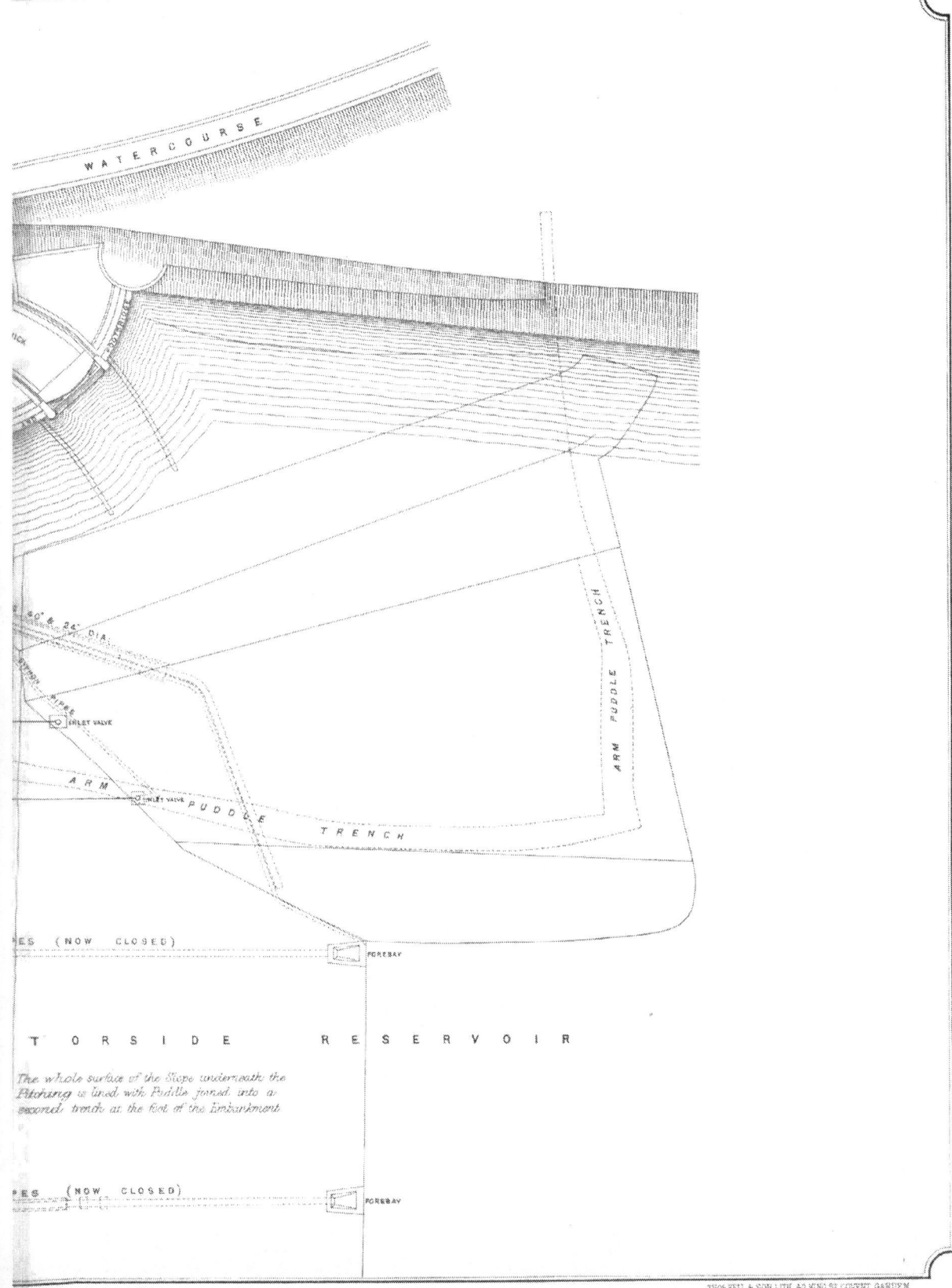

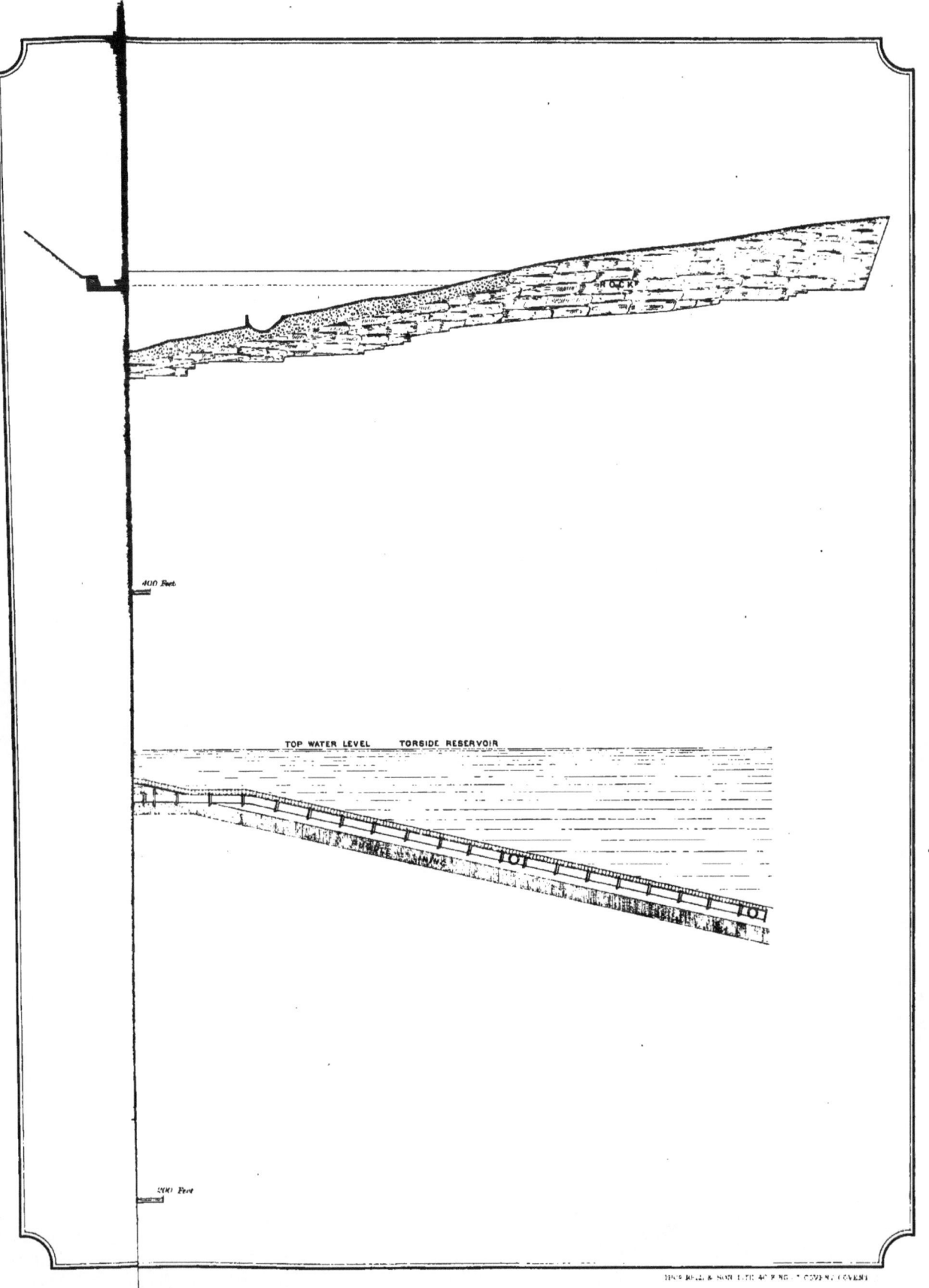

RHODES WOOD RESERVOIR.

PLAN OF EMBANKMENT, DISCHARGE PIPES, SYPHON, WASTE WEIR and FLOOD WATERCOURSES.

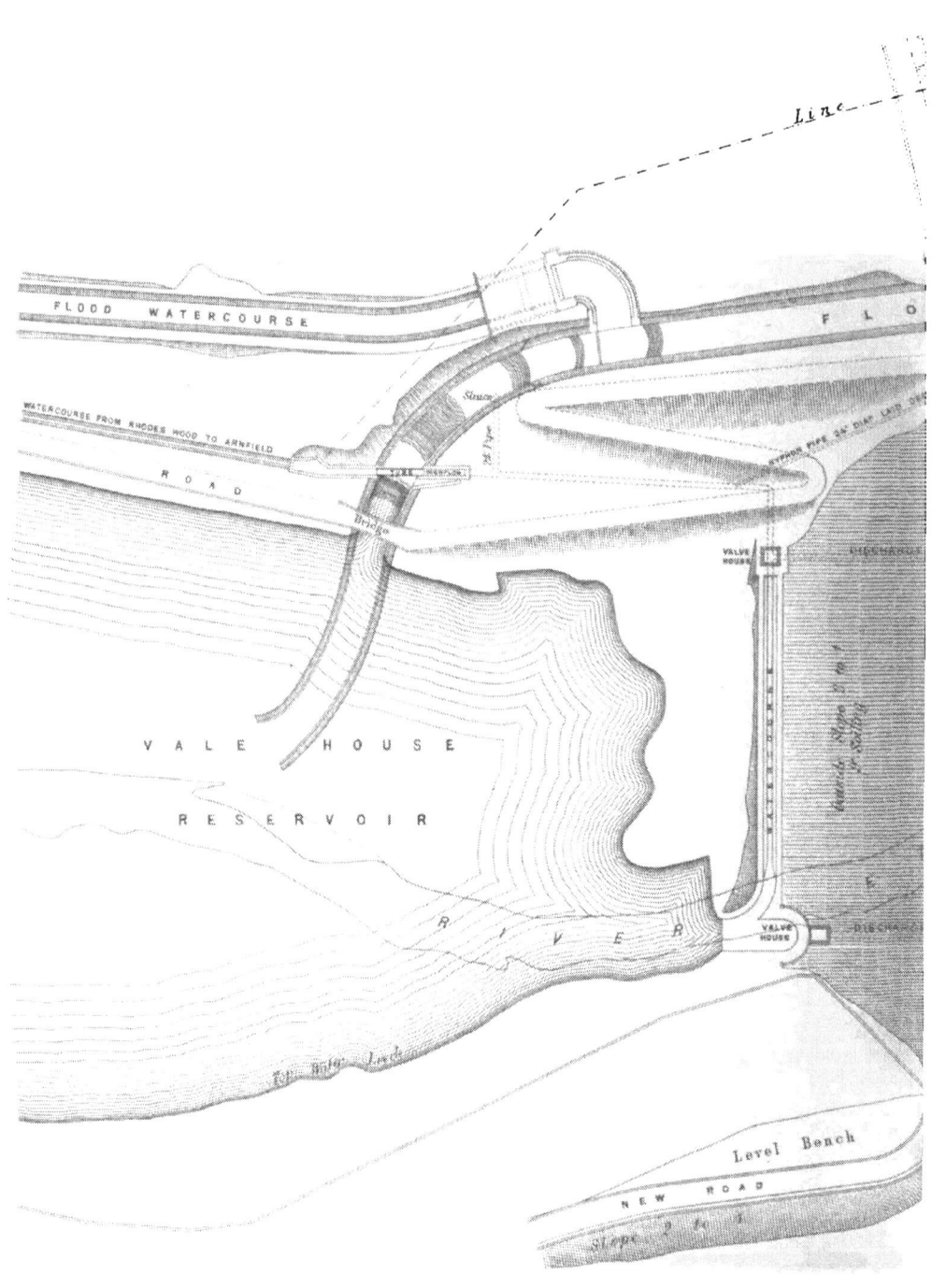

SCALE.

Feet 10 5 0 10 20 30 40 50 60 70 80 90 100   200 Feet

RHODES WO[OD]

LONGITUDINAL SECTI[ON]

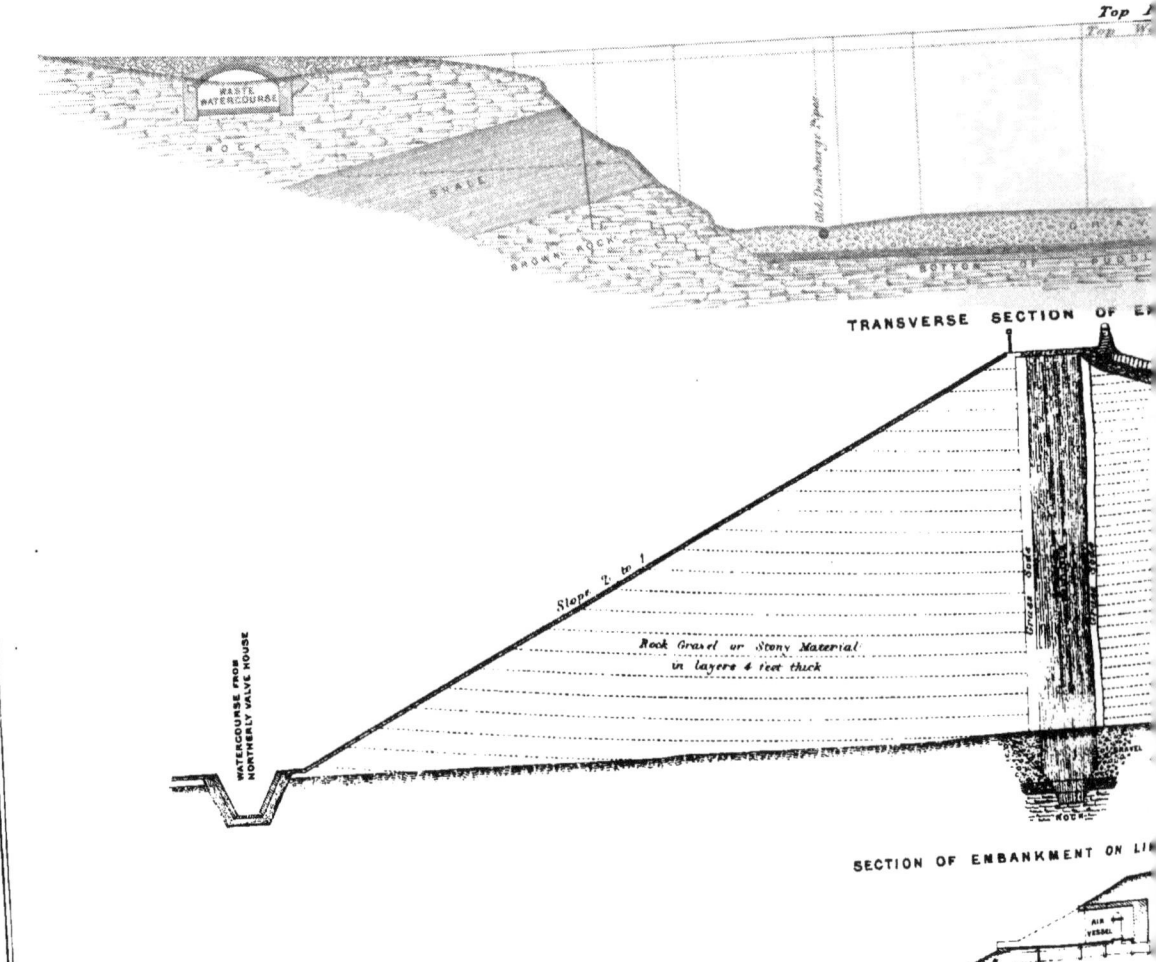

) RESERVOIR.

OF PUDDLE TRENCH.

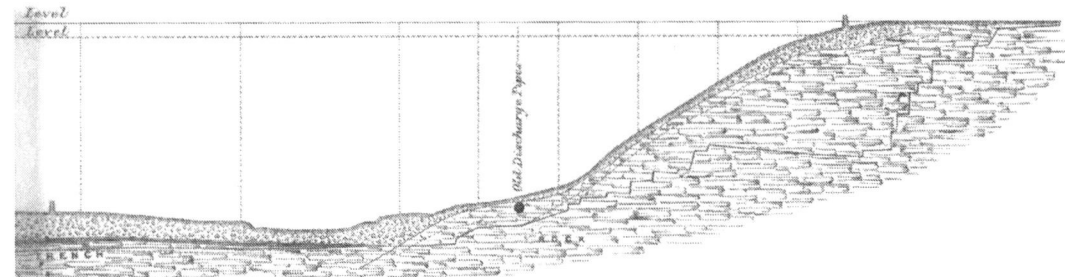

KMENT.

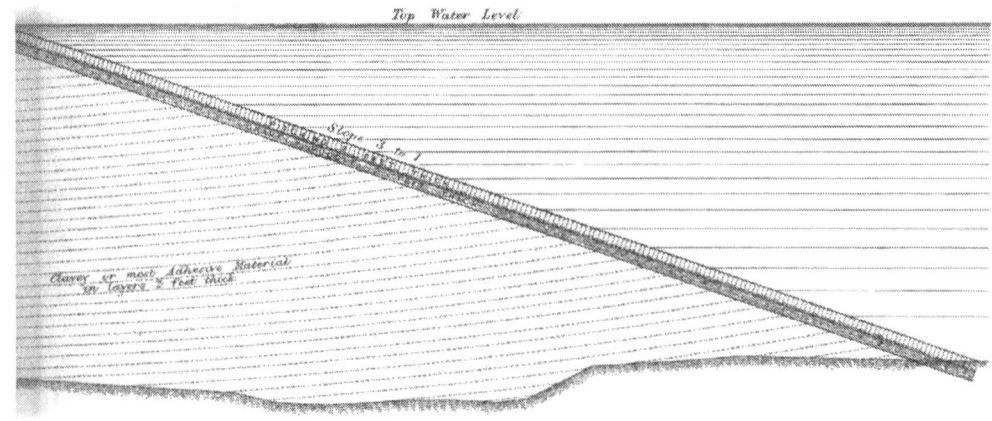

SYPHON.

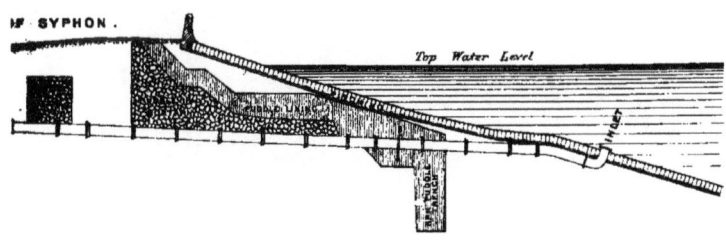

UDINAL SECTION.

VERSE SECTIONS.

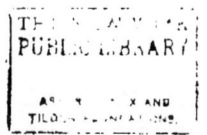

VALE HOUSE

PLAN OF EMBANKMENT, WASTE WATERCOURSE &c.

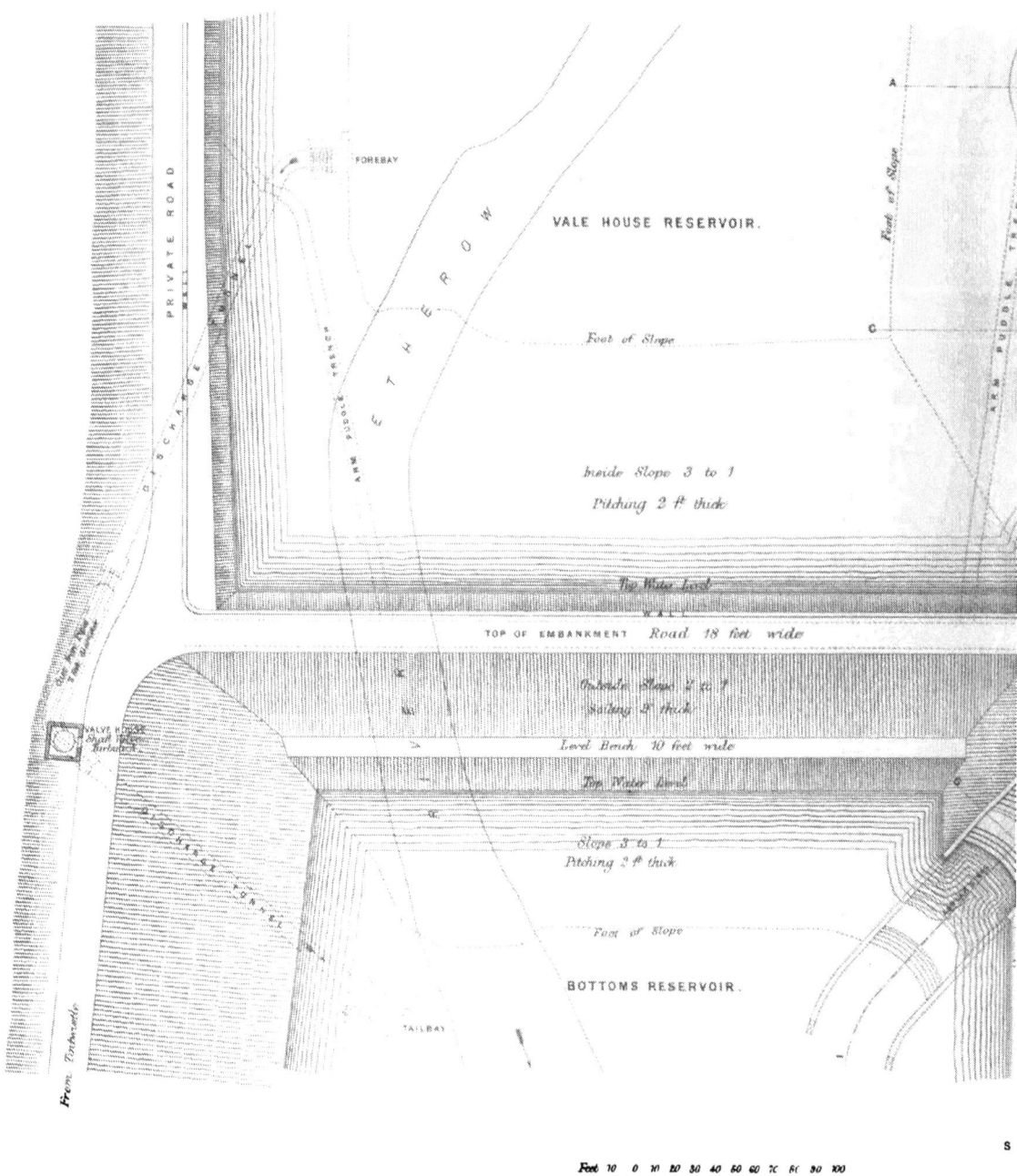

Manchester, T J Day

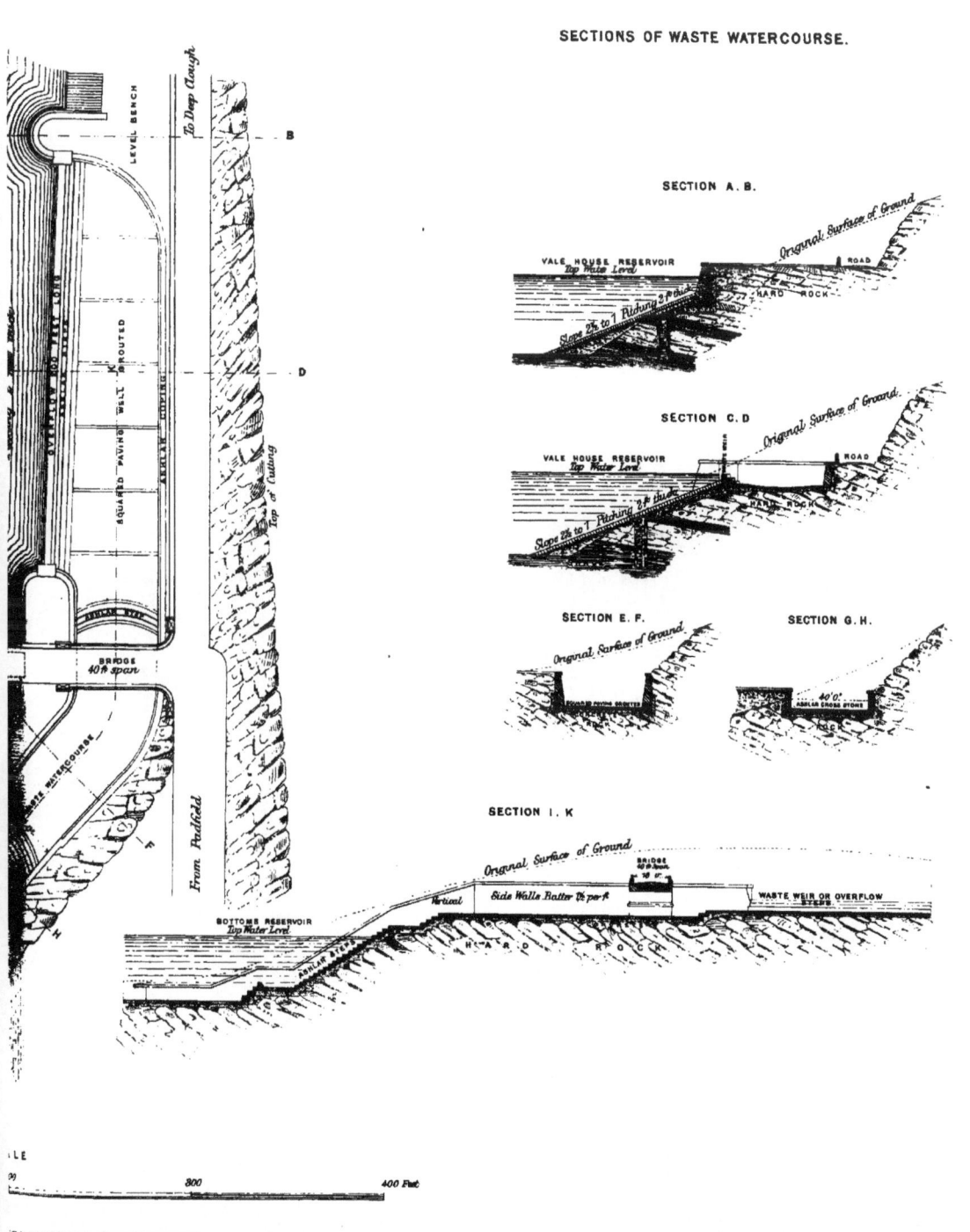

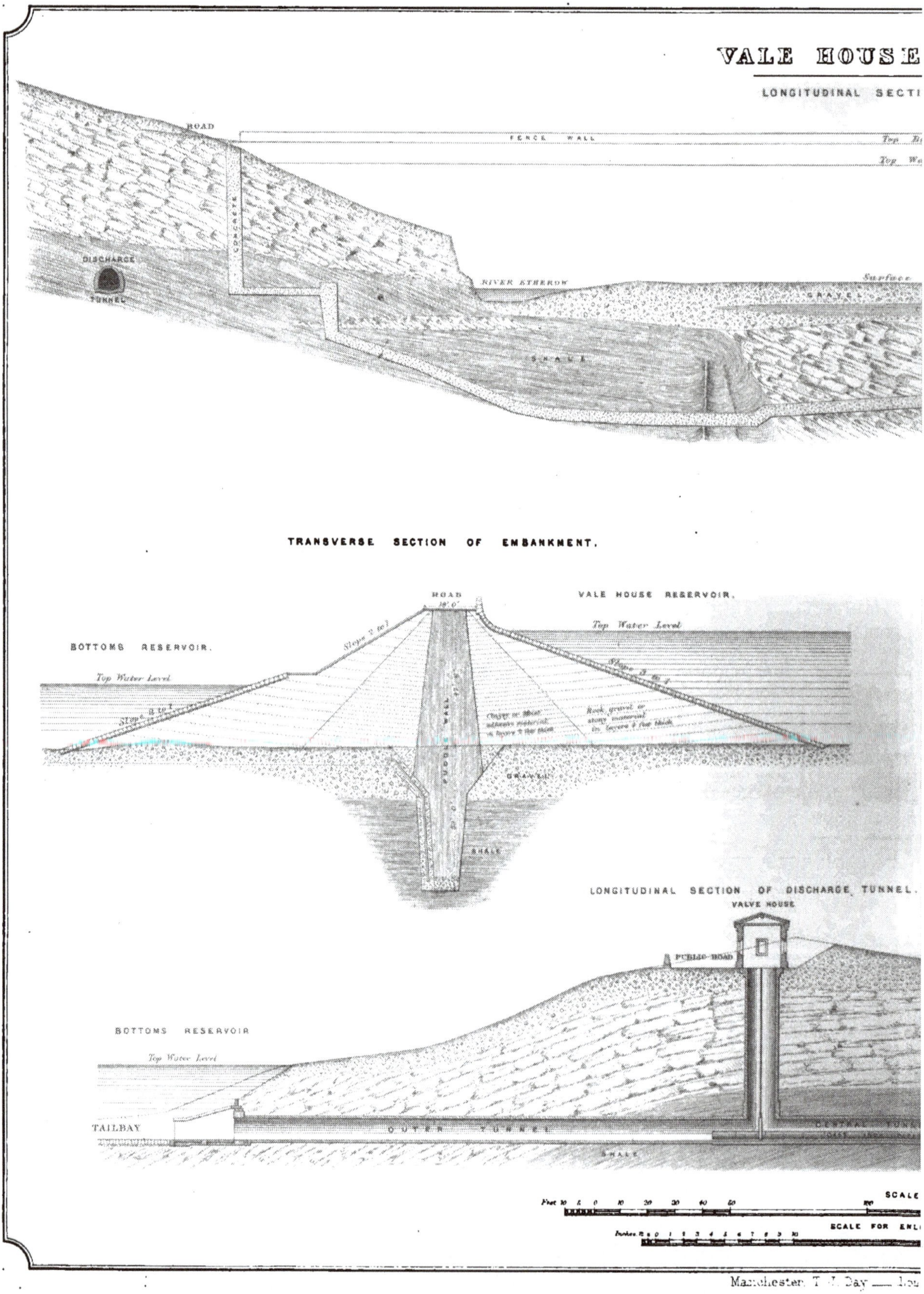

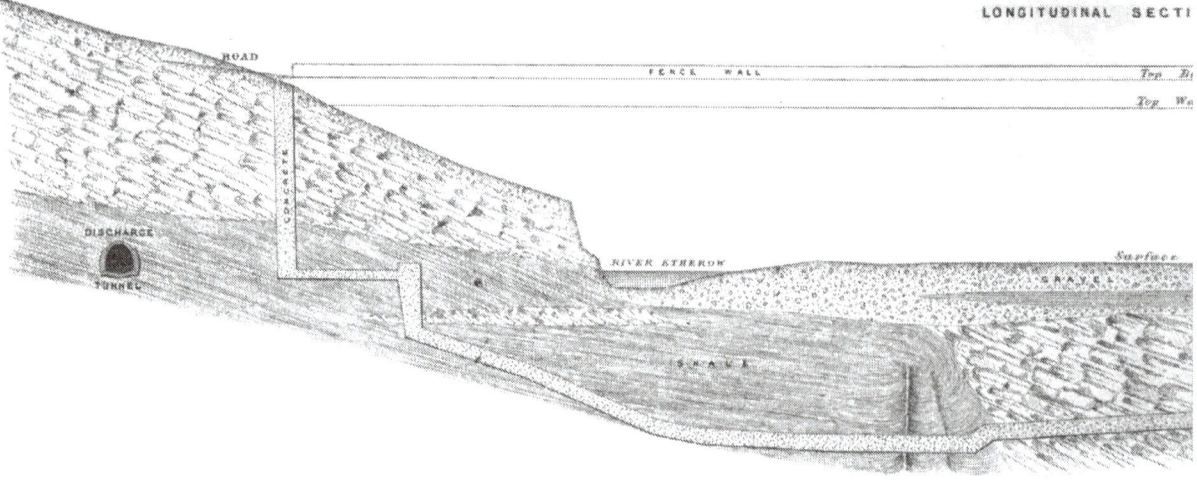

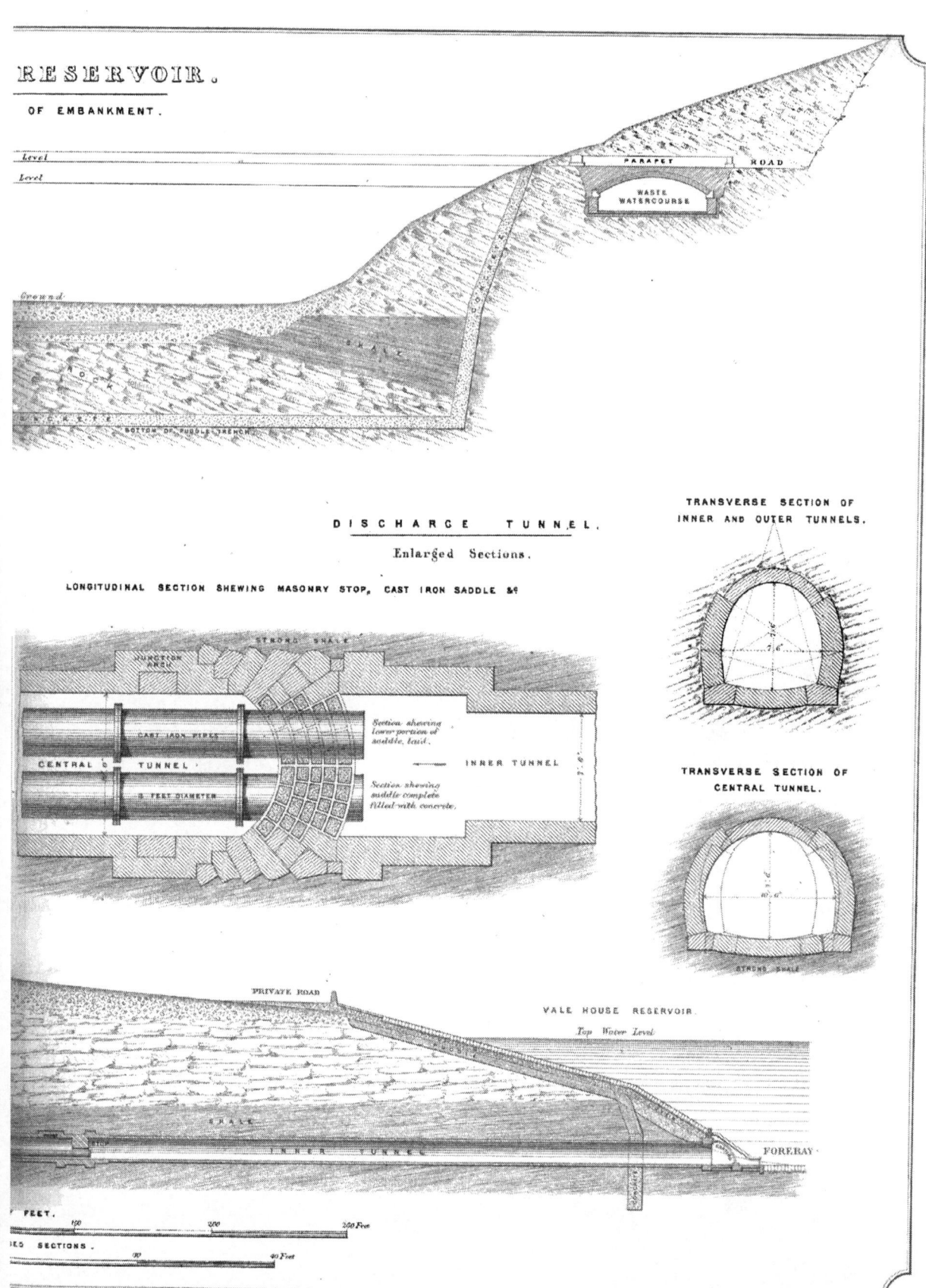

THE NEW YORK
PUBLIC LIBRARY

ASTOR LENOX AND
TILDEN FOUNDATIONS.

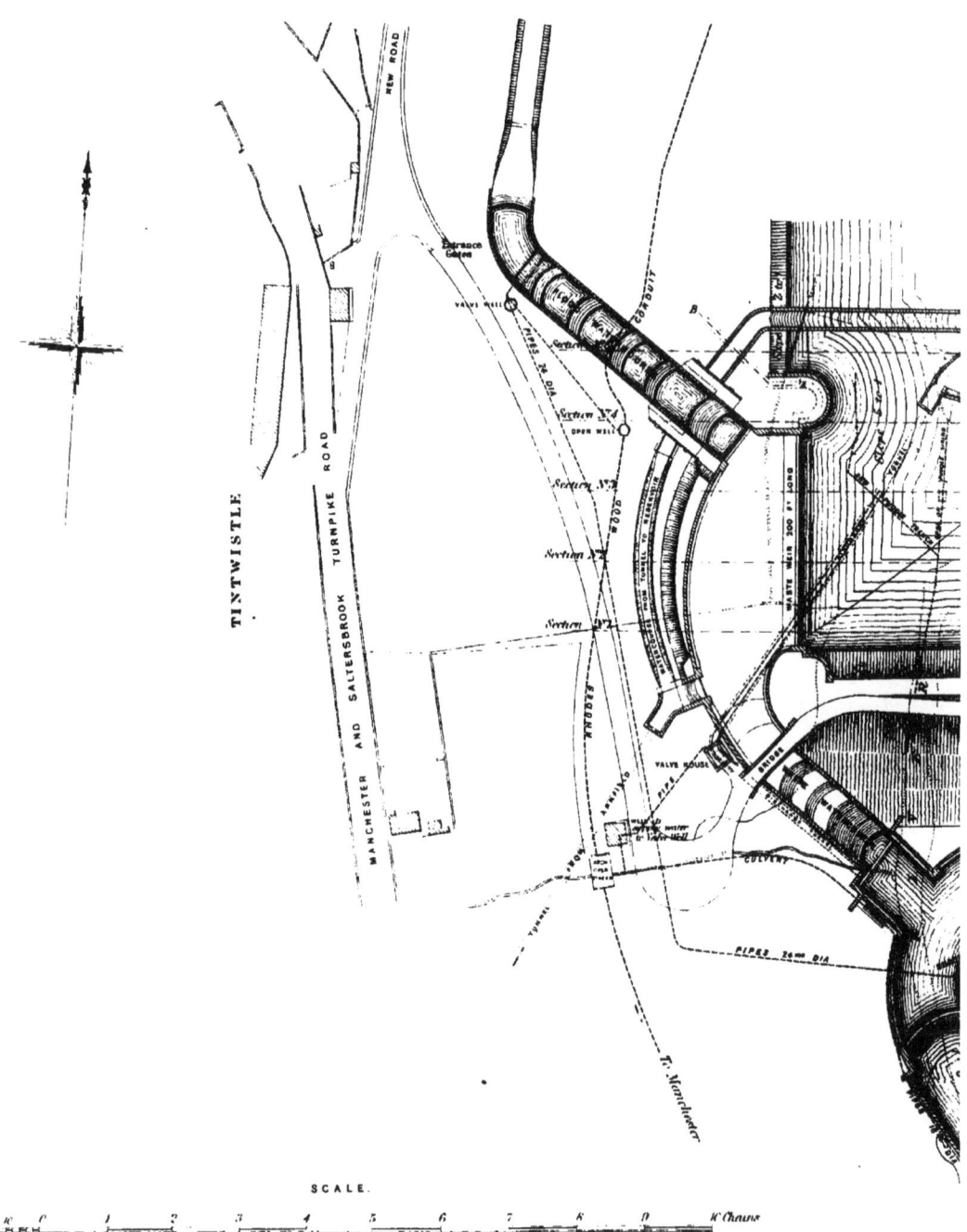

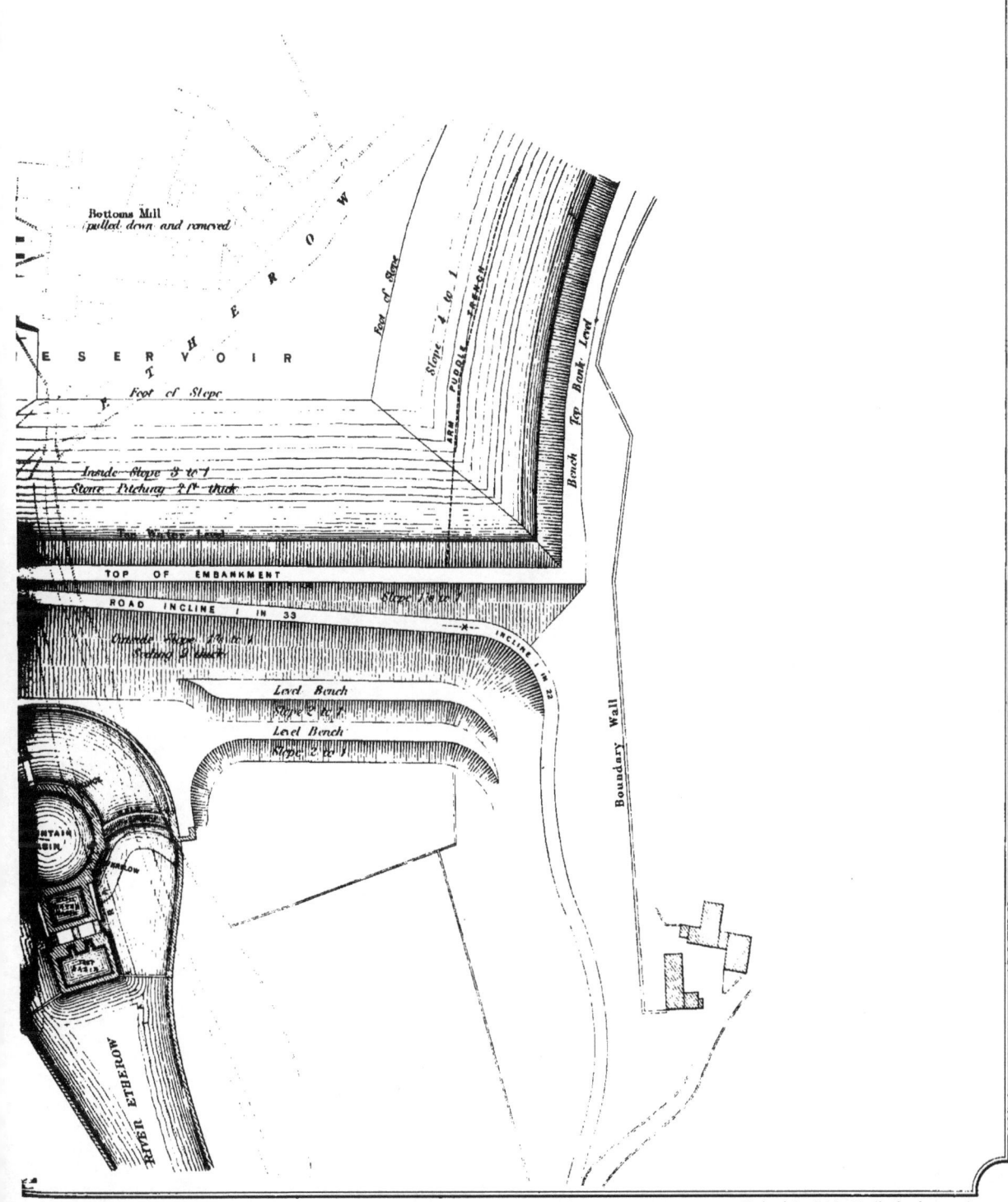

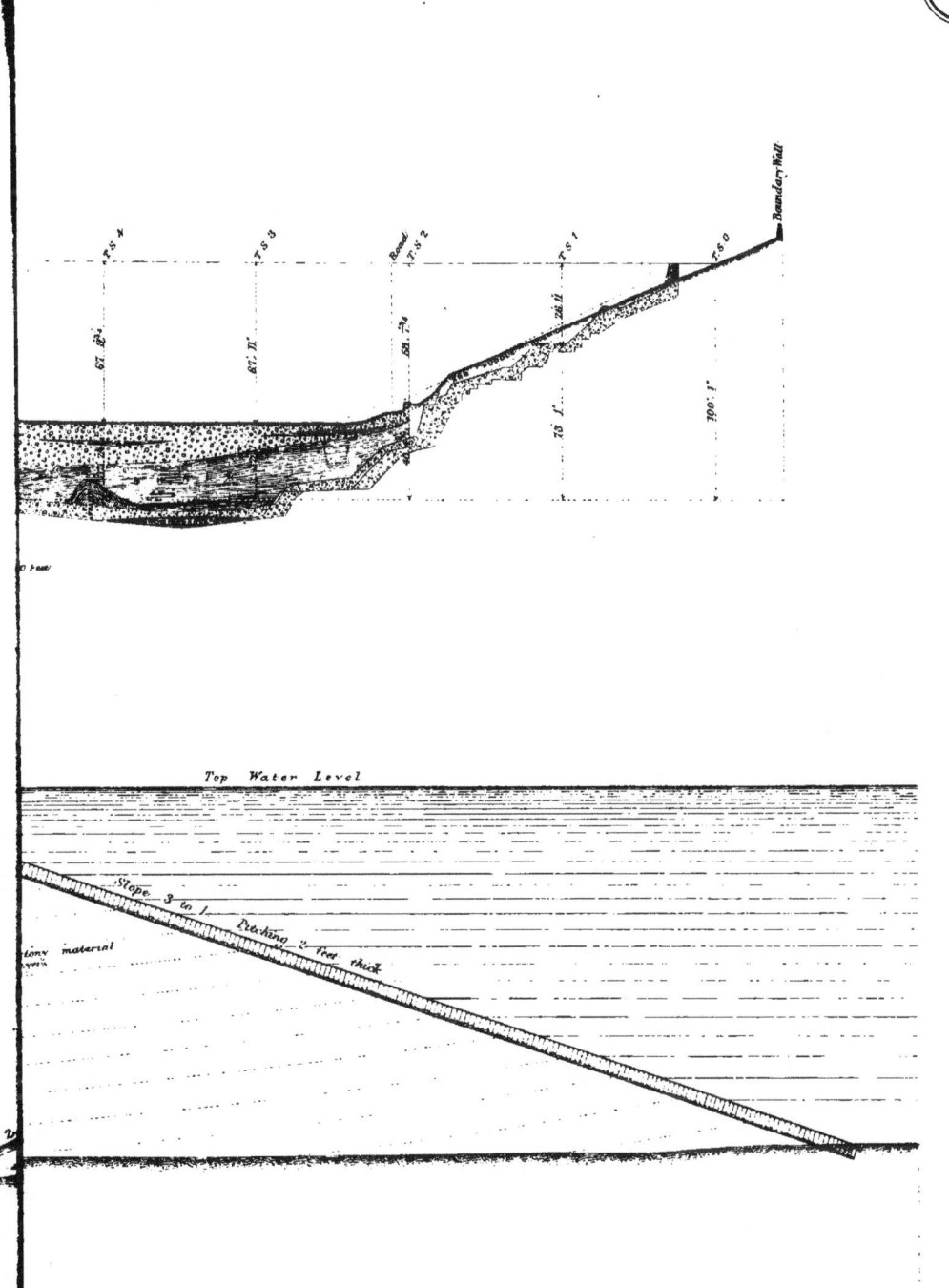

BOTTOMS RESERVOIR.

SECTIONS ACROSS WASTE WEIR.

SECTION Nº 1.

SECTION Nº 2.

SECTION Nº 3.

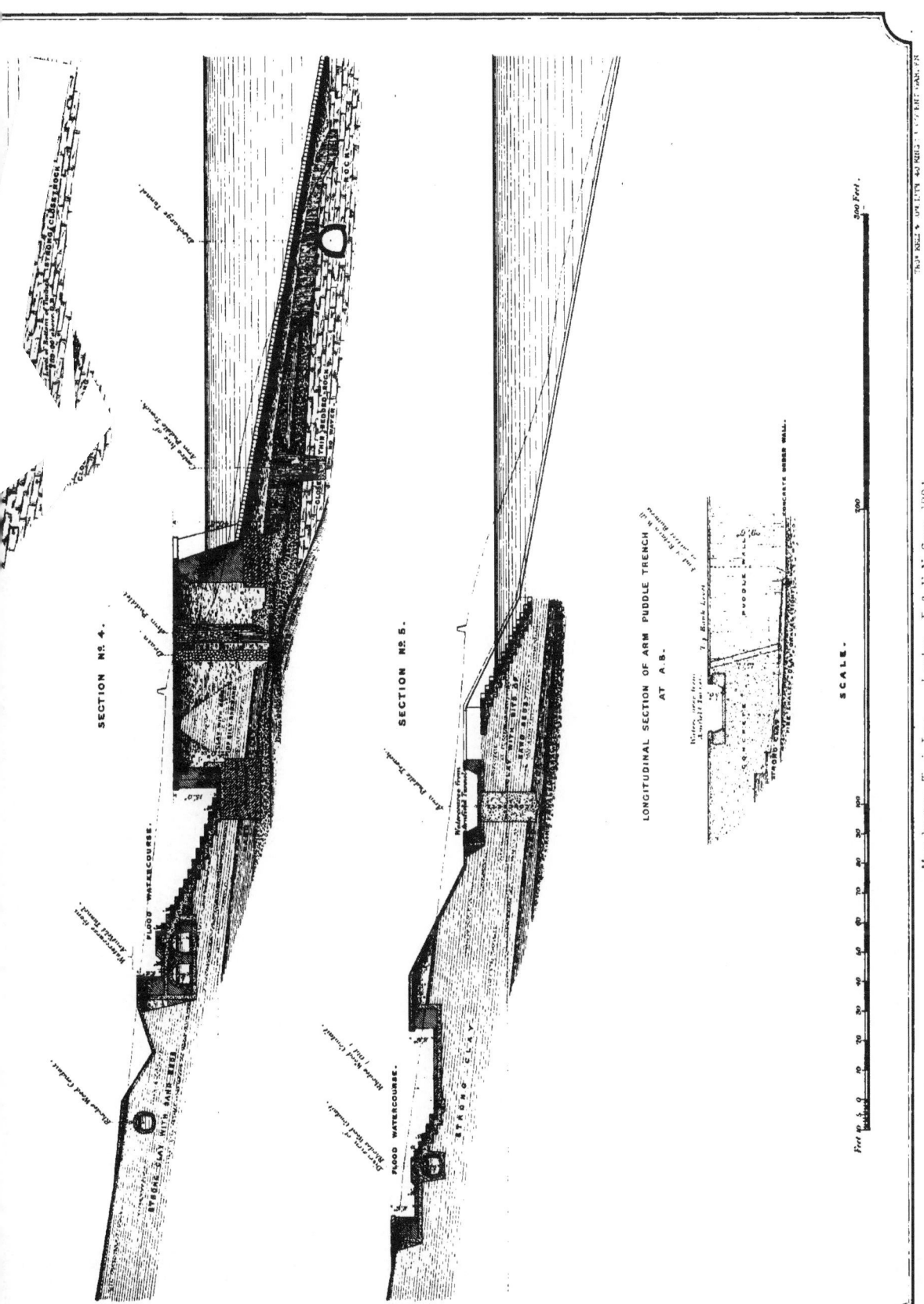

BOTTOMS RESERVOIR.

DETAILS OF VALVE SHAFT, SHEWING ARRANGEMENT OF HYDRAULIC ENGINES FOR WORKING VALVES.

DETAILS.

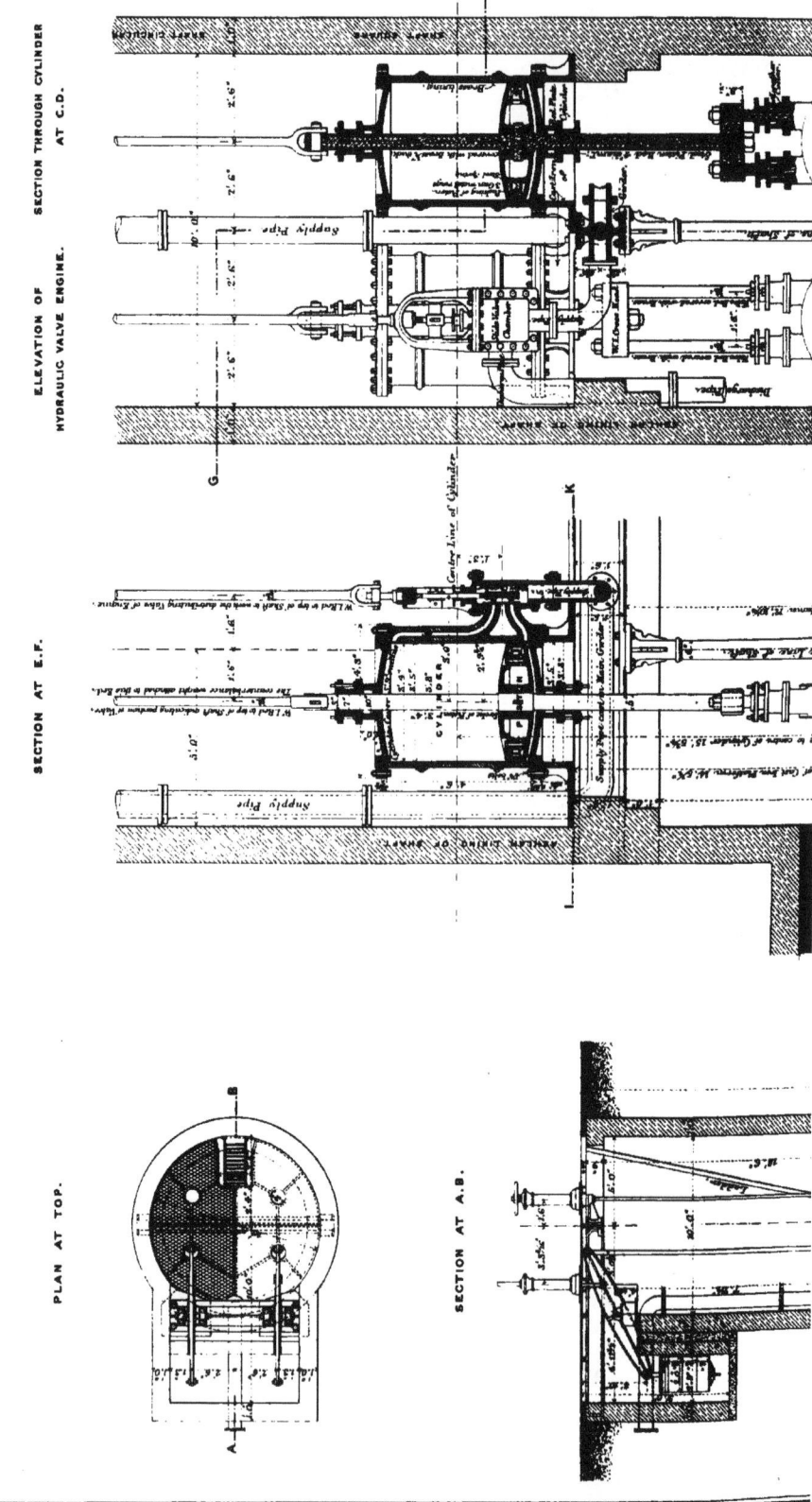

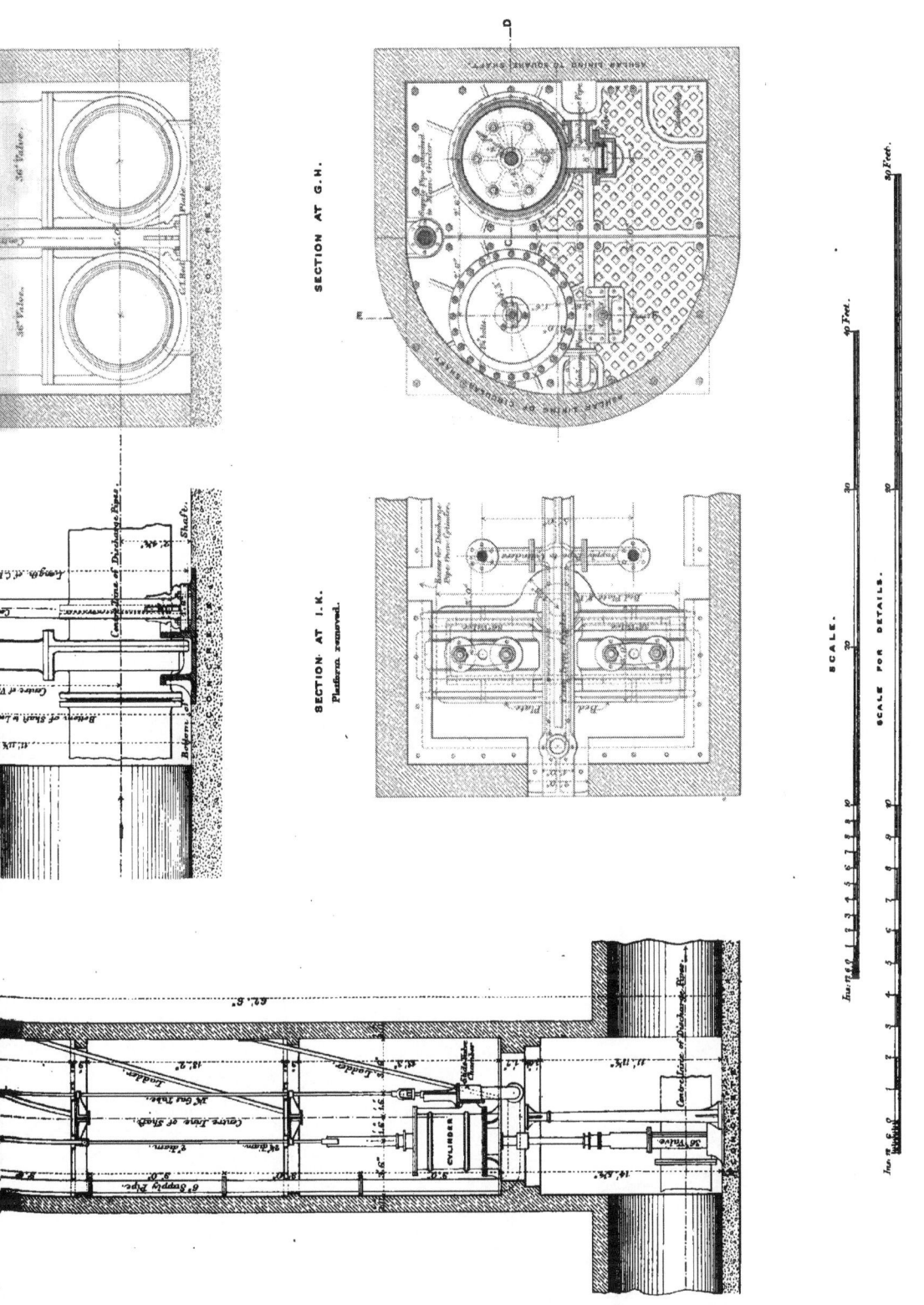

Manchester: T. J. Lay. — London: E. & F. N. Spon, 1884.

BOTTOMS RESERVOIR.

DETAILS OF TEST BASIN &c.

OPENINGS THROUGH WALL BETWEEN FOUNTAIN AND STILL WATER BASINS.

PLAN.

SECTION A.B.

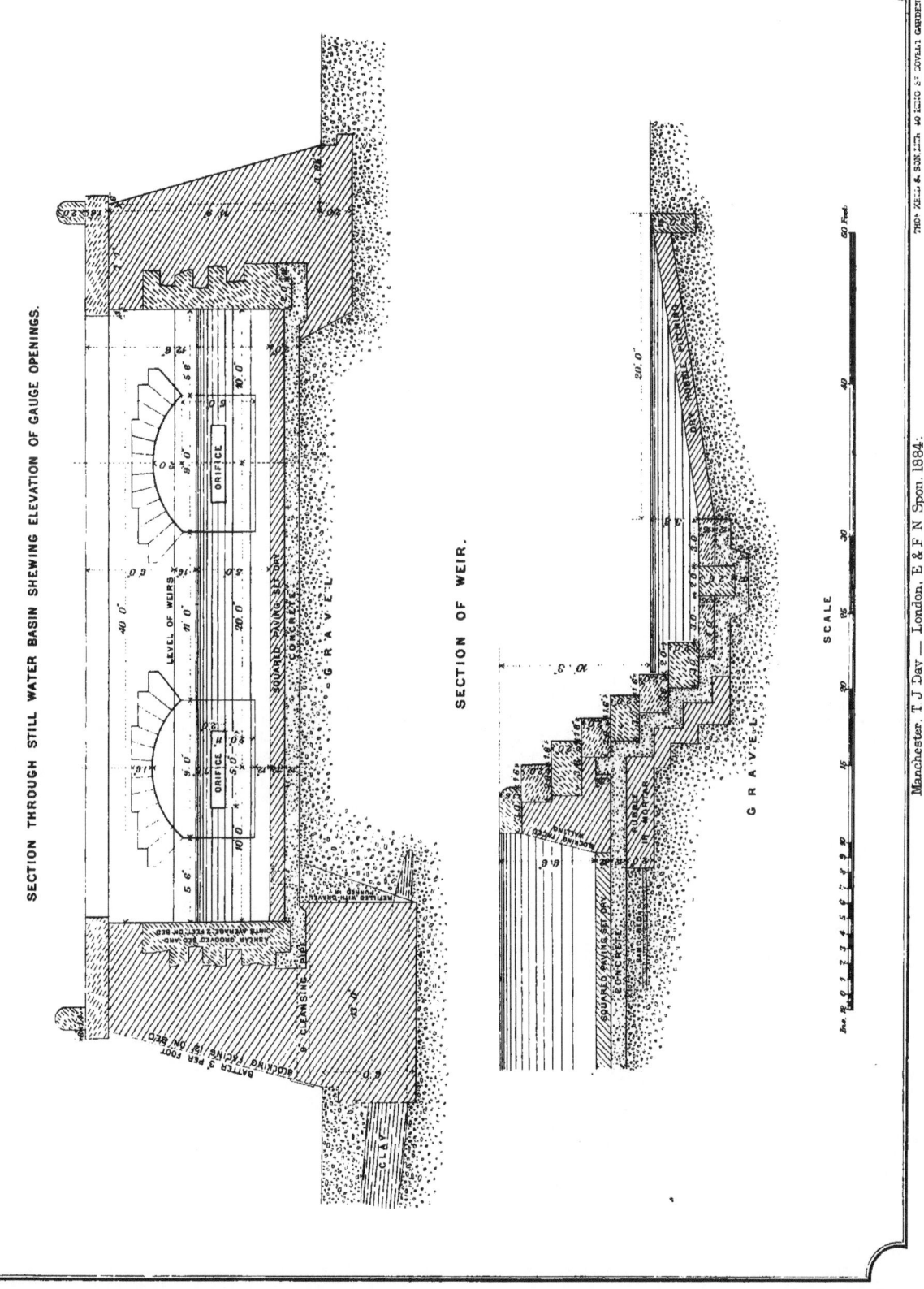

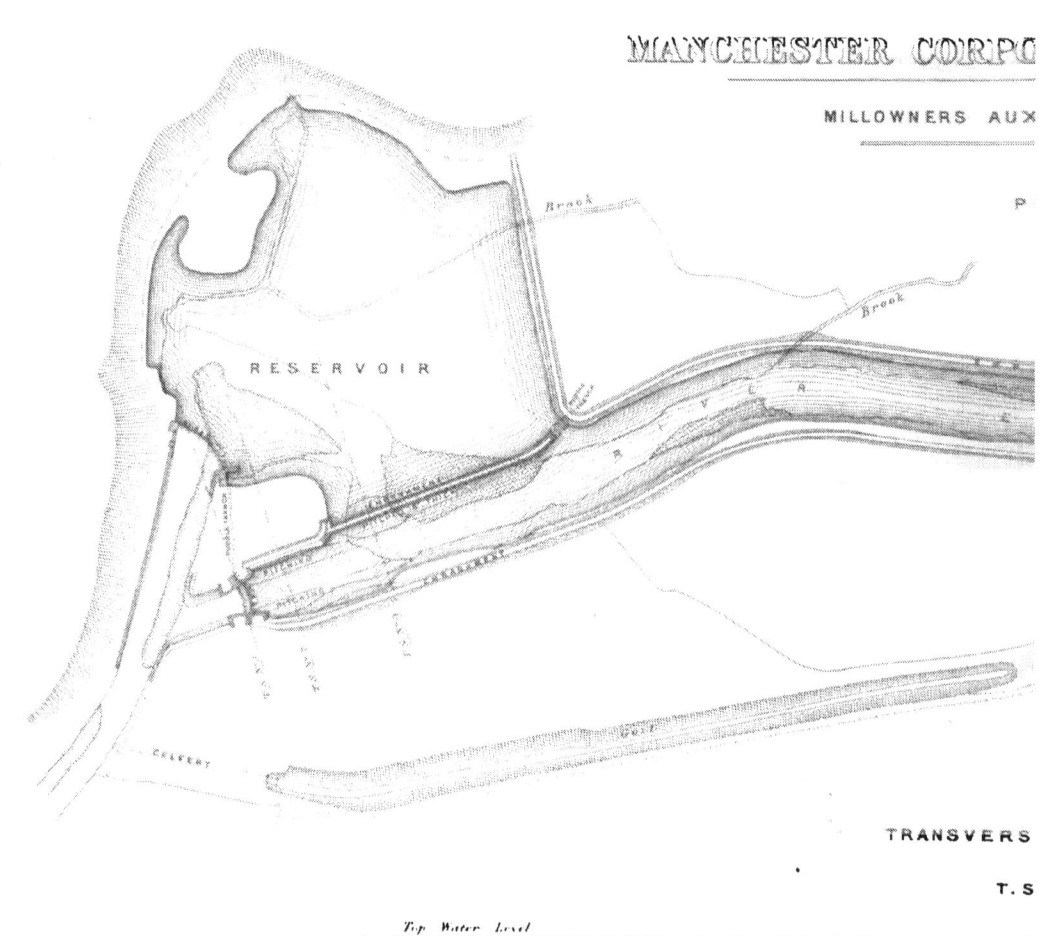

...ATION WATERWORKS.

...IARY RESERVOIR.

...N.

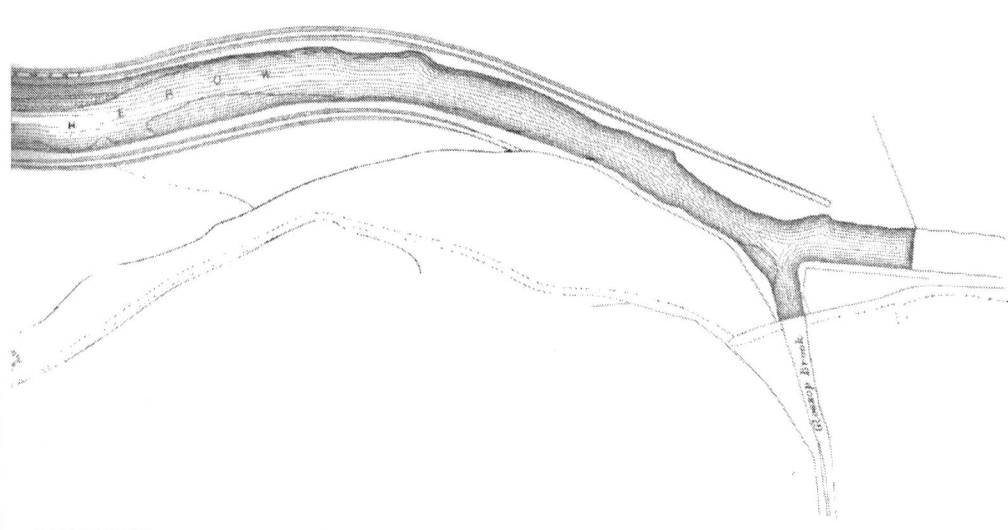

SECTIONS.

N° 1.

N° 2.

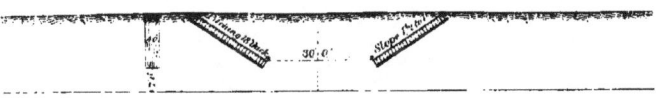

N° 3.

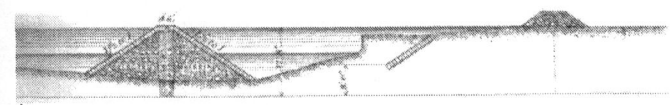

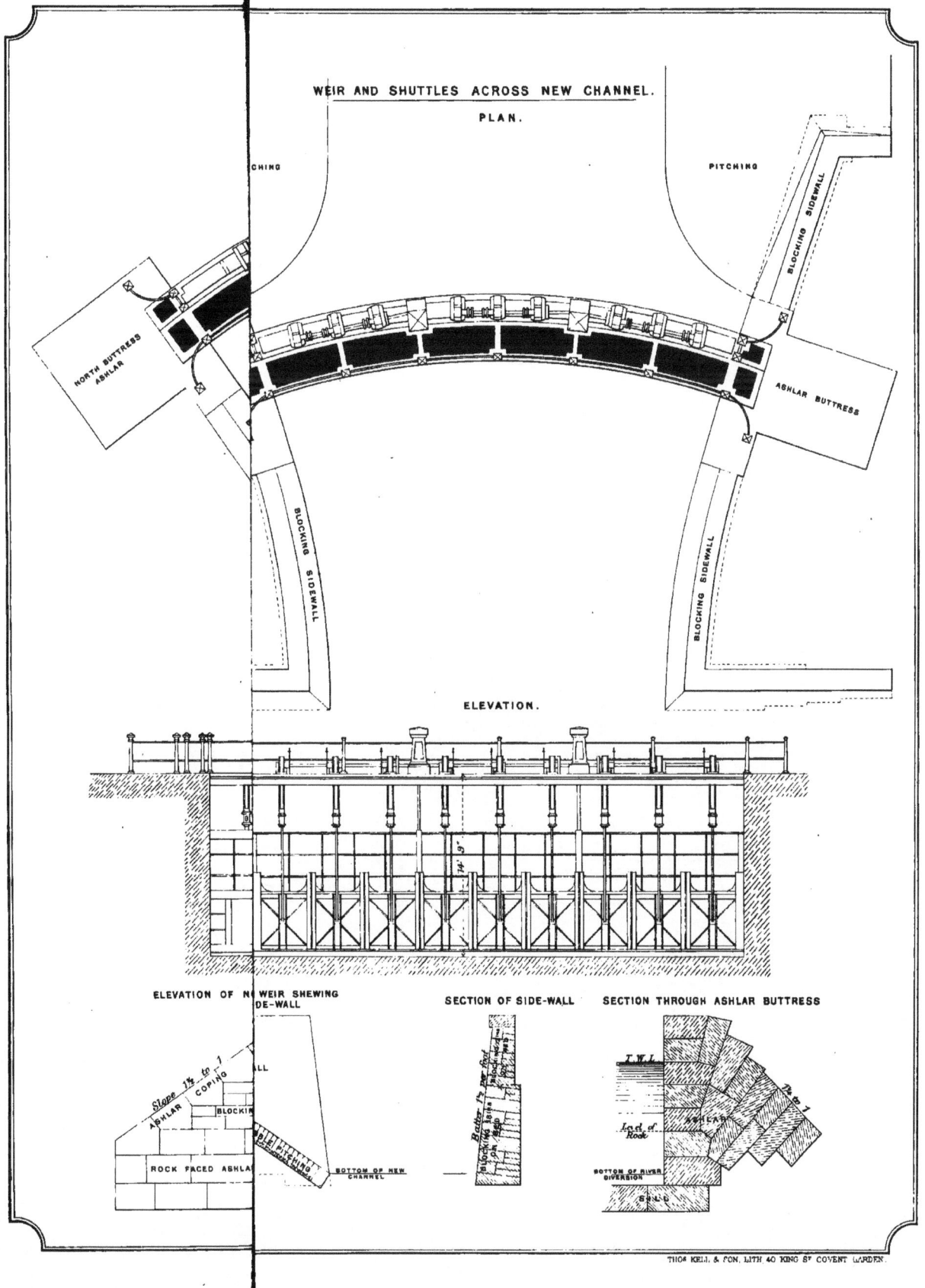

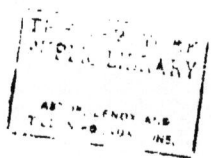

BOTTOMS

DETAILS OF IRONWORK FOR THE GAUGE-SL

LONGITUDINAL SECTION THROUGH TROUGH AND SLUICE.

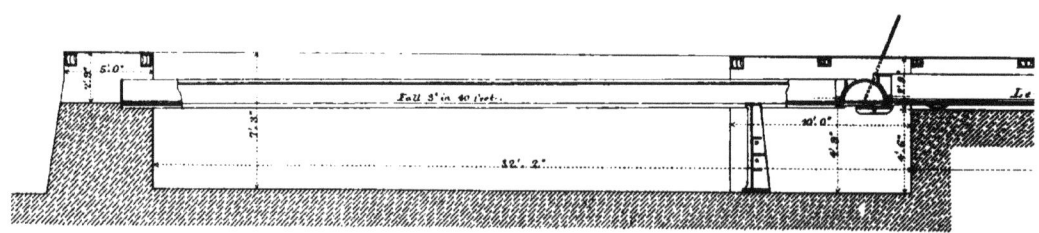

SECTIONAL PLAN.

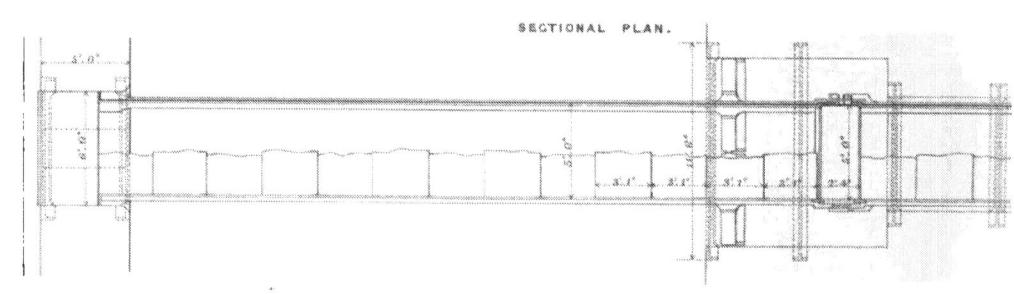

BACK ELEVATION OF STOP PLATE CARRYING SLUICE.

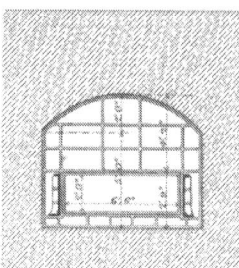

ELEVATION OF SLUICE, STOP PLATE, AND FRAME CASTINGS TO HOLD SAME.

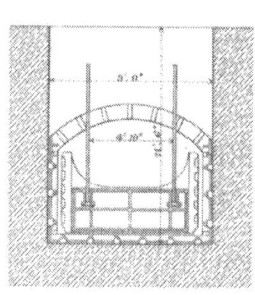

BACK ELEVATION OF PERFORATED STANDARDS CARRYING TROUGH BELOW TUMBLER, AND BACK AND FRONT VIEWS OF OUTSIDE FOOTWAY GIRDER.

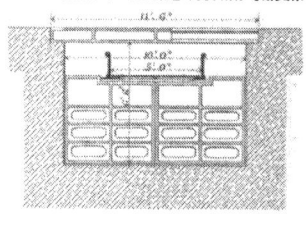

DETAILS TO

DETAILS OF SLUICE FRAME.

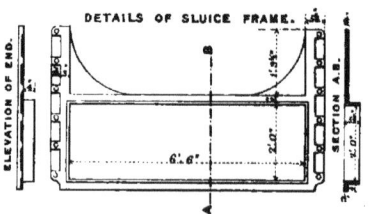

DETAILS OF BOTTOM FRAME CASTING TO HOLD STOP PLATE.

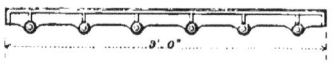

Manchester T. J Day

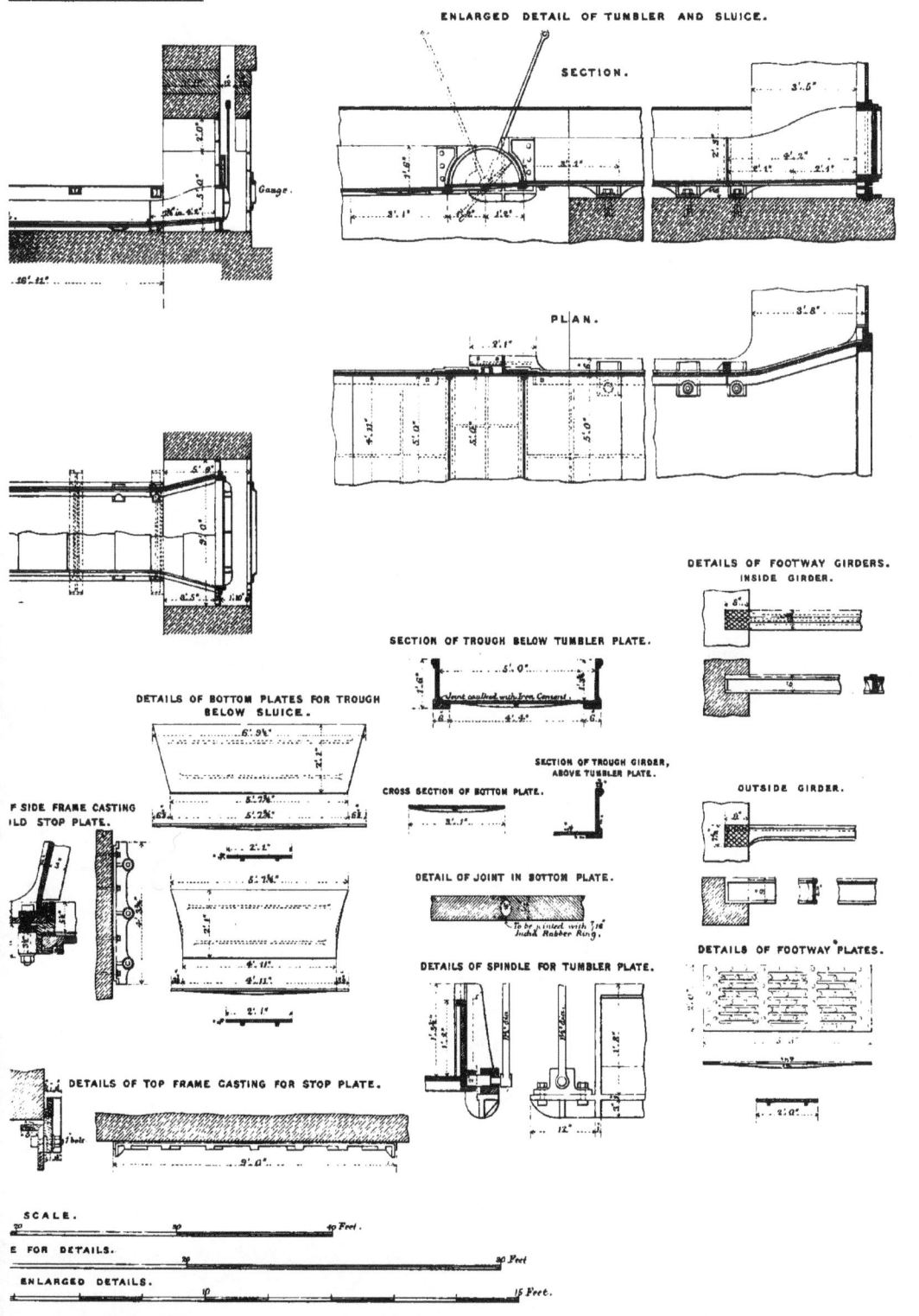

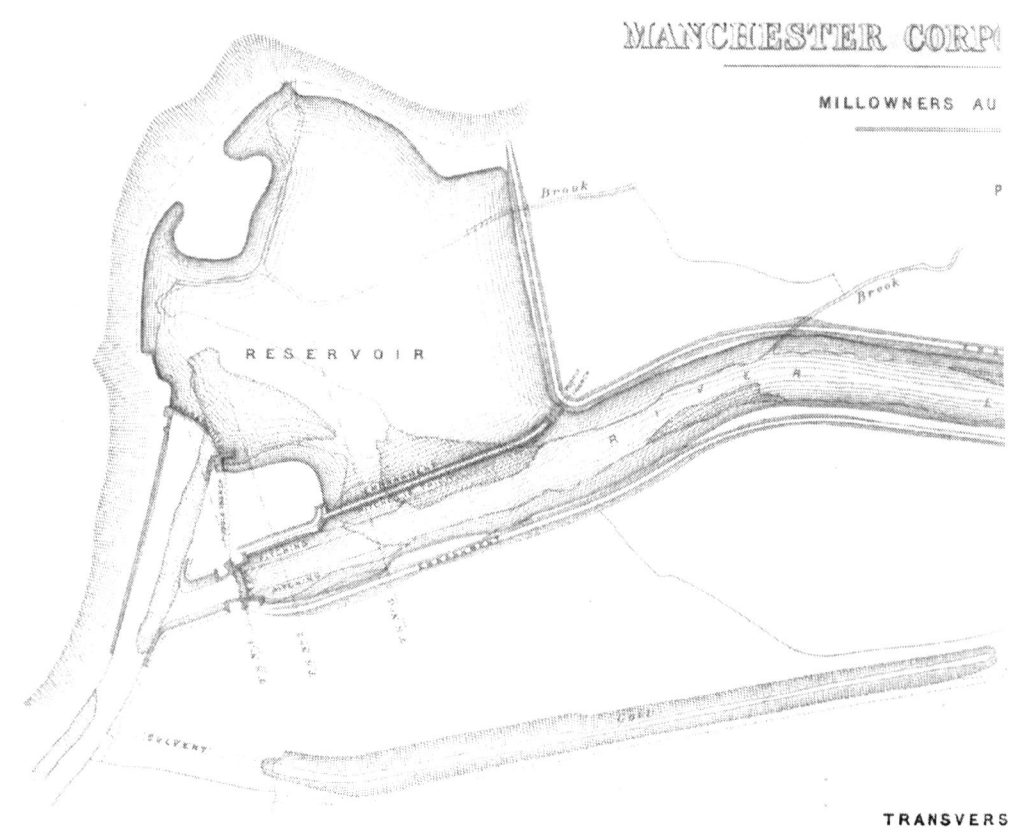

RATION WATERWORKS.

LIARY RESERVOIR.

A N.

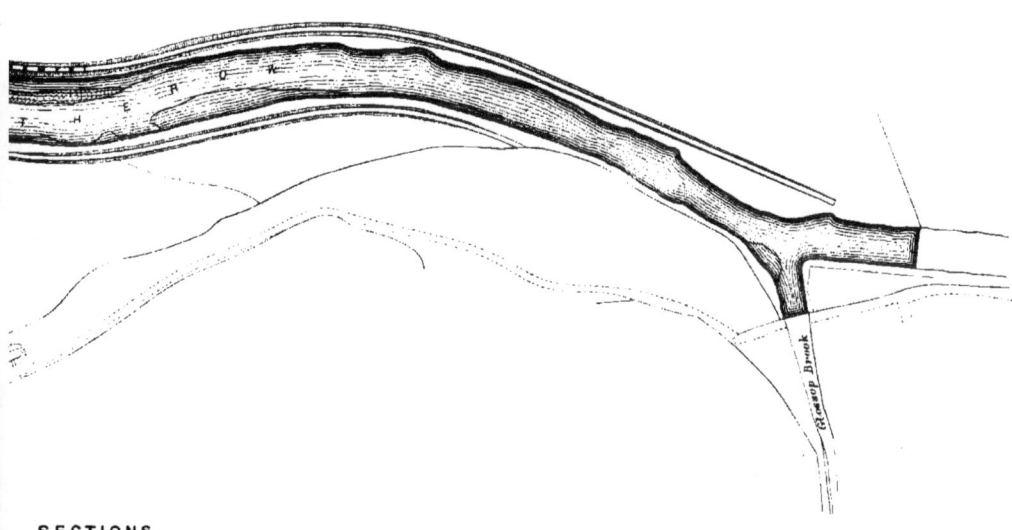

SECTIONS.

Nº 1.

Nº 2.

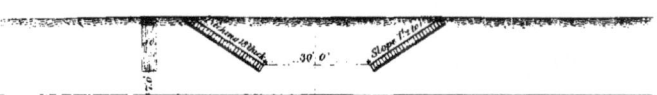

Nº 3.

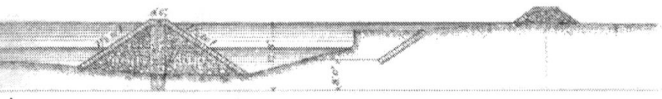

ridon F. & F. N. Spon, 1884. THOS KELL & SON, LITH 40 KING ST COVENT GARDEN

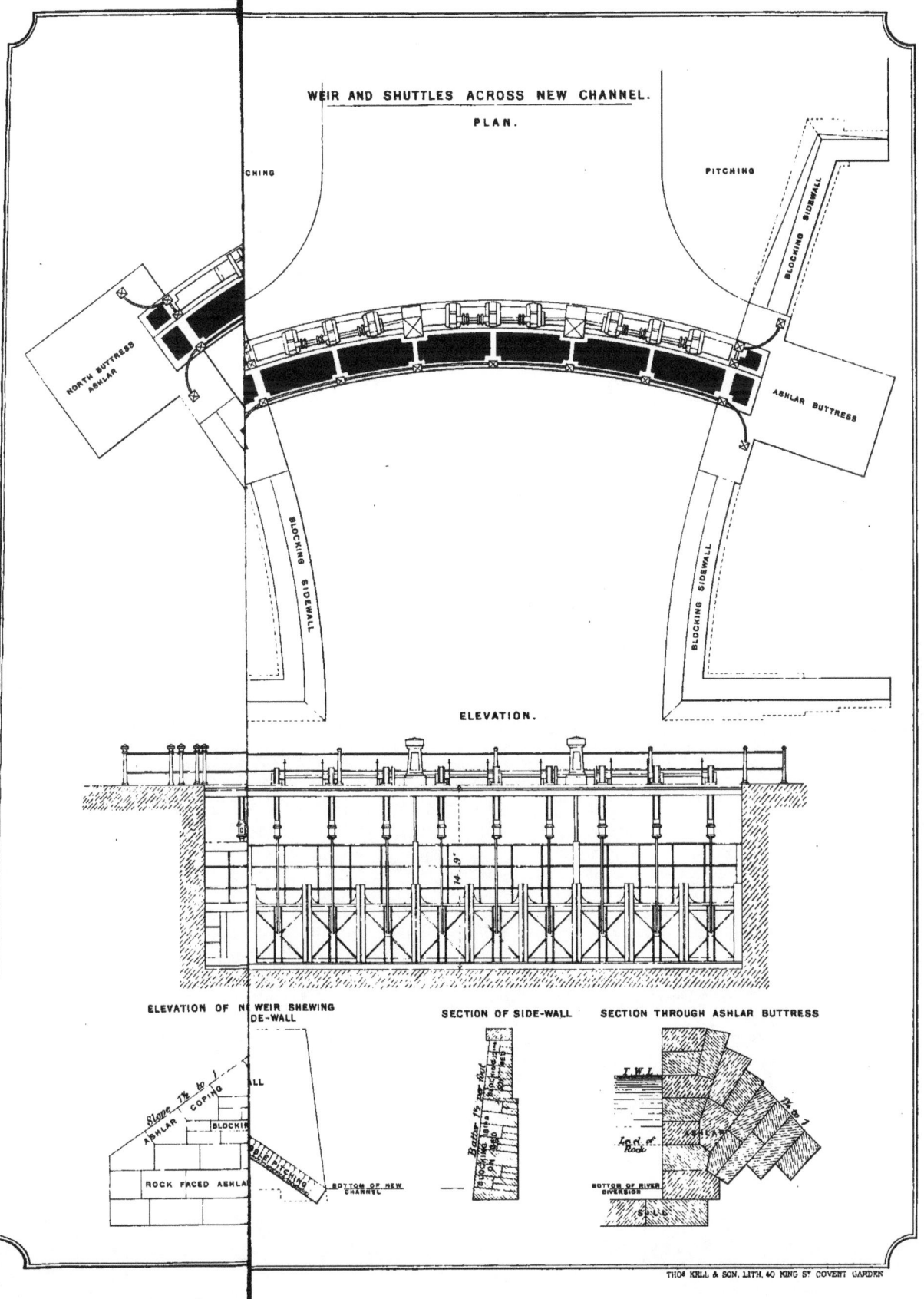

AUXILIARY
SELF-ACTING

ELEVATION.

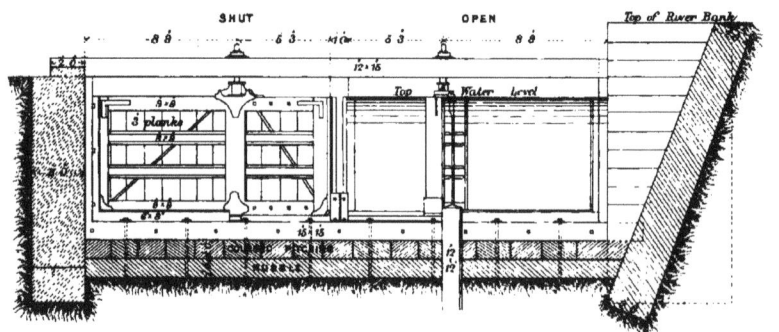

TRANSVERSE

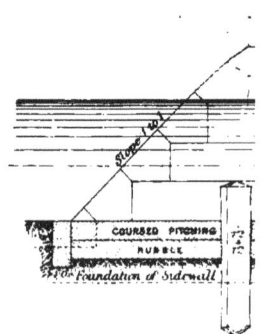

PLAN.

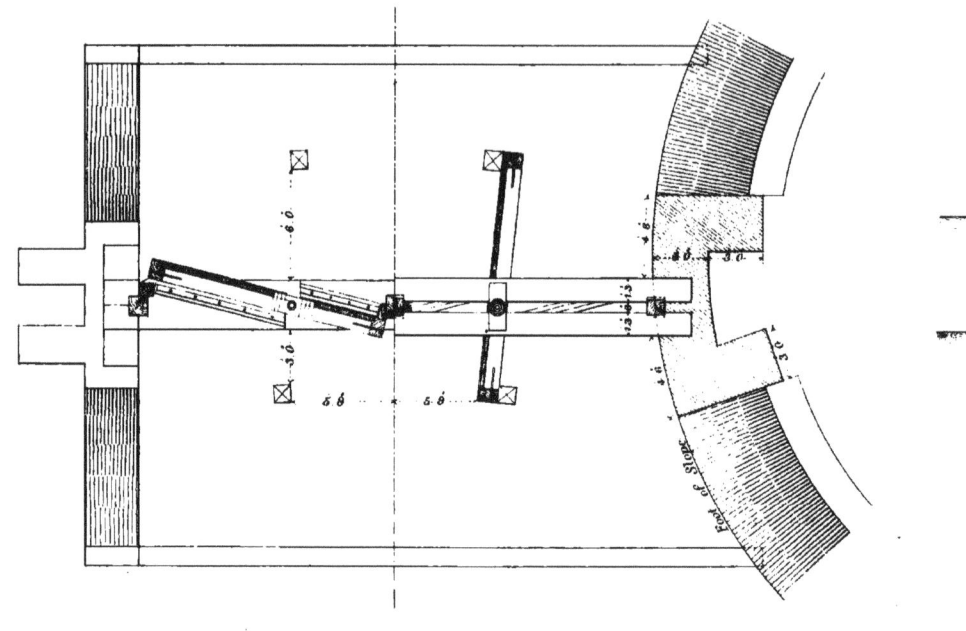

TRANSVERSE

Manchester T J Day

ESERVOIR.
OOD GATES.

SE SECTION.

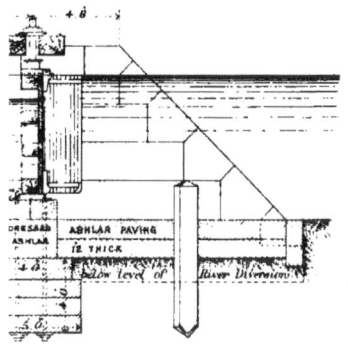

DETAILS.

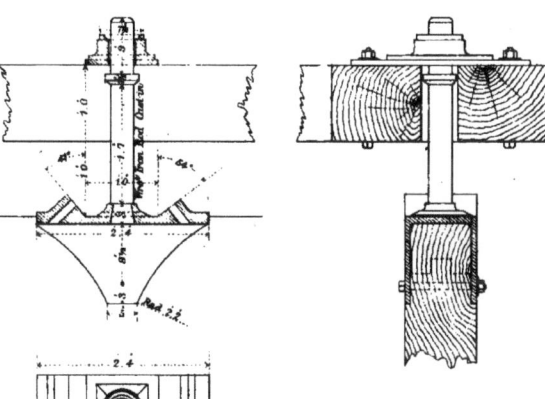

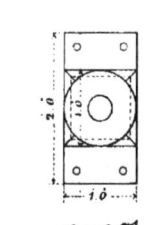

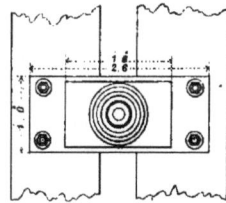

ION OF DIVISION BANK.

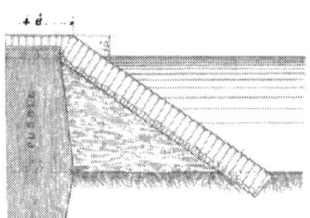

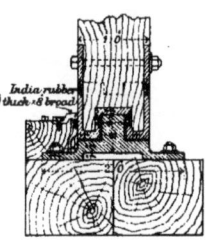

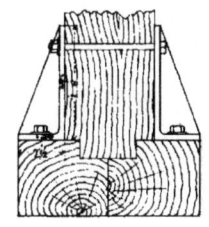

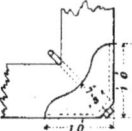

SCALE.

E. & F. N. Spon, 1884.

Thos Kell & Son Lith, 40, King St Covent Garden.

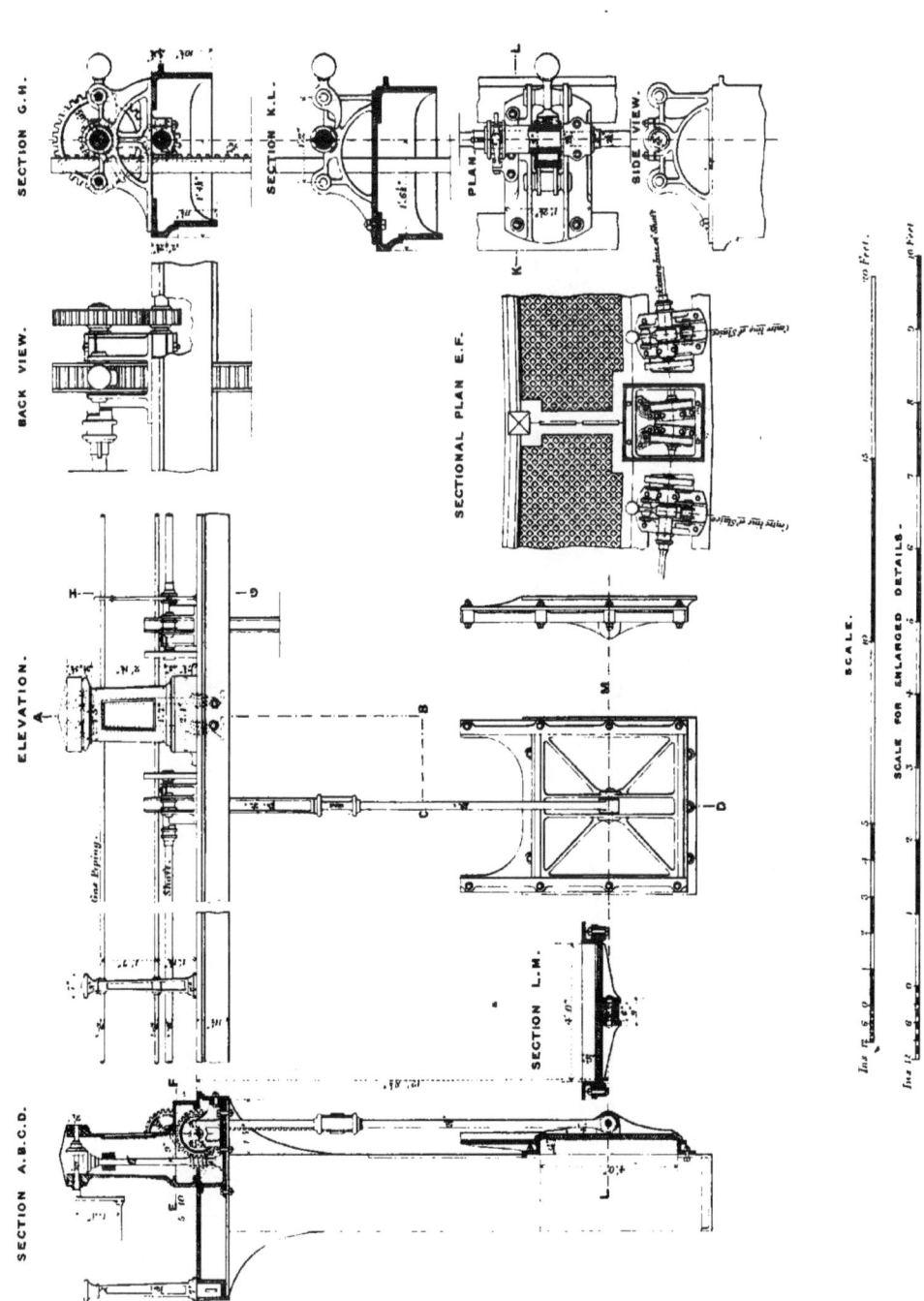

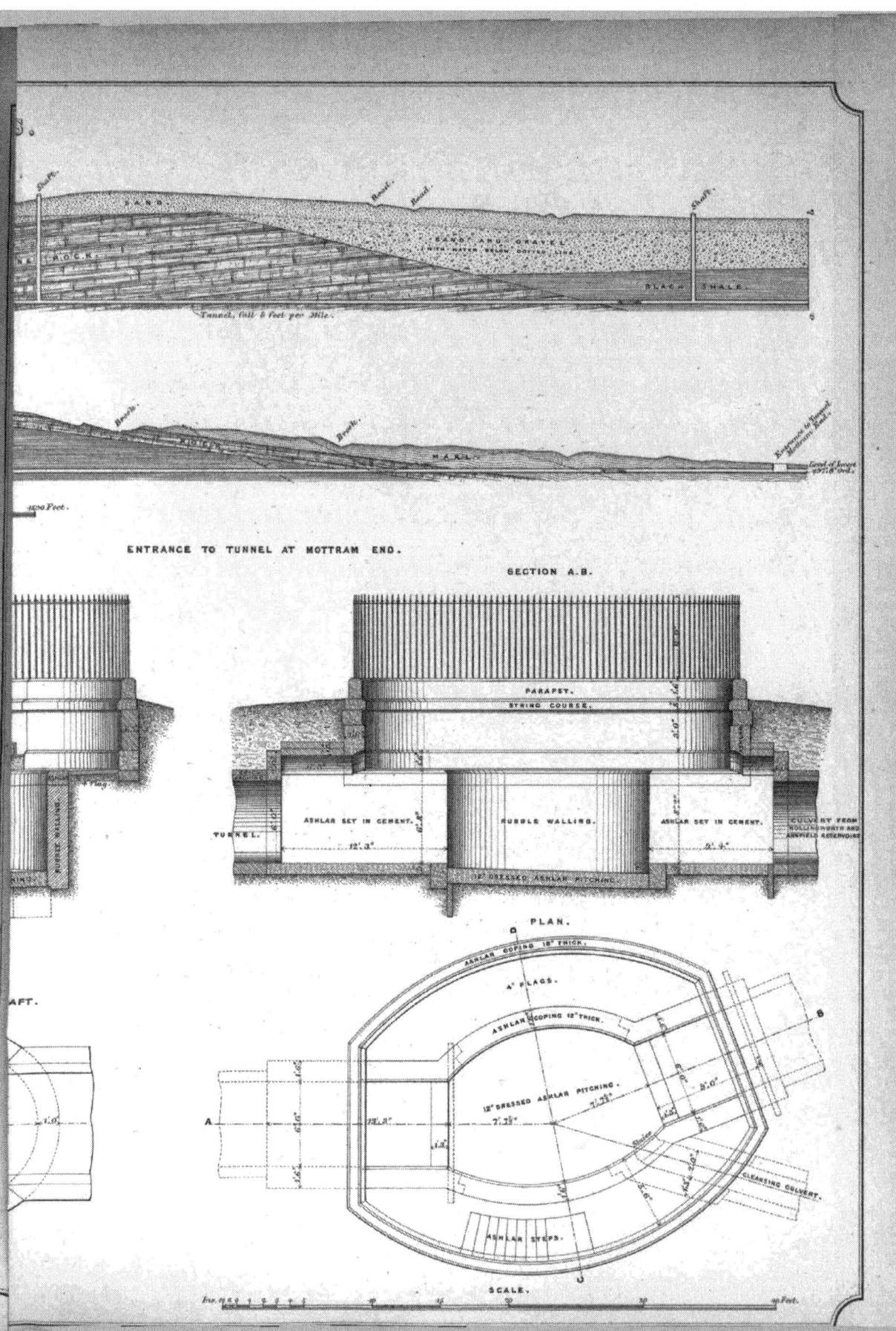

MANCHESTER CORPORATION WATER WORKS.

PLAN SHEWING WORKS AT GODLEY.

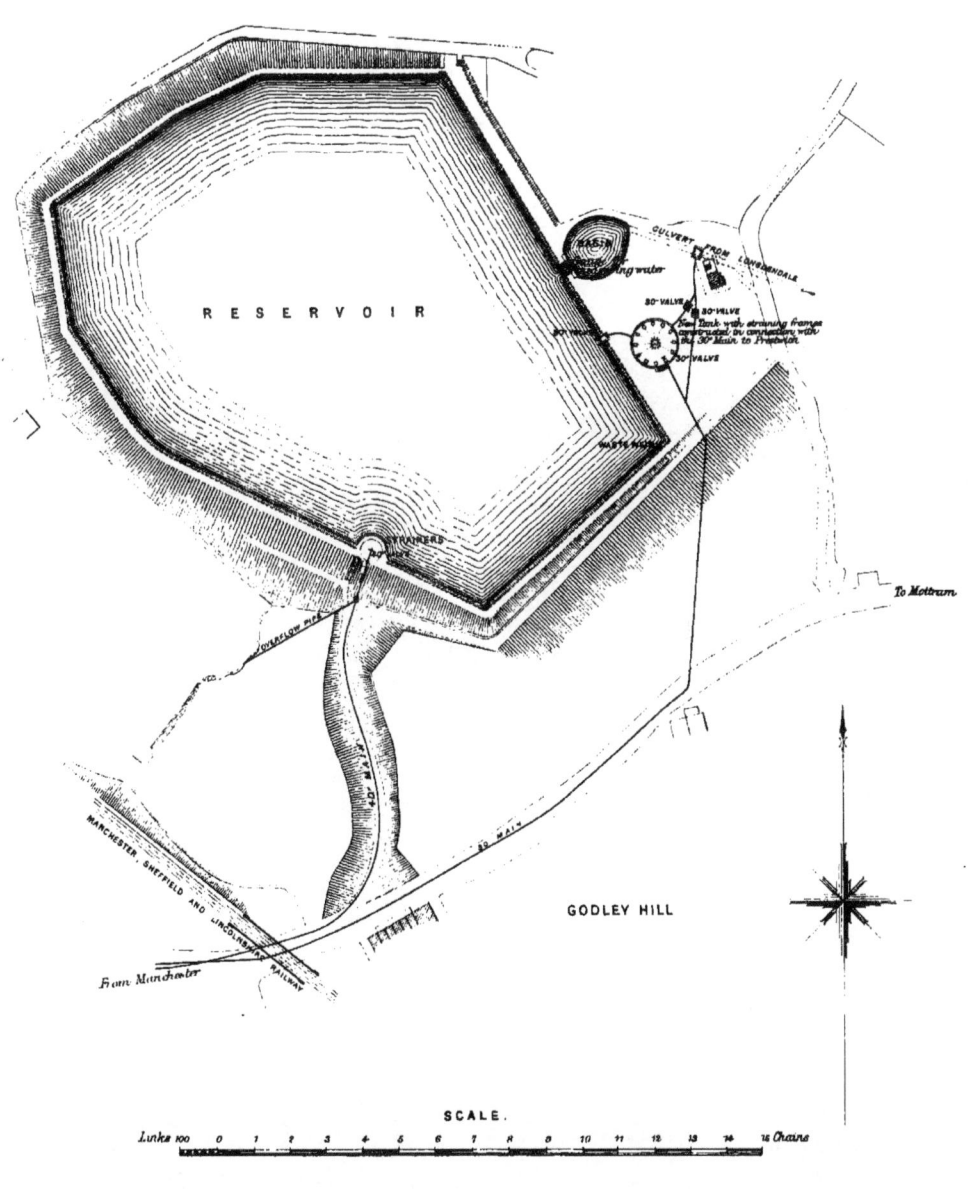

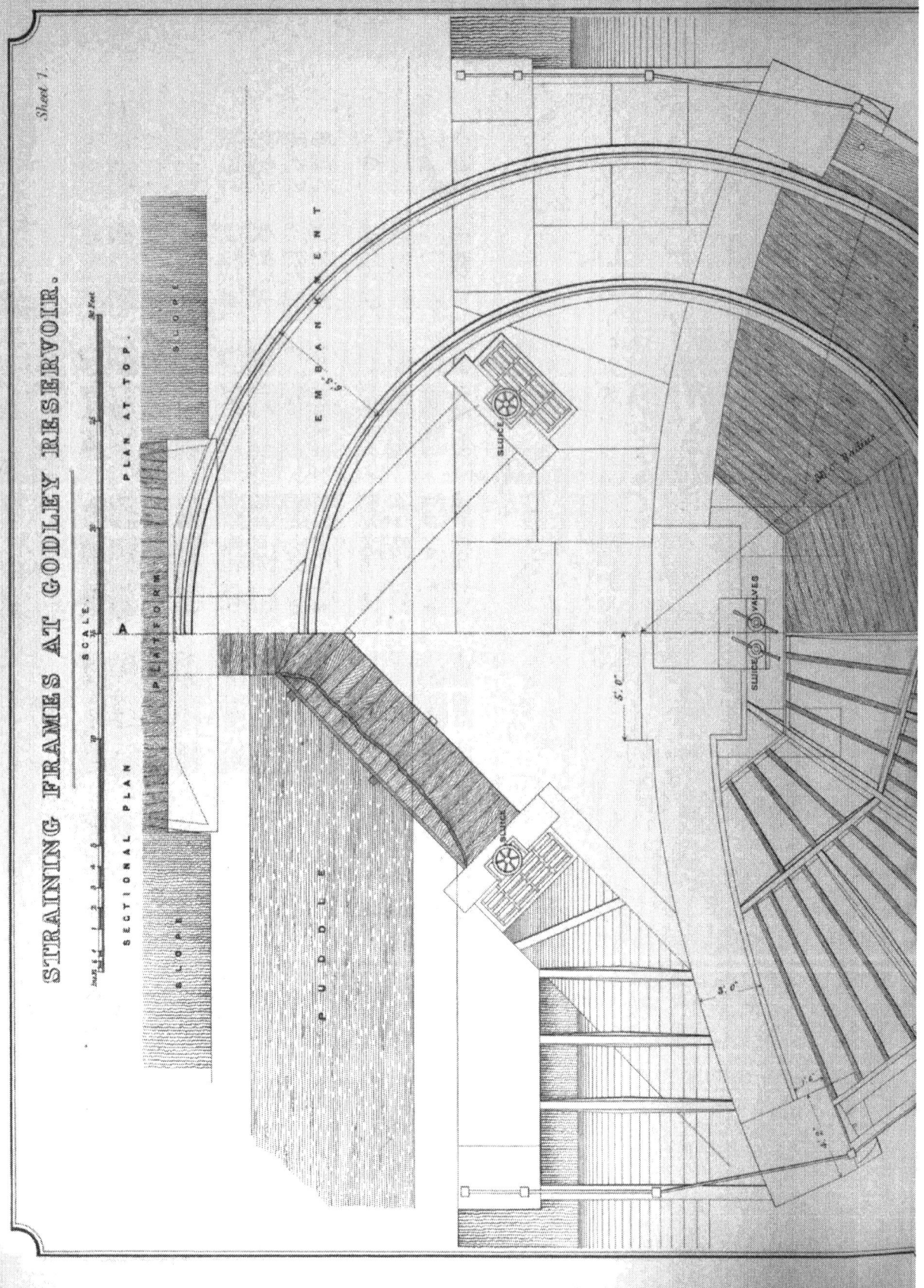

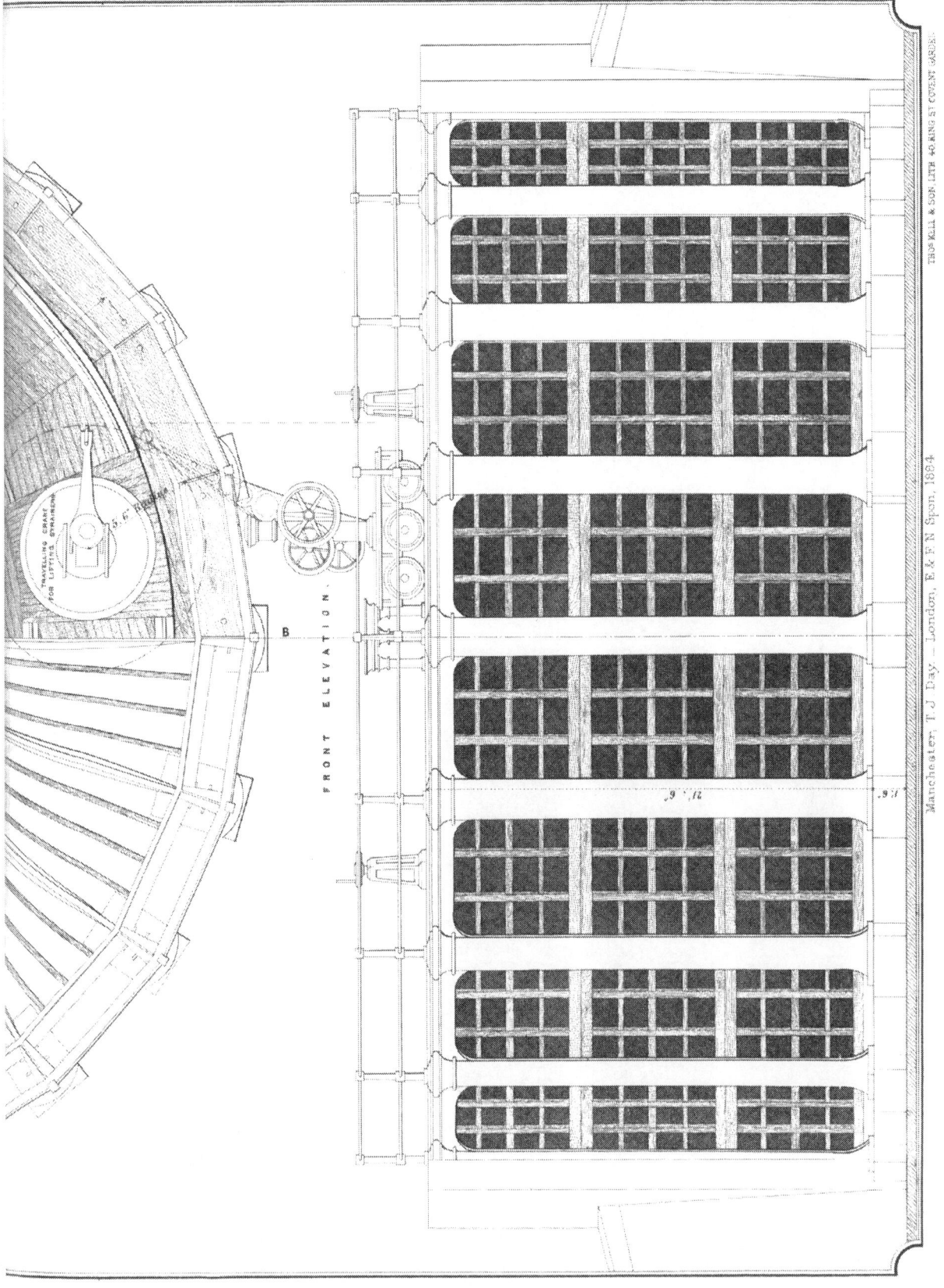

SIDE ELEVATION.

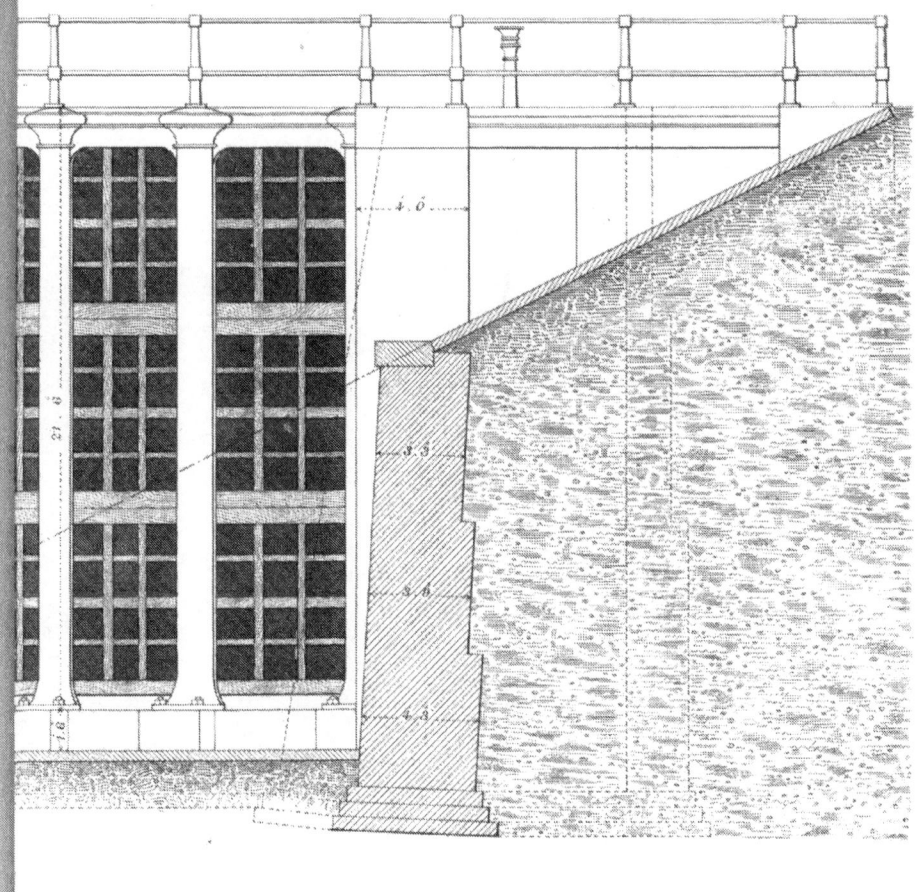

DETAILS OF STRAINING FRAMES AND STRAINERS.

DETAIL OF FRAME

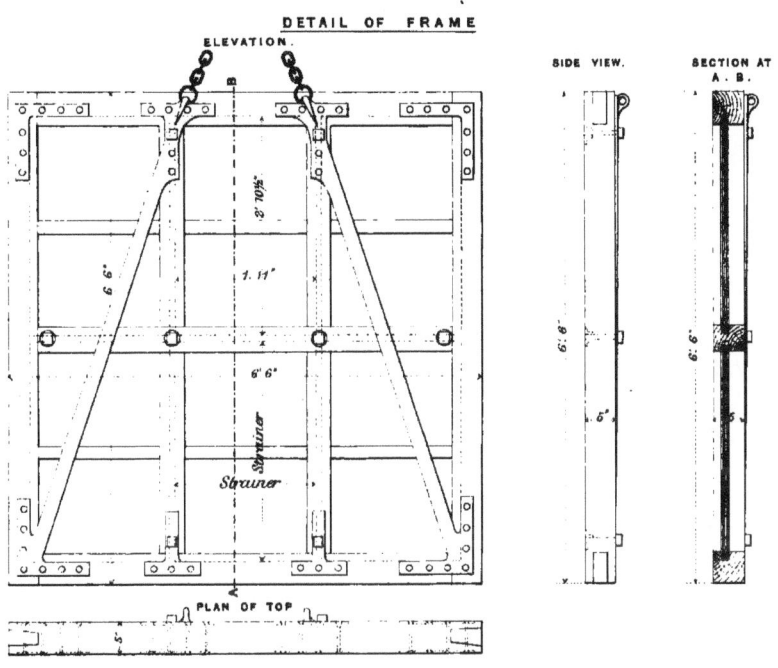

ENLARGED DETAILS OF WIRE GAUGE STRAINERS.

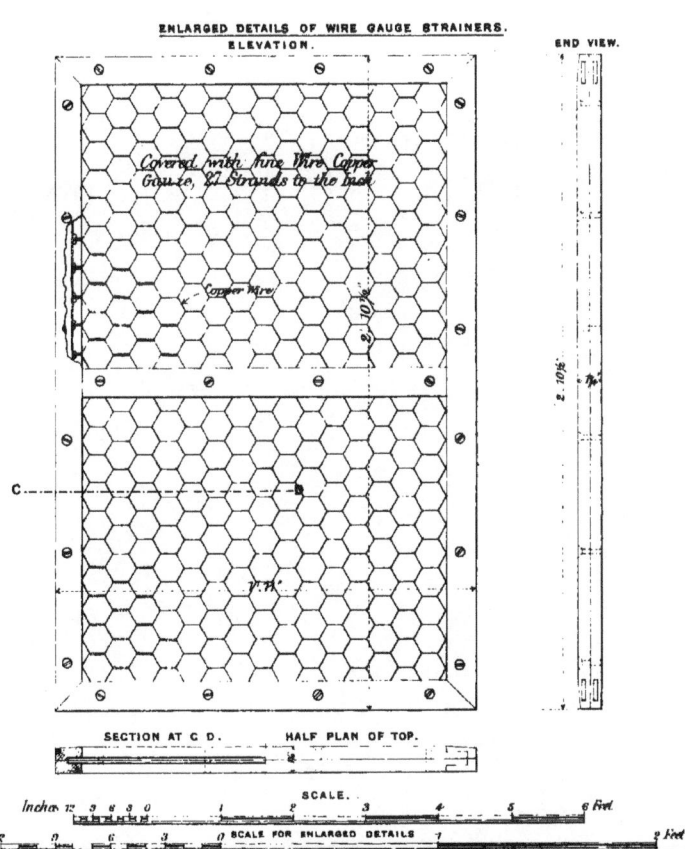

Manchester, T J Day — London, E & F N Spon 1884.

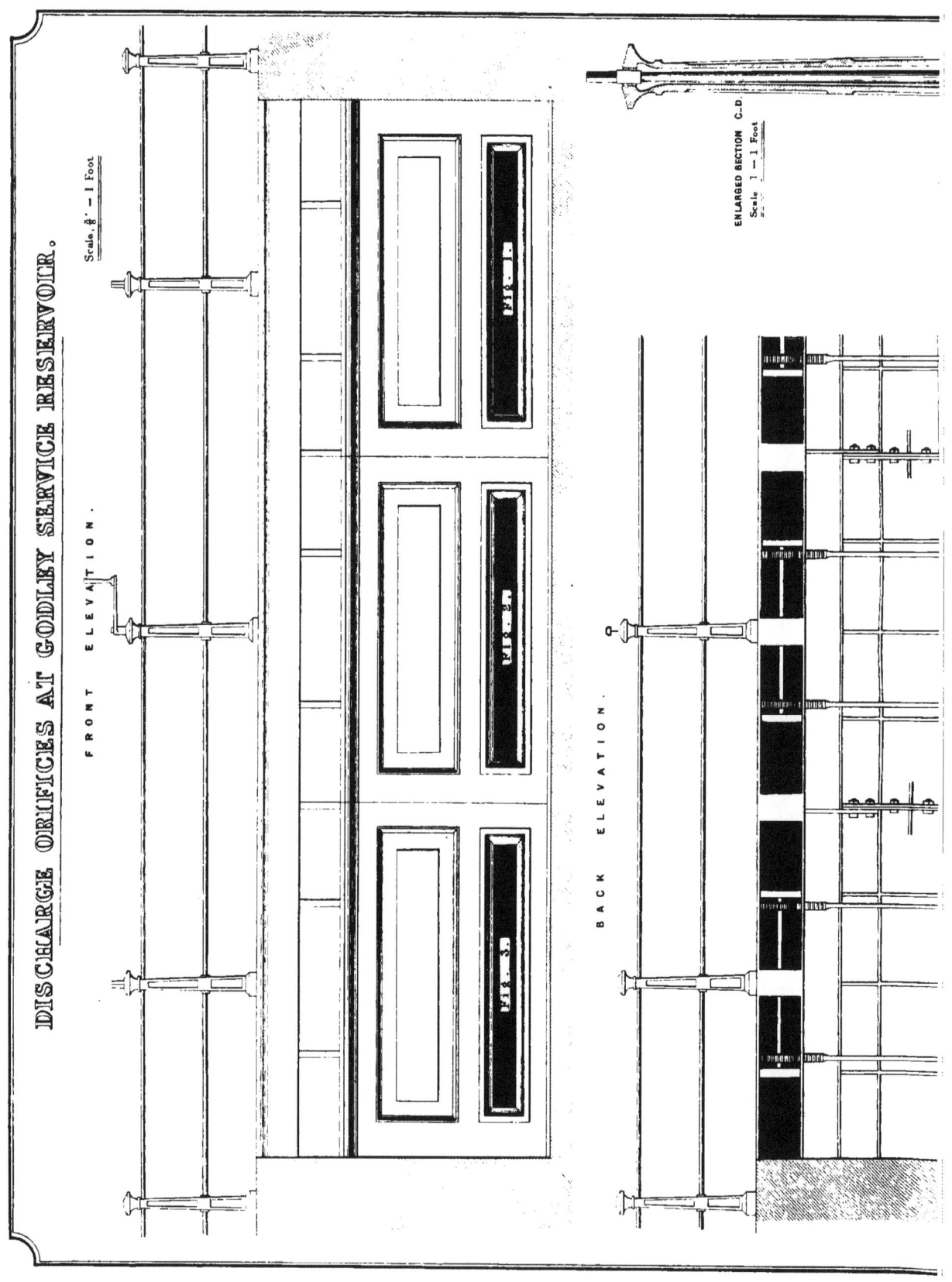

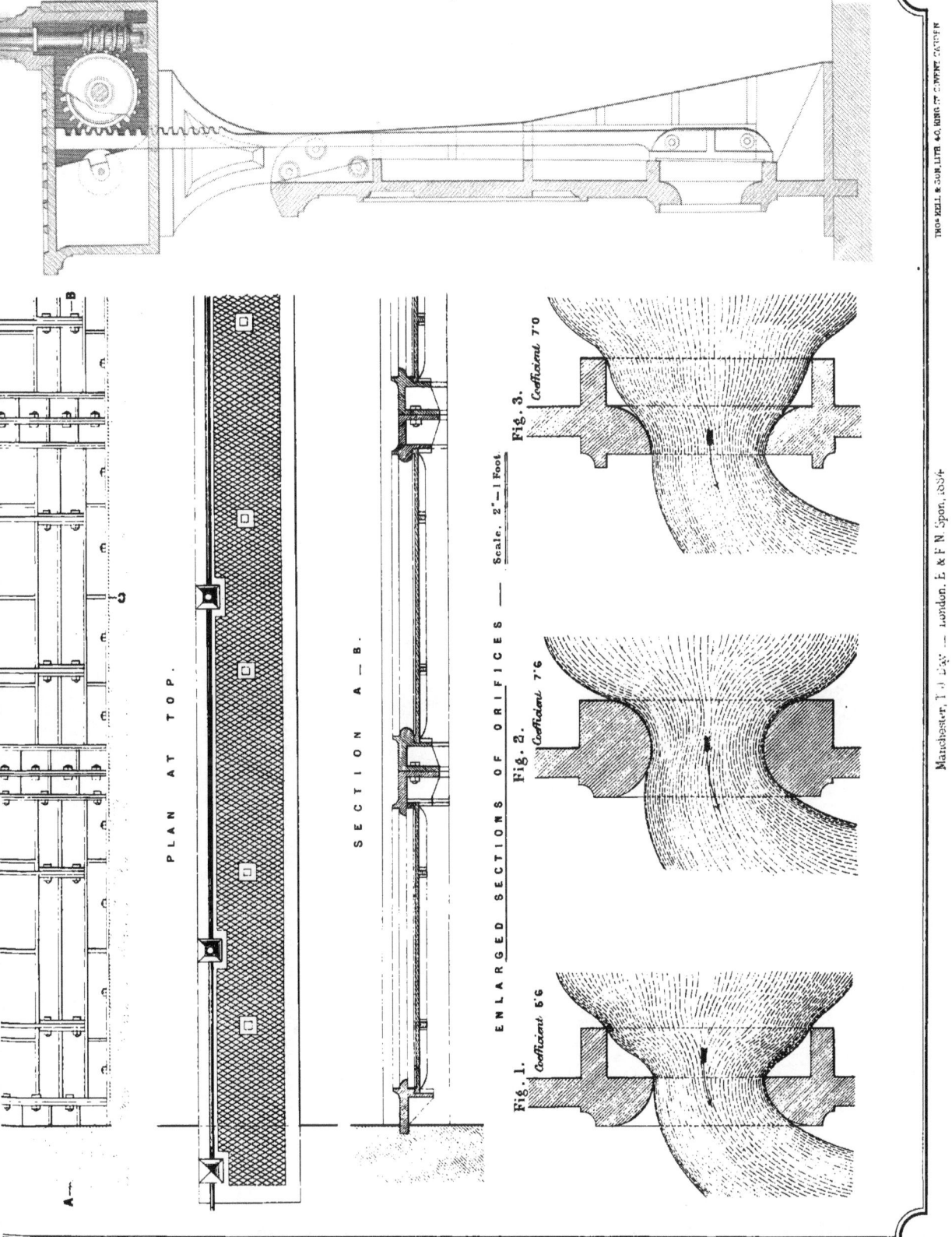

THE NEW YORK
PUBLIC LIBRARY

ASTOR, LENOX AND
TILDEN FOUNDATIONS

MANCHESTER CORPOR

PLAN SHEWING WORKS

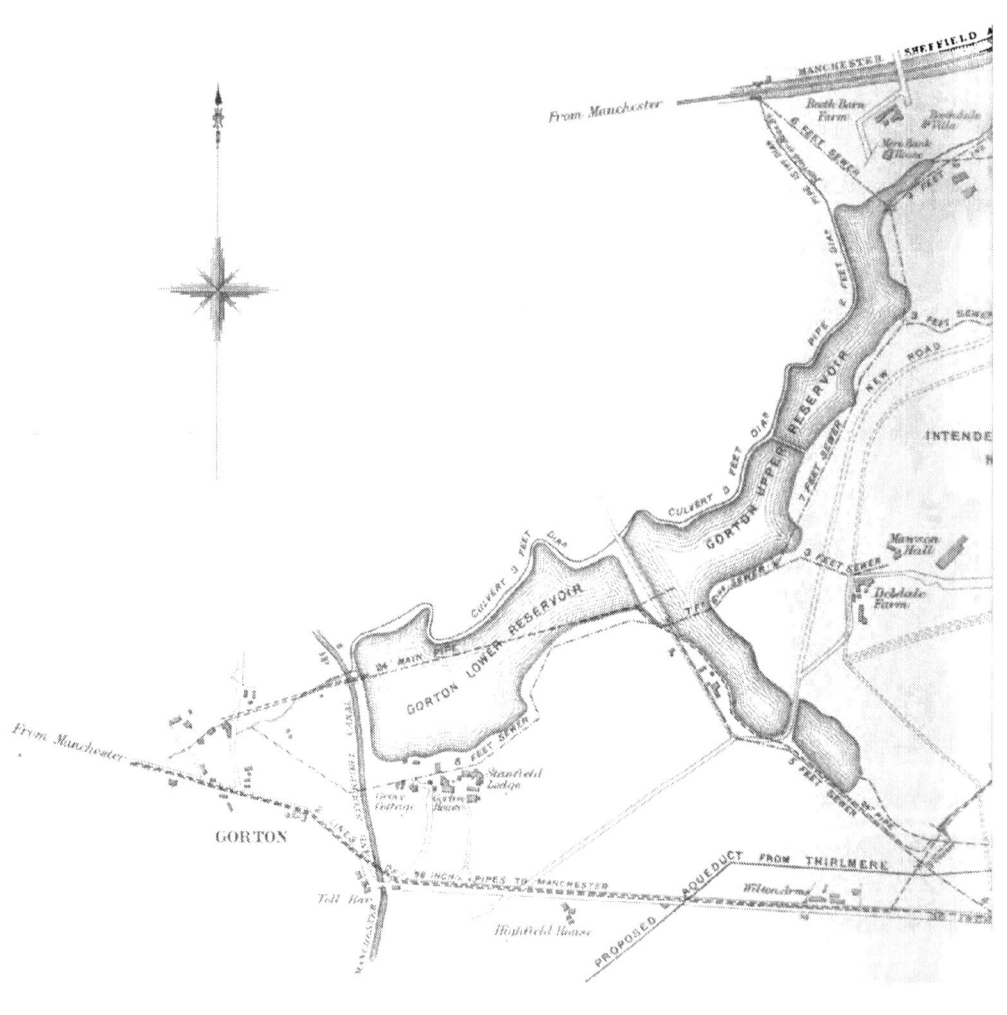

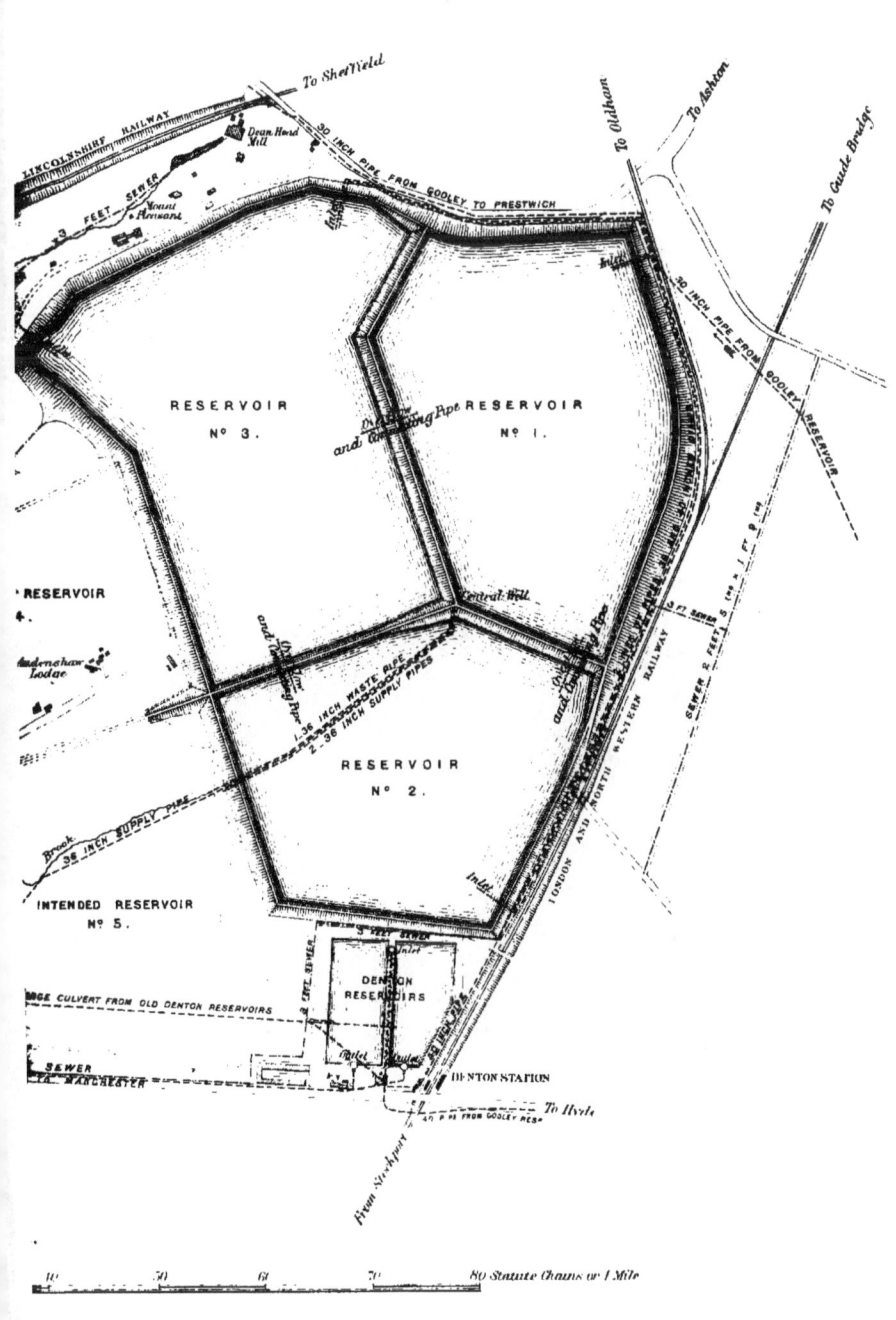

SECTIONS of NEW RESERVOIR EMBANKMENTS at DENTON.

RESERVOIR Nº 1. EAST BANK BY RAILWAY.

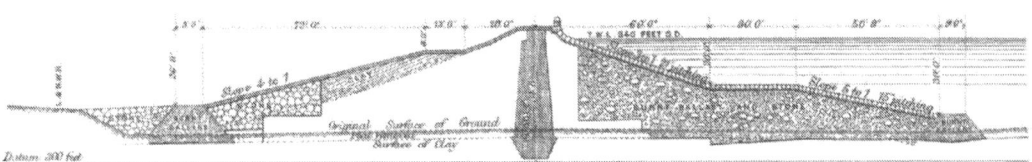

RESERVOIR Nº 2. WEST BANK.
ORIGINAL SECTION AS DESIGNED.

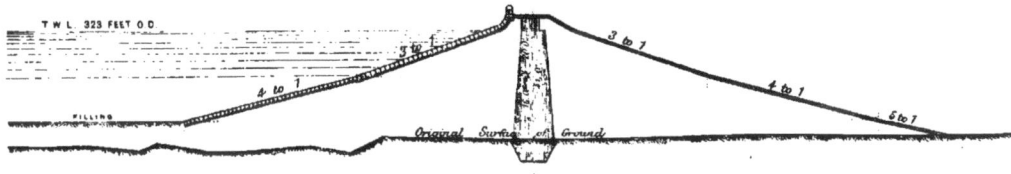

RESERVOIR Nº 2. WEST BANK.

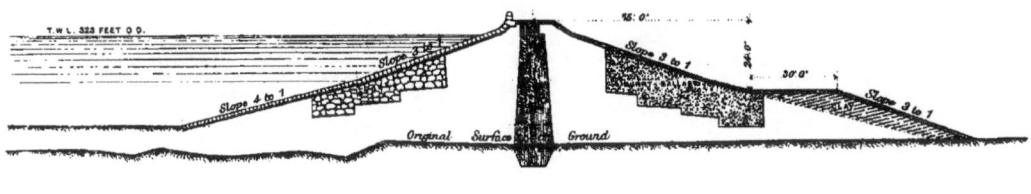

RESERVOIR Nº 3. SAMMY CLOUGH.

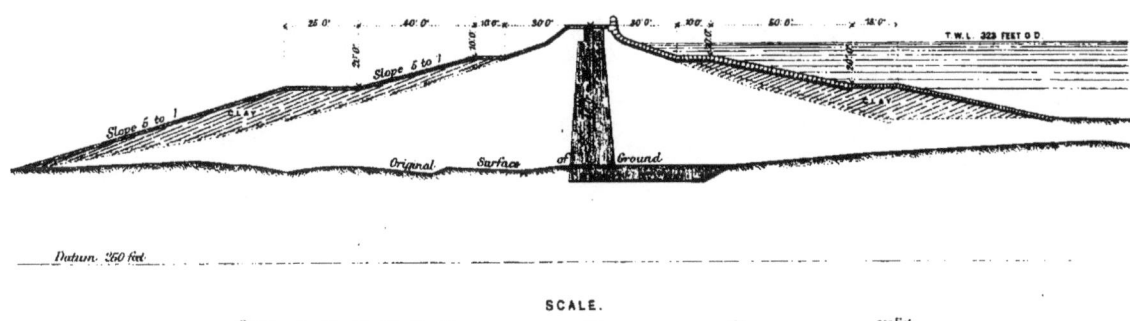

SCALE.

Manchester T J Day — London, E. & F N Spon 1884

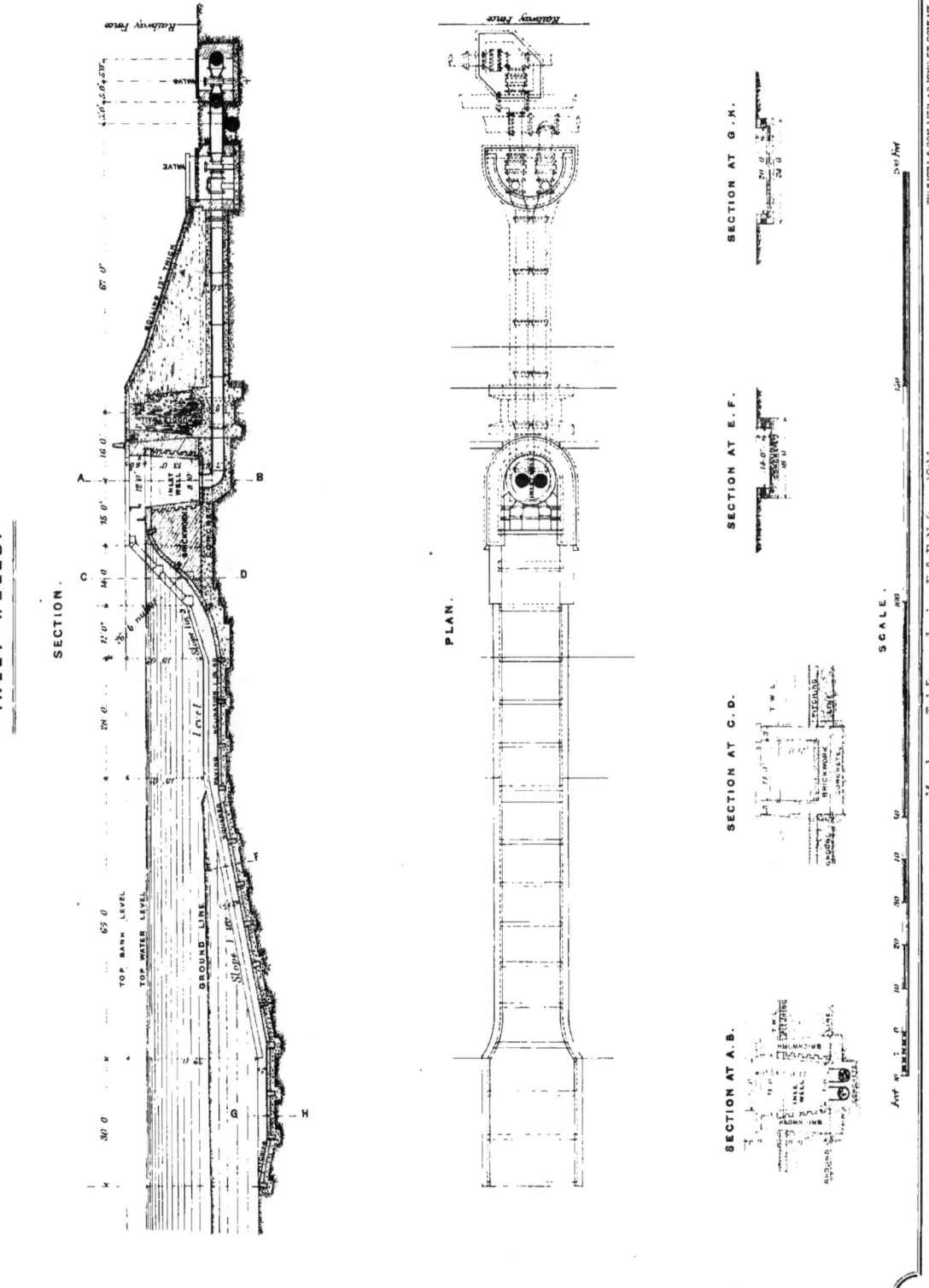

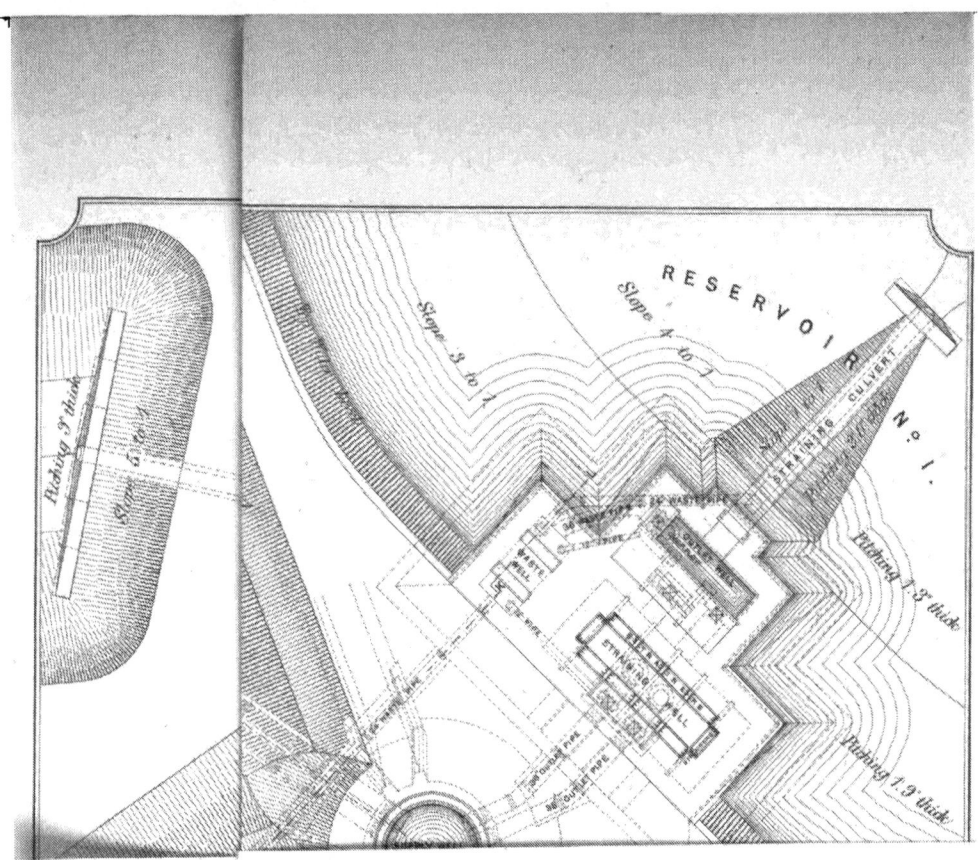

THE NEW YORK
PUBLIC LIBRARY

WORKS AT GOR[T]
SECTIONS OF STRAIN

SECTI[ON]

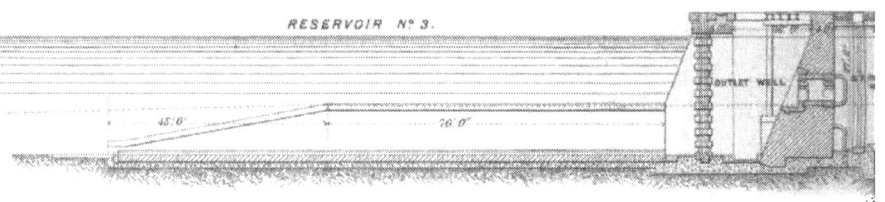

SECTION D.E.F.

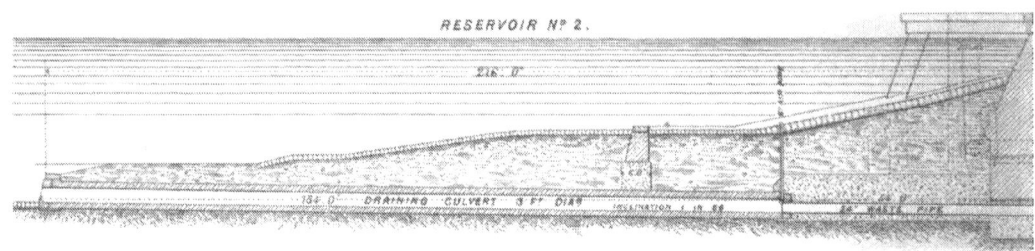

SECTION I.K.L.

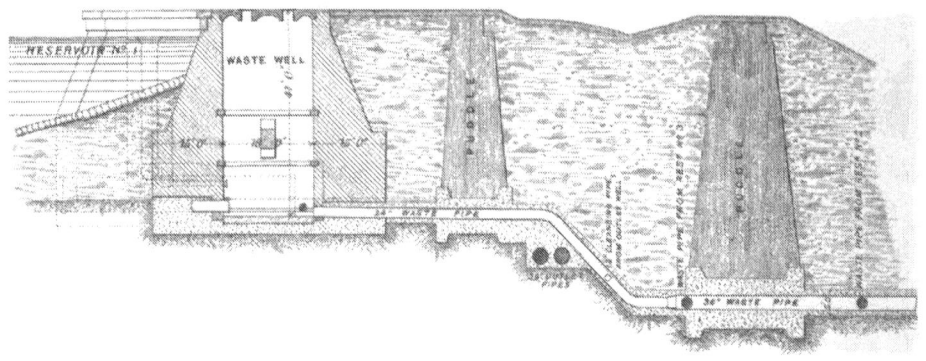

SECTION M.N.

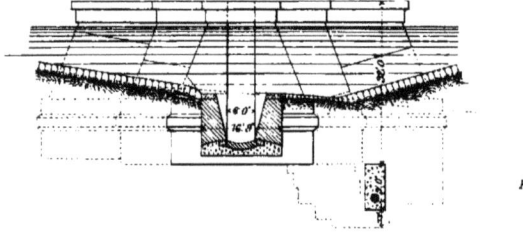

SECTION O.P.

SCALE.

SCALE FOR DETAILS

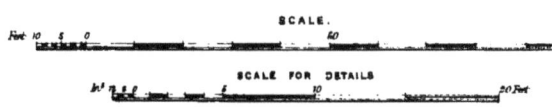

Manchester, T J Day

ON AND DENTON.
G AND OUTLET WELLS.

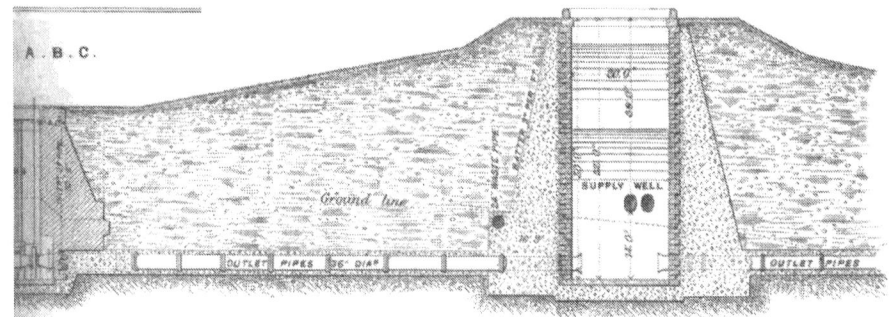

A.B.C.

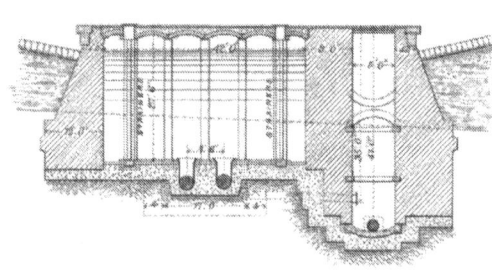

SECTION G.H.

DETAILS OF SUPPLY WELL.

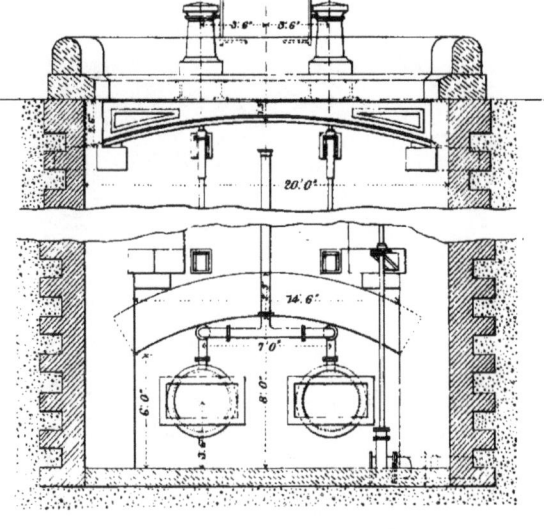

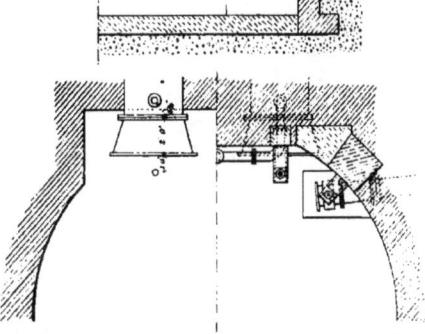

THE NEW YORK
PUBLIC LIBRARY

ASTOR, LENOX AND
TILDEN FOUNDATIONS

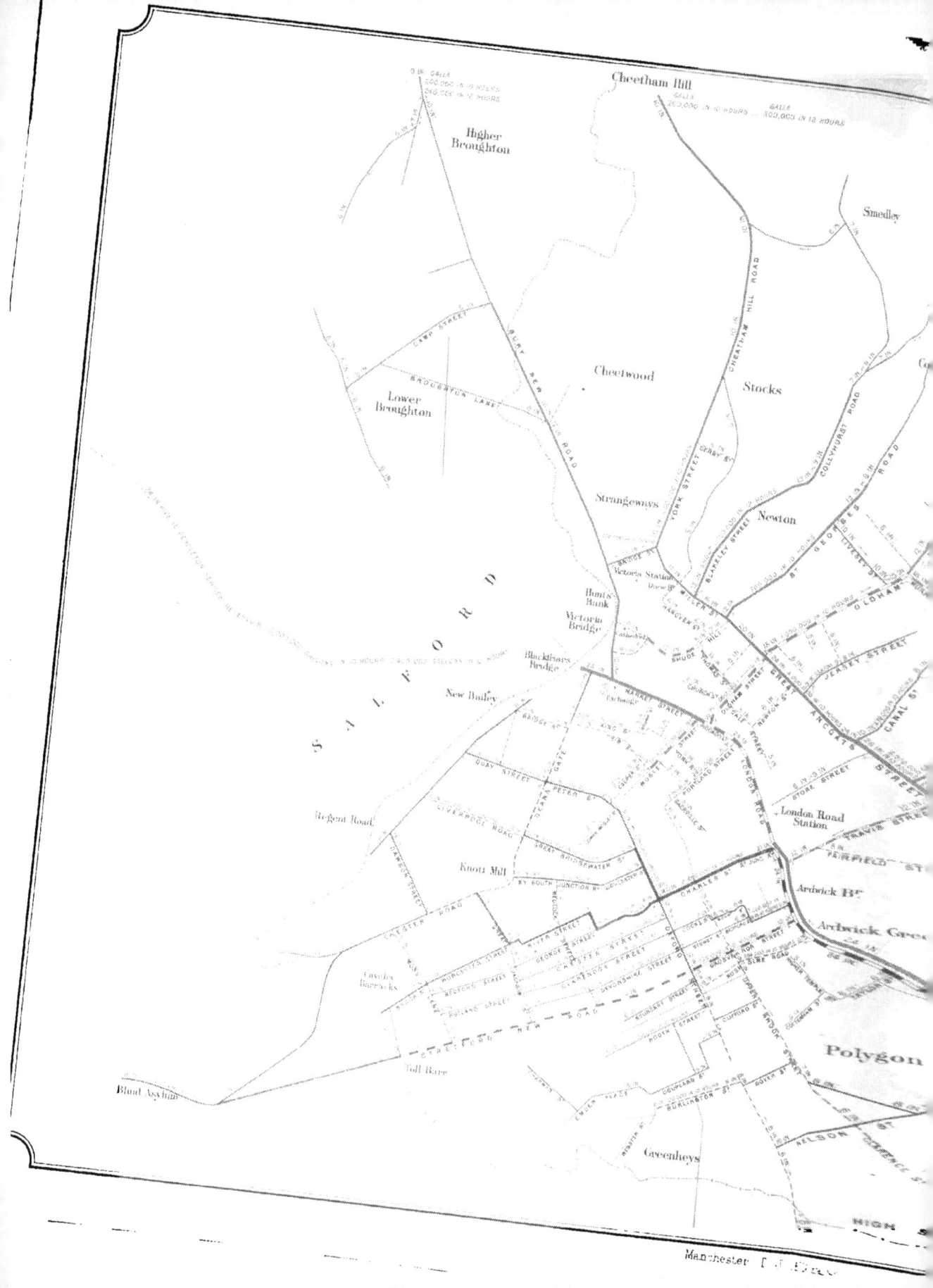

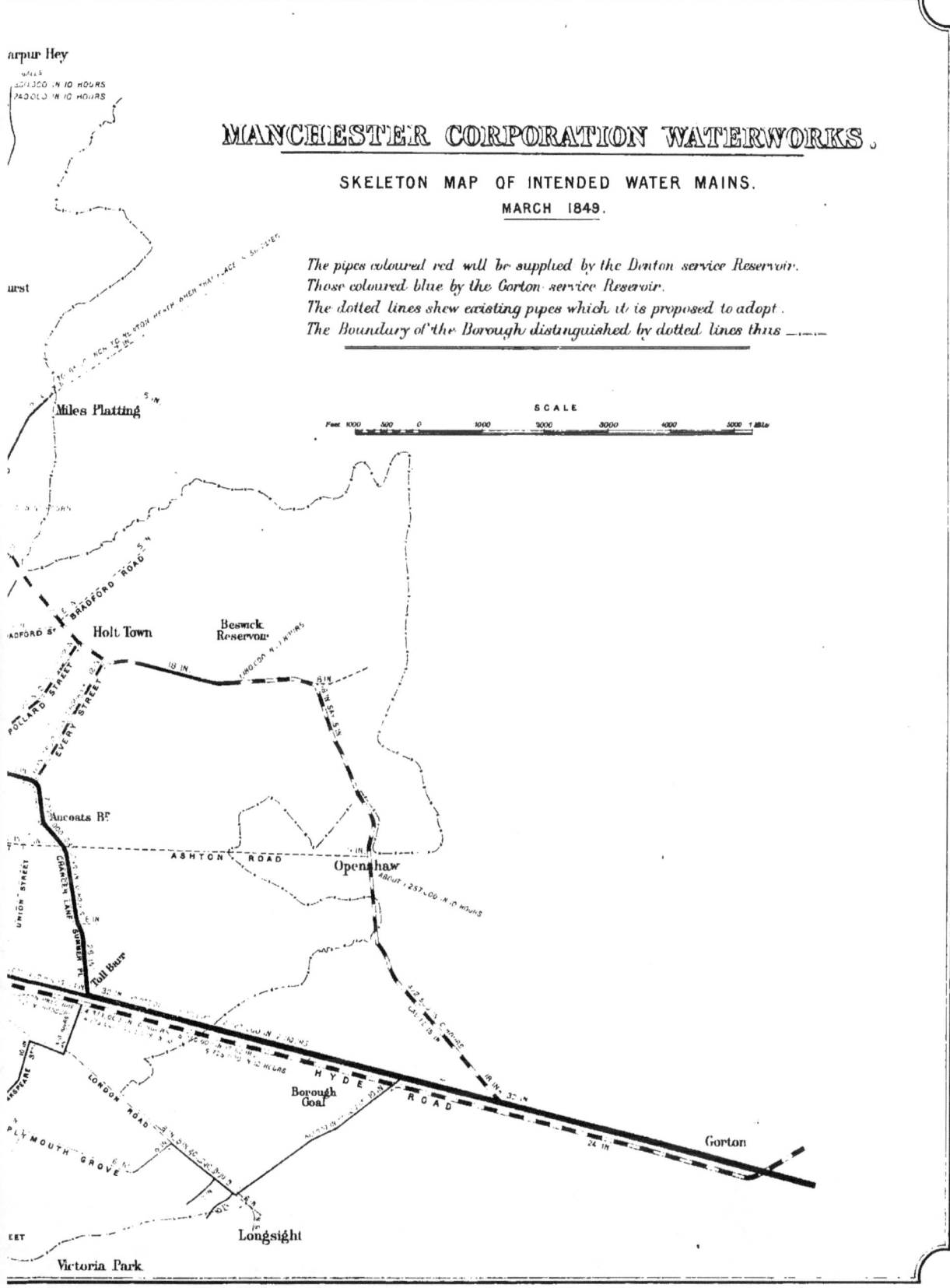

MANCHESTER CORPOR

DIAGRAM SHEWING THE AVERAGE QUANTITY OF WATER

DIAGRAM SHEWING THE YEARLY RAINFALL A

Manchester T. J. Day — Lond

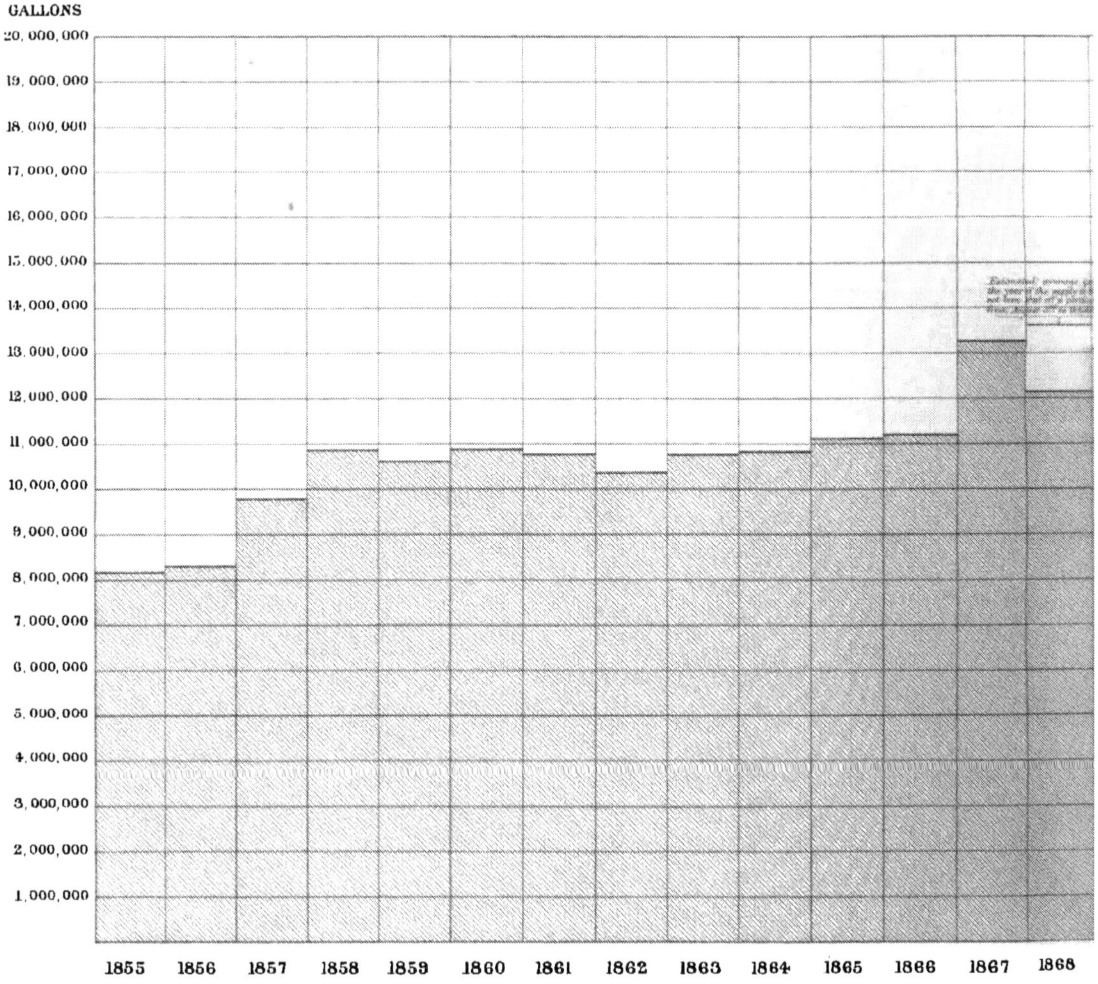

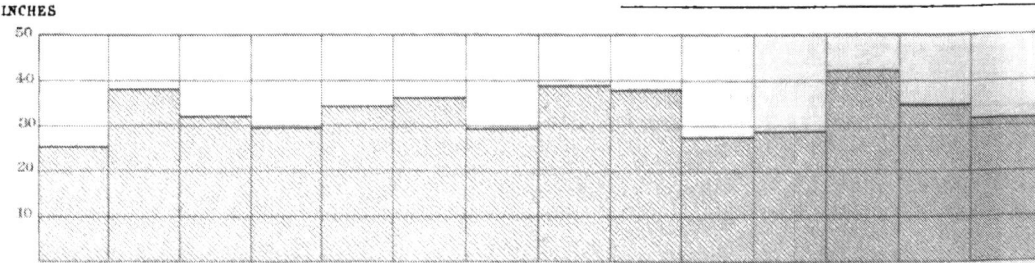

RATION WATERWORKS.

SUPPLIED PER DAY IN EACH YEAR FROM 1855 TO 1882.

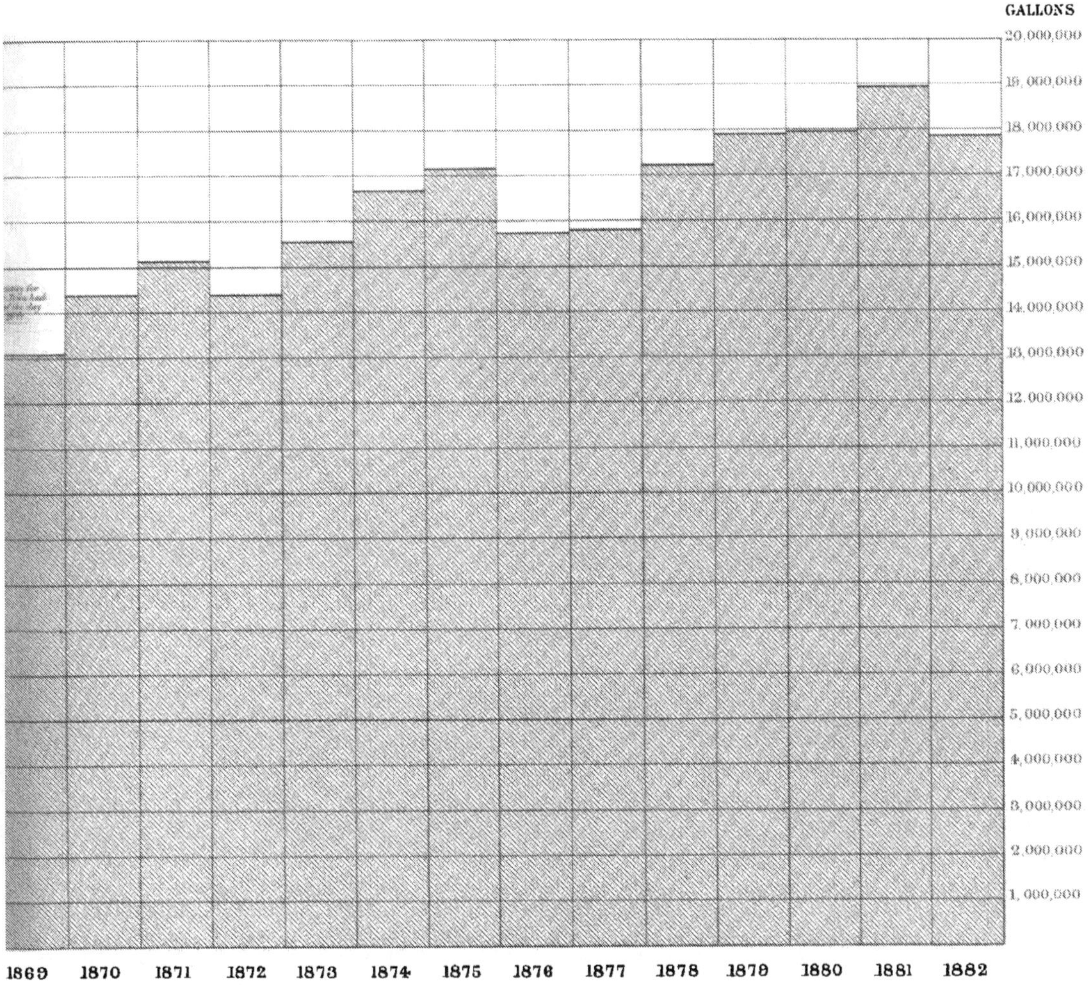

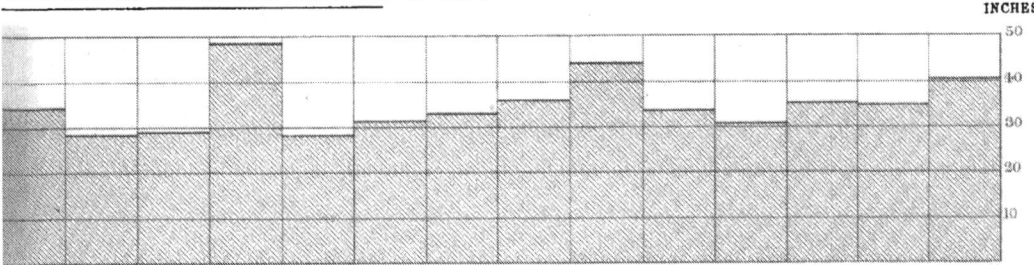

THE GORTON RESERVOIRS FROM 1855 TO 1882.

E. & F. N. Spon, 1884.

THOS KELL & SON, LITH 40 KING ST COVENT GARDEN

SELF ACTING BALL AIR VALVES.

FOR DISCHARGING AIR DURING FILLING OF PIPES, AND THAT WHICH ACCUMULATES UNDER PRESSURE WHEN THE PIPES ARE FILLED WITH WATER.

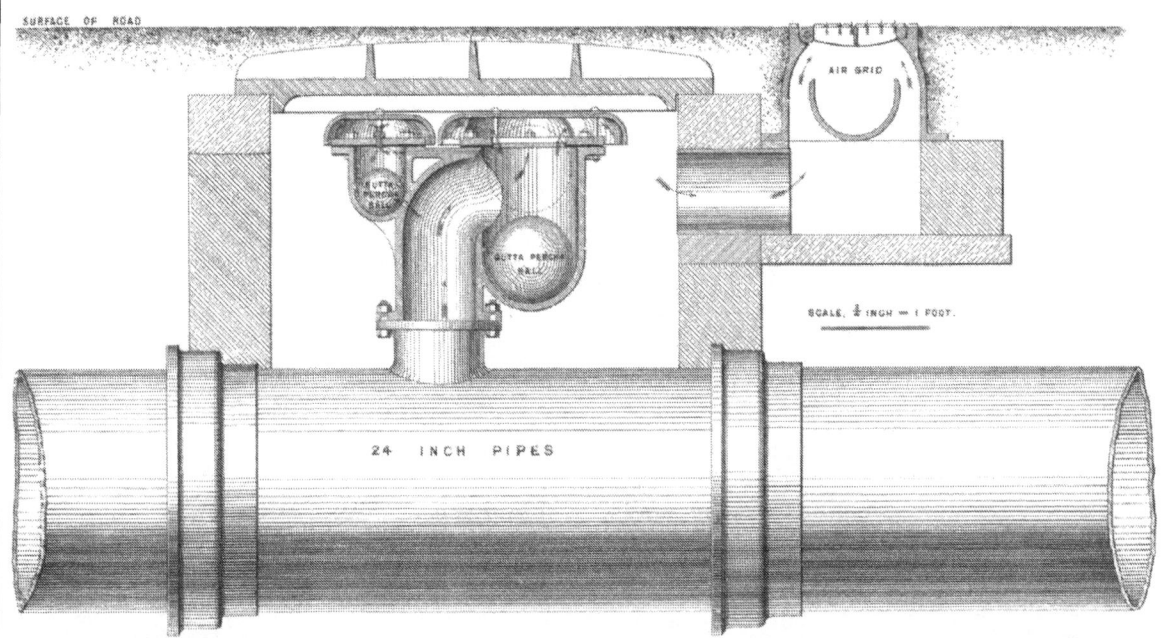

ELEVATION.

SECTION OF AIR VALVE.

SECTION.

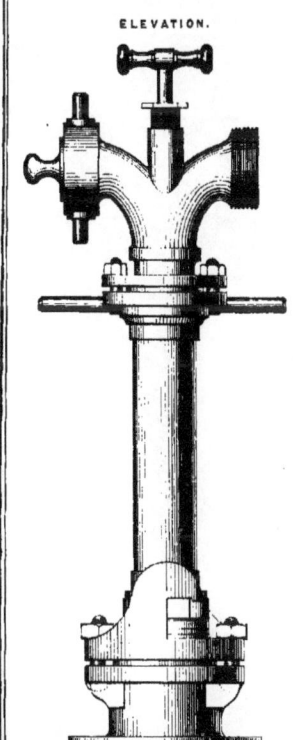
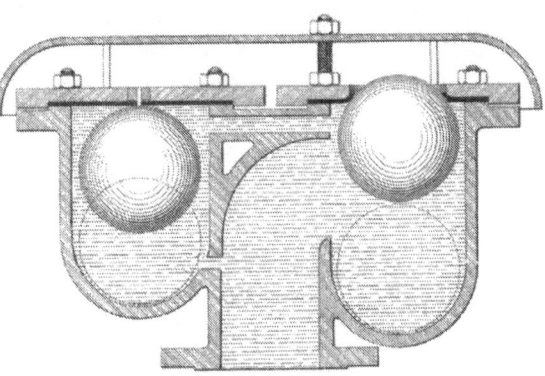
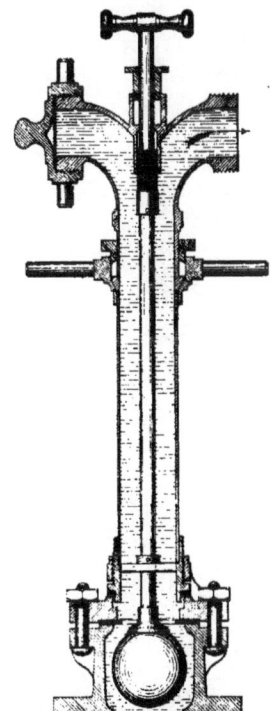

HYDRANT OR FIRE COCK

SECTION SHOWING VALVE CLOSED.

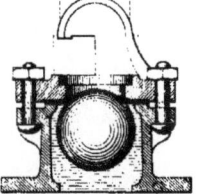

SCALE.

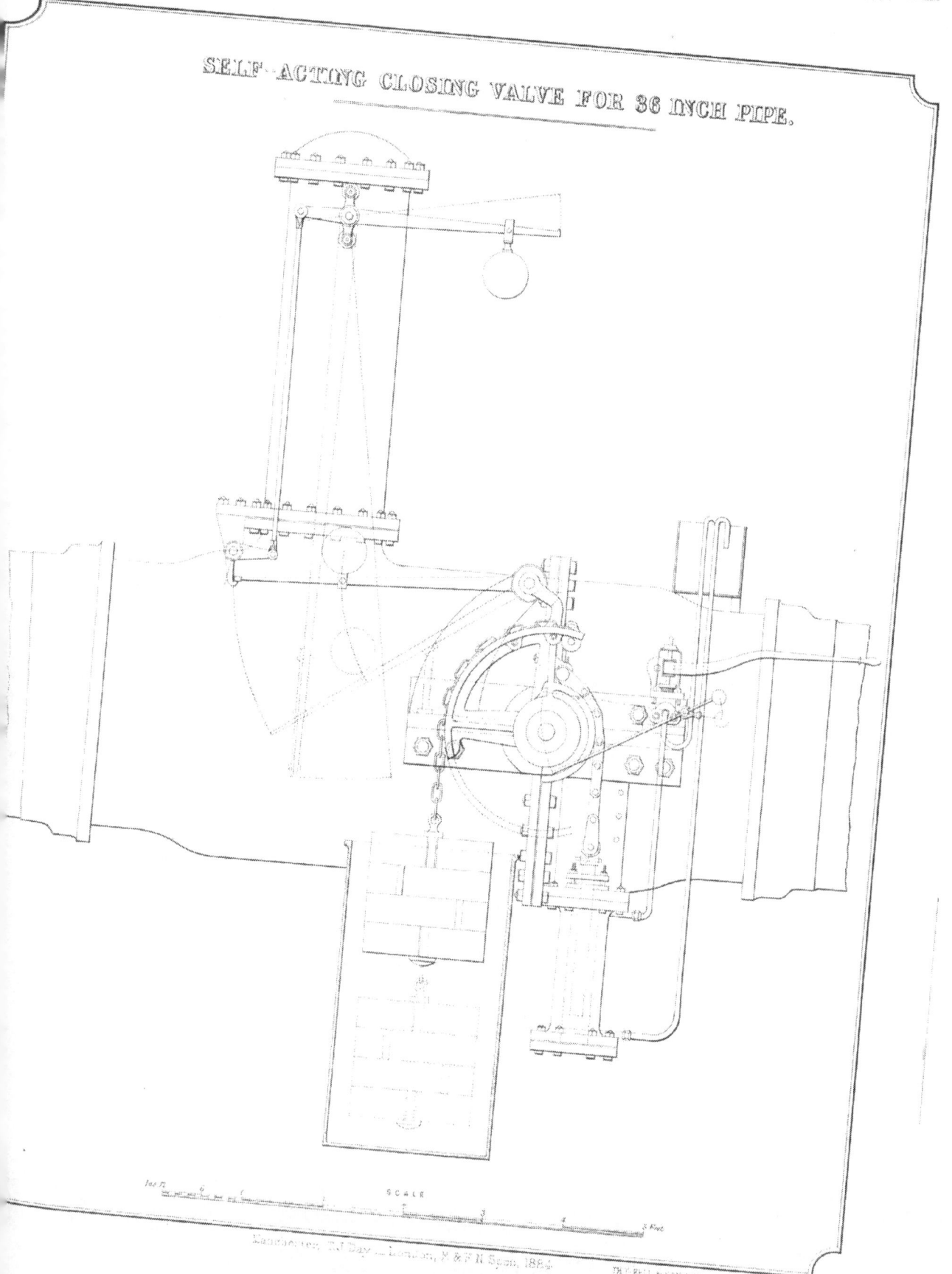

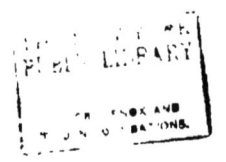

21 INCH HORIZONTAL SLUICE VALVE.

(TWO SLIDES)

PLAN.

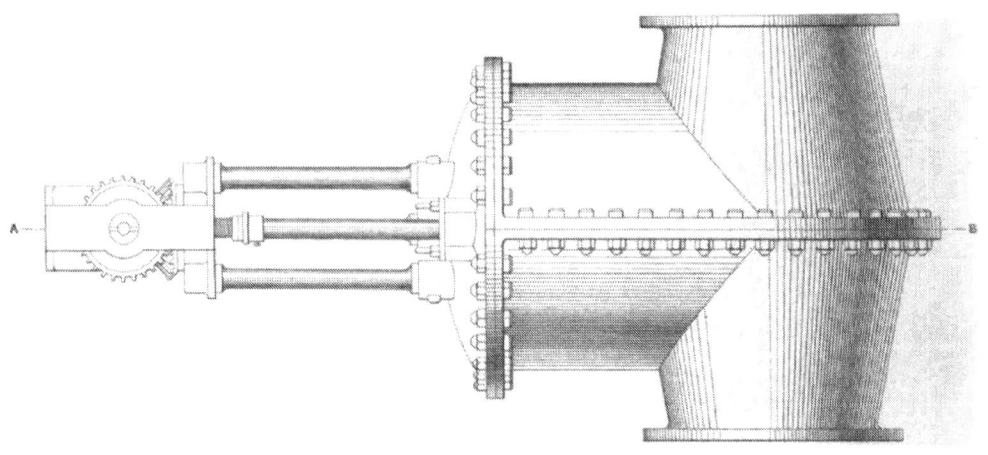

SECTION A-B.

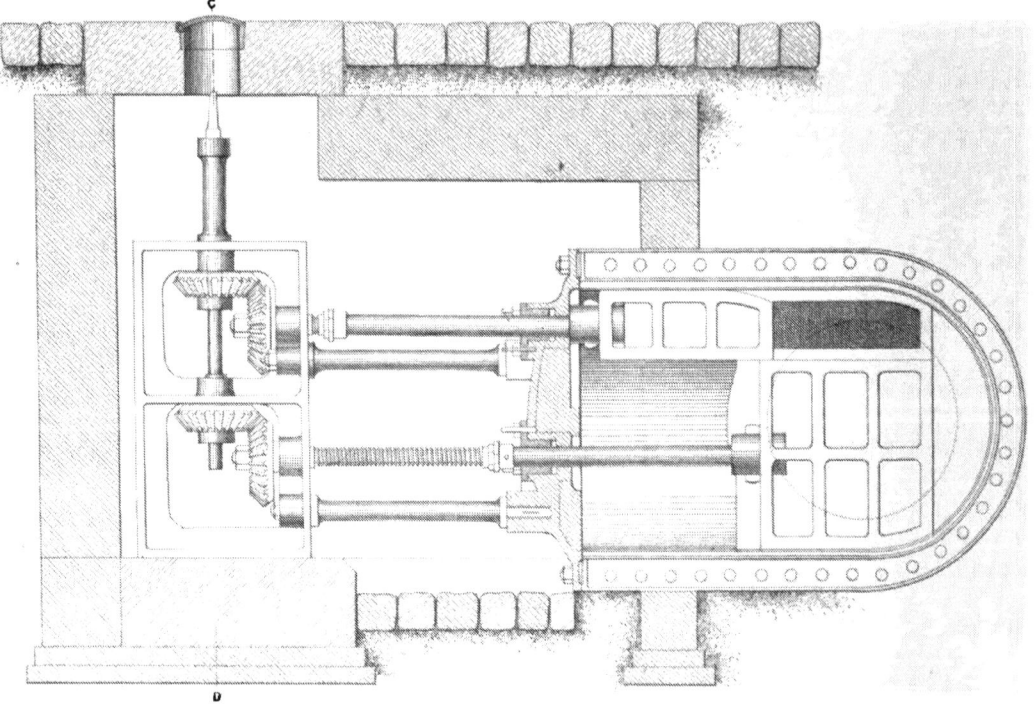

Manchester T J Day

40 INCH REFLUX VALVE.

SECTION. ELEVATION.

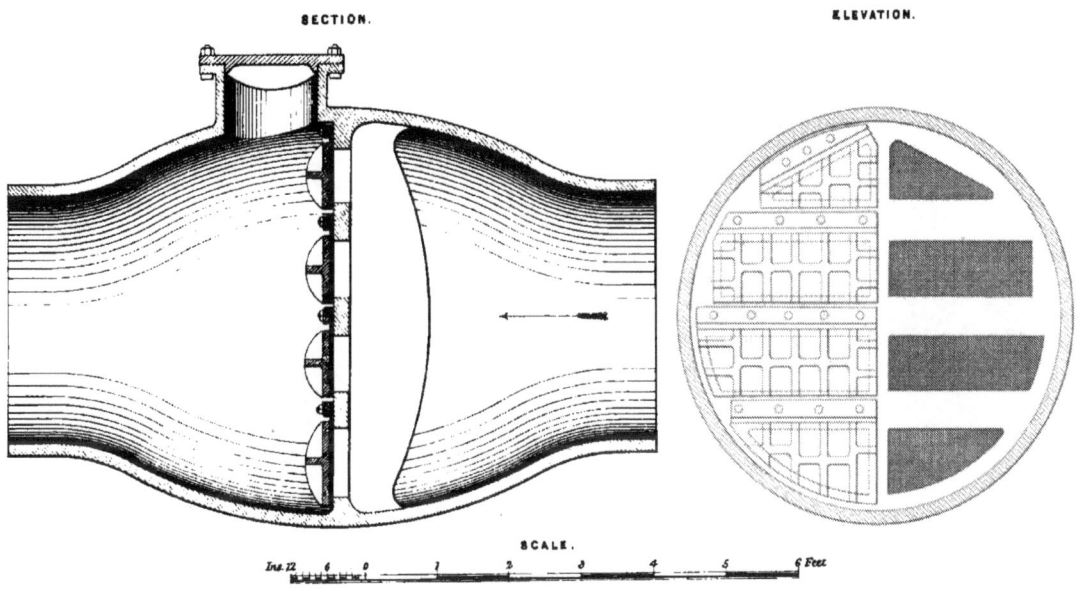

SCALE.

SECTION C-D.

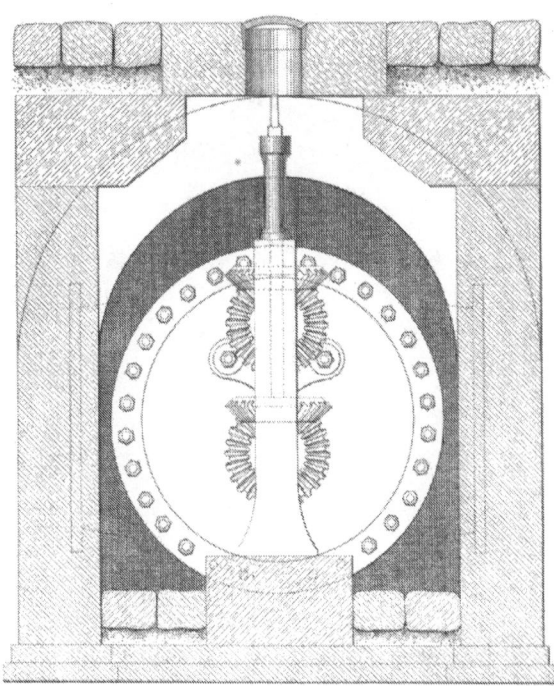

London E. & F. N. Spon, 1884.

REVERSING TUMBLER IN DISCHARGE TROUGHS.

FIG. 1. ORDINARY OPEN POSITION.

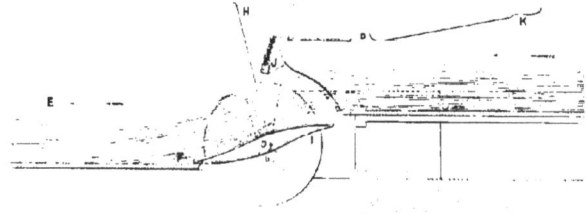

FIG. 2. TUMBLER REVERSED DISCHARGING INTO TEST BASIN.

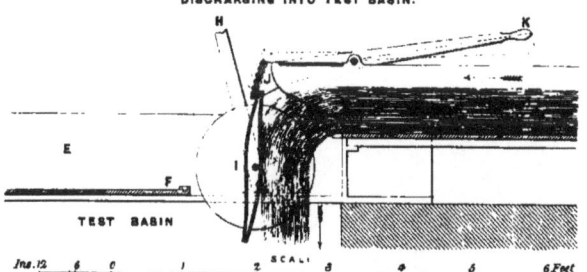

EXPLANATION.

In the bottom of the trough E, Fig. 1., is placed a tumbler I in a horizontal position, turning on an axis in the centre, and this tumbler ordinarily forms the floor of the trough and the water passes over it; but on drawing back the hand lever H into the position shown by the dotted line, so that the extremity of the tumbler just clears the edge F of the trough, the tumbler is instantaneously reversed by the stream of water and turned vertically across the trough, where it is caught by the stop J, as shown in Fig. 2. In this position the water is discharged through the opening in the bottom of the trough into the test basin below, and at the same time the tumbler opposes an effectual barrier to its passing along the trough beyond the opening. The previous level of the water in the basin being noted, together with the time at which the stream is turned into it, the tumbler is again replaced at the end of a given interval in its original position, shown in Fig. 1., by raising the stop J by the handle K so as to release the tumbler; the discharge of the water into the test basin is thus instantly arrested, and the water allowed to pass along the trough E, as before, into the river below. The height to which the basin has been filled during the time noted is then ascertained, and the quantity discharged is thereby accurately determined.

GAUGE SLUICE IN WATERCOURSES.

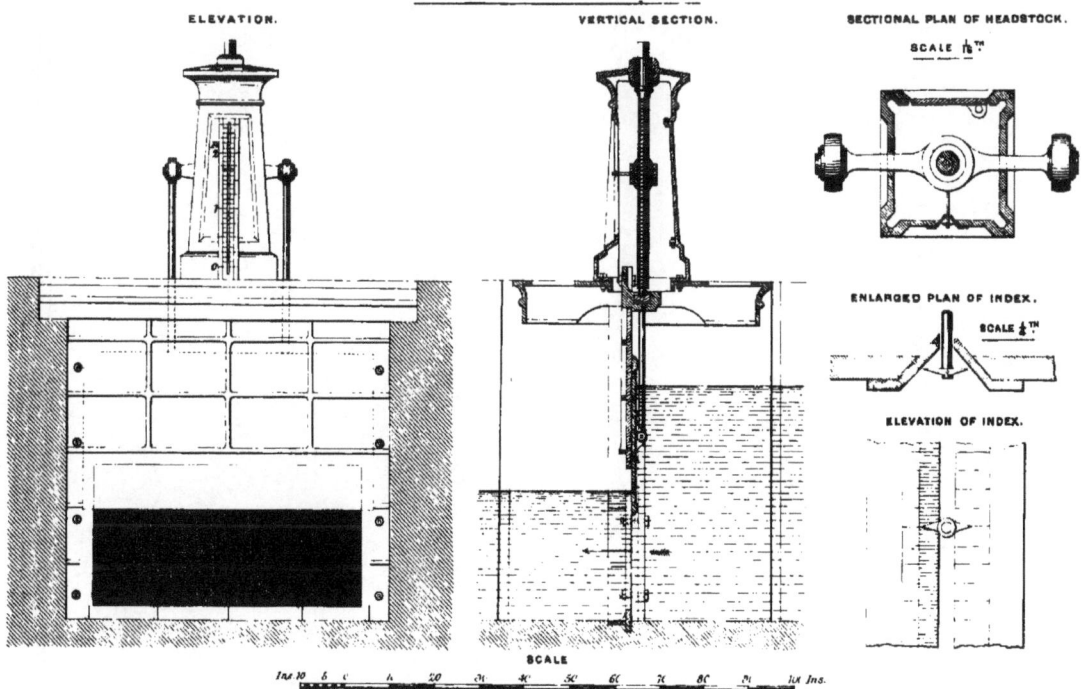

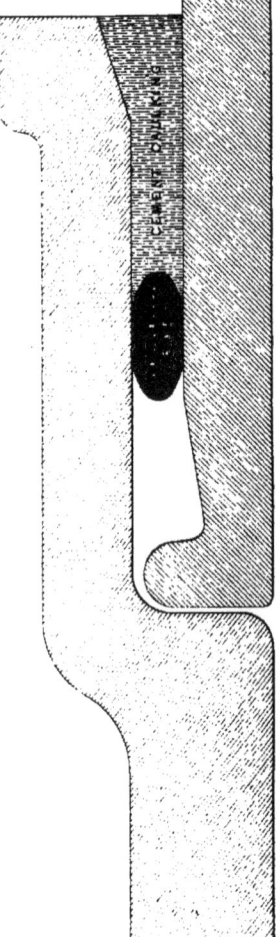

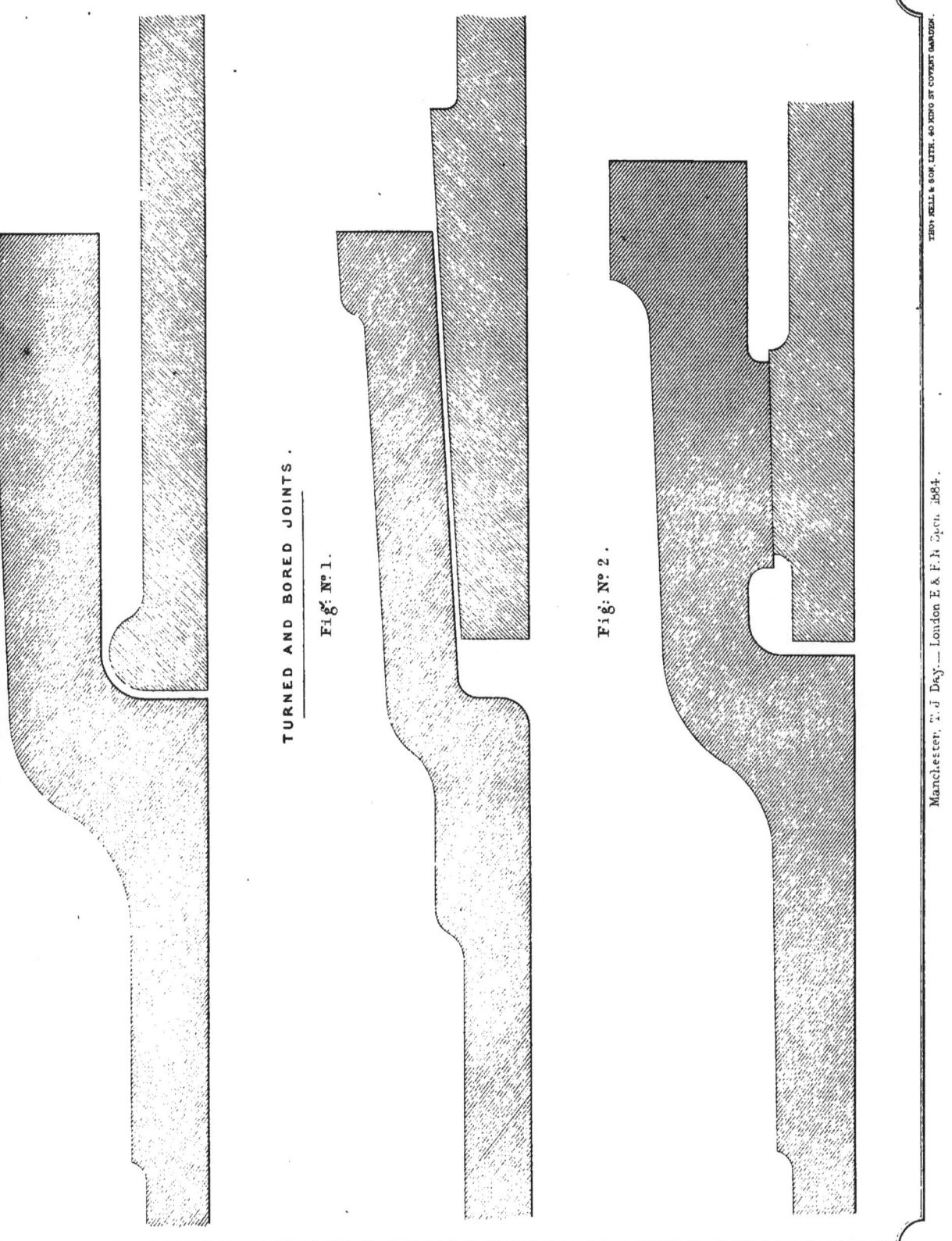

CORPORATI
NG THE PROPOSED LINE
HIRLMERE TO MANC

JW

Lightning Source UK Ltd.
Milton Keynes UK
UKHW030642060223
416537UK00015B/2908